Voice Processing

Other McGraw-Hill Communications Books of Interest

AZEVEDO • *ISPF*

BALL • *Cost-Efficient Network Management*

BERSON • *APPC: A Guide to LU6.2*

BLACK • *Network Management Standards*

BLACK • *TCP/IP and Related Protocols*

BLACK • *The V Series Recommendations*

BLACK • *The X Series Recommendations*

CHORAPAS • *The Complete LAN Reference*

COOPER • *Computer and Communications Security*

DAYTON (RANADE, ED.) • *Integrating Digital Services*

DAYTON • *Telecommunications*

FOLTS • *McGraw-Hill's Compilation of Open Systems Standards*

FORTIER • *Handbook of LAN Technology*

GRAY • *Open Systems: A Business Strategy for the 1990s*

HELDMAN • *Global Telecommunications*

INGLIS • *Electronic Communications Handbook*

KESSLER • *ISDN*

KIMBERLEY • *Electronic Data Interchange*

KNIGHTSON • *Standards for Open Systems Interconnection*

LUTZ • *Large Systems Networking with VTAM*

MCCLAIN • *The Open Systems Interconnection Handbook*

MCCLIMANA • *Communications Wiring and Interconnection*

NAUGLE • *Local Area Networking*

NEMZOW • *The Ethernet Management Guide*

OWEN • *Digital Transmission Systems*

POTTS • *McGraw-Hill Data Communications Dictionary*

RADICATI • *Electronic Mail*

RANADE • *Advanced SNA Networking*

RANADE • *Introduction to SNA Networking*

RHEE • *Error Correction Coding Theory*

ROHDE • *Communications Receivers*

RORABAUGH • *Communications Formulas and Algorithms*

ROSE • *Programmer's Guide to Netware*

SARCH • *Integrating Voice and Data*

SARCH, ABBATIELLO • *Telecommunications and Data Communications Fact Book*

SCHLAR • *Inside X.25*

TUGAL • *Data Transmission*

UNGARO • *Networking Software*

WATERS • *Computer Communications Networks*

WHITE • *Interworking and Addressing*

Voice Processing

Gordon E. Pelton

McGraw-Hill, Inc.

New York San Francisco Washington, D.C. Auckland Bogotá
Caracas Lisbon London Madrid Mexico City Milan
Montreal New Delhi San Juan Singapore
Sydney Tokyo Toronto

Library of Congress Cataloging-in-Publication Data

Pelton, Gordon E.
    Voice processing / by Gordon E. Pelton.
        p. cm
    Includes index.
    ISBN 0-07-049309-X
    1. Speech processing systems.   I. Title.
TK7882.S65P48 1992
006.4'54—dc20   92-21417
                                                                       CIP

1 2 3 4 5 6 7 8 8 9 0 DOC/DOC 9 6 5 4 3

ISBN 0-07-049309-X

*The editors for this book are Neil M. Levine and Sally Anne Glover, the
director of production is Katherine G. Brown. This book is set in
Century Schoolbook.*

Printed and bound by R.R. Donnelly

*For more information about other McGraw-Hill materials,
call 1-800-2-MCGRAW in the United States. In other
countries, call your nearest McGraw-Hill office.*

Contents

Chapter 9. Vocabulary Production   289

Appendix A. MAX, The Check-in System   321

Preface

I was first introduced to computers in 1958 as a college senior majoring in mathematics. From that day until this, I have participated in the computer revolution, the whole time fascinated by the thought that computers would encroach further and further into the intellectual domain—an arena previously thought to be reserved strictly for humans. I even designed my own graduate program founded on the notion that interdisciplinary study was the only preparation for the design of intelligent automata. During my years as a graduate student—and as a programmer and analyst working on the development of assemblers and compilers—I watched with growing fascination our progress toward the day, which I had come to believe would inevitably arrive, when machines would outmatch human intelligence. Later, working with artificial intelligence and exotic human-machine interfaces, my thoughts and beliefs about intelligent computers solidified. Never, until the late 1970s, did it occur to me that we would actually make computers talk—much less teach them to understand our speech. It wasn't that I didn't believe it possible; it was just that, in my certainty of the computer's eventual role as an artificial brain, it simply had not occurred to me that we would communicate verbally with the things. Talking computers. Imagine!

The intellectual capability of computers continues to grow slowly, though inexorably, toward something. However, the computer's verbal skills have virtually exploded, developing in a single decade from limited, hesitant, monotonic mumblings to nearly natural, understandable dialogues—from a mere curiosity to a sought-after capability that today graces many thousands of computer applications. In the late 1970s, when I first learned of the technological advances that were to make computer speech possible, I felt a rare wave of excitement and intellectual stimulation, the thrill that comes with the realization that you're about to embark upon something important, something both worthy and meaningful. I had experienced that rush of feelings only twice before in my life. The first time was when I was involved in a Navy electronics curriculum in the early 1950s and first glimpsed the subtle promise of electronics. I experienced this thrill again a few years later as a UCLA undergraduate—at the initial meeting of that institution's only computer programming course. However, this third time, as I read in a technical journal about the development of integrated circuits designed for digital speech compression, I knew instantly that I must immerse myself in the world of computer speech technology. For more than a decade, along with many other people, I have done just that. We've studied the literature dealing with linguistics, phonetics, signal processing, telecommunications, and various other related disciplines, and we've launched into the business of creating voice processing devices, tools, and applications. We've taken many a false step, made some mistakes, and had our failures, but we've found the way and produced numerous successes. Our efforts continue. Now, thousands are involved in the field of voice processing, with more coming in every day.

This book was written to share the benefits of experience gained and lessons learned over the past decade. The book brings together, in a single volume, discussions of the foundations, tools, and techniques necessary to the development of voice processing systems. While the implementation of voice processing capabilities is similar in many ways to interfacing any piece of hardware into new products or applications, the techniques needed to produce an effective telephone interface have only recently been developed and are not yet widely known. Computers that talk to people over the phone and respond to their speech or to Touch-Tone inputs differ greatly from systems that interface with users via a keyboard and display screen. Thus, it's necessary to learn new techniques and new disciplines for the development of these systems and their voices. Numerous books dealing with the fundamentals of telecommunications and speech technology are readily available in any good library or technical bookstore, but objective material covering voice processing hardware and software has been scarce—and almost nothing has existed to help developers or to give a top-level overview. This book will provide anyone, regardless of education or background, a broad understanding of the concepts and tools important to voice processing. At the same time, it contains highly technical detail that's targeted to those already conversant in the computer field. This book takes the reader in three related yet separate directions. One provides a background in the fundamentals and basic concepts upon which voice processing is founded. A second is intended to furnish a generic understanding of the hardware and software tools that can be obtained in the marketplace or developed for use in voice processing systems. The third introduces a number of concepts, techniques, and features commonly found in such systems.

Chapter 2 provides a comprehensive survey of human attempts to produce machines that talk. That discussion is included because it seems to me that a distinctly human obsession with this topic has existed almost since the beginning of recorded history. I found this human fascination with speech fascinating in itself and wanted to share that excitement with others. All of the material presented in chapter 2 is available to any diligent researcher through scattered and diverse sources, but much of it's difficult to obtain. Every chapter contains material of value to anyone interested in the field of voice processing—particularly those developing, selling, managing, or acquiring systems. Developers and integrators might benefit most from the chapters dealing with fundamentals, hardware products, software development tools, application features and techniques, and audio speech production. Those involved in selling in the voice processing arena will be especially interested in the chapters providing background on the foundations of telecommunications and speech technology, or with the chapters on hardware and software tools—or the chapter covering implementation features. Managers and buyers might choose to read lightly over the technical sections, but they can gain valuable insights from the historical and background materials found at the beginning of almost every chapter. Those who might be contemplating a venture into the world of talking computers and voice processing will find much of value in every chapter.

Acknowledgments

I want first to acknowledge my gratitude to Uyless Black of Information Engineering, Inc., for his early encouragement, for the confidence he has shown in me, and for choosing this book to include in his important series on Computer Communications. I also recognize the contributions of many who worked with me in two companies, forging numerous concepts, approaches, and techniques that are discussed in the book—you know who you are. To Rick Pelton of IBM for reviewing parts of the manuscript and suggesting needed improvements, I give my heartfelt thanks. I am also grateful to Dr. Michael O'Malley of Berkeley Speech Technologies, not only for his critical reading of parts of the manuscript pertaining to text-to-speech, but also for several lengthy discussions on compression, speech recognition, and speech hardware. I thank him also for his suggestions concerning the structure and content of the book. I also owe a debt of gratitude to Elisabeth Peters of Berkeley Speech Technologies, who reviewed much of the material on text-to-speech and, before and during the writing of this book, shared her viewpoints and insights relating to many aspects of voice processing. Dr. James Baker of Dragon Systems graciously agreed to review the chapter on speech recognition, and I am greatly indebted to him for the changes he suggested.

Finally, I owe much to Gayle, my wife and best friend. Only those who have undertaken a project of this kind—and those who live with them—can truly comprehend the enormous contribution that Gayle has given in time, patience, understanding, and encouragement. Thank you, friend.

1

Introduction

One of the most important inventions of the nineteenth century was the telephone. Early in the twentieth century, development of the automobile, and later of the airplane, expanded our horizons and made possible a highly mobile society. The combined effect of these inventions was to shrink our world. Then, at the midpoint of the twentieth century, the invention of the digital computer amplified the power of our minds, enabled us to think and work more efficiently, and made us more productive than we ever could have imagined. Now, several new technologies have empowered us to teach computers to talk in our native languages and to listen to us as we speak; haltingly, computers have begun to understand what we say.

Having given our computers both oral and aural abilities, we've been able to produce innumerable computer applications that further enhance our productivity; not only can we communicate quickly and easily with each other from a distance, our computers now converse with us over the telephone. Such capabilities enable us to route phone calls automatically and to obtain and update computer-based information by telephone, using a group of activities collectively referred to as *voice processing*. At the foundation of these activities are a body of prior research and development, a group of technological fundamentals, numerous hardware devices and systems, several comprehensive software development tools, and a dozen or so audio techniques and practices. These are the subject of this book.

For many years computers have been sending information via modem over the telephone. To access such information, you must have use of a terminal that includes a display monitor and a keyboard. Voice processing applications, though, require no such equipment; these applications have made the marriage of computers and telecommunications simple and inexpensive, requiring only a basic telephone instrument. Voice processing has placed the power of the computer at the fingertips—and at the ears and mouth—of anyone with access to a telephone. Not all voice processing applications, however, involve telecommunication; the same technologies are found in calculators, pocket dictionaries, language translators, games, toys, appliances, vending machines, automobiles, and aids for the handicapped. The future will bring many more useful applications of voice processing to nontelephone devices.

Just as the advancement of data processing in the earliest days of computers grew a little bit at a time as new algorithms and new technologies evolved, so it is with voice processing. Almost from the beginning, scientists attempted to give voice to computers. When, finally, humans were able to place digitally recorded human speech in a computer's memory, speech segments could be pieced together to produce a few unnatural-sounding words spoken in a crude, tentative, mechanical, barely understood voice. Entire verbal messages could be stored to be accessed later by telephone. As speech technology improved, the quality of voice output from computers reached a point where it could barely be discerned from the real thing. By this time, computers could even read from text, pronouncing the synthesized words without the aid of humans or their recorded voices. Now, computers are able to listen to human speech and, with limitations, derive its meaning or produce a textual transcription. These abilities have evolved only after many years of study and experimentation—and they continue to evolve.

Speech Technologies

Three primary speech technologies are used in voice processing applications: stored speech, text-to-speech, and speech recognition. *Stored speech* involves the production of computer speech from an actual human voice that's stored in a computer's memory and used in any of several ways. In one, entire verbal messages are converted in realtime to a form suitable for computer storage. These can be played back on demand in a process we know as *voice messaging*. In another version of stored speech, segments of spoken utterances are placed in the computer's memory to be called up and pieced together in realtime when instructions or prompts are to be spoken. Speech can also be synthesized from plain text in a process known as *text-to-speech*, which enables voice processing applications to read from textual databases. *Speech recognition* is the process of deriving either a textual transcription or some form of meaning from spoken input. A related activity, though not strictly part of speech recognition, is the process we call speaker verification, whereby the identity of a speaker is learned or verified from samples of his or her speech.

While these technologies share common principles, each is a different aspect of computer speech, employing its own distinct technology whose details might vary from implementation to implementation. For example, in most stored speech applications, speech is compressed to reduce the amount of digital data that must be stored. Any of a dozen or so distinctly different compression algorithms can be used. Furthermore, text-to-speech can be implemented either as a purely synthetic product or by concatenation of very short subword, recorded human speech segments. Any or all of these speech technologies can be used alone or in combination and are frequently integrated with other technologies such as facsimile. A voice mail system, for example, uses both stored voice messages and stored voice prompts. It can employ speech recognition for control functions and is often combined with facsimile capabilities. Stored speech and text-to-speech are also used together, text-to-speech only for speaking names and addresses that might be too numerous to be recorded for stored speech. Most voice processing applications use Touch-Tone for data input and menu selection. But, rotary-dial sensing devices are sometimes optionally available for input because so many of the world's telephones still don't have Touch-Tone dialing. Speech recognition is still limited as an input medium, especially for telephone use, but its application for numeric input and menu selection is becoming commonplace.

Voice Processing Applications

Applications for voice processing technology are varied and far-reaching. There are numerous implementations for automobiles, hand-held language translators and similar devices that don't involve the telephone. Those designed for telephone access can be implemented on personal or larger computers and can stand alone, be a LAN node, or be linked to a host computer. Voice processing applications can operate with either a PBX or telephone key system with only a handful or hundreds of normal dialup, toll-free 800, or pay-per-call 900/976 lines attached. Their purpose can be to distribute incoming calls among operators in a call center, to take orders for a manufacturing firm, to provide the address of a retailer's nearest location, to obtain sales leads for a real estate firm, to convert E-mail messages to voice mail, or to record and relay voice messages among employees of an aerospace company—to name only a few.

To help explain the extent of voice processing and provide an understanding of its place in the world, a number of applications are summarized in this section. Voice processing applications can be classified according to the hardware they use, by the number of telephone lines handled, according to speech technology features employed, by functions performed, or by any of numerous other schemes. For purposes of this discussion, they're classified according to their intended function. Some arbitrary choices must be made in such a classification because boundary lines separating system functions can't be clearly defined. With that reservation in mind, the subsequent sections are intended to provide an overview of the voice processing industry through descriptions of a few applications in each of the several classes. Applications not requiring the telephone are touched upon only briefly. A longer discourse on these is omitted because, with few exceptions, most voice processing applications being implemented access information or perform operations in connection with the worldwide telephone network.

Telephone-based applications are perhaps more familiar because they have become commonplace and touch the working lives of many of us almost every day. A large variety of telephone-based systems are in operation throughout the world today, and most of these can be thought of as falling into one of three categories: call processing, voice mail, or interactive voice response. The latter category can be further subdivided into transaction processing, audiotex, and telemarketing applications. As mentioned earlier, the boundaries between these categories are blurred and, to a great extent, arbitrary. Furthermore, many voice processing implementations include multiple functions taken from more than one category. A brief discussion of nontelephone applications is provided in the following section.

Nontelephone applications

Speech output can be integrated inexpensively into devices that are quite small and lightweight, devices such as calculators, pocket dictionaries, and toys. Both text-to-speech and stored speech can be implemented with a few integrated circuits and a small power source. While talking dolls that say "Mama" have been familiar companions to children for many years, Texas Instruments' "Speak-and-Spell" in 1978 was the first speaking toy based on digital technology to be produced for the consumer market. Since that time, the market has seen talking calculators that speak their results and repeat each digit as it's entered, hand-held dictionaries and language translators that pronounce words entered on a keyboard, elevators that announce floors as they're approached, and talking vending machines and appliances. Perhaps even more interesting is the fact that some people are awakened every day by clocks that actually do tell them the time.

Voice-controlled cellular phones are available that can be dialed or answered without taking your eyes from the road or your hands from the steering wheel. And, if you try to leave your car without taking the keys, today's cars can speak authoritatively to you, saying something like "keys are in the ignition." If the oil is low or a door is ajar, your automobile can inform you of that by voice too. Some of the most useful nontelephone voice processing products are those that give speech or speech understanding to the handicapped. Reading machines employ text-to-speech to read books or other printed materials aloud. Synthetic speech is also generated by button-operated speaking prostheses for those unable to talk. Many other nontelephone talking devices will be produced in the future. Some will be mere novelties, but others, like the speaking machines for the speechless and the blind, will offer capabilities previously unavailable and will find eager buyers.

Call processing

Natural applications for voice processing computers are those concerned with routing incoming phone calls. Included in this category, called call processing, are operator services, call sequencers, automatic call distributors, automated attendants, and similar applications. As with other voice processing applications, call-processing functions are often grouped and the distinctions between them obscured. Many services normally provided by telephone company operators have been automated—in particular, those dealing with information services, credit card calls, and calls from public telephones. Call sequencers do just what their name implies. As calls arrive, the call sequencer plays one of a group of messages before putting the call on hold, pending availability of an agent. A different message can be played, depending on the time of day, the day of the week, or another factor. The sequencer keeps track of all calls in the hold queue and, while on hold, callers hear music, news, or announcements. When an agent in the call center is available, the next call in the queue is routed through. Statistical and call detail reports are displayed or printed to help management identify trends and future staffing requirements.

Automatic call distributors (ACDs) are similar in basic function to call sequencers but tend to be more intelligent, passing the call and detailed calling-customer information from a company database to an agent. In addition to telephone equipment, video displays and keyboards are available on the agents' desktops in the call center. Either automatic number identification (ANI, a service in which the calling party's telephone number is sent to the ACD by the telephone company) or a front-end interactive voice response (IVR) system is used with the ACD, which is also interfaced to the company's host database computer. The calling-customer's phone number, account number, social security number, or other identification that can be prompted by the IVR identifies the caller so that database information can be obtained from the host. With data screens showing past orders and other account information already displayed, an agent is able to sound knowledgeable from the very first moment contact is made with the caller. ACDs increase call center productivity by shortening both the length of calls and agent idle time. They can also feature predictive dialing for outbound calling (predictive dialing is described later, under Telemarketing). Features such as personalized announcements, faxback, voice mail, and others can also be included in ACDs. As with most call-processing systems, ACDs provide call detail reporting and other management and statistical reports.

Automated attendant systems are familiar to most people today; these systems take the place of a company's operators, attending to incoming calls and routing them to a department, an individual extension, a live operator, or to an appropriate voice mailbox. When a call arrives, it's answered, a greeting and a menu of options is played, and the caller is asked to enter an extension or to choose from among a list of departments or other organizations by depressing a Touch-Tone key. When the selection is made, the automated attendant rings the appropriate extension. If it's busy or unanswered, other options such as transfer to a live operator or to a voice mailbox can be offered to the caller. Automated attendants are often integrated with PBXs, voice mail, or other systems and usually include a myriad of options, management screens and reports.

Voice messaging

The concept of voice messaging is to digitally record telephone callers' voices, store the resulting messages on a disk, catalog them, and play any subset of them over the telephone when requested to do so. The term "voice messaging" is used here rather than "voice mail" to emphasize the fact that messaging is more appropriately thought of as a function than as an application or a system. Today, many voice processing systems running a variety of applications also include voice messaging functions. There are, to be sure, comprehensive and feature-laden, dedicated voice mail systems but, except for the extent of their options, these share much in common with the voice messaging functions found in nondedicated systems. Voice processing systems featuring voice messaging typically have subscribers (who are known to the system in advance) and callers (who might not be known ahead of time). Each subscriber has a password and has been assigned a voice mailbox—which doesn't actually exist as a physical entity. A voice mailbox is no more than an accounting artifice that enables the system to later locate all messages for a subscriber. Callers' messages are digitally recorded as they're spoken, and some systems allow callers to review and change or rerecord their messages. Subscribers can call to review their messages and, after a particular message is heard, it can be forwarded to other subscribers (sometimes with annotations), deleted, or saved. Numerous control options are available, including limitation on length of messages, message date/time stamping, subscriber directories that can be heard by callers, playback speed control, message quick scan, and many others.

Systems with voice messaging functions, whether or not they're dedicated voice mail products, offer the usual statistical and management reports. They also permit a system manager to add and delete subscribers, assign mailboxes, and review, and perhaps purge, message storage, which can grow beyond reason if subscribers save or propagate messages too freely. A particularly interesting feature of some voice processing systems is the use of text-to-speech software to convert electronic mail (E-Mail) messages to voice messages. Systems with this feature can also send the E-Mail message by FAX. A fascinating twist on this idea is found in some voice processing systems that use a scanner to convert incoming FAX text images to E-Mail (or other textual representation). Text-to-speech software can then be used to convert these to voice messages.

Interactive voice response (IVR)

Interactive voice response applications are those in which a caller (or callee) converses with the application, inputting information and making selections either by voice or by Touch-Tone. Almost all telephone-based voice processing applications are interactive in the sense that callers control the flow by pressing Touch-Tone keys; but the term interactive voice response is used here to define applications in the following three categories: transaction processing, audiotex, and telemarketing.

Transaction processing. Transaction processing applications conduct some form of transaction over the telephone—usually updating either local or host processor databases. Examples are applications that enable account holders at a bank to transfer funds between accounts, collect information on the day's receipts for a chain of auto supply stores, or enroll students for classes at colleges. Transaction processing applications usually begin with input of callers' personal identification numbers or other identifying information and might even require a password for access—especially when they update databases. A database can be local and maintained by the voice processing computer, or it can exist on a separate host processor.

Interfacing to a host computer is a common function for such systems and can be done by direct connection through a standard industry serial or parallel port, by implementation as a node on a LAN, or through emulation of one of the host's standard terminals. Some of these approaches require database access software that must be developed especially for the host. To avoid this complication, the preferred interface is terminal emulation, in which standard access screens already available on the host are used by the voice processing system, and online user keystrokes are emulated for access to the host's database.

Primary among transaction-processing systems that interface with host databases are those concerned with financial transactions: account status, funds transfer, stock quotations and the like. There are, however, some that might be considered more interesting. In the United States, the IRS has implemented a tax-filing system for taxpayers who would otherwise file a short form. Callers to the government's 800 number are prompted for earnings, tax prepayments, and other pertinent W-2 information. While on the phone, they're told the amount of tax they owe and the amount of their refund, if any. Callers reportedly receive their refunds more quickly than those filing by mail. Other examples involving host databases include employee benefit inquiries, delivery reminder calls from department stores, jury scheduling and notification, and many others.

Some general voice processing platforms have provided features for creation and maintenance of local databases—most provide for access to industry-standard databases such as dBASE. Stand-alone application systems are often conveniently implemented with a local database that can periodically be offloaded to another processor or accessed via online processes. Examples of such applications using local databases are numerous. An insurance company enables its agents to phone its dedicated automobile liability insurance binding system at the time of a sale to fix the exact time and date that a policy is put into force. Information regarding the policy and the insured are entered by the agent via Touch-Tone keypad and recorded with a date/time stamp in a local database that is daily offloaded to the company's central data processing facility.

Another example can be found in substitute teacher scheduling systems. These are usually used in secondary school districts to automatically find substitute teachers to fill in for those reporting sick. Absence reports usually occur early in the morning when time is of the essence. A teacher awakes too ill to go to work and phones a voice processing system to report the absence. The system immediately searches its database for substitute teachers qualified to fill in for the absent teacher and begins calling them. When one agrees to fill in, the substitute is given all pertinent details by the voice processing system. The database is updated to reflect two transactions (one—regular teacher is absent, and two—substitute teacher is working that day). This type of application is also used for nurses and many other staffing situations.

Another interesting transaction processing application with a local database occurs with security guard check-in systems. The voice processing system's local database contains information on each guard, each client, each post to be covered, and the times when guards at posts are scheduled to check in by telephone. At appointed times, guards phone the system and enter their personal identification number to complete their check-in. If that call doesn't come within a specified time, a missed check-in is queued and an outbound call is placed to a supervisor or other management person to report the event. There are many other examples of transaction processing applications.

Audiotex. Applications in the audiotex class provide information to callers. They're passive in the sense that they dispense information but collect none. Examples of information that might be obtained from audiotex systems include baseball scores, plane or bus schedules, financial yields, mortgage rates, weather and highway conditions, health tips, show times, equipment troubleshooting tips, classified ads, recycling information, current news, restaurant reviews and hundreds more. Typically, a caller is first presented with an oral menu of selections. After working down a hierarchy of menus, picking from each menu by pressing the appropriate Touch-Tone key, the caller hears the information provider's message.

Audiotex applications are frequently associated with the 900 and 976 pay-per-call industry, where each caller is billed by the telephone company at a given per-minute rate. Receipts are shared between the telephone company and information provider. Toll-free 800 numbers also provide access to many audiotex applications. Some offerings by information providers are most appropriately classed as entertainment and some are interactive, asking callers to answer questions and offering rewards for correct answers. The audiotex industry has brought many colorful applications to the world, including gab lines, "dial-a-porn," sports scores, trivia games, horoscopes, and race results. Large numbers of audiotex applications are designed to be updated remotely by telephone, often in realtime, because they must be modified frequently to provide ongoing interest to callers.

Telemarketing. Voice processing systems capable of automatically placing outbound calls have been a boon to organizations that depend upon selling by telephone. Using mailing lists or other sources, telemarketing systems dial prospects, whose answered calls are automatically routed to a pool of agents or operators. These systems interface with PBXs and host processors and can handle from a handful to hundreds of telephone lines and dozens of agents. Such applications, in addition to automatic dialing, provide many of the same features found in ACDs.

One of the objectives of a telemarketing voice processing system is to achieve a high rate of agent "talk time" with qualified prospects while maintaining a low ratio of calls that must be placed on hold because no agent is available when the call is answered (these are referred to as "no-op" calls). No-ops not only result in customer dissatisfaction, but also in a higher number of abandoned calls. No-ops are controlled by pacing call attempts at a rate that's "just right" for the number of agents logged on. If the rate of call attempts is too slow, not enough calls are completed in a given period of time and agents have too much idle time between calls. If the rate is too fast, more calls are answered in a given period and the ratio of no-ops to call attempts grows unacceptably large. Telemarketing applications use a range of dialing methodologies, with names such as auto-dialers, preview-dialers, progressive-dialers, power-dialers, and predictive-dialers. Telemarketers have found that, because of their impact on talk time and no-ops, the sophistication of dialing algorithms has a significant effect on cost and selling effectiveness.

All automatic dialers handle telephone dialing tasks, but the best know when a human has answered, recognizing the difference between a human voice and an answering machine, modem, or facsimile machine. The best of the best even distinguish business responses from household responses.

Preview dialers don't dial until instructed to do so by an agent—who is probably reviewing prospect files before making each call. Progressive dialers monitor agents' calls and begin dialing the next one as soon as the current call ends. Power dialers are similar to progressive dialers, except that they attempt to improve an agent's talk time by undertaking multiple call attempts for each agent in a pool, recognizing that a certain percentage of calls dialed will be busy, unanswered, or intercepted by the telephone company. Power dialers greatly improve talk time but usually result in a larger ratio of no-ops to call attempts. In spite of the fact that agents and their supervisors constantly tweak call pacing rates, power dialers can still log soaring no-op ratios. Predictive dialing algorithms go a step further and apply computer-based intelligence to the call pacing problem. They continually adjust pacing rates by considering the number of agents, average per-call talk time, and the ratio of completed (live answer) calls to call attempts. They try to predict when the next agent will be available and pace call attempts so that the next live answer call will occur at just the right time. Predictive dialing algorithms can double the amount of agent talk time over what's possible with manual systems, while still keeping no-ops within reasonable limits.

Telemarketing voice processing applications consider called time zones and time of day to avoid disturbing people at inappropriate times. They also have provisions for blocking calls to such places as hospitals, police and other government offices, and to prospects who have specifically asked not to be called. A full range of management reports are possible with telemarketing systems to provide operational statistics and other information regarding the success of marketing campaigns.

Application Acquisition

Organizations wishing to offer a voice processing application for their employees, clients or customers have several options. Some of the more common applications are available as turnkey systems, needing only to be installed and customized before going into production. Others can be implemented on generic voice processing platforms using software development toolkits or application generators. Such implementations can be accomplished in-house or contracted to a system integrator. A third option is to contract with a service provider who can handle both application development and system operation.

Development of high-quality voice processing applications can require considerable effort—much of which will be familiar to veteran computer system developers. Among other tasks, it can involve determination of system or application requirements, production of specifications, system design, selection and acquisition of hardware and operating system, selection and acquisition of software development tools, script design, system and script prototyping, auditioning and selection of announcers, programming or application generation, script recording and editing, system integration, beta testing, and documentation. Using an application generator (or even a development toolkit), application developers can be spared most of the tough technical work—which will already have been done by software tool developers.

The fundamentals of voice processing are covered in the following chapters. They include details relating to speech digitization and compression, voice recognition, and vocabulary production. Separate chapters on telecommunications, voice processing hardware and development software are also included. Chapter two provides a history of human attempts to create speaking automata and offers a sense of historical perspective and a glimpse of the human drive that has lead to endeavors that we now call voice processing.

2

History of
Talking Automata

As with all great developments, voice processing technology grew not from a single root, but from several. This new and emerging discipline owes its existence to a number of separate and distinct bodies of knowledge, some of which have been evolving almost since the dawn of civilization. Two important fields that have developed fairly recently are computer science, which did not exist as recently as 1940, and telephony, which began about 1876. Voice processing, however, could not have developed had it not been for the contributions of those who for centuries have endeavored to understand the means by which humans speak, and those who experimented with machines that emulate speaking. Most of us are somewhat familiar with the invention of the telephone, and many of us have lived with the birth and growth of the computer. The roots of the search for an understanding of human speech, on the other hand, reach back through the ages; the search has entwined a surprising variety of contributors that has included academics, clerics, artisans, mechanicians, engineers, scientists, and even charlatans. The origins of our accumulated body of knowledge concerning human speech and artificial talking machines are not widely known, but they do provide a fascinating history.

Speaking Idols of the Ancients

The earliest evidence of attempts to produce artificial talking comes to us from the ancients. It probably started with the desire to exploit superstition and impart authenticity and godlike power to religious idols. Later, in the Middle Ages, a handful of learned people crafted talking heads of bronze and other materials, apparently with no other purpose than to amaze and impress others and to differentiate themselves from the masses. Several mechanicians, all working at about the same time in the eighteenth century, were motivated by the desire to advance science—principally the study of phonetics and articulation. Over the next hundred years, advances in acoustics and in basic electricity occurred. The telegraph, the telephone, then the radio were invented. From that time forward, dozens then hundreds of engineers dedicated their lives to discovering more efficient means of using telephone lines and other communication channels. Though its means have changed over the years, that work continues today and has given birth to our present efforts to provide ever more human voices for computers.

Ancient Greek priests a few centuries before Christ were known to create talking oracles—no doubt to exercise divine control over believers. They fitted huge statues with long tubes so the idol could "speak" directly to the masses (who couldn't see the hidden priest speaking into the other end of the tube). The Oracle of Orpheus on the Isle of Lesbos spoke in this way and is said to have predicted, although in an equivocal pronouncement, the violent death of Cyrus the Great in 529 B.C. during his upcoming campaign against the Scythians. Another possible example comes to us from among the writings of ancient Egypt. These writings claim that the Statue of Memnon emitted musical sounds every morning at sunrise, just as solar rays fell upon its lips. The sounds, it was said, could be compared only to the breaking of the string of a lyre. An inscription on the left leg of the monolith suggests that priests sometimes also made the idol speak. Musical sounds issuing from the base of the statue were observed and reported in recent centuries by Europeans traveling in Egypt. They didn't report hearing the idol speak.

Talking Heads in the Middle Ages

Before the advent of experimental science, some thought it would be possible to trap a voice in a hollow tube or in a trunk. It could be released at a later time when the words would, it was supposed, emerge in full voice and proper sequence as though they had just been spoken. I imagine that this idea, being so easily tested, gave disappointing results. Sylvester II, who was Pope from 999 to 1003, built a speaking head of brass and was rewarded for this ingenuity, as were most mechanical innovators of his day, by being accused of magic. A German theologian, Albertus Magnus, a Dominican who was later sainted, constructed a talking head of earthenware in the thirteenth century. Apparently, Magnus demonstrated the head to one of his disciples, Thomas Aquinas, who is said to have been so unnerved at hearing the fragile head speak that he shattered the thing. Supposedly, Magnus had worked for forty years on his creation. Roger Bacon, an Oxford scholar who later became a Franciscan and is considered a founder of experimental science, is said to have also built a bronze speaking-head during the thirteenth century. One author, writing four-hundred years later, doubted that Bacon's contrivance ever existed and felt that if it did, it probably had a human voice and hidden tubes. Others apparently thought, however, that the motives of all of these gentlemen were not to deceive, but rather to evince their mechanical ingenuity.

Some Contrivances of the Seventeenth and Eighteenth Centuries

A famous Jesuit, Athanasius Kirsher, dabbled in acoustics in the seventeenth century. He gave us written descriptions of the Eolian harp and the speaking trumpet and also wrote of his confidence that an individual statue could be made that would pronounce articulate sounds and whose mouth, tongue, lips and eyes could be made to move. Reports claimed that he had intended to make such a statue for Queen Christina; history doesn't record whether or not he succeeded. Several bona fide speaking machines were about to appear, but in the meantime the deceptions continued.

A subject of Charles II, one Thomas Irson, demonstrated to the king and his court a multilingual speaking head that answered questions that were whispered into its ear. One of the king's pages, however, discovered a speaking tube leading to a Popish priest in the next room. Sometime in the eighteenth century, a figure of Bacchus seated on a barrel was exhibited at Versailles. Speaking in a loud voice, the statue pronounced the days of the week and wished the audience a good day. The demonstrator encouraged inspection of the barrel, in which could be seen bellows, wheels, wind-chests, organ-pipes, cylinders and the like. On one occasion, a concealed dwarf who was speaking into a voice-tube was discovered in one of the wind-chests. Similar frauds were perpetrated a number of times throughout Europe and can be attributed in part to an infatuation with public exhibitions of automata, which persisted for several centuries.

Professor Kratzenstein's Prize

Late in the eighteenth century, a great interest in the study of the mechanics of articulation flourished. The scientific activity attendant to this interest included several serious efforts to create artificial speaking machines. In 1779, the Imperial Academy of St. Petersburg posed two questions for its annual competition:

1. "What is the nature and character of the sounds of the vowels a, e, i, o, u that make them so different from one another?"

2. "Can an instrument be constructed like the *vox humana* pipes of an organ, which shall accurately express the sounds of the vowels?"

A Russian named Christian Gottlieb Kratzenstein, who was born in Germany and who at some time became Professor of Physiology at Halle then later at Copenhagen, won the prize by constructing a set of acoustic resonators that simulated the human mouth. The resonators (depicted in Figure 2.1) varied in shape, depending on the vowel to be emulated, and all were excited by means of a vibrating reed meant to simulate the human vocal chords. His scheme, it was reported, reproduced each of the vowels with "tolerable accuracy." Robert Willis, while researching synthetic vowel production in 1829, demonstrated that Kratzenstein could have accomplished the same result using a single tube whose length was adjusted for each vowel. It's interesting that the type of reed invented by Kratzenstein for this competition apparently later found a use in harmonicas. In 1786 Kratzenstein showed an acquaintance in Paris parts of a speaking machine that he had made using a pin cylinder drive. Apparently, the machine was able only to say the vowels and a few words like mamma and papa, but little more.

The Speaking Machines of Wolfgang von Kempelen

Over the period of two decades, from 1769 through 1790, Wolfgang Ritter von Kempelen of Vienna created the first complete speaking machine. In the process, he actually built three different models, all hand-operated, and in 1791 described this work in a thoroughly illustrated book. Before beginning his speaking machines, however, he was involved in a curious hoax that at first cast doubt on his later accomplishments. von Kempelen was born in 1734 in western Hungary in the town that's now called Bratislava. He was born into an age of increased scientific curiosity, an age that valued experimentation as the path to knowledge. This was also a time of fascination with machines. In Europe, that fascination probably began even before the fourteenth century, when hundreds of master clock makers were already plying their craft, creating exotic timekeeping machines driven by complicated clockworks.[1]

By von Kempelen's day, various automata, many driven by a wound spring, were being built to produce particular motions that could be studied. Others were built solely for the amusement of their creators and audi-

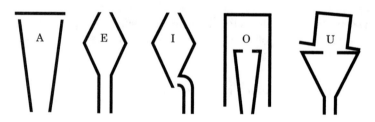

Figure 2.1 The prize-winning vowel resonators of Professor Kratzenstein.

ences. Around 1736, a Frenchman by the name of Vaucanson created a machine (which he called an android) in the figure of a man; the machine appropriately moved its fingers, lips and tongue while playing the flute. It was said that the performance of the machine was surprisingly accurate in its imitation and was probably as good as that of a live performer. When the flute player was first demonstrated in Paris, it might have been viewed skeptically. Not long before that, an organist from Troyes had exhibited to the French court an "automaton" that played the harpsichord. The "works" for this device were found to have consisted of a talented five-year-old musician concealed within the machine. Vaucanson later created other human-like automata. One played a shepherd's pipe, which it held in one hand while the other hand beat on a tambour. A few years after creating the flute-playing automaton, the same man, perhaps with some hostile motivation, created what must have seemed the world's most bizarre automaton. The machine was built in the form of a duck—probably following the example of General Degennes, a French officer who had earlier produced a peacock with similar though less exact capabilities. Vaucanson's device closely resembled a live duck, and behaved as a duck, even emulating muscle and bone movements. The duck walked, quacked and flapped its wings in a natural way. When it drank water, it piddled. It would stretch its neck to nibble kernels of corn, swallow them, then eliminate them in an altered form using chemicals contained therein for the purpose. Other mechanists later imitated some of these ingenious machines. Vaucanson later proposed to Louis XVI the construction of an automaton that would emulate the entire human circulatory system. The king gave orders for a voyage to Guyana, where an expert botanist was to construct the blood vessels from the gum of a tree indigenous to that area. Vaucanson encountered technical difficulties before the voyage, however, and the project was cancelled.

It was into this receptive, and perhaps credulous, atmosphere that von Kempelen launched an audacious deception in 1769 that astonished much of Europe. In only six months he built and began to exhibit his famous chess automaton. Seated at a desk in front of the chess board across from a hu-

---

[1]One early such example was constructed at the Cathedral of Strasbourg in the year 1350 and improved two-hundred years later. When first completed, it included a moving calendar and an astrolabe with indicators tracking movements of the sun, moon, and planets. In an upper section the three Magi, accompanied by a melody of bells, bowed in turn to the Virgin Mary. Then a large wrought iron cock standing on a gilded base and sporting a copper comb opened its beak, extended its tongue, flapped its wings, and crowed. After being enhanced in 1574, the magnificent clock also featured a calendar showing movable feasts, a Copernican planetarium with revolving planets, moon phases, eclipses, apparent and sidereal times, precession of the equinoxes, and equations for translating sun and moon indicators into local time. Saint's days were noted on a special dial. Figures representing the ages of man (Infancy, Adolescence, Manhood, and Old Age) struck each of the four quarter hours. The days of the week were marked by seven chariots among the clouds, each carrying the appropriate pagan god. At noon every day the twelve Apostles paraded by to be blessed by Christ.

man opponent, a turbaned figure in the image of a Turk held a long-stemmed pipe in one hand. Grinding and clanking of internal machinery could be heard from within each time the Turk methodically looked over the board, then moved his piece. Occasionally, Professor von Kempelen would wind the crank a few turns. Whenever his human opponent made an illegal move, the Turk would shake his head, replace the errant piece, and take his own move. On checkmate, the Turk's head would nod exactly three times. Skilled opponents chosen from the audience rarely beat the stiff Turk, who was even rumored to once have beaten Napoleon. Wolfgang von Kempelen commented that his creation was not really an automaton, that its only outstanding feature was in the skill of the deception.

There were several serious attempts to explain von Kempelen's hoax. A pamphlet appeared in Paris in 1785, conjecturing that a famous chess player, a dwarf, scrambled about within the machine under the Turk's petticoats, concealing various limbs as von Kempelen methodically opened and closed successive compartments for observers. Another conjectured that a former Polish army officer named Worouski, a legless chess master, was concealed within. It's interesting to speculate on von Kempelen's motivation for the ruse. It might have been for money, but he was exceptionally skilled in mechanics and had other respectable talents. He was a gentleman, a man of education, and never pretended the machine itself played chess; perhaps he found some wry magician's satisfaction just getting away with the trick. Even so, one can only wonder with what suspicion von Kempelen was viewed soon thereafter, when he began demonstrating his talking machines.

The combination of a growing interest in experimentation in science, the public's fascination with mechanized works, and longstanding human concern with the physiology of speech production probably provided the incentive for an accomplished machinist like von Kempelen to become obsessed with creating a machine that could emulate the human vocal tract and actually speak. At least one author felt that von Kempelen also had some thoughts about the problem of teaching deaf-mutes to speak. Interest in the problems of deaf-mutes figured critically in the invention of the telephone and had an important connection with the eventual creation of electronic speaking devices; I'll say more about this later.

Wolfgang von Kempelen felt that to make a speaking machine, he should first be able to reproduce the vowel sounds. He started by searching for an appropriate sound source, a mechanical substitute for the vocal chords. He considered the vibrating reeds used in musical instruments and, though not entirely satisfied, settled on the drone reed used in bagpipes as the one sounding the most human. Sound from the reed was played into a bell-shaped device with a baffle at the mouth, which was moved to create the different vowels. Unsatisfied with the result, von Kempelen used his hand in place of the baffle and, although better, the resulting vowel sounds were not what he wanted. He started over. The second model anticipated the need to have various resonant devices for the variety of sounds required. This version was modular in that it featured an ensemble of up to thirteen resonators, each with its own musical reed, and each removable so that different ones could be tried. These were each attached to one of thirteen channels provided on the machine's console. Any of thirteen piano-like keys could be pressed to introduce a stream of air into one of the channels, causing that channel's reed to vibrate. A foot pedal was provided to work the common bellows.

Wolfgang von Kempelen seems to have tried a variety of resonators. The representation of his second machine, shown in Figure 2.2, includes closeup views of two mechanisms: a clamshell-shaped device and a pyramid-shaped device with a movable baffle. Four other clamshells with dif-

Figure 2.2 Wolfgang von Kempelen's second talking machine.

ferent-sized openings and two square resonators are shown plugged into the console. With this machine, von Kempelen claims to have been able to produce reasonable versions of the vowels a, o, and u, and nearly acceptable sounds for the consonants p, m, and l. In a monotonic voice, the new machine was able to say words like "mama" and "papa," but it still had two major problems. First, the vowels (and some of the other voiced sounds) evidenced a problem familiar to later researchers in that they started explosively, introducing an extra k-like sound. Furthermore, when the individual keys were pressed, the sounds seemed separate and distinct and didn't flow smoothly together as in natural speech. To solve the first problem, he padded the reeds with soft leather, realizing that use of a single reed rather than individual ones was needed to achieve a smooth blending of sounds. This latter solution would require a complete redesign of his creation. If von Kempelen felt discouraged, he didn't let it stop him. Again, he started over.

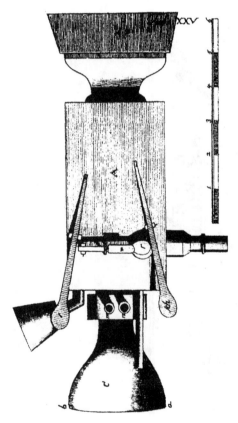

Figure 2.3 Von Kempelen's third and final talking machine.

Each of von Kempelen's three speaking machines had to be "played" like a musical instrument. His third and final machine differed in appearance from the second one, as shown in Figure 2.3. Lungs were simulated by continually pumping a bellows up and down with the right elbow. Vowels could be produced by closing the "nostrils" of the machine with the right hand, pumping the "lungs" with the right elbow, and interrupting the resonant characteristics of a large bell-shaped affair with the palm of the left hand. Only through acquisition of great skill obtained by much practice could each of the vowels be produced reliably. Consonants required even more practice. There were special controls for five of the consonants, and the fingers of the right hand operated these while the arm worked the bellows. Sounds for F, H, V, W and some of the others, for example, were created by various manipulations of devices that could close or open at certain places to allow air to escape. For certain consonants, these had to be held with exactly the right pressure to vibrate a reed just so—and for other consonants, so it would not vibrate—all the while pumping the bellows with the right elbow at a correct speed and pressure.

Wolfgang von Kempelen claimed the machine could produce all the vowels and nineteen consonants. It still could not make sounds for several consonants. Even though the machine's bellows were capable of moving six times the amount of air in a human's lungs, it was capable of saying only short phrases before running out of air. Each sound had its own configuration of finger, hand, arm, and elbow positions and movements. One can only imagine the patience required to attain the skill necessary to make the device speak despite the fact that von Kempelen wrote that if a person were to stick to Latin, French, and Italian he could have a good start on learning to "play" the machine in about three weeks. German, he said, would take longer because that language is more scarce in vowels and richer in consonants than the other languages.

In 1791 von Kempelen published in both German and French *Mechanismus der menschlichen Sprache nebst der Beschreibung seiner sprechenden Maschine*, describing in 456 pages, with many illustrations, the results of his twenty years of work on speaking machines.

Two Talking Heads of the Abbe' Mical

In France, at about the same time that von Kempelen worked to perfect his speaking machines, the Abbe' Mical is said to have constructed a pair of large, brazen speaking heads featuring two pin-cylinder drives similar to those found in music boxes. One cylinder was able to play a number of fixed utterances with natural phrasing and prosody. The other produced all the sounds used in the French language. It was common in that time to view such exhibits with suspicion, and Mical had his detractors who thought him a fraud too. It's not known whether or not his talking heads were authentic.

Further Efforts in the Nineteenth Century

Hermann Helmholtz, one of the world's leading acoustical scientists in the mid-nineteenth century, constructed an electro-mechanical device consisting of multiple tuning forks, electrical coils, and resonators that synthesized a composite sound that was a credible approximation of human vowel sounds. This device probably didn't provide an important link in the chain of inventions that led to the development of speaking machines. However, its existence did provide encouragement to Alexander Graham Bell, whose work gave rise to so many inventions that were important in the chain.

At about the same time that Helmholtz was doing so much to further our understanding of acoustics, others worked and experimented in diverse ways to develop the body of knowledge upon which speaking machines would eventually be built. Sir Richard Paget constructed plaster models of the vocal tract in order to study the production of speech. Interestingly, Paget became so adept that he was able to emulate vocal tract configurations with his hands and make them speak by blowing into his articulating cupped palms through vibrating lips. Melville Bell, the father of Alexander Graham Bell, was at this time teaching elocution. He experimented broadly, and his writings on the science of speech are well known to this day.

It's impossible to ignore the work of Sir Charles Wheatstone, the man who is best known to first-year electrical engineering students for inventing the "Wheatstone Bridge." In England, Wheatstone is considered the father of the telegraph, an honor generally recognized in the United States as belonging to Samuel Morse. Wheatstone grew up helping his father in the family music shop in London. In 1821, at the age of nineteen, Wheatstone demonstrated his "Enchanted Lyre," an instrument in which tuned metal rods were excited by a source (located a small distance away) whose vibrations were transmitted via solid conductors. A periodical of the day reported that "words of speech may be susceptible to the same means of propagation." Alexander Graham Bell was to take this lead a few years hence.

In 1835, Wheatstone demonstrated to the Dublin Association for the Advancement of Sciences a speaking machine that he had constructed along the principles set down in von Kempelen's book. A representation of this machine is shown in Figure 2.4. Wheatstone's version of the machine was also hand-operated and included a bellows for maintaining pressure in a compressed air chamber, a vibrating reed, several levers and whistles, and a hand-manipulated leather resonator. Wheatstone's machine was said to have been capable of higher-quality speech than Von Kempelen's.

The Automaton Speaking Figure of Professor Joseph Faber

In about 1846 in London, Professor Joseph Faber of Vienna demonstrated his "Euphonia," a wax head perched atop a draped bust that spoke with an artificial tongue and a hinged jaw. Concealed from the audience behind the

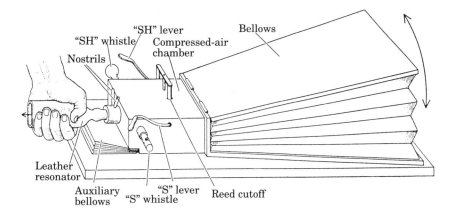

Figure 2.4 Wheatstone's version of Von Kempelen's third talking machine. *(From "The Synthesis of Speech," by James L. Flanagan. Copyright (c) 1972 by Scientific American, Inc. All rights reserved. Reprinted by permission.)*

drape was an apparatus that had the appearance of a small weaving loom (see Figure 2.5). Also out of sight was the female operator who, with the help of a sixteen-lever keyboard and foot-operated bellows, played the device like an organ. Not only could the machine speak whole sentences while varying its pitch, it could also whisper, sing, laugh, sigh, and cry. When Professor Faber died in the late 1860s, his niece and her husband came into possession of the machine and continued to demonstrate it under Faber's name throughout Europe and the United States. In 1873, when interest in the demonstrations all but disappeared, they petitioned some of the well-known acoustical scientists of the day for financial aid. When not much was forthcoming (other than a $500 loan from Alexander Graham Bell), Professor Faber's "Wonderful Talking Machine" became an historical curiosity. It's thought to have been destroyed in a warehouse fire in Boston, a dead-end except for the influence it might have had upon the man behind the greatest invention of the nineteenth century.

The Contributions of Alexander Graham Bell

Alexander Graham Bell is best known as the inventor of the telephone. Bell was born in Edinburgh in 1846. A number of factors combined to encourage his strong interest in the science of speech. His father and grandfather were both well-known elocutionists and phoneticians, both taught speech, and both were also named Alexander Bell. Alexander Graham Bell's uncle, David, was also a teacher of elocution. Bell's grandfather, a Shakespearian actor of some repute, had already published *Elegant Extracts*, a book that was present in all the best homes.

Figure 2.5 Professor Faber's speech organ.

When Alexander Graham Bell was three, his father, who went by his middle name, Melville, published a book called *A New Elucidation of the Principles of Speech and Elocution*. Melville Bell would soon publish widely on the subject of "visible speech," a universal phonetic alphabet that he had invented. Besides being born into a family already wholly immersed in the mechanics of speech, young Bell grew up in the British Empire at a time when the path to social and business advancement required an impeccable speaking style, faultless pronunciation, and a correct accent.[2]

---

[2]George Bernard Shaw's Professor Henry Higgins used the visible speech system developed by Bell's father to improve speech and transform the guttersnipe Eliza Doolittle to a lady in his 1913 classic play, "Pygmalion." In fact, Shaw might have gotten the idea for Henry Higgins' character from a play, "The Bride," which was published in 1847 by Bell's grandfather. Shaw was a boyhood friend of Alexander's cousin and was a frequent visitor in the home of Bell's uncle, David.

In 1862 at the age of fifteen, Bell went to London to live with his grandfather. A year later, Bell's father arrived to fetch the young Bell. Melville had seen Faber's speaking machine some years earlier in London and remembered being told at that time of Wheatstone's improved version of von Kempelen's machine. So, before leaving London with the boy, Melville took Alexander to a demonstration of Faber's famed machine and also to visit Wheatstone. It had been twenty-five years since Wheatstone had built his device, but, after removing more than two decades of dust, Wheatstone managed to make the machine talk. Melville and young Alexander listened as it pronounced a few mechanical-sounding words and sentences. When they left London, the two Bells took with them Wheatstone's own copy of von Kempelen's book. Back in Edinburgh, Melville encouraged Aleck (as Alexander was then called) and his two brothers (Melly, two years older than Aleck, and Ted, a year younger), to build their own speaking machine. Ted demurred; his interests ran more to art than to technical matters.

After a careful study of von Kempelen's book, the boys organized the task: Aleck would be responsible for constructing the tongue and mouth, and Melly would make the lungs, throat, and larynx. In the interest of science (and failing an adequate anatomical understanding of the larynx), they decided to autopsy their pet cat. Wishing the cat's end to be painless, they summoned a friend of Melly's, a medical student, who botched the job. In the end, they obtained the larynx of a lamb from a local butcher, vowing never again to resort to such expedients. Melly was able to arrange two thin pieces of rubber at an angle and attach them at one end of a tin tube. Thus, he had the throat and larynx that worked by blowing into one end of the tube. They would use their own lungs. Aleck took his grim assignment seriously. He made impressions of a human skull, and thought of creating a full cranium and face. He even considered using a wig. He soon thought better of it, however, and in the end crafted jaws, teeth, pharynx, and the nasal cavity from gutta-percha and settled for rubber lips and cheeks.

To create a tongue that could take on a variety of shapes, Aleck crafted a wooden replica, sliced it into six sections, padded each with cotton, and covered the whole with a sheet of rubber. Each section could be individually moved to produce a desired shape. The palate, which could be worked from outside by means of a lever, was also padded with cotton. When the parts of the apparatus were finally assembled, the boys found it easy to produce a human-sounding cacophony with Melly puffing into the tin tube and Aleck manipulating the lips, palate, and tongue. With experience, they were able to find the proper configurations for some consonants so that, by closing and opening the lips as Melly blew through the tin tube to produce a sustained vowel, their talking head could be heard to loudly articulate the word "mama." They had to be excited by this first word as they repeated the feat over and over in their attempt to perfect its pronunciation. They must have been even more thrilled when an upstairs tenant who heard the sounds scurried down the stairs expecting to help a poor, lost child find its mother.

Soon after they had lost interest in their talking apparatus, Aleck trained a Skye Terrier, a stray they named "Trouve," to growl while he manipulated the dog's mouth and throat. By "playing" the dog in this way, Aleck could make the dog growl out utterances that sounded like "ow, ah, ooh, ga, and ma." Aleck and the dog even learned to put it all together into the single utterance "How are you, Grandmama?" Of course, without Aleck, the dog couldn't talk at all.

At age nineteen Bell unknowingly repeated some of Helmholtz's acoustical experiments. When Helmholtz's work was brought to his attention, he acquired a French translation of the German scientist's book *On the Sensations of Tone*. Bell mistakenly thought that the tuning-fork device could electrically transmit vowel sounds, and in the process of correcting his thinking, he acquired the conviction that any sound could be transmitted electrically.

In 1875, at the age of twenty-nine, working with Thomas Watson on a device that Bell hoped would enable telegraph wires to carry multiple simultaneous messages Bell happened upon (and recognized the importance of) the principle that would enable him to construct the first telephone.[3] Bell and his employees would go on to other inventions such as: the harmonic telegraph, a device that was a precursor of the iron lung, a probe for locating bullets in the body, various devices to improve Edison's phonograph, a scheme for transmitting voice using light rays, and others. He would also found the companies that were to become Bell Laboratories and AT&T.

Developments in the Early Twentieth Century

On that day in 1876 when Bell displayed his telephone in Philadelphia's Centennial Hall, an entire science was born. Its objective was to further the effectiveness and efficiency of telephone communications. The need to maximize the information-carrying capacity of telephone and telegraph lines produced an economic pressure that eventually gave rise to the technology necessary to the synthesis of speech by electronic means. However, first scientists had to find better and better means for converting speech to an electrical analog, for transmitting it through a wire, and for converting it back to talking at a distant place. All of this had to be done with minimum expense and with minimum loss of fidelity.

It's impossible to cover all the work that has occurred since the early twentieth century that has contributed to (or even been a prerequisite to) the development of talking machines. However, J. L. Flanagan has reported some work that followed the thinking of Helmholtz and tested a variety of

---

[3]On Sunday, June 26, 1876, as General George Custer and his troop of soldiers were mounting their last stand on the Little Big Horn River before five-thousand braves of Chief Sitting Bull, Alexander Graham Bell demonstrated his new telephone for the first Centennial Exhibition in Centennial Hall at Philadelphia.

means for synthesizing vowels. These attempts included the use of organ pipes, multiple sirens, and tuning forks vibrating with appropriate amplitude at selected frequencies. Flanagan also reported the ideas of R. R. Riesz. In about 1937, Riesz proposed a finger-operated mechanical talker. The design emulates the vocal tract, with keys to control the configuration of lips, teeth, tongue, and pharynx. Two more keys control the use of voiced or unvoiced excitation. With practice, the machine could be made to emulate connected speech. Other mechanical devices were used to emulate and study characteristics of the vocal tract, but soon the interest in mechanical models for analysis of talking gave way to electrical ones.

Given the curiosity and inventiveness of humans, it was natural that once we achieved the means for converting an electrical analog back to speech with adequate fidelity (as was eventually done with the telephone), we would try to produce the electrical analog without benefit of the original speaker. The creative process often results in the means being produced before its application is recognized. Accordingly, it was also natural that humans would soon recognize the advantages of combining several of the new technologies: the ability to convert talking to an electrical analog, to store an electrical signal for later use, to process and modify electrical signals, and to convert electrical analogs back to talking. Thus, out of the creative processes born of the telegraph and telephone would eventually emerge the ability not only to offset talking in both time and space, but also to alter and improve the sound of that talking. During that process, however, many small advances would occur. In 1939, one of them would amaze the public.

Pedro the VODER

In a departure from the usual motive for funding such efforts, The Bell System (with the participation of the Bell Telephone Laboratories) prepared a spectacular exhibit for the 1939 New York World's Fair and also for the Golden Gate International Exhibition held the same year on Treasure Island in San Francisco Bay. The exhibits featured a speaking machine named Pedro the VODER, which consisted of electrical components used in everyday telephony. A skilled "player" was required to make Pedro talk. The speaking machine was named after Dom Pedro, the Emperor of Brazil, who was present at the 1876 demonstration of Bell's telephone at the first Centennial Exhibition in Philadelphia. Upon hearing a voice coming from the telephone receiver, Dom Pedro exclaimed, "My God, it talks." The name VODER was chosen from letters appearing in the words Voice Operated DEmonstratoR.

The exhibits took place in a high, circular area about eighty feet in diameter, with a balcony extending around most of the circumference (Figure 2.6).The space was bare except for VODER's platform, whichjutted into one end of the room. The audience, who was free to enter or leave the room at any time, stood during the performance, which was continuous but repeated itself about

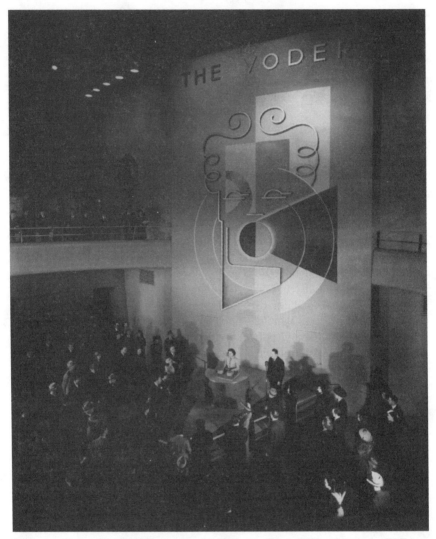

Figure 2.6 Pedro the VODER at the New York World's Fair in 1939. *(Courtesy AT&T Archives.)*

every six minutes. On the platform with VODER were a man with a microphone, who carried on a dialogue with the machine, and a woman seated at the console, who "played" the VODER like a piano or an organ. As a boy of six, I was fortunate to be present with my father at one of the San Francisco demonstrations.

VODER represented a masterful piece of work in 1939. It appears to have been created as a showcase for the large body of research and development in speech, acoustic theory, electrical engineering, and other disciplines that had been conducted up to that time. The immediately preceding achievement (by one of VODER's designers) was an electronic machine that altered the voice of any speaker in realtime. That machine could change the pitch, convert voiced phrases to whispered ones, alter the energy, and even change the quality of a person's voice. VODER added finger-operated keys as the control elements. Because VODER was not a mechanical analog but rather an electrical one, it had no parts that bore physical resemblance to the human vocal tract. Instead, it had functional equivalents, as suggested in Figure 2.7. VODER included two energy sources: a relaxation oscillator to provide excitation for voiced sounds, and a random noise generator for unvoiced sounds. These were switched by the human operator by means of a wrist bar and fed into the resonance circuit that consisted of ten band-pass filters, each with its own control key to adjust the amplitude of its contribution. The outputs of each band-pass filter were mixed to form a single "speech" signal that was then amplified and played through a loudspeaker. The machine was also fitted with several special keys to aid the operator with stops and other difficult sounds.

VODER spoke in simple, flowing sentences with a voice that sounded somewhat human but had a definite electronic quality. Its numerous speech impediments and the difficulty in understanding what it was saying could not be blamed entirely on the women who played VODER. Almost two years in advance of the exhibitions, Bell employees built twelve VODERs, established an extensive training program, and, out of a field of over three-hundred telephone operators, screened and selected twenty-four for extensive training on VODER. Their training consisted of six half-hour sessions on VODER every working day, with a lesson every other day. It took six months to learn to produce all the sounds of English and six more to acquire a satisfactory measure of naturalness and intelligibility. Figure 2.8 shows one of the players at VODER's console.[4] Such training was probably intense and must have often seemed like something right out of Buck Rogers. At times, pairs of these precocious machines were heard speaking to each other, and one could eavesdrop on complete conversations that in 1938 must have seemed eerily human.

Within a few years of the New York World's Fair and San Francisco exhibitions, a variety of electrical devices for studying speech were being developed. A class of machines called VOCODERs (VOice CODER) originated at Bell Laboratories. Like the VODER, VOCODERs used the resonant characteristic of speech to generate a coded electrical signal that embodied information regarding the excitation source and resonant features of the original

---

[4]The principal inventor of VODER, H. W. Dudley, retired from Bell Laboratories in 1961 after forty years of speech research. An old VODER machine was resurrected from storage and dusted off in time to speak at his retirement party. One of the original women players was enlisted, and, after a hiatus of more than twenty years, she and VODER produced a tolerable performance.

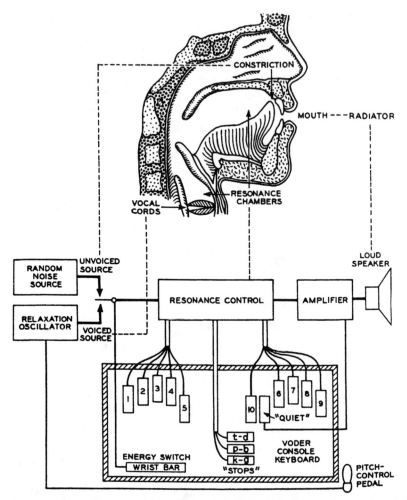

Figure 2.7 Pedro the VODER's electrical equivalents to the human vocal tract. *(Courtesy Journal of the Franklin Institute.)*

speech. VOCODERs consisted of a collection of band-pass filters, separate sources for voiced and unvoiced excitation, and a means for encoding the pitch of the original speech, which was reproduced from information describing settings for these devices. These slowly changing parameters required less bandwidth for transmission than the original waveform, but the gains in transmission efficiency were partially offset by a loss of fidelity.

In 1931 the Audichron Company created a machine that might qualify as the world's first voice processing application: it automatically spoke the time and temperature over the telephone. When a patron phoned, the ringing telephone was sensed by a microphone that triggered a motor that lifted the telephone receiver. Voice for the time and temperature was played from a pair of 78 RPM records. At about this same time, the British Post Office featured a speaking clock that used synchronized rotating optical disks to store utterances for the hours, minutes, and seconds of the day. Other interesting electrical devices soon appeared. Among them, sound spectrographs for displaying speech patterns on a cathode-ray screen. L. O. Schott

Figure 2.8 Pedro the VODER demonstrated by Mrs. Harper. *(Courtesy AT&T Archives.)*

in 1948 described a mechanism for mounting frosted lucite replicas of sound spectrograms on a large drum. A fluorescent light shone from inside as the drum turned to excite a bank of thirteen photoelectric cells whose outputs were fed to a synthesizing circuit and then to a loudspeaker. The patterns could be altered so that their effects could be heard and studied.

Milestones in the World of Telephone Communications

The introduction of Touch-Tone dialing in the early 1960s and a landmark ruling by the FCC in 1968 were to be key milestones in the march toward widespread acceptance of voice processing technologies. In the early days of the telephone, signaling was accomplished with ringers that operated by hand crank. Later, rotary dialers became available. Rotary dialers, still much in evidence today, don't allow signaling beyond the central office. In the early 1960s, DTMF (dual-tone multifrequency) dialing would be offered by telephone companies. DTMF dialing employs pairs of tones and are easily transmitted throughout the telephone network. As one of those accidental occurrences of good fortune, the use of DTMF has greatly accelerated the pace of development of voice processing.

In 1968 the FCC handed down a decision called the Carterphone Ruling. On petition of a Texas firm, Carter Electronics, the FCC ruled that direct connection of non-telephone company equipment to the telephone network would be permitted if operation of the network was not adversely affected. To ensure that requirement, the FCC required all such attachments to use a telephone company coupler. But in 1975, a registration program was instituted permitting direct attachment of devices that met network requirements. These decisions eventually led to deregulation and set the stage for stiff competition among manufacturers of telephone equipment and accessories.

The Digital Computer and Voice Processing

One of the first commercial attempts to apply the digital computer to voice processing applications was IBM's 7770 Audio Response Unit, which used a rotating drum to store speech data. By the early 1980s, there were other voice processing systems available that were based either on mainframe computers or on minicomputers. Using these systems, several financial institutions offered some services automatically by telephone. When the development of the integrated circuit enabled the use of small, inexpensive computers and special-purpose speech-processing circuits, the interest in voice processing applications began to grow rapidly. The proliferation of inexpensive hardware and software products to support voice processing followed almost immediately. Today, as we shall see in the following chapters, the growth continues at an almost explosive rate.

3

Speech Technology

In this chapter, I'll explore the features of speech production and some of the speech technology concepts that lie at the foundation of voice processing. In particular, I'll consider topics relevant to speech analysis and to speech synthesis. *Speech analysis* can be thought of as that part of voice processing that converts human speech to digital forms suitable for transmission or storage by computers. *Speech synthesis* functions are essentially the inverse of speech analysis—they reconvert speech data from a digital form to one that's similar to the original recording and suitable for playback. Speech analysis processes can also be referred to as *digital speech encoding* (or simply coding), and speech synthesis can be referred to as *speech decoding*. Despite the fact that one or more of the concepts discussed in this chapter are applied in one form or another in every voice processing product, the use of these concepts is transparent to users. Nevertheless, familiarity with the similarities, differences, advantages, and disadvantages of the various processing techniques discussed in this chapter will give you an acquaintance with the basics of speech technology and enable a broader understanding of voice processing.

By no means is the following treatment of speech technology an exhaustive one. Most of the common schemes or approaches are presented, while, in some cases, less popular ones are omitted. The intent is to introduce you to speech technology, discuss the important speech coding and decoding disciplines, touch on their good and bad points, and provide a glimpse into the complexities that lie therein. The references listed in the bibliography for this chapter are excellent reading for those who desire an in-depth study of the subject.

Production of Speech Waveforms

When a person speaks, compressed air from the lungs is forced through the vocal tract and emanates from the lips as a *sound pressure wave*—compressed air that varies with time in response to lung pressure and the configuration of the vocal tract. It's this wave, this acoustic wave, that's interpreted as sound when it falls upon a person's ears. To record a person's voice, we first convert the sound pressure wave to an electrical analog using a microphone. When we speak into a telephone receiver, a small microphone in the instrument converts the acoustic wave into an electrical analog, a signal that can be transmitted through the telephone network. The electrical signal output from a microphone varies in amplitude over time and is referred to as an *analog signal* or an *analog waveform*; if the signal results from speech, it's known as a *speech waveform*. Speech waveforms have the characteristic of being continuous (as opposed to discrete) in both time and amplitude, their amplitude varying in proportion to the density of air in the originating sound pressure wave.

Analog speech waveforms are rich with information that enables another's ear and brain to discriminate among its features and characteristics to discern the speaker's meaning. Many of these same features and acoustic cues are detected and used by machines during speech analysis and synthesis. Because it's helpful to understand some of the more important of these features, what they are, how they're produced, and what they mean, we'll briefly examine the acoustic operation of the human articulatory system.

Consider the vocal tract depicted in Figure 3.1. Speaking begins at the bottom of the diagram, as air under pressure from the lungs causes the folds of skin known as the *vocal chords* to vibrate. The elongated orifice between the vocal chords is called the *glottis*. The effect of the vibrations is to release repeated bursts of compressed air into the vocal cavities at frequencies that vary with the vibrations. The bursts of air proceed through the cavities, reflecting off the walls, eventually emanating from the lips and nostrils as a speech sound pressure wave. Articulators in the vocal tract are manipulated by the speaker to produce various effects. The vocal chords can be stiffened or relaxed to modify the rate of vibration. Or they can be turned off and the vibration eliminated while still allowing air to pass. The *velum* acts as gate between the oral and nasal cavities. It can be closed to isolate or opened to couple the two cavities. The tongue, jaw, teeth and lips can be moved to change the shape of the oral cavity. The nature of the sound pressure wave radiating outward from the lips depends upon these time-varying articulations and upon the absorptive qualities of the vocal tract's materials. The sound pressure wave exists as a continually moving disturbance of air. Particles move closer together as the pressure increases, or further apart as it decreases, each influencing its neighbor in turn as the wave propagates at the speed of sound. The amplitude of the wave at any position distant from

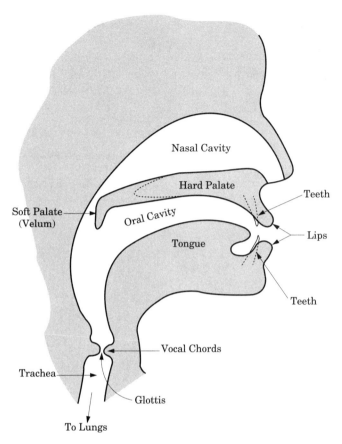

Figure 3.1 The human vocal tract.

the speaker is measured by the density of air molecules and grows weaker as the distance increases. When this wave falls upon the ear, it's interpreted as sound with discernible timbre, pitch, and loudness.

Air under pressure from the lungs moves through the vocal tract and comes into contact with various obstructions including the palate, tongue, teeth, lips, and lining. Some of its energy is absorbed by these obstructions; most is reflected. Reflections occur in all directions so that parts of waves bounce around inside the cavities for some time, blending with other waves, dissipating some of their energy, and finally finding their way out through the nostrils or past the lips. Some waves resonate inside the tract according to their frequency and the cavity's shape at that moment, combining with other reflections of themselves, reinforcing the wave's energy before exiting. Energy in waves of other, nonresonant frequencies is attenuated rather than amplified in its passage through the tract.

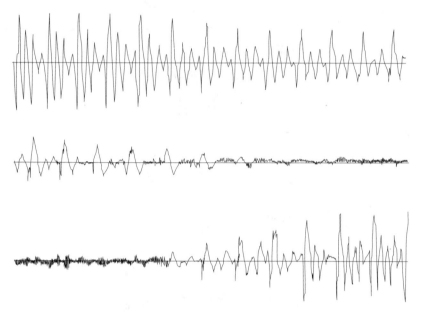

Figure 3.2   Analog waveform showing voiced and unvoiced speech.

The vocal tract is excited by air from the lungs and the excitation source is either voiced or unvoiced. During voiced speech, the vocal chords vibrate at a rate known as the *fundamental frequency*—this is what we experience as the pitch of a voice. You can feel the vibrations by putting your hand to your throat while you speak. Unvoiced speech is created when the vocal chords are held firm so they don't vibrate. Instead, the air is either aspirated through the vocal tract or, a constriction at the glottis, tongue, teeth or lips creates turbulence as the air is forced past. Thus, at any given instant, the complex sound pressure wave escaping the lips is a composite of voiced or unvoiced waves of varying frequencies and intensities. It's this complex sound pressure wave that's sensed by a microphone to produce an analog speech waveform.

Figure 3.2 illustrates an analog waveform for an utterance containing both voiced and unvoiced speech. The voiced part of the waveform consists of cycles that appear to be inexact copies of their neighbors. These cycles are repeated at the pitch period and appear in Figure 3.2 in the front and end sections, their wide excursions fading and reemerging as the articulators ease into and out of unvoiced sections. A large number of frequencies are combined as a result of voicing, and many of these can be seen in the waveform as higher frequency excursions superimposed upon those of the fundamental frequency. Notice how the waveform drops significantly in amplitude and consists entirely of high-frequency components during unvoiced speech.

While analog speech waveforms like those we've been discussing can be used to magnetize recording tape or to modulate transmitted radio or telephone signals, they must be converted to a stream of discrete values before use in a digital computer. It's therefore important to know something about the digitization process, the conversion of an analog waveform to one that's discrete in both time and amplitude.

Digitization of Analog Waveforms

Two processes are required to digitize an analog signal: sampling, which discretizes the signal in time, and quantizing, which discretizes the signal in amplitude. During digitization, an analog waveform is "sampled" at a fixed rate. Quantization takes place at each sample time when the waveform's amplitude is measured. From the measurement, a discrete value approximating the amplitude at that instant is selected as the output

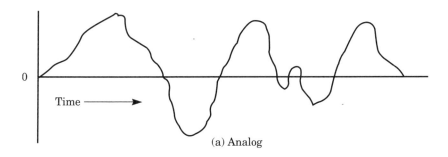

(a) Analog

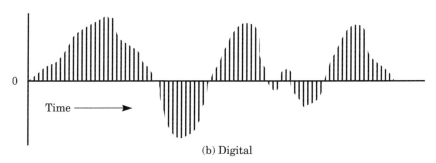

(b) Digital

Figure 3.3   An analog waveform with its digitized derivation.

quantity. As time progresses, the resulting stream of outputs represents the analog waveform and is called the digital waveform. The waveform in Figure 3.3a represents an analog waveform, and Figure 3.3b represents the digital waveform. Notice that the waveform in 3.3a varies continuously over time, while the waveform in 3.3b consists of a series of quantities, each approximating the amplitude of the analog waveform at a discrete time. The electronic devices that accomplish digitization are *A/D (analog to digital) converters*. The reverse process, conversion of digital signals to analog, is performed by *D/A converters*. Electronic devices that perform both processes are called *codecs* (for coder/decoder). A/D and D/A devices are discussed in chapter 7.

The objective of digitizing is to derive from an analog waveform a digital waveform that can be used in digital machines as a faithful representation. Naturally, it's desirable to do this with the smallest quantity of data that meets the objective. The ideal situation is to be able to pass a digitized waveform through a D/A converter and obtain a reconstructed analog waveform that very closely approximates the original. For speech, this means the resulting analog waveform, when played through an amplifier and speaker, should produce sounds that are nearly indistinguishable from the original talking. A trade-off occurs between this objective and the need to store and move the digital waveform as economically as possible, so we frequently settle for reconstructed speech that's merely intelligible. The trade-off can be thought of as one between maximization of quality and minimization of data rate. Differing demands affect the balance of these two objectives and have resulted in a variety of speech analysis schemes. Discussion of some of them follow. They all start with sampling and quantizing.

Sampling analog waveforms

When sampling an analog waveform at fixed intervals of period T seconds, the sampling frequency (also called *sampling rate*) is $1/T$ Hz (Hertz—cycles per second). For example, if a waveform is sampled once every 1/8000th seconds, the sampling frequency is 8000 Hz. The *Sampling Theorem*, a fundamental theorem of telecommunications, tells us that if the digital waveform is to uniquely represent the analog waveform, then the sampling rate must be at least twice the highest frequency present in the analog signal. That is, if the sampling frequency is F Hz, then the largest frequency present in the analog waveform cannot be greater than $F/2$ Hz (referred to as the *Nyquist frequency*). Suppose, for example, we wish to digitize a speech signal whose greatest frequency component is 3.4 kHz, then the sampling frequency must be 6.8 kHz or greater. While speech waveforms are not sine waves, the sine waves of Figure 3.4 serve to demonstrate what can happen when the sampling frequency is less than twice the Nyquist frequency. The

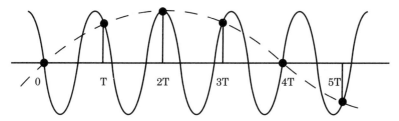

Figure 3.4 Sine wave with aliases.

figure illustrates how the series of samples taken from a given sine wave at fixed intervals greater than one-half the wave's cycle period can also define an entirely different sine wave of a lower frequency. The resulting ambiguity, the dual wave representation, is known as *aliasing*. A stream of digital quantities can represent (e.g., could have been obtained from either of) two sine waves with different frequencies. Either of the waves of Figure 3.4 could be reconstructed from the sequence of samples. If frequencies higher than one-half the sampling frequency are present in the speech waveform being sampled, then aliasing can occur, and higher frequency components will be folded back upon the lower frequencies to distort the result. In fact, if the Nyquist Frequency is F, then any frequency, f, such that $f > F$, will map to frequency $F - f$ under sampling. In other words, a frequency above the Nyquist frequency maps to one that's as far below Nyquist as the original is above.

To avoid aliasing, analog speech waveforms are filtered before digitization to remove unwanted higher frequencies. Filters used for this purpose are variously called antialiasing, band-pass, low-pass, presampling filters, etc. The speech spectrum contains frequencies beyond 10,000 Hz, but because most applications of digital speech involve transmission over the telephone network, higher frequencies can be safely filtered prior to digitization. The telephone network is designed to eliminate frequencies above about 3.4 kHz. (This causes a loss of some information from the transmitted signal, but the remaining frequencies still result in intelligible speech.) Typically, then, analog speech signals are filtered to eliminate frequencies above about 3000 to 4000 Hz, then sampled at 6000 to 8000 Hz. Because the cutoff frequency for most filters is not sharp (energy slants off in the neighborhood of the cutoff frequency), some aliasing is bound to occur, but most of it is low energy and maps into the reduced energy, high-frequency range where it causes a minimum of distortion. The result is often referred to as "telephone quality" or "toll quality" speech. It doesn't compare to what we expect from our home audio systems, but because it's what we experience every time we talk on the telephone, we've become used to it and consider it acceptable.

Quantizing analog waveforms

Whereas sampling makes an analog waveform discrete in time, quantizing makes it discrete in amplitude. It measures the analog signal at each sample time and produces a digital quantity in the form of a binary code word representing the amplitude at that instant. Quantizers are also called *coders* and require a decoder to perform the inverse process of reconstructing the original waveform. In selecting a quantization strategy, two important objectives are traded off: minimization of data rate and maximization of quality. Data rate is measured as the number of bits per second (bps) required to define the waveform, the product of samples per second and bits per quantized sample. Because sample rate is already fixed by the sampling theorem and the Nyquist Frequency discussed earlier, data rate minimization means reducing the number of bits per sample to as few as possible (e.g.: the quantizer's code-word bit size must be held to a minimum). This bears directly on the measurement resolution of the analog signal at each sample time, and this, in turn, affects quality (fidelity of the reconstructed waveform).

Maximization of quality means production of a digital waveform that can be reconverted to analog with only a small error. When the reconstructed voice waveform is played, it sounds very much like the original voice. Sampling, by itself, doesn't result in a loss of information. Quantization, on the other hand, resolves a continuum of amplitudes into a finite number of discrete quantities. This necessarily results in a loss of information and the consequent introduction of noise, called *quantization noise* or *quantization error*. Signal-to-noise ratio (SNR) in decibels (dB) is an accepted measure used to discuss voice quality. If the signal-to-noise ratio of a speech signal is low, the listener will experience intelligibility loss, fatigue, and other uncomfortable effects normally associated with a reduction in speech quality. For our purposes, we can think of the signal-to-noise ratio of a set of quantized samples whose mean is zero as the sum of the squares of sample values divided by the sum of the squares of quantization noise. To get signal-to-noise ratio in decibels, we take the logarithm of that result. For a set of N samples whose mean is zero where $x(n)$ is the nth sample, and $e(n)$ is the quantization error for that sample, then the signal-to-noise ratio in decibels, E, for the set is given by the following equation:

$$\frac{\sum_{i=1}^{N} x^2(i)}{\sum_{i=1}^{N} e^2(i)}$$

What's generally accepted as telephone-quality speech has a signal-to-noise ratio above 30 dB over most of its range. Furthermore, the addition of one bit per sample increases a quantized waveform's signal-to-noise ratio by about 6 dB. Likewise, a reduction of one bit in code word reduces the signal-to-noise ratio by 6 dB. So, maximization of quality means keeping quantization noise low relative to signal amplitude. The following sections discuss several quantization schemes.

Uniform quantization—uniform PCM. Input to the quantizer comes in the form of an analog voltage provided by the sampler. For a quantizer whose code word has n bits, the range of voltages is divided into 2^n regions; a unique digital code word of n bits is associated with each. The width of each region is known as the step size. The quantizer determines the region into which each input falls and outputs the corresponding code word. If the signal falls outside the quantizer's range, it's clipped (truncated at maximum), and the code word for the top region is output. The number of regions is usually a power of two because this helps to minimize the digital bit rate. In uniform quantization, all regions are of the same width. The step size must be small to minimize quantization noise but large enough to give the quantizer an adequate range. The range, R, of an n bit quantizer with step size, s, is given by the following equation.

$$R=2^n{\cdot}s$$

If the range is not large enough, clipping occurs more frequently, and this, of course, is another source of quantization noise. Both code word size and step size are chosen in consideration of the data-rate versus quantization-noise trade-off.

Figure 3.5 illustrates one of many versions of the process for a 3-bit uniform quantizer with step size s. Note that it's unimportant how the digital codes are assigned as long as the decoder mirrors the assignment. Code assignment in the figure permits interpretation of the left-most bit as a sign bit. It has been established that, for uniform quantization of zero-mean speech signals, an 11-bit quantizer provides the best trade-off between data rate and quality and can produce telephone-quality speech for signal amplitudes above 1 percent of the quantizer's range.

When an analog voltage is quantized, assuming it's not clipped, the value of the output differs from that of the input by no more than one-half the step size. (If it were greater, it would fall into an adjacent region.) Thus, assuming a negligible number of samples are clipped, quantization noise for speech waveforms oscillates mildly around a mean of one-half the step size. For the signal-to-noise ratio to be high, quantization noise must be low relative to signal amplitude. But quantization noise in a given uniform quantizer is essentially constant. Therefore, such a quantizer will produce digital waveforms whose quality varies directly with the amplitude of the incoming signal. Amplitude variations are common and are attributed to differences

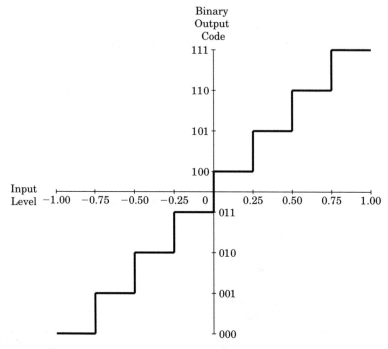

Figure 3.5 Uniform quantizer step function.

among speakers, normal features inherent in speech, head movement or other tendencies of the speaker to alter loudness. It can be seen from an examination of Figure 3.5 that a drop in input amplitude by half is equivalent to a 1-bit reduction in the width of the output code word (half the code words are not used). That 1-bit reduction corresponds to a 6-dB reduction in signal-to-noise ratio. It's easy to see why we must start with an 11-bit code word in uniform quantization. If the input signal amplitude were always near maximum, 6-bit or 7-bit coding would be sufficient to assure a high-quality output.

A scheme in which quantization noise is independent of signal level would avoid the uneven speech quality resulting from uniform quantization. Logarithmic quantization provides such a scheme.

Logarithmic quantization—log PCM. The objective of logarithmic quantization is to maintain a nominally constant signal-to-noise ratio over a broad range of analog amplitudes. Signal-to-noise ratio will not vary with incoming signal amplitude if, instead of quantizing the analog value, we quantize a log function of the value. Signal-to-noise ratio will depend only upon step size. For example, for analog values, x, the equation

$$y = 1 + k \log x$$

provides such a log function. This function is applicable only when x is greater than zero. A piecewise linear approximation to the function can be devised that's valid both for zero and negative values. Logarithmic quantization is a compression process; it reduces the dynamic range of a signal according to a logarithmic function. After compression, a reverse process, exponentiation, is required to recover a facsimile of the original; the entire cycle is often referred to as *companding* (for compressing/expanding). Indeed, logarithmic quantization is called *instantaneous companding* because it requires only current samples. The next section introduces companding techniques that take into account the signal's history and therefore require memory.

Figure 3.6 shows a logarithmic curve and its linear approximation. The horizontal axis portrays the input level in proportion to the quantizer's full scale. The piecewise linear approximation is divided into eight sectors— four positive and four negative, a division convenient for implementation as a 6-bit logarithmic quantizer. Quantizers, however, produce discrete values, so the linear approximation of each sector must itself be approximated. The

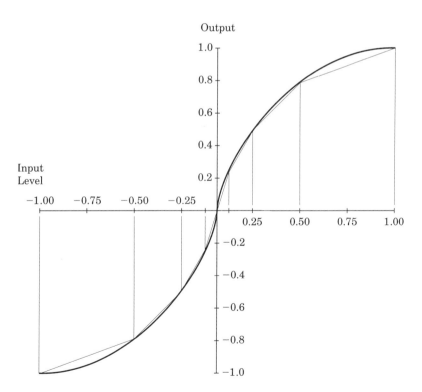

Figure 3.6 Piecewise linear approximation to logarithmic function.

most natural way to do this is with step functions (similar to those used in uniform quantization). Two familiar questions arise concerning step size and the number of steps for each of the linear sections. These questions have already been answered for two well-known schemes commonly used throughout the world. In North America, the preferred scheme is called μ-Law, but in Europe a similar approach called A-Law is popular. Both employ 8-bit logarithmic quantization (sixteen sectors and sixteen steps per sector) and are similar in concept to the 6-bit examples used in Figures 3.6 and 3.7.

Note that the sectors of Figures 3.6 and 3.7 increase in size as input values move further from zero. In fact, each succeeding sector is twice the size of the preceding one. This is true in both the positive and the negative directions. Each of the eight sectors of Figure 3.7 is uniquely identified with a 3-bit binary number. This figure also shows stepwise approximations to the linear components within each sector. It's efficient to select an identical number of steps for each sector so that the number is a power of two. I've chosen to divide each sector into eight steps; each step within a sector can be uniquely identified by a 3-bit binary number. The assignment of binary codes is arbitrary as long as the decoder's reconstruction follows the as-

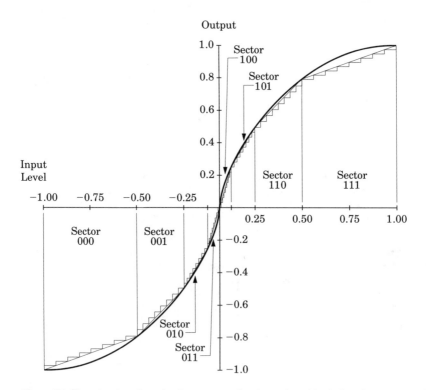

Figure 3.7 Discrete-step piecewise linear approximation to logarithmic function.

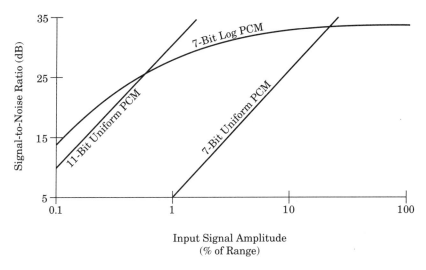

Figure 3.8 Quality of 7-bit and 11-bit uniform and 7-bit log PCM. (*Copyright (c) 1957, AT&T. Reprinted with permission.*)

signment scheme. In the example of Figure 3.7, it's convenient to assign the binary sector number to the left-most three bits of the code word and the step number within the sector to the right-most three bits. Thus, using a 6-bit code word, each step, regardless of its sector, is uniquely identified. In this assignment scheme, as in that of Figure 3.5, the most significant bit of the code word can be considered a sign bit—a feature that can be useful later during digital signal processing of the waveform. The step size within each sector is one-eighth of the sector as required by code word size and number of sectors. The step size is small for input values close to zero but grows larger as the value moves toward the maximum or minimum of the quantizer's range. Thus, as the signal shrinks in amplitude, quantization noise shrinks in response, providing a more constant output quality.

Figure 3.8 compares the quality of 7-bit μ-Law PCM quantization with both 7-bit and 11-bit uniform PCM quantization as a function of input signal amplitude. Incoming signal level is shown as percent of the quantizer's full range. Signal-to-noise ratio for 7-bit μ-Law remains high and fairly constant across a wide range of signal levels. It rises steeply from one-tenth of one percent of full range and attains telephone quality speech (about 30 dB) for signal levels slightly above 1 percent of the quantizer's range. This is a savings of approximately four bits over uniform quantization at toll quality. At a sampling rate of 8 kHz, the savings amounts to a difference of 32 kbps in the data rate. The difference between 7-bit μ-Law and 7-bit uniform PCM is striking. Seven-bit uniform quantization fails to achieve telephone quality speech for signal strength that's 10 percent of range or below. The quality of PCM derived from

7-bit μ-Law logarithmic quantization is considered by many to be a standard for telephone-quality speech. In spite of this, the telecommunications industry generally adds one bit and employs 8-bit μ-Law to provide a margin as telephone messages, passing through successive links, are converted back and forth between analog and digital.

Adaptive quantization. Further reductions in data rate (or the equivalent 6-dB-per-bit gain in signal-to-noise ratio) are achieved by dynamically adapting quantizer step size in response to variations in signal amplitude. The objective is to maintain a quantizer range that's matched to the input signal's dynamic range. Techniques that adapt step sizes are referred to as *adaptive PCM* or APCM. Step size adaptation is accomplished for both uniform and nonuniform quantizers, and conditions for adaptation are based on several signal statistics—all related to amplitude. There are many different adaptation algorithms, but all attempt to estimate the slowly varying amplitude of the input signal. Many of them are called *syllabic companding* techniques (as differentiated from *instantaneous companding*) because their quantization characteristics change at about the same rate as syllables occur in speech. All must balance the need to increase step size to attain adequate quantizer range against the loss in signal-to-noise ratio that results from larger step sizes.

Several adaptation approaches calculate signal amplitude statistics over a relatively short span of samples and adjust step size accordingly. Two approaches, *feed forward adaptive PCM* and *feedback adaptive PCM* are used in adjusting step size. In both, adjustments are based on calculations involving short-time energy, variance, standard deviation, dynamic range, or other such measurements made over a block of incoming samples. The term *block companding* also refers to these techniques. In feedback adaptation, step size calculations are performed on each sample as it arrives for processing. Let's assume there are N samples per block. After N samples have been processed (using the previous step size), the new step size resulting from these samples is used in processing the succeeding N samples. The procedure continues throughout the sample train, always applying a step size that's N samples old. Feed forward adaptation, on the other hand, uses a given step size only in processing those samples from which it was calculated. A block of N samples is first accumulated, step size calculations are made on the block, then every sample in the block is processed using that step size. Feed forward schemes require buffering a block of data samples and thus incur a quantization delay sufficient to accumulate the required values. Another disadvantage of feed forward encoding schemes is that side-information concerning step size must be transmitted or stored with the quantized data (usually only once per block). This, however, leads to one of the advantages of feed forward quantizers: step sizes are not subject to quantization noise because they're produced from unquantized samples and explicitly passed to

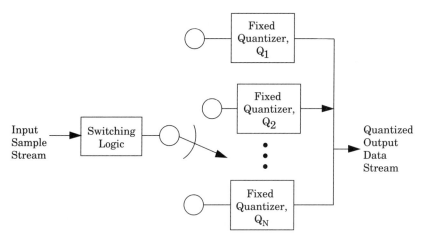

Figure 3.9 Switched adaptive quantization with fixed quantizers.

the decoder. In contrast, while feedback adaptive PCM enjoys the advantage of being instantaneous, its step size estimates are sensitive to quantization noise because the decoder must compute them from quantized samples.

Figure 3.9 illustrates the concept of switched quantizers that compose a bank of separate fixed-quantizers, an interesting approach to implementing step size adaptation. When the system adapts, the appropriate fixed quantizer is switched into the processing stream, and the others are switched out. With a bank of no more than two fixed quantizers, switched systems demonstrate gains over nonadaptive ones with the same number of bits. Most adaptive quantizers produce improvements over their nonadaptive counterparts, saving approximately one bit in output word size or increasing signal-to-noise ratio by about 6 dB.

Analysis/Synthesis in the Frequency Domain

The analog and digital speech waveforms we've been discussing exist in the time-domain; the waveform represents speech as amplitude versus time. The time-domain sound pressure wave emanating from the lips is easily converted by microphone to a speech waveform, so it's natural that speech analysis/synthesis systems operate directly upon this waveform. Other approaches, ones that operate in the frequency domain, offer their own advantages. The objective of every speech-coding scheme is to produce code of minimum data rate so that a synthesizer can reconstruct an accurate facsimile of the original speech waveform. Frequency domain coders attempt to reach this objective by exploiting the resonant characteristics of the vocal tract. As we'll presently see, there's much information to be exploited in time-varying speech spectra obtained from the time-domain waveform.

Spectrum analysis of speech waveforms

A speech spectrum represents the frequency distribution of energy present in speech over a period of time; examples are shown in Figures 3.10a and 3.10b. Smoothed traces are shown superimposed on the frequency spectra in the figures to emphasize the net contour. As shown in Figure 3.10a, energy in voiced speech decreases as frequency increases. In fact, the rate of energy decay in the frequency spectrum of the signal emanating from the lips is about 6 dB per octave; it actually decays about 12 dB per octave in the vocal tract, but radiation at the lips adds 6 dB per octave. Figure 3.10b gives an example of the frequency spectrum for unvoiced speech. It shows the unvoiced spectrum to be rather flat, with a slight peak near 3 kHz.

Formants.   Certain frequencies resonate within the vocal tract, depending upon its size and shape. The energy in those frequencies is reinforced when reflections of the wave coincide and boost each other; energy in other frequencies tends to dissipate—rapidly at antiresonant frequencies in which energy is damped. Resonant frequencies appear in the spectrum as humps and are called *formant frequencies* or simply *formants*. The first few formants can be readily discerned in the example spectra of Figure 3.10a. A voiced speech waveform contains many formants, but only the first few are important to the analysis of speech signals. The later formants, their energy being small relative to their predecessors, are usually either ignored or just estimated as a group. The nasal cavity was shown in Figure 3.1. It has its own resonant and antiresonant frequencies and, when the velum is open, the nasal cavity acts as a separate but coupled parallel acoustic path with the oral cavity and mixes its own formants into the waveform. Coupling of the subglottal system (lungs and larynx) also affects the acoustic brew—but this occurs only during part of the pitch period (when the glottis is open) and is generally ignored except in very precise analyses. If the resolution of the frequency spectrum is high, a fine ripple is superimposed over the formant humps. These ripples are representations of the excitation source and appear at the pitch frequency and its harmonics. An example of this phenomenon is shown in Figure 3.10a.

The frequency spectrum changes continually during speech, responding to motions of the articulators. Naturally, formant frequencies and bandwidths vary in the process. Formant frequencies also vary from person to person according to head size and other factors. The first formant, the one with lowest frequency, occurs in a range from about 200 to 1200 Hz. The second falls into an overlapping range from about 500 to 3000 Hz. The first two formants go a long way toward identifying vowels.

Filters.   Filters are commonly used to derive the frequency spectrum from part of a speech waveform. Filters operate on analog signals to pass only

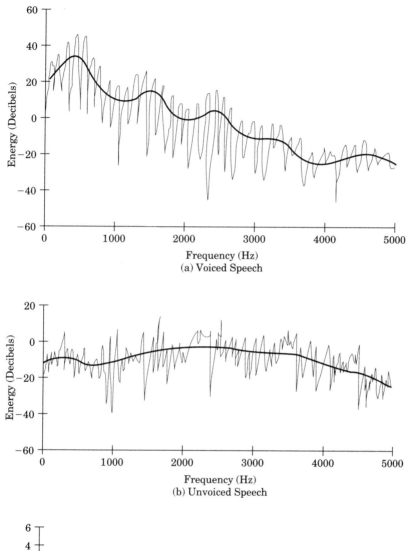

(a) Voiced Speech

(b) Unvoiced Speech

(c) Cepstrum of the frequency spectrum of (a)

Figure 3.10 (a-c) Frequency spectrums.

certain frequencies and filter out all others. I've already discussed the use of filtering in connection with preprocessing of speech analog waveforms. Unwanted frequencies can be those that lie above a given level, those below, or both. Filters that perform these transformations are called respectively, *low-pass, high-pass*, and *band-pass* filters. A band-pass filter can be used to determine energy in its band; a bank of such filters, each set to pass adjacent (or overlapping) bands, will give the frequency spectrum of an input waveform. A single speech spectrum is generally derived over only a short portion of the waveform, perhaps a section extending no more than 10 to 25 ms. As the pass bands are made smaller, finer and finer frequency resolution can be obtained.

Sound spectrograms. A graph of an utterance's frequency variation over time can be obtained from a sound *spectrograph*, a spectral analyzer that inputs a speech waveform and plots the energy in frequency bands over time. An example spectrogram is shown in Figure 3.11. The sound spectrograph has long been used by analysts in speech research. Energy is portrayed by the heaviness of the vertical striations. The vertical lines represent individual openings of the vocal chords during voicing; as pitch changes, the distance between adjacent lines changes as well. Notice the broad swath each formant traces through the graph and the absence of formants during unvoiced speech. Unvoiced sections produce a more solid appearance at higher frequencies.

Discrete Fourier transforms—DFT. Mathematical procedures exist for filtering waveforms digitally. Discrete Fourier transforms, for example, are excellent mathematical filters; they're used to calculate correlation functions and to produce frequency spectra from discrete waveforms of finite length. In calcu-

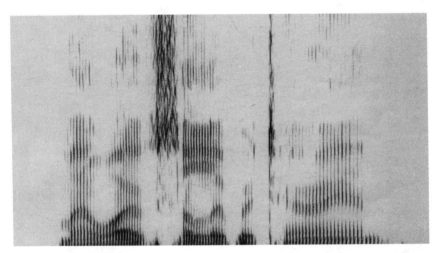

Figure 3.11 Spectrogram.

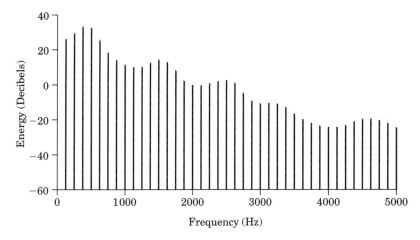

Figure 3.12 Short-time frequency spectrum for voiced waveform (125 Hz pitch).

lating frequency spectra, a waveform of N samples is input. The DFT divides the spectrum from 0 Hz through the sampling frequency into N equal steps and provides an energy value for each. However, the outputs are symmetric about the center of the frequency range (half the sampling rate), so only $N/2$ values are used. The DFT assumes the input samples to comprise one cycle of a periodic waveform, and it interprets the data accordingly. It might, therefore, seem reasonable to isolate a single pitch cycle for input to the DFT, but, finding the start and end of a cycle is not always possible in speech waveforms.

Formant estimation. Formant frequencies can be determined from the digital representation of a frequency spectrum by intentionally misinterpreting that data. The representation is itself a set of digital values. By considering this set to be a time-domain waveform rather than data in the frequency domain, it too can be processed through the DFT. First, though, the ripple resulting from the pitch frequency and its harmonics must be removed. This is done by taking the logarithm of the frequency spectrum data set, passing that through the DFT, setting the high frequency components to zero (e.g., filtering them out), and using an inverse DFT to convert the result back to a frequency spectrum. What results from this is a smoothed version of the spectrum in which the first few formants should be prominent—as illustrated by the humps in Figure 3.12.

The result of DFT processing of the logarithm of a frequency spectrum is called a *cepstrum*. Interestingly, this name was coined from "spectrum" by reversing the order of the first four letters—sort of symbolic for the way the process operates. A sometimes valuable side effect of calculating the cepstrum is that it has a significant peak at the fundamental frequency and lesser ones at its harmonics, so it can be useful in determining pitch. Figure 3.10c is a representation of the cepstrum for the spectrum of Figure 3.10a. Note from the ripples in Figure 3.10a that the spectrum has a fundamental frequency of about 125 Hz. As expected, the cepstrum shows a prominent peak at 8 ms, the exact period of a 125 Hz signal.

Parametric coders—vocoders. Parametric coders model speech production mechanisms rather than the resulting waveform. They're based on the notion that the vocal tract changes slowly, and its state and configuration at any instant can be closely modeled using a small set of parameters. They take advantage of the vocal tract's slow rate of change, allowing one set of parameters to approximate the true state over a period up to about 25 ms. Parametric coders are also called vocoders (from VOice CODERs). Most vocoders characterize the frequency spectrum and vocal tract excitation source (lungs and vocal chords) with only a handful of parameters. These include about ten or fifteen filter coefficients that define vocal tract resonance characteristics, a simple two-valued parameter specifying whether the excitation source is voiced or unvoiced, a value for excitation energy, and one for pitch (during voicing only). Vocal tract state is deduced by analyzing the speech waveform every ten to twenty-five milliseconds and calculating a new set of parameters (a data frame) at the end of the period. A succession of data frames is later used to control synthesis of a facsimile waveform. Vocoders include the ability to switch between two separate excitation sources: a variable-period impulse source for voiced speech and a white noise (high-frequency) generator for unvoiced. During playback, one of the two excitation sources is passed to a filter network that's tuned using each frame's filter coefficients.

The earliest vocoder is attributed to Homer Dudley of Bell Telephone Laboratories and dates back to the late 1930s. Pedro the VODER (described in chapter 1) was similar in its synthesis section to a vocoder and is also attributed to Homer Dudley. Pedro featured ten parallel band-pass filters whose inputs came from finger keys rather than from analytical parameter sets. Figure 3.13 is a block diagram of a simple vocoder. Switching between voiced and unvoiced speech is controlled by a two-valued parameter in the data frames. The pitch parameter controls the rate of impulse generation for voiced speech. Unvoiced excitation requires no control; when switched into the system it always produces the same white noise excitation. Loudness control, driven by the gain parameter, adjusts the amplitude of the excitation signal entering the filter network whose tuning, in turn, is adjusted with each new set of filter coefficients.

Complications arise from factors relating to the nature of speech. For example, the block diagram shows a simple two-valued switch that doesn't allow voiced and unvoiced excitation to occur together. Synthesis of aspiration, however, requires unvoiced excitation. But voiced aspiration also occurs in speech. Accommodation of details like this requires a complexity of design beyond that shown in the block diagram.

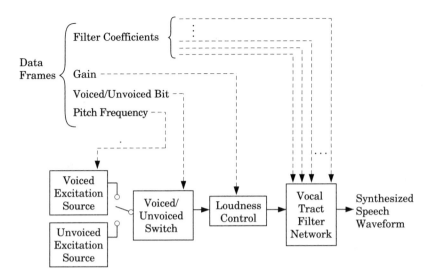

Figure 3.13 Typical VOCODER.

Separation of excitation and vocal tract parameters. In addition to its low data rate, one of the advantages of vocoders is its separation of excitation parameters. Pitch, gain, and voiced/unvoiced bit are themselves parameters in the data frame, so these variables can be modified before or during synthesis. Thus, for example, entirely different amplitude and pitch contours can be computed for an utterance. Or, voiced speech can be changed to a whisper by setting the voiced/unvoiced bit to a constant unvoiced. It's also possible to modify the resonance parameters to alter the speech itself, but this is a fairly complex operation because the effect of a change to any particular filter coefficient depends upon the values of all the others.

Excitation sources. A periodic impulse generator and a pulse-shaping circuit compose the excitation source for voiced speech. The impulse period adjusts to follow the original pitch contour according to the pitch frequency parameter. The glottal pulse-shaping section helps form an excitation waveform approximating a normal glottal pulse. A number of pulse shapes have been studied and, not surprisingly, a higher degree of naturalness is attained when the synthetic pulse shape mirrors a natural glottal pulse. The frequency spectrum for unvoiced speech (Figure 3.10b) is nearly flat, so a random noise generator serves adequately for the excitation source. During unvoiced speech, the pitch frequency parameter in the data frame is meaningless and not used.

Vocal tract filter network. The vocal tract filter network emulates resonance characteristics of the original vocal tract. The synthetic glottal waveform entering this section of the synthesizer is transformed to a speech waveform approximating the original. There are several different types of vocoders, and they can be categorized according to the design of the filter network. It might be designed to reproduce formants, as with the *formant vocoder* or simply divide the spectrum into ten or fifteen bands, as in the *channel vocoder*. Formant vocoders include a filter for each of the first few formants, then lump all higher formants into one final filter. A *homomorphic vocoder* relies upon calculation of a cepstrum every 10 or 20 ms for coding of both excitation and vocal tract parameters. *Phase vocoders* consider the phase of a signal in addition to its magnitude in an attempt to achieve a lower data rate for the same voice quality. *LPC vocoders* and *voice-excited (RELP) vocoders* are discussed in later sections.

Several different architectures are used in filter network design of vocoder synthesizers, including series and parallel structures. The series design features a filter circuit for each frequency band. Excitation sources are input to the first filter, whose output goes to the second; output of the second goes to the third, and so on until a synthesized waveform emanates from the final stage. With a parallel design the excitation source is simultaneously input to all filters whose outputs are combined to produce the output waveform. One advantage of a parallel architecture over a series architecture is that parallel architecture facilitates inclusion of nasal effects, which, in a natural vocal tract, combine with those of the oral tract in a parallel fashion.

Data rates and speech quality. Vocoder data rates run from about 1200 bps to 9600 bps; they depend upon the frame rate and upon the accuracy with which each parameter is coded. Speech quality for an example vocoder is discussed in more detail in a later section titled "Linear Predictive Coding—LPC." Speech quality varies depending on many factors, but vocoder speech is generally inferior to most of the other speech compression approaches discussed.

Subband coding—SBC

Subband coding subdivides the speech spectrum into a small number of frequency ranges (subbands) and codes each individually. Several advantages accrue when coding in a reduced frequency range. Every subband can be translated downward in frequency, thus reducing the largest frequency component and the Nyquist rate. As a consequence, a lower sampling rate can be used. Furthermore, not all frequencies in the spectrum contribute in the same measure to speech intelligibility; quantization accuracy within each subband can be tailored to its contribution. In fact, frequencies with little or no energy can be omitted entirely. Various coding schemes, including PCM or ADPCM, can be used within subbands. Figure 3.14 illustrates how the spectrum might be subdivided.

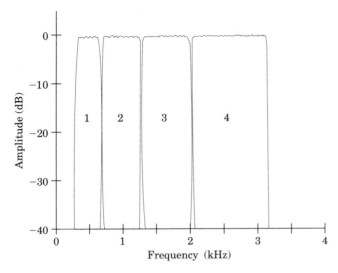

Figure 3.14 Partitions in the frequency domain for subband coding. *(Copyright (c) 1976, AT&T. All rights reserved. Reprinted with permission.)*

Much study has been devoted to determining how best to choose the number of subbands and their frequencies, bandwidths, and boundaries. Some designs have four subdivisions, others eight or more. Center frequencies are often fixed, but there are designs in which some of them float. Boundaries might overlap, or gaps might occur between them. Formant frequencies contribute most to speech quality. This fact is used in variable-band implementations wherein the positioning of the first two subbands are allowed to fluctuate with the formants. Of course, the formants must be located in such an implementation, and this increases complexity and cost of the coder.

In performance tests with a group of twelve listeners, 16 kbps SBC was preferred about 90 percent of the time over ADPCM at the same data rate. When 26 kbps SBC was compared with 24 kbps ADPCM, it was preferred only 35 percent of the time. In similar tests, 9.6 kbps SBC was compared with ADM at about 10 kbps and 17 kbps. In both tests SBC was preferred—about 90 percent of the time in the first case and 65 percent in the second.

Analysis/Synthesis in the Time Domain

I've discussed sampling and quantization of a speech waveform. These processes together compose digitization of a speech signal to produce a digital speech waveform that consists of a string of digital values spaced over a period of time. The waveform is said to exist in the time domain. As previously discussed, it can also be converted to a form that exists in the frequency domain. The speech waveform (whether analog or digital, frequency domain or time domain) contains a significant amount of redundant information about the speech that it represents. By exploiting these redundancies, and removing some of it through further processing, we're able to produce a waveform with a lower data rate that still represents the original speech and allows a reasonably faithful reconstruction of it. Techniques for finding alternate, lower data rate representations are said to code the digital waveform, and the algorithms and devices used to accomplish it are called *coders*.

It's generally true of coded speech waveforms that data rate and quality are directly related, that quality rises as the data rate rises, and that a reduction in data rate results in a proportionally poorer quality speech. The objective of all of these techniques, however, is to beat that equation, to get ahead of the curve, so to speak, and reduce the data rate as much as possible without the proportional reduction in quality. This is as true of the frequency-domain coders previously discussed as it is for the time-domain coders that follow.

Differential coding

Digital speech waveforms sampled at (or above) the Nyquist rate are highly correlated from sample to sample. In fact, they're moderately well correlated over a span of several samples. In practical terms, this means that values of adjacent samples don't differ greatly. It also means that, given some number of past samples, it's possible to predict with some accuracy the value of the next sample. This fact leads to differential coding techniques that, rather than coding the input waveform directly, code the difference between that waveform and one reconstituted from linear predictions of past quantized samples. These approaches are also called *linear prediction*. At sample time n, they code $e(n)$, where

$$e(n) = y(n) - y'(n)$$

and where $y(n)$ is the input sample and $y'(n)$ a predicted value of the input. The prediction, $y'(n)$ is obtained from p past samples according to the relationship

$$y'(n) = a_1 y(n-1) + a_2 y(n-2) + ... + a_p y(n-p)$$

which can be written

$$y'n = \sum_{i=1}^{p} = a_i y(n-i)$$

The quantities a_i in the preceding equation are known as prediction coefficients. The output quantities, the prediction errors, $e(n)$, have a smaller dynamic range than the original signal so they can be coded with fewer bits (or achieve a higher signal-to-noise ratio with the same number of bits). The signal-to-noise ratio varies with the order of the predictor (that is, the value of p—which is the number of prediction coefficients) and, with fixed predictors, can reach from about 8 to 12 dB above comparable PCM systems; the higher the order, the greater the gains.

These techniques are called *linear predictions* because, as the preceding equations show, the predictions involve only first-order functions of past samples. The prediction coefficients are selected so as to minimize the total squared prediction error, E, where

$$E = \sum_{i=0}^{n} e^2(i)$$

and where n is the number of samples. The quantity, E, depends upon the character of the speech waveform and thus upon the speaker and the loudness and content of the speech. E is time-varying, so it follows that for optimum performance, the coefficients must also vary with time. It's not necessary, however, for the coefficients to be recalculated with each new sample. Thus, a trade-off can be made by adapting the coefficients less frequently in response to the slowly changing speech signal. In fact, predictor coefficients are adapted every 10 to 25 milliseconds, a rate slightly faster than syllabic. Once computed, the coefficients are used with all samples until they're recalculated. The quantity, n, in the preceding equation is the number of samples over which the error signal is minimized. In conjunction with the sampling rate, it specifies the time span over which minimization takes place. This time is not always the same as the adaptation interval.

As with adaptive quantization, adaptive prediction is performed with either a feedback or feed-forward approach. In the case of feedback predictive adaptation, the adaptation is based on calculations involving the previous set of n samples, with the disadvantage that the prediction coefficients are used for a succeeding set of samples rather than for the ones from which they were derived. With feed forward predictive adaptation, a buffer is required by the predictor to accumulate n samples before the coefficients can be calculated. A delay sufficient to allow accumulation of the samples is introduced into the process. Typical for speech signals are tenth-order adaptive feed-forward predictors with $n = 128$ and a sampling rate of 8 kHz.

For order four and higher, adaptive predictors achieve signal-to-noise ratios of 3 or 4 dB more than their nonadaptive counterparts, and almost 14 dB over PCM. Devices that use this technique are referred to as *APC*, adaptive predictive coders. One APC design that can't be described as simple, the *Atal-Schroeder adaptive predictor*, takes advantage of the spectral nature of speech and also of its periodicity to achieve a signal-to-noise ratio of about 20 dB more than that of PCM coders.

Differential PCM—DPCM. A simple realization of linear prediction is to be found in DPCM coding. Rather than quantizing samples directly, the difference between adjacent samples for speech waveforms can be quantized with almost one less bit while maintaining the signal-to-noise ratio. In fact, the signal-to-noise ratio can be improved by scaling the earlier of the two samples. If $y(n)$ is the value of a sample at time n for a PCM waveform, then the DPCM sample at time n is given by $e(n)$, where

$$e(n) = y(n) - a'y(n-1)$$

and where a' is a scaling factor. But this is equivalent to the equations previously given for linear prediction with a first-order predictor (the prediction is made from one previous sample).

Differential PCM is also called *differential quantization* or *differential coding*. The dynamic range represented by the differences from sample to sample doesn't vary as widely as the signal itself. Hence, for the same number of bits, the difference signal can be represented with an improvement of 4 or 5 dB.

Adaptive differential PCM—ADPCM. Additional gains over DPCM are obtained by including adaptation. This is done either by incorporating adaptive quantization or by adjusting the scaling factor (at syllabic rate), or both.

Delta modulation—DM. A simplified realization of differential coding is found in delta modulation, where the code word is reduced to one bit. Delta modulation, then, is another form of first-order linear prediction, one in which a 1-bit code word is used. Delta modulation is called *linear delta modulation* or LDM when the step size is fixed. A single sign bit representing the direction of the difference between the input waveform and the accumulated output is stored at sample time. The bit's used by the decoder to determine whether to increment or decrement the output waveform by one step size. *Slope overload* distortion occurs whenever the input signal's slope exceeds the maximum slope attainable by the coder. *Granular noise* distortion occurs whenever variations in the input signal are small relative to step size. These distortions are illustrated in Figure 3.15; distortion magnitudes are represented by the shaded areas.

Slope overload can be lessened by a higher sampling rate, a larger step size, or both. Granular noise, on the other hand, is reduced only by lessening step size. For voice waveforms, *oversampling* (sampling at a rate higher than the Nyquist rate) helps to control slope overload distortion. With the proper balance of sampling rate and step size, delta modulation

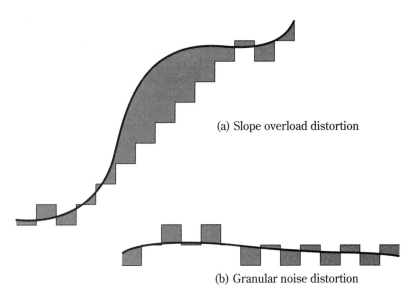

(a) Slope overload distortion

(b) Granular noise distortion

Figure 3.15 Delta modulation.

can result in a smaller data rate for a given signal-to-noise ratio than logarithmic quantization, but this is true only for lower-quality speech that's less than about 16 kbps. Therefore, in spite of the fact that some gains are obtained by adapting step size, delta modulation is used only in applications where something less than telephone-quality speech is acceptable and a very simple coder is desired.

Adaptive delta modulation—ADM. The step size in delta modulation can be adapted according to a number of algorithms, all of which have as their objectives more accurate tracking of the input signal. This means increasing the step size during periods of slope overload and decreasing it when slope overload is not occurring. A comparison of Figures 3.15a and 3.16 illustrates how adaptation of the step size can reduce coding distortion. A common approach is to modify the step size, S, at sample, n, by multiplying it by one of two constants, depending on present and past bits in the delta modulation bit stream. A constant larger than one is used whenever a string of identical bits occurs—for instance, when the 3-bit stream made up of the current bit and the two previous bits is either 1, 1, 1 or 0, 0, 0. The multiplier is made smaller than one for all other bit patterns. Thus, the step size increases whenever the quantizer is in a slope overload condition and decreases at times when granular noise is occurring. While it's advantageous to adapt step size increases fast enough to keep up with steep excursions in the input signal, granular noise is smaller when adaptations occur at syllabic rates.

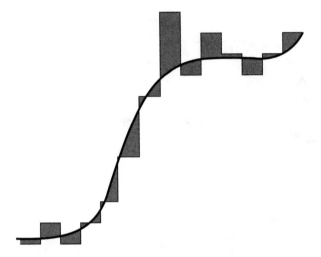

Figure 3.16 Adaptive delta modulation slope overload.

With adaptive schemes, maximum step size can be larger than for linear delta modulation, and the minimum can be smaller so that both slope overload and granular noise distortions are reduced. At a given data rate, ADM can result in as much as a 10 dB improvement in signal-to-noise ratio over linear implementations, but for telephone quality speech, all delta modulators require a higher data rate than PCM. The advantages of ADM are that it can be implemented simply and that it's robust in the presence of noise. It's most attractive in environments where less than toll-quality speech is acceptable. An often-used delta modulation adaptation approach results in the technique called continuous variable slope deltamodulation described in the next section.

Continuously variable slope deltamodulation—CVSD. A variation of adaptive delta modulation, CVSD features exponential adaptations to step size in its attempt to respond quickly to excursions in the voice signal. Step size adaptation is accomplished according to the following equation. For a new step size, $S(i)$, and the previous step size, $S(i-1)$,

$$S(i) = AS(i-1) + B$$

where A is a constant between 0 and 1, and B takes on one value during periods of slope overload and a smaller value otherwise. Step size is limited. Because A is less than 1, step size will degrade to its minimum when the signal slope decreases. The rate of fall is determined by B. Likewise, slope overload causes step size to grow, but only to its maximum. The values of A and B can be set so that growth in step size is near instantaneous, but reductions occur at a syllabic rate. CVSD, as with other ADM variations, is efficient in cases where robustness is required and speech below telephone quality is satisfactory.

Linear predictive coding—LPC.   Linear prediction, as previously discussed, is the foundation of the parametric coding scheme known as linear predictive coding, LPC. Recall that parametric coding devices are called vocoders. I've already discussed several coding schemes that employ linear prediction, but the term LPC is applied to those coding schemes that represent the excitation source parametrically (e.g., vocoders) and that use a higher-order linear predictor. LPC vocoders are further differentiated by the broader goal taken in their design—a goal that goes beyond the notion of a residual-minimizing predictor. LPC analysis has important advantages in the estimation of speech parameters such as its spectrum, formant frequencies and their bandwidths, pitch, and vocal-tract area.

LPC analysis is conducted as a time-domain process, but its result can be interpreted in the frequency domain. Ignoring nasal-tract effects and losses due to heat, vibration, and other factors, the vocal tract can be modeled as a sequence of concatenated cylinders of time-varying diameter that are excited at one end by a synthetic glottal waveform, a periodic impulse source for voiced speech, or a random noise source for unvoiced. Figure 3.17 illustrates

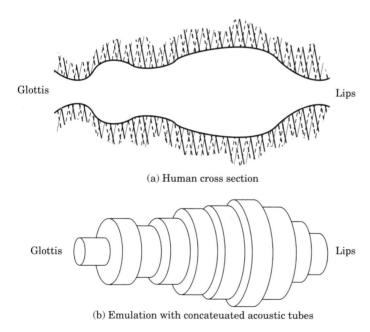

(a) Human cross section

(b) Emulation with concateuated acoustic tubes

Figure 3.17   Oral tract.

the concept of concatenated acoustic tubes and their relationship to the oral tract. Note that the nasal tract is ignored in this model. As the excitation waveform propagates through the acoustic tubes, it bounces off cylinder walls, reflects from edges, resonates at certain frequencies, antiresonates at others, and radiates from the other end as a complex waveform. If the number of cylinder sections is properly chosen and other features are selected carefully, the easily formulated frequency-domain mathematics characterizing the concatenated cylinder model also approximates the vocal tract.

The good news about LPC is that it can be interpreted directly in terms of the acoustic tube model and therefore provides a method for estimating frequency-domain acoustic tube parameters from the speech waveform. LPC prediction coefficients calculated from the waveform can be converted to reflection coefficients representing a set of concatenated tubes. This means that frequency-domain estimations that approximately describe the vocal tract can be obtained in the time-domain using linear mathematics. The N prediction coefficients of an Nth-order predictor can be calculated by solving a system of N linear equations in N unknowns. The N reflection coefficients that appear in equations describing resonances in a concatenated acoustic tube model of $(N–1)/2$ sections can be calculated from the N prediction coefficients. Furthermore, although it's the most difficult part of LPC analysis, excitation parameters can be derived from the residual waveform. LPC analysis thus yields a set of reflection coefficients, excitation energy, a voiced/unvoiced bit, and fundamental frequency (if voiced). Figure 3.13, referenced in the discussion of vocoders, adequately represents synthesis in LPC vocoders.

As with other vocoders, LPC coding produces a set of data (a data frame) at a rate of about 40 to 100 frames per second. Naturally, lower frame rates produce lower-quality speech. The size of the frame depends upon the number of coefficients (e.g., order of the predictor) and the accuracy to which each of the frame's parameters is quantized. Speech synthesized from LPC analysis is most sensitive to the first few coefficients (just as the first few formants are the most crucial). This implies that the coefficients need not all be quantized with the same accuracy. Clearly, quantization for voiced frames is much more important than for unvoiced. A standard 2400 bps LPC scheme known as *LPC-10* was defined by the U.S. government in 1976. According to this standard, a 10th-order predictor is used (hence the name LPC-10) and, because the standard was designed to be robust in communication environments, some redundancy is built in to help minimize the very significant reductions in intelligibility that could result from transmission errors. At 44.4 frames per second, LPC-10 codes the first four coefficients in five bits; this accuracy is successively reduced for subsequent coefficients until only two are used for the tenth one. Pitch is coded in seven bits and energy in five. Fifty-four bits are required for voiced frames, but unvoiced frames don't include coefficients beyond the fourth, so 21 bits in these frames are available for error correction information. Other LPC implementations exist in which the effective data rate is close to 1000 bps. These additional savings are not all achieved by sacrificing quality. Major reductions result by ignoring error correction and allowing a different frame size for unvoiced frames. Error correction, while important in communications applications, is not so crucial for applications in which speech is stored in a computer and played out on command. Further reductions are obtained through several other expedients such as:

1. Eliminating the voiced/unvoiced bit and using zero pitch for unvoiced speech.
2. Defining a zero-gain frame as silence.
3. Including a repeat bit to enable a fourth frame format that includes only pitch and gain.

The repeat frame takes advantage of slowly varying parameters and produces a shorter frame whenever the coefficients have not changed from the previous frame. This feature is especially efficient for unvoiced speech and vowels that frequently persist unchanged for three or four or more frames. Significant reductions are accounted for by using a frame that includes only the repeat bit and energy (set to zero) during the periods of silence that occur so often in connected speech.

It might seem that synthesis from LPC parameters would first require reflection coefficients to be converted back to predictor coefficients. This, however, is unnecessary because generation of speech directly from reflection coefficients is possible using *lattice filters*. The advantages of LPC lie primarily in its usefulness in deriving important speech parameters and in its reduced data rate. LPC is used in low bit-rate speech encoders but, as with other vocoders, it doesn't produce telephone-quality speech and doesn't gain much in the contest between data rate and quality.

Residual-excited linear prediction—RELP. Instead of deriving pitch, gain, and the voiced/unvoiced decision from the prediction residual as is done in LPC, a filter network can be driven directly by the residual waveform. RELP and other schemes that do so are also referred to as *voice-excited linear prediction*. This idea might sound familiar because it has already been discussed for linear prediction or differential coding. The difference here is that reflection coefficients are used (as in LPC) instead of prediction coefficients. Recall that LPC excitation parameters were derived from the residual signal. With RELP, that step is eliminated and an important source of noise is avoided. The consequence is higher-quality speech than LPC—and the requisite increase in data rate. The LPC residual waveform consists of data occurring at the sampling rate, perhaps 8 kHz, whereas reflection or filter coefficients occur at frame rates between 40 and 100 kHz. RELP must deal with both data types, but can still be accomplished with data rates of about 4000 bps and with speech qualities better than LPC. RELP doesn't produce telephone-quality speech.

Vector quantization—VQ. Vector quantization replaces a vector with a single value or symbol that represents a clustering of vectors that are "close" according to some distance measure. A vector can consist of a block of accumulated digital samples, a set of LPC reflection coefficients (with or without excitation parameters), or any other collection, frame, or block of parameters. Given a set of continuous vectors, M clusters can be defined such that each vector is a member of some cluster. Membership in a cluster can be specified by rule—some sort of n-dimensional distance measure in vector space is generally used. Each cluster can be represented in a *codebook* by one of its members or by some new symbol or vector defined for the purpose (e.g., perhaps the cluster's centroid). Prior to operation, training sessions are conducted with representative data to define the clusterings, select representative vectors, and construct the codebook. The codebook contains M entries, one for each cluster. The clusters and codebook are chosen during training sessions so as to "best" represent the original collection of vectors. At runtime, each time a vector is presented, the vector quantizer decides which cluster it "belongs to" according to the same distance measure and substitutes for it the appropriate symbol or value (perhaps the codebook entry's index). Quantization noise is measured by the "distance" between the codebook entry and the input vector.

The codebook can be improved (made to more closely fit the expected vector stream and minimize quantization noise) by providing more representative data in training sessions and by increasing the number of clusters. Clearly, the key to an effective vector quantizer lies in the design and training of its codebook.

Consider the simple vector quantization example represented in Figure 3.18. In this example, input data composes a stream of two-dimensional vectors, each with two four-bit coordinates. The designer has decided to subdivide the vector space into eight clusters (thus the codebook contains eight entries). The training vectors are enumerated in Figure 3.18a and plotted in the two-dimensional vector space in Figure 3.18b. Eight clusters are shown in the vector space surrounded by dashed lines. Figure 3.18c lists the codebook vectors that are plotted in the vector space as solid circles. The clusters and codebook vectors result from the training data. If more training vectors were to be added in additional training sessions, they could be combined with those already shown, the clusters refined, and new codebook vectors chosen. The data rate reduction in this example would be appreciable, going from eight bits to three for each vector. It's clear that the example depicts a very coarse and unrealistic design, however, and would

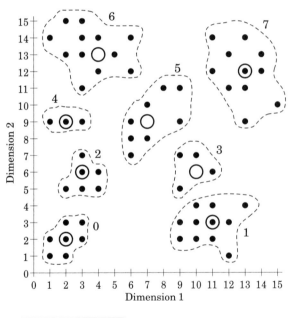

<table>
<tr><th colspan="5">Training Vectors</th></tr>
<tr><td>1,1</td><td>3,5</td><td>6,7</td><td>9,9</td><td>12,1</td></tr>
<tr><td>1,2</td><td>3,6</td><td>6,8</td><td>9,11</td><td>12,3</td></tr>
<tr><td>1,9</td><td>3,7</td><td>6,9</td><td>10,2</td><td>12,11</td></tr>
<tr><td>1,14</td><td>3,9</td><td>6,12</td><td>10,3</td><td>12,13</td></tr>
<tr><td>2,1</td><td>3,11</td><td>6,14</td><td>10,4</td><td>13,4</td></tr>
<tr><td>2,2</td><td>3,13</td><td>7,8</td><td>10,7</td><td>13,9</td></tr>
<tr><td>2,3</td><td>3,14</td><td>7,10</td><td>11,2</td><td>13,11</td></tr>
<tr><td>2,5</td><td>3,15</td><td>8,11</td><td>11,3</td><td>13,12</td></tr>
<tr><td>2,9</td><td>4,5</td><td>9,2</td><td>11,4</td><td>13,14</td></tr>
<tr><td>2,13</td><td>4,6</td><td>9,3</td><td>11,6</td><td>14,12</td></tr>
<tr><td>2,15</td><td>4,12</td><td>9,5</td><td>11,12</td><td>14,13</td></tr>
<tr><td>3,2</td><td>4,14</td><td>9,7</td><td>11,14</td><td>15,10</td></tr>
<tr><td>3,3</td><td>5,13</td><td></td><td></td><td></td></tr>
</table>

(a) Training vectors

(b) Clusters in two-dimensional vector space

Codebook	
Index	Vector
0	2,2
1	11,3
2	3,6
3	10,6
4	2,9
5	7,9
6	4,13
7	13,12

(c) The codebook

Figure 3.18 Vector quantization.

involve significant quantization noise. Consider, for example, the input vector (6,4) that would be replaced in the quantization by codebook entry 2. By any distance measure this result involves more quantization noise than any member of the training data. Use of vector quantization in speech analysis/synthesis systems has not been preferred over scaler coders because of their complexity and because the simpler coders previously discussed have proven adequate. Nevertheless, effective vector quantization designs are possible and are often used in speech recognition systems.

Evaluation of Coding Schemes

Figure 3.19 summarizes the relative voice quality of speech coders discussed in this chapter. Voice quality is measured in terms of signal-to-noise ratio on the y-axis versus data rate as a logarithmic scale on the x-axis. Both solid and dashed traces appear in the figure and respectively represent objective and estimated results—all of which are approximations. Many possible implementations of these schemes are possible, each with its own objective result that differs from other realizations within its class. This figure does help to illustrate the relative positioning of each coder category. When dealing with a notion as subjective as voice quality, you should not attempt too fine a resolution.

Some comments and general observations can be made from an examination of Figure 3.19. CVSD and ADM share the same trace in the figure because CVSD is a specific realization of ADM. LPC is not shown explicitly in the figure but is included in the vocoder category. Log PCM appears to have the steepest slope, so you could expect that technique to produce the highest-quality speech at high data rates. Recall, however, that most voice processing applications are conducted over the public switched telephone network, which filters out speech above about 4000 Hz. For such applications, it's counterproductive to spend for signal-to-noise ratio gains beyond telephone quality (about 30 dB). This limit can be reached at a lower data rate with a complex ADPCM coder. But the lower data rate must be traded off against complexity and cost of the coder. If data rate is not so important, log PCM might still be the best choice (in fact, telephone-quality speech can be attained with a simple linear delta modulation coder at about 200,000 bps). Telephone-quality speech is not required in every voice processing application—as evidenced by the fact that there are many voice processing systems in existence that use CVSD and other lower-quality schemes. Devices that implement subtoll quality coders are often more robust in a given application or less expensive, or both. LDM, CVSD, and other ADM schemes, for instance, are simple to implement and are less subject to distortion from single-bit errors.

The best use of Figure 3.19 is as a rough gauge of the merits of these approaches relative to one another. Listener tests, which furnish another sub-

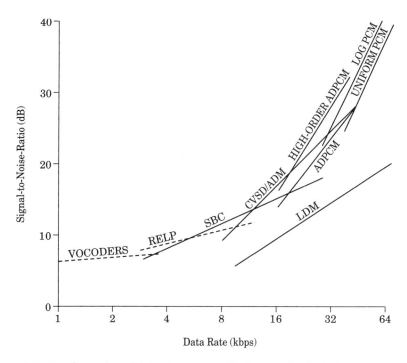

Figure 3.19 Comparison of data rate versus quality for several coding schemes.

jective measure of voice quality, have been conducted for many of the coders discussed; some are reported in the references listed in the bibliography. More is said about the impact of voice quality in the chapter on vocabulary production.

Text-to-Speech

True speech synthesis needs no human recorded voice—it's generated (synthesized) essentially from scratch. Using linguistic, phonetic, and acoustic knowledge, ordinary text such as what you're reading now can be converted to speech. These processes are popularly called text-to-speech and, because most are rule-based, are also referred to as synthesis-by-rule (one process that has been implemented is not actually synthetic because it relies on an inventory of small segments of recorded human speech). A very attractive advantage of text-to-speech is that any text can be read—vocabulary is not restricted to utterances that have been decided upon beforehand.

The task of text-to-speech systems is to convert plain text into speech that fairly represents the meaning conveyed in the text. To be deemed useful, the resulting speech must achieve a high degree of intelligibility and naturalness. Furthermore, if it can be delivered with a lively rather than a dull interpretation, it will find greater acceptance by its users. With these issues in mind, and considering the complexity of human speech, it's clear that a better result could be obtained if the conversion software were able to comprehend text; nevertheless, an adequate, intelligible, reasonably natural text-to-speech conversion can be obtained without understanding.

Among the various text-to-speech schemes that have been tested are some that concatenate prerecorded words, but these are always limited to vocabulary selected in advance. Text-to-speech systems that produce speech by concatenating subword segments such as syllables, morphemes, phonemes, diphones or triphones generally accept unrestricted text, but, even though they might have a somewhat natural-sounding rhythm and intonation, their speech quality varies widely. Output can be highly intelligible, especially after you gain listening experience, but no text-to-speech system has been able to produce results comparable with stored speech systems of even moderate quality. Text-to-speech output tends to sound mechanical and definitely stilted, but great improvements have been made since the first appearance of these products; further improvements can be expected—though probably at a somewhat slower rate than that experienced to date.

In the discussions that follow, some of the problems of synthesizing high-quality speech by concatenation of subword speech segments are covered. Through years of research and experimentation, it's been found that some approaches yield more easily to solutions than others. Regardless of the approach, each of a set of specific yet difficult tasks must be accomplished—usually in realtime at normal speaking rates. Discussions of the problems to be addressed and some of the solutions follow.

Linguistic issues

The smallest distinguishable sound in a dialect of a language is a *phoneme*, which defines a family of sounds rather than a single sound. The actual sound produced varies according to surrounding phonemes. A specific instance of a phoneme as spoken is called an *allophone*, and there are many allophones for each phoneme. I. A. Witten, in his book *Principles of Computer Speech*, gives the definition of phoneme as ". . . a set of sounds whose members don't discriminate between any words in the language under consideration." This definition says that the sound for "c" in "cat" and the sound for "h" in "hat" can't be of the same phoneme because they're precisely the sounds that distinguish the two words. Dialects of most languages, English included, require between forty and fifty phonemes. Figure 3.20 shows a set of 41 phonemes for English.

An utterance can be recorded as a string of phonemes with stress, duration, and intonation marked throughout. Such a representation provides a

Phonemes for English

Letter Representation	Example
/AA/	almost
/AE/	hat
/AH/	nut
/AO/	gone
/AW/	now
/AX/	about
/AY/	slide
/EH/	met
/ER/	absurd
/EY/	date
/IH/	sit
/IY/	seed
/OW/	tome
/OY/	joy
/UH/	look
/UW/	loot
/HH/	hat
/L/	lamp
/R/	rage
/W/	win
/WH/	when
/Y/	yes
/M/	maybe
/N/	no
/NX/	rung
/DH/	than
/F/	fun
/S/	sun
/SH/	shop
/TH/	think
/V/	vast
/Z/	zip
/ZH/	leisure
/B/	bat
/D/	dumb
/G/	gold
/K/	cold
/P/	peck
/T/	tone
/CH/	chip
/JH/	jam

Figure 3.20 A set of phonemes for English.

convenient intermediate transcription between text and speech, but, to accurately represent an utterance as it would most naturally be spoken, a number of adjustments must be made to account for context. For instance, consider the different sounds made for "s" in the words "lease" and "please," which have the final five letters in common. As another example, the sounds for "ie" differ in the word "pie" as it's pronounced in each of the following two sentences. "Eat the pie." "Eat the pie now." Pronunciation differences due to context exist when a suffix is added—for instance, when "indicate" becomes "indicative." The suffix itself can be subject to different pronunciations according to the preceding phoneme—as when the plural "s" is added to words like "thought" and "dream." Other phonemes, too, acquire different pronunciation depending upon context—as with the "t" in "part" and "partner." Pronunciation of a phoneme might even differ according to a word's meaning. *Homonyms* are words that have the same spelling but different meanings and pronunciations. English has many of them; examples include "bow," "record," "construct," "offense," "invalid," and "contest." Many more examples of homonyms exist. To complicate the conversion of text to speech even further, the same pronunciation might be used for various spellings or, different pronunciations for the same spelling. Consider the word "the" in the following two sentences. "Eat the pear." "Eat the extra pear." A *homophone* is one of a group of words that are spelled differently but pronounced the same. The words "aloud/allowed," "wrote/-rote," and "to/too/two" are examples. English is replete with such difficulties that must be considered by high-quality text-to-speech systems.

When text is read by human speakers, pitch rises and falls, syllables are enunciated with more or less intensity, vowels are elongated or shortened, and pauses are inserted to give the passage a definite rhythm. These features are part of those we refer to as *prosody* in speech. Ordinary text contains little direct prosodic information to guide those reading aloud, so prosodic features are produced by each reader according to his or her interpretation of the material. As a result, different people read with different rhythm and intonation, emphasizing different syllables, words, or passages in conformance with their knowledge of the language, their emotional state, and their understanding of the content of the text. To produce voices that seem natural and are intelligible, text-to-speech systems must be able to emulate as nearly as possible these interpretive capabilities of human readers and generate natural-sounding prosody. Fortunately, linguists have derived rules for many languages that, generally if sometimes crudely, encode the way humans intone, enunciate, and emphasize or deemphasize when reading aloud.

Living languages are continually changing. They evolve through usage, sometimes over thousands of years. Today there are more than 3,000 languages, each continuing to evolve and adapt to the needs of its speakers, who imprint upon language individual nuances of pronunciation and word choices. New words are coined, borrowed from other languages, or derived by compounding existing words. The words "codec," "transistor," and "diskette" have been added to the English vocabulary in the past half-century. Meanings are expanded or changed through need, misuse, or common usage—as with the word "premises," which once meant "matters previously set forth" and referred to real estate only when that was the matter previously set forth. Regional dialects and accents affect the way words are used, their order in a sentence, and the way they're pronounced. Words, when they're no longer relevant in our lives, become obsolete from disuse and are forgotten. While words like "liege," "breeches," and "doublet" might still be found in modern dictionaries, they're seldom heard today. Other words, such as "freme," (which once was used to mean "benefit,") and "hoaten," (the Old English word for "command,") have totally disappeared from modern English. It's even possible for a phoneme to become obsolete. English, as spoken at the time of Chaucer 600 years ago, had a phoneme similar to the frictional sound produced in the back of the throat and used in the German word "nacht." That phoneme has disappeared from modern English, which has been evolving for over 1,500 years and is hardly recognizable as the same language that was spoken in England only half that many years ago.

Regardless of which language is being spoken, pronunciations of speech segments differ at their boundaries because of the sluggishness of human articulators, which are preparing for the next sound to be enunciated before they have completed the preceding one. Lips, tongue and jaw can't change configuration instantly, so transitions from one phoneme to the next are smoothed out. This effect is called *coarticulation* and is most noticeable in phrases such as, "Would you give me something?" which usually sounds more like "Woodja gimmee sumpun?" Our tendency to speak rapidly when we expect to be understood by listeners tends to accentuate the effect of coarticulation, which must be emulated if synthetic speech machines are to sound natural.

I mentioned earlier that text-to-speech systems must emulate the human ability to read aloud from text. What do humans do when abbreviations or acronyms are encountered? How are lists read? How are numerals or mathematical formulae read? What happens to speech when the text being read contains a period, a comma, or an exclamation mark? Abbreviations such as Mr., Ms., St., and many others occur frequently in text. In many cases, the correct meaning of the abbreviation can be derived only from the context. Consider the sentence "Dr. Johnson lives at the corner of Bingham Dr. and St. Claire St." The words "Doctor," "Drive," "Saint," and "Street" must be spoken in the proper sequence in the foregoing passage; the correct result can't be obtained merely by analyzing each word individually. Acronyms such as NAACP are used in typed or printed text and must be handled appropriately by text-to-speech systems. American English text strings such as "$23,809.15," "490,397," "4.75," and "7:23 a.m." should be spoken as "twenty-three thousand, eight-hundred-nine dollars and fifteen cents," "four-hun-

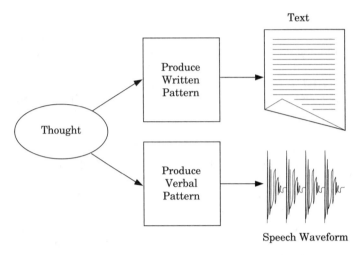

Figure 3.21 Text and speech as external manifestations of thought.

dred-ninety thousand, three-hundred and ninety-seven," "four point seven-five," and "seven twenty-three aye em" respectively. Furthermore, commas and periods appearing in such contexts must not be confused with those marking a break or the end of a sentence.

The conversion process

A thought can be written (or typed), and it can also be verbalized so that text and speech are two distinct manifestations of the same thought. Text is a train of symbols that follow, more or less, the flow of the corresponding speech sounds. The ability of machines to convert text strings to speech depends upon these facts. Figure 3.21 depicts the idea that a thought might be represented by a string of written symbols or by a corresponding train of uttered sounds—or both. A human or a machine reading aloud performs a text-to-speech conversion process like that represented in Figure 3.22. When written language first came into being, it used a distinct symbol for each word—as Chinese and other languages still do today. But word vocabularies commonly reach from fifty to several hundred thousand entries. It was soon realized that a smaller inventory would be sufficient, with fewer characters to remember if written symbols represented individual sounds rather than words. Through time and usage, though, spoken and written representations of every language diverge, driving the correspondence between phonemes and alphabetic characters further apart. But the sequential part of the relationship still holds, and text can be converted to appropriate speech even by readers unfamiliar with textual content. This is done by human readers through the application of thousands of rules—rules that any native speaker has learned and applies without much conscious thought.

The foregoing discussions have touched on some but not all of the issues that must be addressed by high-quality text-to-speech conversion software. Though on the surface it appears that most text-to-speech systems must perform the same functions, today's systems handle the details in different ways and obtain similar but varying results. Although the following sections present a kind of generic approach to synthesis-by-rule text-to-speech conversion, it should be recognized that the processes discussed might not proceed in the sequence given and, in fact, might be intermingled to some extent rather than being performed in order. Furthermore, alternative approaches are possible for most functions. The various implementations each have their advantages and disadvantages. For example, some might feature improved speech quality but have other negative attributes—such as being difficult to adapt to other languages. Figure 3.23 summarizes the processes discussed in the following.

Text normalization. A *text normalizer* is a preprocessor that scans text, replaces certain sequences of characters with letters, and replaces symbols and other special constructs, spelling them out in full alphabetic form so that no ambiguity regarding pronunciation is passed on to succeeding stages. An unrestricted text sequence might contain abbreviations, numbers, homonyms, acronyms, dates, times, lists, formulae, special characters, and other constructs that require special handling. Each of these must be interpreted and its proper pronunciation determined. For example, "Mr. Johnstone" in the input text would be expanded to "Mister Johnstone" and "$123.45" would be replaced with "one hundred twenty three dollars and forty five cents." "Dr. Brown" would become "doctor brown" and "123 Brown Dr." would be changed to "one twenty three brown drive." Because initial capitals are irrelevant for this processing (after sentence delimiters are unambiguously located), the normalizer may replace them with their lowercase equivalent to simplify later processing. Punctuation may also be resolved to prosodic pauses of appropriate duration or to other text when required. Periods, besides marking the end of-sentences, also appear at the end of abbreviations, as decimal points, and as separators in file names. An abbreviation might come at the end of a

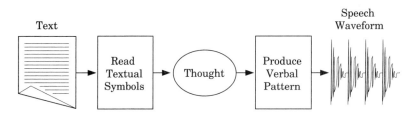

Figure 3.22 Reading aloud.

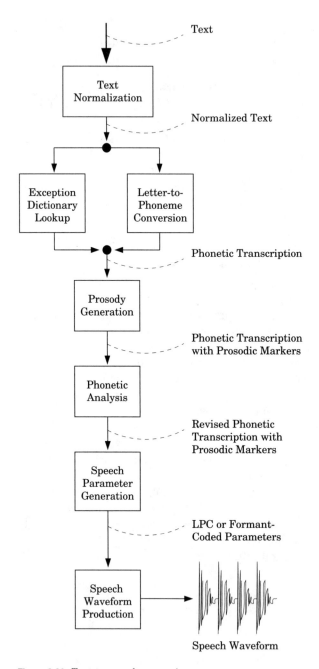

Figure 3.23 Text-to-speech conversion.

sentence, with a period serving two purposes. Commas signify pauses in sentences, but they might also be place separators in numbers. The normalizer also deals with various uses of apostrophes, hyphens, dashes, and special symbols such as the ampersand and percent sign, analyzing their surrounding context and inserting replacements as required.

A sequence of numerals might be interpreted in any of several ways, and the normalizer must resolve the issue and produce an appropriate alphabetic string. The string "3267" might be replaced with "thirty two sixty seven" if it appeared, for instance, as the final four digits of a telephone number or as a street address. It could be converted to "three thousand two hundred and sixty seven" if it were preceded by a dollar sign or if the word "dollars" followed it in the text. The same input string might, alternatively, be replaced by "three two six seven" if it were preceded by a decimal point. Abbreviations such as "Dr." for "Drive" or "doctor," and "esq." for "esquire" might be expanded to their textual equivalents if they appear in a system abbreviation list available to the normalizer. To facilitate this process, conventions are established for certain text constructs such as abbreviations (which might require a succeeding period) and acronyms (which might be required to appear as strings of uppercase letters). Thus, a text sequence such as "ABC" can be changed to "aye bee cee" and "CIA" might become either "cee aye ey" or "central intelligence agency" depending upon whether or not it is present in the normalizer's abbreviation list.

Exception dictionary lookup. The next step after normalization in the conversion process is to obtain a prescription for basic pronunciations of each word in the normalized text. This is produced in the form of a phonetic transcription showing the sequence of phonemes to be pronounced. Text in alphabetic languages can be read and properly pronounced by native speakers who conform to thousands of pronunciation and prosodic rules (usually without knowing they're doing so). Many of these rules have been transcribed to forms that are convenient for use on computers. Still, every set of rules has its exceptions, including those rules governing linguistic issues in every language. Many exceptions are learned without much conscious effort by native speakers, and the exceptions are themselves often stated as rules. However, some exceptions are too rare to merit a rule. Furthermore, new words, new pronunciations, and new exceptions are added frequently to living, growing languages. Names, jargon for particular disciplines, and certain dialects almost always lead to exceptional pronunciations. Consequently, some means for correctly pronouncing exception words must be implemented in high-quality text-to-speech systems. English could never sound natural and fluent if exceptions were ignored and pronunciation always followed its linguistic rules. Pronunciation exceptions are handled in text-to-speech systems by placing words or word segments in exception dictionaries (also called lexicons) with explicit phonetic transcriptions (and sometimes duration, stress, and part-of-speech information). For example, the following entries showing a word and its phonetic transcription with accent marks might appear in an exception dictionary. The phonemes listed between the slashes correspond to those shown in Figure 3.20.

```
A = /AX/
OUGHT = /AO/' T/
THEREBY = /DH EH'/ R B AY/
```

Dictionaries need not always be based on whole words, but can also contain subword segments. Early text-to-speech systems developed at MIT and elsewhere employ morpheme dictionaries. *Morphemes* are the smallest syntactic units of a language, and their orthographic representations are called *morphs*. For example, the morphs of "trying" are "try" and "ing." The morphs of a word consist of its prefixes, its root, and its suffixes—all of which can be contained individually in the dictionary along with pronunciation information and, if desired, duration and part-of-speech information for use at a later stage of text-to-speech conversion. Naturally, if morph dictionaries are employed, a prior process will have decomposed each word in the text string into its morphs. Pronunciation of a word is obtained by concatenating pronunciations for each of its morphs. There are, however, many complications involved in the decomposition of words into morphemes and in the derivation of pronunciation by this method. (For example, morphemes must frequently be modified at their boundaries due to the effects of concatenation with other morphemes.) It has been estimated that an English morph dictionary would contain about 10,000 entries, but such a dictionary would serve 100,000 or more words.

Besides exception words, high-frequency words might also appear in the exception dictionary to save time that would otherwise be used in a later process for letter-to-sound conversion every time they're encountered. Of course, for unrestricted text, there are too many words for the pronunciations of all of them to be derived from dictionaries, so a scheme of letter-to-sound conversion must be invoked for many (if not most) words or morphs. Normally, though, before pronunciation rules are applied, exception dictionaries are searched (sometimes more than one). If the item is found, its pronunciation and other information is taken from the dictionary—but, if it's not found, a letter-to-phoneme conversion process is invoked.

Letter-to-phoneme conversion. *Phonemes* are the sounds of a language, and letter-to-sound rules provide a prescription for deriving the phonemes represented by a string of letters. Phonemes result from empirical studies of words or morphemes and their pronunciations as produced by native speakers of a language. A rule in English, for instance, states that a vowel followed by a consonant in a single syllable word containing no other vowels is given its short pronunciation. Operation of this rule can be heard with such words as "hat," "red," "bit," "odd," "hut," and many, many more. Another rule specifies that the preceding vowel in a word ending in silent "e" is to be given the vowel's long pronunciation— this is the rule that enables distinctions to be made between "hate" or "bite" and two of the words in the previous example. Other rules might deal with adjustments due to the addition of prefixes or suffixes. Some rules specify different pronunciations for the same letter (or group of letters) depending upon their context—that is, depending upon the letters immediately to the left or right in a word or subword segment. Rules are often stated in a form suitable for computer processing and might appear in the following form.

```
left-context [letter-set] right-context = phoneme string
```

This form specifies the left-context (the letter or letters that immediately precede those under consideration), the set of letters being considered (which might be a single letter or several), and the right context (letters that immediately follow those under consideration). A letter-set under consideration might consist of one or more letters—for example, the letters "t," "ch," "ien," "ng," or any others might be considered as a group. During letter-to-sound processing, a subset of rules is tested against a letter-set in some specific sequence one at a time. Any time an exact letter-set match is found and the left-context and right-context are exactly as stated in the rule, the search is terminated and the phoneme string taken to represent the letter-set. If a rule is tested and found to not apply, the next rule in sequence is tried. Once a rule is applied, the phoneme string specified in the rule is passed to the phonetic transcription output. The letter-set (indicated between brackets in the rule) is passed over in the input text, and the next letter-set following immediately to its right is tested. The process continues until all text has been transcribed to phonemes.

Examples of letter-to-sound rules stated in this form are given by the following.

```
C[O]N= /AA/
[IER]= /IY ER/
#:[E] = / /
```

Only three rules are shown here, but, in fact, many hundreds are needed to produce high-quality English language text-to-speech. Phoneme designations to the right of the equal sign refer to phonemes shown in Figure 3.20.

Letters in the rules are printed as uppercase, but either uppercase or low-ercase might appear in the text being converted. The first rule states that wherever the contiguous letters "con" appear in a word, the "o" is to be pro-nounced like the "a" in "almost." The second rule states that pronunciation of "ier" in a word requires two phonemes in succession: the "ee" in "seed" followed by the "ur" in "absurd." Notice that the second rule states no con-text. Thus, the rule applies to "ier" no matter in what context it might ap-pear. Words containing this sequence include "tier," "bier," "chandelier," and "financier." In the third rule, left-context is specified by two special symbols: "#" stands for any one or more vowels and ":" means that any num-ber of consonants (including none) might appear at that position. Right-context is shown as a blank character that means that the letter-set must be final with no letters following in the word. The symbols "/ /" in place of the phoneme in that rule indicates that no phonemes are pronounced when the rule applies (e.g., the rule states that in a word with at least two vowels, a final "e" is silent).

High-frequency words are often placed in an exception dictionary to re-lieve the system of repetitive conversions. On the other hand, dictionary items sometimes alternatively appear as individual rules; the rule format pre-viously illustrated seems well-suited to this approach. The letter-to-sound conversion process might also produce other information that's passed along with phoneme output to aid later processing. By identifying suffixes (and by other means), part-of-speech can be determined and relevant grammatical information included in the phonetic transcription—as can phoneme dura-tions and even stress patterns. Some text-to-speech software accepts input forms other than text in an effort to eliminate some of the conversion processes previously discussed and thus improve speech quality; the as-sumption is that humans can do a better job of these processes than ma-chines. (Assuming that machines must accomplish them in realtime, while humans might do them iteratively, the assumption is correct.) A pre-pre-pared phonetic transcription with interspersed prosodic markers can be in-put at this point in the process rather than text being input to the normalizer. These shortcut approaches don't accomplish unrestricted text-to-speech, but they do result in higher-quality output and offer great advantages for some applications. Regardless of how it's generated, the phonetic transcrip-tions with prosodic markers is passed along to a prosody generation module, where silences are inserted and pitch contours determined.

Prosody generation. The word *prosody* refers to features of speech whose effects extend beyond a syllable and smaller speech segments—features like rhythm, pitch, and amplitude. Prosodic features are also referred to as suprasegmental features. Most text-to-speech systems attempt to synthe-size a natural-sounding rhythm and an acceptable pitch contour while hold-ing amplitude constant and ignoring other prosodic features. Indeed, judgments regarding the naturalness and intelligibility of synthetic speech are significantly affected by its prosody. Emphasis (or stress) affects both phoneme durations and pitch contours. In live speech, it also impacts amplitudes, but this feature of stress is so much less important to intelligibility and naturalness that it's usually ignored in text-to-speech systems. Emphasis is provided to spoken passages by stressing certain syllables; stress is manifested as an elongation of a syllable, an increased pitch, and (with live speech) a higher amplitude. Rhythm is accomplished, in part, by setting durations of pauses, but also by establishing the pattern of pitch changes throughout an utterance. Adequate pitch contours can be synthesized from an appropriate set of rules that usually result in a dull but correct reading of text passages. So, a prosody is generated for synthetic speech by establishing those points in the phonetic transcription where pauses must be inserted, determining their durations, and specifying the pitch trajectories to be used for an intonation contour.

Much of the meaning conveyed in a conversation between two people is carried in its prosodies. The same is true, but usually less so, for textual materials read aloud. A reading delivered by a speaker who understands the material and who might even feel passionately about it, might be totally unambiguous, while the same text read with a more neutral prosody, such as when read by machine, might require interpretation by the listener. Prosody can't be adequately conveyed in normal written text; when text is read aloud, prosody is created by the reader. An intelligent reader, one who understands the material, can emphasize or deemphasize words, pause to highlight the beginning of a new thought, or change inflection to highlight a passage. Many of these things are usually beyond the ken of text-to-speech systems, which generally attempt to generate acceptable prosodies that are not incorrect for the material but contribute little to its understanding.

Prosody is generated by a text-to-speech system using knowledge of the language (embodied in a set of prosodic rules) along with punctuation marks and whatever other grammatical, syntactic or semantic information it has been able to glean from the text. Accent marks and other information added in various processing steps are carried through, along with punctuation, to the phonetic transcription where they serve as prosodic cues. Pauses whose durations depend upon the punctuation are inserted at each comma, period, semicolon, colon, question mark, and exclamation mark. While not signaled by a unique mark, the end of a paragraph can be easily detected in text and can be used by text-to-speech systems like an actual punctuation mark. These cues are used as guideposts for placing pauses, varying pitch, and lengthening or shortening phonemes. For example, questions that contain "what," "where," "when," "why," "who" or "how" usually end in a rising pitch, while other questions and sentences are spoken with a falling pitch. This rule alone is not sufficient for generation of intonation; however, much more complex analyses are conducted. Pitch contours might be fitted to multiword sections that are usually (though not always) smaller than a sentence—let's call these sections prosodic units. Each prosodic unit contains a syllable that's stressed more than the others. To create emphasis on this syllable, it's elongated and the pitch contour made steeper. Throughout a phrase or sentence, there might be several stressed syllables and one, the tonic syllable, is meant to predominate. Pitch might either increase or decrease to provide emphasis on the tonic or other syllables; the more rapid the rate of change in pitch, the more emphasis is perceived.

A pitch contour might be derived for a group of prosodic units (covering one phrase or a whole sentence) with the contour for each being designed according to the location of stressed syllables within it and the unit's position relative to the tonic syllable. Besides determining where each prosodic unit begins and ends, the text-to-speech system must also locate the syllables to be stressed and decide the relative stress to be given to each. The punctuation marks mentioned above usually define the end of one prosodic unit and the start of another—though other less obvious cues might also mark prosodic unit boundaries. The type of punctuation encountered has an effect on the pitch contours selected for the surrounding prosodic units. For example, periods (at the end of sentences) and most commas cause the preceding prosodic unit to drop some in pitch at the end of the unit. This is followed by a short burst of silence—longer for a period than for a comma. A paragraph ending generally signals the beginning of a new thought, so the preceding prosodic unit is read with a deep declining pitch and is followed by a longer pause.

Only a few of the many details associated with the creation of prosodies have been suggested in this section. I encourage you to read aloud and observe the prosodic effects as they're generated.

Phonetic analysis. A final adjustment of phonemes must be accomplished to account for phenomena resulting from contextual influences at concatenated phoneme boundaries. Human articulators assume a different configuration for each phoneme produced but can't move instantly between them, so, during the time taken for the change, sounds made for adjacent phonemes merge near their boundaries. The process is called *coarticulation*, and its effects occur at segment boundaries regardless of what speech units are joined. Because of coarticulation with the preceding phoneme, the /l/ phoneme in "ball" and "bullet," for example, is pronounced differently in each instance. Consider the different pronunciations of the "s" appended to "beds," "socks," and "corpses," and of the past participles in the words "kissed," "prospered," and "cranked." The rule-based phonetic analysis module accounts for these effects by prescribing modifications to phonemes in the phonemic transcription—for instance, by specifying shortening, lengthening, or deletions to be carried out when speech parameters are generated. Naturally, the details of the process vary for different languages.

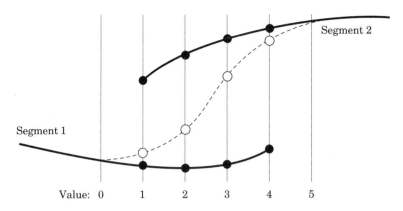

Value: 0   1   2   3   4   5

Figure 3.24 Parameter smoothing for co-articulation.

Speech parameter generation. From a phonetic transcription that includes embedded information to guide the conversion, parameters can be produced that drive a vocal tract model. A parametric speech representation (e.g., LPC or formant coding) is most convenient for speech synthesis systems because speech parameters such as pitch can be controlled individually. They also facilitate the modifications required for coarticulation because individual speech parameters are isolated and can be mathematically smoothed over several frames to emulate changing articulators. Figure 3.24 shows a graphic representation of smoothing as it might be performed on the various parameters within LPC or formant frames. Lengthening and shortening of speech segments can be easily accomplished with parametric representations by adding or deleting frames. Figure 3.25 shows how speech segment shortening might be coupled with coarticulation.

An inventory of phonemes (stored as LPC frame sets, for instance) can be accessed, modified, and concatenated in accordance with phonetic and prosodic information contained in the enhanced phonetic transcription. The inventory might be derived from human recorded speech or might be entirely synthetic. Some text-to-speech systems feature an inventory of human speech segments consisting of about 1500 biphones and triphones (phoneme pairs and triples) for each language implemented. Such systems tend to produce less mechanical speech (the voices are, after all, really human), but a separate segment inventory must be prepared for every new language.

Waveform production. An analog speech waveform is produced from the modified speech parameters and a standard vocal tract model of the type described earlier in this chapter (e.g., an LPC or formant vocoder).

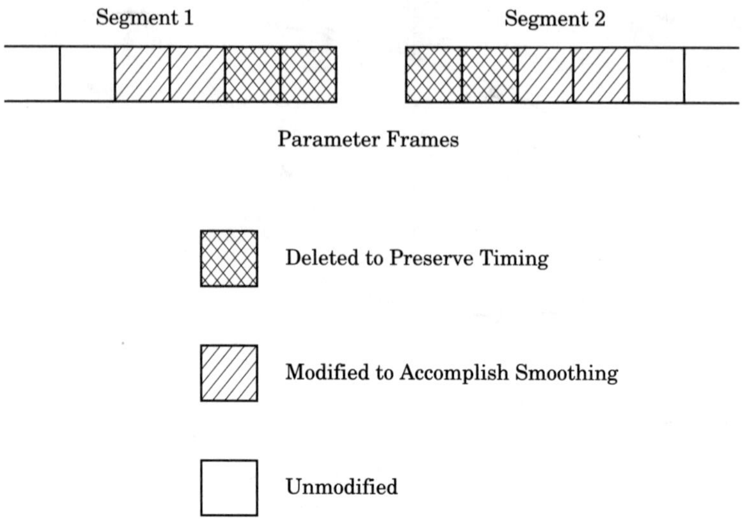

Segment 1   Segment 2

Parameter Frames

Deleted to Preserve Timing

Modified to Accomplish Smoothing

Unmodified

Figure 3.25 Parameter modification for co-articulation.

4

Speech Recognition

In the previous chapter, I discussed output of speech from computers, which is the synthesis of speech from coded signals or text. *Speech recognition* is the inverse process, conversion of speech to text. The objective of human speech is not merely to transfer words from one person to another, but rather to communicate understanding—a thought, concept or idea. The final product is not the words or phrases that are spoken and heard, but rather the information conveyed by them. In computer speech recognition, a person speaks into a microphone or telephone and the computer listens. This, however, doesn't mean the computer understands the meaning of the words it has heard. More often, the computer simply attempts to transcribe the speech it hears into a textual representation. It's possible for a computer to selectively execute an action based on a spoken command, but is this really understanding? Let's assume that computer speech recognition has as its objective the derivation of some representation of the intended word or words.

A related task is called *speaker verification*; although it's not strictly speech recognition, it uses some of the same techniques and is therefore allied with it. In speaker verification, the process of analyzing a speech sample to identify the speaker, there's no attempt by the computer to understand what was said or even to convert the speech to a form that's understandable to humans. The task is simply to compare a sample utterance to one spoken by the subject during a prior enrollment session to determine if, in fact, both utterances were spoken by the same person. Because some of the techniques and processes applied to speech recognition are the same as those of speaker verification, the two functions are sometimes attempted at the same time on the same speech waveforms. However, in the following, I shall generally confine my discussions to issues of speech recognition.

The speech recognition task is complex. It would be complicated enough if every speaker pronounced every word in an identical manner each time it was spoken, but this doesn't happen.

Variations in Speech

The smallest sound units discernible by people are called *phonemes*. It's generally accepted that English has slightly more than forty of them. To produce a given phoneme, the human vocal apparatus momentarily assumes a particular configuration. It then begins to change in preparation for the next phoneme, assumes a new configuration, then almost immediately starts its change for the succeeding one, and so on. Each phoneme and the transitions between them have their correlates in the sound pressure wave and hence in the waveform. A speech recognizer inputs a waveform, extracts information from it, uses that information to hypothesize words chosen from its vocabulary, applies knowledge of the grammar to prune or add word choices, and outputs the recognized word or sequence of words. Speech recognizers must rely upon the waveform's record of speech events to accomplish their task, but the waveform also contains unwanted, irrelevant, or ambiguous information that works to confound the recognizer. The recognition process is further complicated because the production of phonemes and transitions between them is not uniform from person to person or from instance to instance with the same talker. This lack of uniformity seriously complicates the task of automatic speech recognition.

Vast differences among people affect the way they speak. Accents, regional dialects, sex, age, speech impediments, emotional state, and other factors cause people to pronounce the same word in different ways. Phonemes are added, omitted, substituted, or shortened. Consider, for example, the word "America." As pronounced in parts of New England it often sounds more like "Americar." Phonemes are frequently omitted entirely in fluent speech by people everywhere. "Come on" is almost always spoken as "c'mon" and "how are you today?" can sound like "ha'er ya t'day?" There are dozens of such examples. The rate of speech also varies from person to person. This can result from habit, regional convention, or for physical or other reasons. The difference in rate is serious enough by itself, but also, the faster the rate of speech, the more likely are phoneme omissions. Vocal tract size and shape vary widely from speaker to speaker and impact the pitch, quality, and precision of speech. Background sounds and noisy recording or communication channels can add acoustic material that's not only irrelevant but might seriously obscure other important sounds. Careless articulation also adds unwanted sounds such as smacks, clicks, breath, and others.

A word or phrase spoken by the same individual differs from instance to instance. Illness, tiredness, stress, frustration or other conditions usually cause differences in the way a word is spoken. Even under normal circumstances, a given individual doesn't pronounce words identically each time they're spoken, and even the smallest difference must be accommodated by the recognizer. Meaningless insertions such as "ah" and "eh" might occur anytime within an utterance. The position of the talker relative to the microphone, the acoustic nature of the surroundings, or the quality of the recording devices have an important impact on the resulting waveform and can drastically alter the performance of the recognizer. In addition, homonyms such as "wait" and "weight" or "sun" and "son" introduce complications at another level.

Some differences can actually aid in the speech recognition process by adding information to the waveform. For example, prosodic features such as intonation, stress, and cadence provide useful clues. An imperative statement has a different pitch contour and probably stresses different syllables than a question. Stressed syllables are often spoken louder and slower and enunciated more carefully, so some automatic speech recognizers cue on them. Furthermore, stressed syllables often provide syntactic and semantic clues that can be exploited.

Classification of Systems

Every speech recognition application is designed to accomplish a specific task. Examples include: to recognize the digits zero through nine and the words "yes" and "no" over the telephone, to enable bedridden patients to control the positioning of their beds, or to implement a VAT (voice-activated typewriter). Once a task is defined, a speech recognizer is chosen or designed for the task. Recognizers fall into one of several categories depending upon whether the system must be "trained" for each individual speaker, whether it requires words to be spoken in isolation or can deal with continuous speech, whether its vocabulary contains a small or a large number of words, and whether or not it operates with input received by telephone. Speaker-dependent systems are able to effectively recognize speech only for speakers who have been previously enrolled on the system. The aim of speaker-independent systems is to remove this restraint and recognize the speech of any talker without prior enrollment. When a speech recognition system requires words to be spoken individually, in isolation from other words, it's said to be an *isolated-word system* and recognizes only discrete words and only when they're separated from their neighbors by distinct interword pauses. Continuous speech recognizers, on the other hand, allow a more fluent form of talking. *Large-vocabulary recognizers* are defined to be those that have more than one thousand words in their vocabularies; the others are considered *small-vocabulary systems*. Finally, recognizers designed to perform with lower bandwidth waveforms as restricted by the telephone network are differentiated from those that require a broader bandwidth input. Consider the effects of some of these distinctions.

Speaker dependence

An issue of utmost concern is whether or not a recognizer must be trained for the voice of each user. If so, the recognizer is said to be *speaker-dependent*, and it must know each talker's identity. Training consists of an enrollment procedure whereby the talker is prompted by the system to speak a number of words or sentences. A substantial amount of spoken training material might be required—with many repetitions. Undertraining results from too little variety in the training material or from too few repetitions and causes inferior performance of the recognizer. Speaker-dependent recognizers sometimes blend every repetition of a given training word for an enrollee into a single unit. Others treat each one as a separate word and add it to its inventory as it's spoken—you can imagine the amounts of storage and search time required by these recognizers.

Training for some systems must occur hours in advance of use, and retraining might be required periodically. Even after the most rigorous training, an individual's voice might not be recognized if the talker is ill, tired, or stressed. Other factors can intervene to defeat recognition. It might fail if the talker's mouth is oriented differently relative to the microphone or when background noise interferes. Training sessions conducted in the morning might be found unsuitable later in the day when the voice tends to reflect fatigue. Or conversely, evening training might be found wanting in the morning. The robustness of a recognizer is a measure of how well it adapts to changes of this kind. Some speaker-dependent systems attempt to update enrollee-trained data every time the person uses the recognizer, but this can still cause problems for reasons already stated. The most effective speaker-dependent recognizers attempt to closely model actual operating circumstances, requiring training and frequent retraining under varied conditions.

Speaker-independent recognizers don't require individual training. They can be used by many different people who might even be talking to the system for the first time. Enrollee training is not required because the recognizers are pretrained with large amounts of training speech from a cross section of many individuals representing the target user population. As with speaker-dependent recognizers, undertraining results in poorer performance.

Speaker-dependent recognition is easier to accomplish than speaker-independent recognition. Accordingly, speaker-independent systems realize a higher rate of recognition error than speaker-dependent systems applied to the same task. (In some cases, the error rate is as much as five times higher.) This is especially true as larger and larger vocabularies are used. Better and more effective approaches to speaker-independent recognition are continually being sought. The search includes attempts to identify speaker-invariant speech features that can be extracted from the waveform. That such features exist is suggested by the fact that expert spectrogram readers are able to "decode" spectrograms visually; also suggested is application of expert systems and knowledge engineering to the problem. To date, these approaches have not been overly successful when applied to any but very limited tasks. Experimentation with clustering algorithms that attempt to group words or subword units across many speakers has been no more successful. Other attempts have tried to adapt the recognizer for each new talker. The most successful efforts (especially for large vocabulary tasks) are those that employ hidden Markov models or other stochastic processes and operate on speech units smaller than words (as discussed later in this chapter).

Recognizers are classified as either *isolated word* or *continuous speech* systems. Isolated word recognizers require the talker to enunciate each word and to separate it from its neighbor with a pause of from 2 to 500 milliseconds. Continuous speech systems have removed that constraint and allow a fluent, more normal mode of speaking. Continuous speech is preferred because it's natural, the way we all speak normally. Furthermore, it's faster, proceeding at a rate of about 150 words per minute as opposed to about 75 per minute for isolated word speech. When spoken in isolation, words are usually more clearly enunciated and tend to be free of contextual influence. And, of course, word boundaries are more easily located. Recognition of continuous speech is considerably more complex and can require 10 times as much processing. Continuous speech is often rushed with word boundaries smeared and sounds slurred, abbreviated, or omitted. Error rates are consequently much higher in continuous speech recognizers. Even so, accurate continuous speech recognition must be achieved before we can converse effectively with these devices in our natural language.

Vocabulary size

A recognizer with a vocabulary of less than 1,000 words is considered a small vocabulary system. All others are classed as large vocabulary recognizers. Several effects are exacerbated as vocabularies grow. These include the need to store and search through more information, giving rise to a growth (that's not always linear) in memory and processing time. Furthermore, larger vocabularies also contain more words that are similar to each other and are therefore more difficult to discriminate from each other. Such systems are said to have more *confusability*. Confusability grows rapidly for vocabularies greater than 1,000 words.

Large vocabulary systems require their own recognition techniques. Because of the massive amounts of storage and processing power required, large vocabulary recognizers are not able to characterize and train each word individually as is done in small vocabulary systems. Word characterization requires storage of large amounts of information. The more words there are, the more storage space required—and the more words there are to search through. Large vocabulary systems get around this problem by adopting a different segment of speech to characterize, a segment smaller than words. Syllables, demisyllables, phonemes, and other units have been used. The numbers of each of these units is small compared to the number of words in a large vocabulary recognizer. Much storage might still be required to characterize each one of these units, but, due to the smaller number of units, storage space is held to a limit. Every word in the vocabulary still appears in storage, but a minimum amount of information is needed to describe it in terms of the smaller unit—say, as a concatenation of phonemes or syllables. Recognition is achieved by transcribing an input waveform to a sequence of phonemes, syllables, or other subword unit, then matching the string to the word list. Processing times for these approaches are manageable, but performance tends to be degraded over word-based approaches because of the larger number of interunit contextual effects.

Telephone speech

Speech information coded in a waveform normally reaches frequencies of 10,000 Hz and above. The telephone network low-pass filters these signals to less than about 4000 Hz. Additionally, the telephone network can interpose background noise, crosstalk, or distortion. Signal level and quality vary based on the talker, distance from the phone, and the type of handset. Speakerphones are generally unsuitable for recognition by phone. They typically have a small signal-to-noise ratio and might produce an echo. These and other factors combine to confound the recognition process and recognizers not explicitly designed to operate under such conditions produce poor results. Some recognizers, however, have been expressly designed for telephone operation. These are usually speaker-independent. Some allow unconstrained speech but might be restricted to only a few words, often the digits zero through ten and a few commands such as "yes" and "no." Some telephone recognizers are *wordspotting* systems that scan the incoming speech signal, trying only to pick out predefined keywords.

Speech Recognition Technology

Speech is input via microphone or telephone and its analog waveform digitized. The job of the recognition system is to derive from the waveform all information needed to make correct word choices. Ultimately, every recognizer must choose from its vocabulary some word or sequence of words that best matches the original spoken speech. All information concerning the words spoken must be derived from the waveform but guidance in the selection can be provided by knowledge of the grammar. The job is not simple. It's complicated by many factors, some inherent in the nature of speech, some following from our limited knowledge of the brain's speech-understanding process, some dependent upon present-day electronic technology, many (but not all) beyond our control. In spite of this, there are automatic systems that recognize speech. None of them, however, is unrestricted—they all limit both the input speech and their outputs in one or more of the ways already mentioned.

An effective speech recognition technique or algorithm will find its way into numerous implementations. As a result, many systems are philosophically similar and might share approaches, algorithms, and design features. A frequently used approach involves template matching in which vocabulary words are characterized in memory as templates—time-based sequences of spectral information taken from waveforms obtained during training. An unknown word is "recognized" when it's compared with templates of all candidate words in the vocabulary and found to be most like one of them according to some similarity measure. An unknown input word is never pronounced identically with its corresponding vocabulary word. Thus, their waveforms differ—as do the templates. An especially troublesome situation arises when trying to compare the templates of two occurrences of the same word spoken at different rates. Their acoustic cues don't match in the time dimension, so appropriate temporal compensations must be made to effect a comparison. This situation is referred to as *time warping*. The time-alignment or time-normalization problem is frequently addressed with dynamic programming, a tool used to solve operations research problems such as the travelling salesman problem (finding the best route through a network of cities). As you shall see, matching word templates doesn't provide the best performance for many recognition tasks.

As an alternative to template matching, feature-based designs have been used in which a time sequence of pertinent phonetic features are extracted from a speech waveform. These are then resolved into word choices from a lexicon whose word descriptions are stored in terms of their phonetic features. Such designs typically apply a stochastic model to speech, characterizing expected speech variations statistically. Feature-based systems, too, must match unknown words against word prototypes (or other units of speech) stored in memory.

Different modeling approaches are used, but models involving state diagrams have been found to give encouraging performance. In particular, hidden Markov models (HMM) are frequently applied. With HMMs any speech unit can be modeled, and all knowledge sources can be included in a single, integrated model. Furthermore, HMM algorithms are available for speech recognition processing. A variety of HMMs have been implemented with differing results. Some model each word in the vocabulary, while others model subword speech units. Some include knowledge of the grammar or other sources directly in the model. Performance for each of these varies depending upon the recognition task addressed.

Next, I'll discuss hidden Markov models then make a few comments about the selection of speech units before giving an example system to show how some of these concepts are applied to speech recognition.

Hidden Markov Models—HMM

A hidden Markov model can be used to model an unknown process that produces a sequence of observable outputs at discrete intervals where the outputs are members of some finite alphabet. It might be helpful to think of the unknown process as a black box about whose workings nothing is known except that, at each interval, it issues one member chosen from the alphabet. These models are called "hidden" Markov models precisely because the state sequence that produced the observable output is not known—it's "hidden." HMMs have been found to be especially apt for modeling speech processes.

An HMM is represented by a set of states, vectors defining transitions between certain pairs of those states, probabilities that apply to state-to-state transitions, sets of probabilities characterizing observed output symbols, and initial conditions. An example is shown in the three-state diagram of Figure 4.1a. States are denoted by nodes and transitions by directed arrows (vectors) between nodes. At any given time, the model is said to be in one (and only one) state. At regularly spaced, discrete times, the model is said to be clocked, and it changes state. At clock-time, the model might change from its current state to any state for which a transition vector exists. Transitions may occur only from the tail to the head of a vector. Note that a transition can be defined from a state back to itself. Each state node in Figure 4.1a is numbered, and transitions are defined between only some of the states. (Notice there's no transition from either state two or state three back to state one.) A state can have more than one transition leaving it and

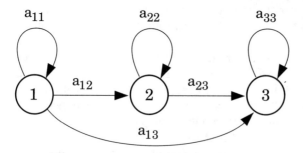

Figure 4.1(a) Hidden Markov model: state diagram.

more than one leading to it. In an ergodic HMM, any state can be reached from any other. A left-to-right HMM is one in which the flow is one-way. Once a node has been entered and exited, it can't be entered again. A null-transition is one that has a transition probability but that neither produces an output nor consumes a clock time.

The value, a_{ij}, associated with a transition from state i to state j, is the probability of that transition being taken axt the next clock time (given the network is in state i). Because probabilities lie between zero and one,

$$0 \le a_{ij} \le 1$$

The sum of probabilities of all transitions leaving any state are equal to one.

$$\sum_i a_{ij} = 1 \text{ for all } j$$

Figure 4.1b gives transition probabilities for the transitions of the example.

Each Markov model has a finite output alphabet that might consist of numbers, letters, or other symbols. Every time a transition is taken, the model can be thought of as emitting or outputting one member of the alphabet—these outputs represent the sequence of observations from the black box. The alphabet for our example consists of six symbols, the capital letters A through F, as shown in Figure 4.1c. At each transition, the HMM is able to emit any member of the alphabet. But it does so according to a probability distribution that's different for each transition. To completely specify the model, these probabilities must be defined. Thus, associated with each transition vector is a set of output probabilities, b_{ijk}, where i and j define the transition vector from state i to state j, and k specifies the kth member in the alphabet. The sum of the b_{ijk} for any vector is equal to one. The following properties hold for all b_{ijk}:

$$0 \le b_{ijk} \le 1$$

$$\sum_k b_{ijk} = 1 \text{ for all } i, j$$

Figure 4.1c shows the output probabilities. In the example of Figure 4.1, the probability that the letter D will be output when the transition is taken from state 1 to state 3 is 0.2. A probability of 0 means that member of the alphabet doesn't occur at the transition in question.

Of primary concern are three problems dealing with the relationship between one or more HMMs and their observable outputs. First, consider the case where an observation sequence that could have been produced by any of several HMMs is known. For each one, you would like to compute the probability that it produced the observed sequence. Another question involves discovering the path through an HMM that has the greatest likelihood of having generated a given observed sequence. The states of an HMM sometimes represent physical entities or phenomena where the solution to

Transition Probability	
a_{11}	0.2
a_{12}	0.3
a_{13}	0.5
a_{22}	0.5
a_{23}	0.5
a_{33}	1.0

Figure 4.1.(b) Hidden Markov model: transition probabilities.

a problem lies in determining the sequence in which these are invoked to produce the observed output. For all but the simplest HMMs, it's possible to produce the same sequence of observable outputs from any of many different paths through the model. In such cases, the sequence of states that produced a given output string can't be known explicitly. Suppose you monitor a black box over five clock periods and observe the following output sequence from the box:

    D B F A A.

And suppose further that the information of Figure 4.1 defines a hidden Markov model of the black box's operation. An examination of the figure reveals numerous paths through the model that will produce the observed output sequence. The probability of the observed sequence being generated by the model is the sum of the probabilities for each possible path. The probability of each path can be calculated and the most likely one identi-

	Output Probability					
Symbol	1,1	1,2	1,3	2,2	2,3	3,3
A	0.2	0.2	0.3	0.1	0.1	0.1
B	0.1	0.2	0.1	0.4	0.1	0.3
C	0.2	0.1	0.1	0.1	0.5	0.1
D	0.1	0.2	0.2	0.1	0.1	0.2
E	0.3	0.1	0.2	0.1	0.1	0.2
F	0.1	0.2	0.1	0.2	0.1	0.1

Figure 4.1.(c) Hidden Markov model: output symbols and their probabilities.

fied. An algorithm known as the *Viterbi Algorithm* calculates the most likely path and remembers the states through which it passes.

You would also like to progressively adjust an HMM's parameters so it approaches a finer and finer approximation of the system being modeled. An observation sequence is presented and the model's parameters tuned to maximize the probability of its having produced the observation sequence. This is the speech recognition "training" problem (the observation sequence presented is the training data). More and more training data can be presented to successively tune a model's parameters. Algorithms exist that deal with each of the three problems just discussed.

So far, I've described discrete HMMs where the alphabets are unique symbols and their probabilities explicitly defined. The concepts and algorithms for discrete HMMs can be extended to continuous HMMs where the observations are sequences of continuous vectors. They differ from discrete HMMs in that their output probabilities, rather than being explicitly listed for each symbol of their alphabet, are modeled on a continuous probability function. Their principal advantage over discrete HMMs is that whereas discrete HMMs require vector quantization in order to model parametrically coded speech, continuous HMMs can model parametric speech directly, thus avoiding the extra steps and the inevitable quantization noise attendant to vector quantization. Continuous HMMs usually result in fewer model parameters than discrete HMMs but require longer training sequences and more computations for recognition. Performance results for speech recognition systems using continuous versus discrete HMMs are mixed and depend on the task.

In subsequent sections you'll see how HMMs are applied in speech recognition. First, let's consider the advantages and disadvantages of adopting various speech segments as the recognition unit.

Choice of speech units

At some point in every speech recognition system, some unit of speech is isolated from its neighbors in the waveform and somehow compared against a stored inventory of fixed units of similar type. Units of speech that have been suggested or tested include word, multiword, syllable, demisyllable, phone (also called phoneme), diphone, triphone, and others. (Diphones and triphones are pairs and triplets of phones taken in context.) An English-speaking adult might have a vocabulary of around 100,000 words. There are about 20,000 different syllables, 2,500 diphones, 1,000 demisyllables, many thousands of triphones, and slightly more than 40 phonemes in English. Multiword units are sometimes used, and the number of these units modeled would depend on the task and could not be expected to be large. Each individual unit in the inventory occupies a sizable piece of storage because it includes details characterizing the unit and differentiating it from the others. The amount of storage required and the amount of processing time for recognition are functions of the number of units in the inventory, so selection of the unit will have a significant impact.

Another important consideration in selecting a speech unit concerns the ability to model contextual differences. Speech can be viewed as a concatenation of phonemes. Contextual changes result in continuous speech when the pronunciation of a phone depends upon either or both its neighbors. Articulators move from one sound to the next in a continuous movement, and the transition is not instantaneous. As the articulators anticipate a succeeding phone, the present one might merge into the next and alter each of them slightly. Phonemes might be omitted entirely, as when "give me" becomes "gimme." To achieve high performance, a recognition system must be able to model these differences.

Another consideration concerns the ease with which adequate training can be provided. Training sequences enable the recognizer's parameters to be adapted for the speech it's expected to recognize. Depending upon the speech unit and other factors, different types and amounts of training data are required. For example, a word-based recognizer must be given training data for every word in its vocabulary, while phone-based recognizers (and those based on other subword units) must train on large quantities of representative sentences—though these need not contain the words they will recognize. Furthermore, a speaker-dependent system must be specifically trained for each speaker. Speaker-independent recognizers, while not required to train every speaker, must be presented with large tracts of training data from a cross section of speakers typical of its intended population. Thus, while training requirements differ in character depending upon the speech unit on which the recognizer is based, they're also dependent upon other factors and are usually extensive. For example, a word-based speaker-dependent system must train every word to be recognized for every speaker. A phone-based speaker-independent recognizer must train many diverse speakers with large numbers of sentences. For any recognizer, no matter which unit of speech is used, inadequate training means inferior performance.

Because the objective of speech recognition is to output a word or sequence of words, it might seem reasonable to adopt the word as the unit of speech. But, because each word in a speaker-dependent system must be trained with every speaker, it's impractical to adopt word units for large-vocabulary, speaker-dependent recognizers. Even with speaker-independent systems, training many words with a large number of speakers would be a formidable task—especially if new words must be added periodically. Furthermore, since each individual unit in inventory requires voluminous storage for templates or other information, large vocabulary word-unit systems require much more storage and processing time than those based on subword units. Searches require processor time, and the larger the inventory, the greater the time. This is usually true even though subword systems generally require additional processing to combine the smaller units into words. There are sometimes, however, advantages to adopting word units. One such case is for a system that recognizes only a few mutually dissimilar words. Recognizers that can be modeled on word units and that have been extensively trained generally outperform equivalent subword systems.

Another seemingly natural recognition unit is the phone (or phoneme), the smallest distinct sound unit of a language. Even though each language has a different set of phones, within any one language the set of phones is always the same. As stated earlier, the English language has slightly more than forty of them. Because of the small number of them, storage requirements are minimized for phones. Training of phone-based recognizers requires only several hundred sentences. A serious disadvantage of phones as a speech unit is that they don't account for contextual differences.

Multiphone units such as syllables and demisyllables can model the effects of context, though not perfectly so. Training of syllable-based systems would be quite impractical due to the large numbers of syllables. Training for demisyllables is also difficult, and results have experimentally shown demisyllables to be inferior to other approaches. Diphone and triphone models both attempt to account for the influence of context by modeling dual or triple phone combinations. Even though multiphone approaches do accommodate context, the main detriment is the large numbers of each and the need to train each instance of the unit individually.

Diverse arrangements of subword units have been conjectured. For example, consider one experiment whose objective was to model a large number of units while still considering context. Kai-Fu Lee at Carnegie Mellon University has described a continuous speech recognizer using hidden Markov models with several different phone units. Both context-dependent and context-independent units were tested with and without an enhancement he calls "Function-Word Dependent Phones." Speech consists of content words and function words such as "the," "is," "it," and "for." In an effort to include context for such words, every version of phones appearing in the set of function words was modeled explicitly. Phones not occurring in any function word were modeled only in their basic version. Function words are numerous in normal speech, so their phones are independent of task and easily trained. Function words in continuous speech are stressed less than 15 percent of the time, and studies have shown that unstressed syllables are the most difficult to recognize. When a speaker stresses a syllable, it's articulated more precisely and produced with greater energy. In experiments cited by Lee, 50 percent of recognition errors occurred in function words, even though they accounted for only 30 percent of those spoken. They usually compose an even smaller proportion of the entire vocabulary. The the-

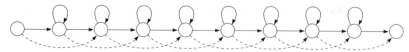

Figure 4.2 Ten-state hidden Markov model for a word.

ory at Carnegie Mellon that better performance can be obtained by explicitly modeling every version of phones as they're pronounced in function words was confirmed in their experiment.

There is strong impetus to create large vocabulary, continuous-speech, speaker-independent recognizers. To achieve the highest performance, such systems must be able to model contextual influences, and it must be practical to provide them with ample training. Word-based systems can't meet these requirements, so the most successful of such systems have adopted some subword unit.

Modeling speech units with hidden Markov models

Suppose you want to design a word-based, isolated word recognizer using discrete hidden Markov models. Each word in the vocabulary is represented by an individual HMM, each with the same number of states. A word can be modeled as a sequence of syllables, phonemes, or other speech sounds that have a temporal interpretation and can best be modeled with a left-to-right HMM whose states represent the speech sounds. Assume the longest word in the vocabulary can be represented by a 10-state HMM. So, let's use a 10-state HMM like that of Figure 4.2 for each word. In our example, let's assume states in the HMM represent phonemes. The dotted lines in the figure are null transitions, so any state can be omitted and some words modeled with fewer states. The duration of a phoneme is accommodated by having a state transition returning to the same state. Thus, at a clock time, a state may return to itself and may do so at as many clock times as required to correctly model the duration of that phoneme in the word. Except for beginning and end states, which represent transitions into and out of the word, each state in the word model has a self-transition.

Assume, in our example, that the input speech waveform is coded into a string of spectral vectors, one occurring every 10 milliseconds, and that vector quantization further transforms each spectral vector to a single value that indexes a representative vector in the codebook. Each word in the vocabulary will be trained through a number of repetitions by one or more talkers. As each word is trained, the transitional and output probabilities of its HMM are adjusted to merge the latest word repetition into the model. During training, the codebook is iterated with the objective of deriving one that's optimum for the defined vocabulary. When an unknown spoken word is to be recognized, it's transformed to a string of codebook indices. That string is then considered an HMM observation sequence by the recognizer that calculates, for each word model in the vocabulary, the probability of that HMM having generated the observations. The word corresponding to the word model with the highest probability is selected as the one recognized.

Discrete HMMs can model any unit of speech, including any subword unit (syllable, demisyllable, phoneme, etc.). Figure 4.3 shows, for instance, how a phoneme might be modeled in a large-vocabulary speaker-independent recognizer. Again a left-to-right HMM is used reflecting the temporal aspect of speech. The leftmost and rightmost nodes are entry and exit states. The three states with self-transitions represent, from left-to-right, a transition into the phoneme, the nontransitional stationary state within the phoneme, and the transition out of the phoneme. The absence of null transitions indicates that none of the three states can be skipped. The self-transitions enable the duration of the segment to be modeled. Because words can be thought of as a concatenation of phonemes, any word can be represented as concatenated strings of the form shown in Figure 4.3. Subword models are trained with representative continuous speech—usually hundreds of sentences spoken by a variety of talkers.

Modeling grammar with hidden Markov models

Every automatic speech recognizer has a purpose that, to only a limited extent, is defined by the broad characterizations discussed previously. The same speaker-independent or continuous-speech system can accomplish a number of different recognition tasks; it can be used for a variety of individual applications. Each recognition application has its own language and grammar that establish the set of legal utterances and defines the scope of the application. These languages specify not only a vocabulary and rules by which words can be combined but also meanings for correctly formed combinations of words. Such languages are usually subsets of a natural language, less complex, and more constrained, serving to structure human-computer communications in service of the specific recognition task.

One goal of automatic speech recognition is to someday enable humans to converse freely and naturally with computers in human language. Natural language grammars never completely codify the rules governing conversational speech. Even if they did, common usage continually evolves the lan-

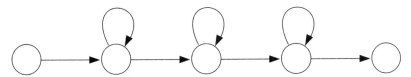

Figure 4.3 Five-state hidden Markov model for a phoneme.

guage, adding new words and constructs. Everyday usage doesn't adhere to rigid rules for language anyway. Nonsense sentences can be syntactically correct and ungrammatical sentences or sentence fragments perfectly sensible. Recognizers, if they're ever to achieve that stated goal, must go far beyond the restrictions of artificial languages and recognize speech that might violate rules of grammar, speech that might include such constructs as "What's up?" and "Just foolin around."

A recognition task's grammar specifies syntax for the task. A recognizer without grammar must evaluate every word or phrase in its active vocabulary at each decision point. A grammar takes away some of the possibilities (or rates them probabilistically) at each decision point and thus eases the workload. Many recognition tasks require no grammar or, only simple grammars. For example, recognition of the digits from zero through nine and a few command words, whether isolated words or connected speech, requires only the simplest of grammars: any word in the vocabulary might be followed by any other within the vocabulary. Some recognition tasks, on the other hand, require fairly complex grammars. *Perplexity* is a measure of the complexity of a grammar, a high perplexity being more complex. Perplexity is roughly based on the number of choices at each decision point (but adjusted by the probability of being at that decision point).

In many cases the grammar can be coded directly in an HMM state diagram, as is done in the example shown in Figure 4.4. In this example, dotted vectors represent null transitions. Valid sentences include "Increase speed to three-fourths throttle," "Reduce to half," "Full throttle," "Stop engine," and others.

Invalid sentences such as "Reduce throttle to quarter" and "Increase speed" are not recognized. This grammar is not perfect because it both excludes some desirable commands and allows constructs that could be thought ambiguous—such as "Half" and "Quarter." It's easy to see how the di-

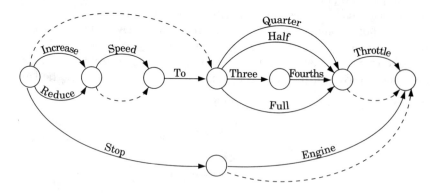

Figure 4.4 Grammar represented in a hidden Markov model.

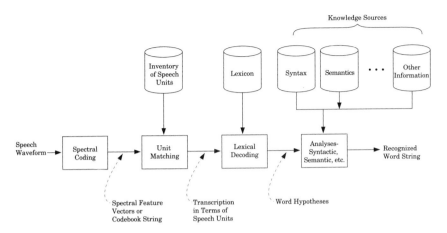

Figure 4.5 A hidden Markov model recognizer.

agram could be changed to allow other useful sentences or to block unwanted forms. Substitutions of word or phoneme state diagrams (like those shown in Figures 4.2 and 4.3) in place of the word transition vectors of Figure 4.4 can be effected to produce an integrated HMM. The resulting state diagram would completely define the recognition task in a single HMM, incorporating all knowledge sources. Thus, recognition for this task can be performed by processing only one HMM network in what's in effect an integrated search—a capability that highlights the power of hidden Markov models.

Acoustic/phonetic example using hidden Markov model

Every speech recognition system has its own architecture. Even those that are based on HMMs have their individual designs, but all share some basic concepts and features, many of which are recognizable even though the names are often different. The following discussions, rather than covering a specific design, are intended as an introduction to some of the concepts frequently found in HMM recognizers. A representative block diagram is given in Figure 4.5. The input to a recognizer represented by Figure 4.5 arrives from the left in the form of a speech waveform, and an output word or sequence of words emanates from the recognizer to the right.

In the following paragraphs, each of the functional blocks of the figure is discussed briefly. For those who desire further study, the references in the bibliography provide a good start toward an in-depth treatment of the subject.

Spectral coding. The purpose of spectral coding is to transform the signal into a digital form embodying speech features that facilitate subsequent recognition tasks. In addition to *spectral coding*, this function is sometimes called *spectrum analysis, acoustic parameterization*, etc. Recognizers can work with time-domain coding, but spectrally coded parameters in the frequency domain have advantages and are widely used—hence the title "spectral coding." As with synthesis, the input speech signal must be digitized and coded for efficient storage and for use in the next stage. Analog input is passed through an antialiasing filter and sometimes a high-frequency preemphasis filter to achieve spectral flattening. It's digitized to 11 or 12 bits at a rate from 6 kHz to 20 kHz or more. The speech spectrum can either be obtained digitally or from a bank of bandpass filters. A parametric representation of the speech is assembled—for example, using LPC coding with a new frame each 10 milliseconds. Typically overlapping frames with a width of 30 milliseconds are used. Either or both the frame rate and width can vary from system to system, depending on design criteria. The set of frame parameters (also called a feature vector) might contain any information derived from the waveform that's pertinent to the recognition tasks that follow. Cepstral coefficients have been found to be a convenient spectral metric and, along with a temporal rate of change measure (e.g., approximated using frame-to-frame variations in the cepstrum), might compose a feature vector of 20 or 30 parameters. Depending upon which speech-unit-modeling techniques are to be used in subsequent sections of the recognizer, the feature vectors might be reduced to a sequence of discrete values using vector quantization whose codebook has been obtained through prior training. Whether feature vectors or codebook entries, the output is then directed to a unit matching module.

Unit matching.   The objective of *unit matching* is to transcribe the output data stream from the spectral coding module into a sequence of speech units. The function of this module is also referred to as feature analysis, phonetic decoding, phonetic segmentation, phonetic processing, feature extraction, etc. The output stream is a time-based sequence of the selected speech units and, at this point in the process, contains numerous errors. If the speech unit is phonemes, then the output of the unit matcher is a sequence of phonemes. If the recognizer uses word units, the output is a string of word candidates. (In this particular case, the unit matching module and the lexical decoding module discussed in the next section are combined.) To accomplish its task, the unit matching module has access to an inventory of speech units (phonemes, words, demisyllables or whatever speech unit's being used), each represented in the database by its individual HMM, whose parameters have been estimated during prior training. Unit matching is highly dependent upon the language, the dialect, and the speaker—each of whose peculiarities are inherent in the waveform and will have been carried through to the unit matching module's input stream. Differences in pronunciation of the units, which must be accommodated, is modeled statistically by the HMM's transitional probabilities.

When an input of unknown speech is presented to the recognizer, it reaches the unit matching module as a sequence of spectral vectors or other correlates of the acoustic signal, where it's tested against each candidate HMM in the speech unit inventory. The input string is considered a sequence of HMM observations and, for each candidate unit in inventory, the probability that the string in question was produced by that model is calculated. The unit corresponding to the HMM with the highest probability is selected as the output token. Note that not every unit in inventory need be a candidate. Other knowledge sources, such as a phonotactic rule base, can be used to eliminate some and nominate other candidates. The unit matching process might also access a rule base detailing legal combinations of phonemes or other units. (If word units are used, the rule base and the grammar are the same.)

Lexical decoding. The function of this module is to match strings of speech units in the unit matching module's output stream with words from the recognizer's lexicon. It outputs candidate words—usually in the form of a word lattice containing sets of alternative word choices. If the speech unit is words, lexical decoding is combined with unit matching into a single module. The lexicon contains the recognizer's vocabulary of words spelled in terms of the speech unit to facilitate matching with the input stream.

Syntactic, semantic, and other analyses. Analyses that follow lexical decoding all have the purpose of pruning word candidates passed along from the lexical decoding module until final word selections can be made. Various means and various sources of intelligence can be applied to this end. Acoustic information (stress, intonation, change of amplitude or pitch, relative location of formants, etc.) obtained from the waveform can be employed, but sources of intelligence from outside the waveform are also available. These include syntactic, semantic, and pragmatic information. Let's consider a simple example showing how some of these sources of information can help to eliminate or promote alternative word choices.

Suppose in an unrestrained task, a large-vocabulary speaker-independent recognizer were presented with a four-word question, and the hypotheses resulting from lexical decoding gave the following sets of candidates for the four words:

```
{White, What} {is} {lore, your} {noon, none, name}.
```

A syntactic analysis would prune the word "lore" from the third position and probably the word "none" from the final position. Semantic analysis would further eliminate the word "noon" from fourth position (and also "none" if not pruned earlier). Acoustic information could reveal that a question was spoken to cause the word "What" to be chosen over "White." Thus, only the sentence "What is your name?" would remain to be selected for output.

Measures of Performance

Successful speech recognition is dependent upon many factors, including the application, the task, speaker-dependence, size of vocabulary, the speaker's physical and emotional state, microphone quality, background noise, channel noise, details concerning language modeling, presence of confusable words in vocabulary, constraints imposed by the grammar, and many others. Despite the many sources of error, it's possible to obtain an estimate of accuracy based on some error-rate measure. In the case of isolated word recognizers, this is a straightforward calculation because each word spoken is either correctly recognized or it's not. With continuous speech recognizers, there can be three different types of errors: insertion, deletion, and substitution. Clearly, a missing word (deletion) is an error. A substitution (selecting the wrong word) is also an error. But, there's controversy over whether or not every insertion should be counted as an error. Consider the case where "Saturday?" is spoken but "Is that your day?" is recognized. You could say this error has resulted in one substitution and three insertions. Is it to be counted as one error or four? When dealing with performance claims for recognizers, it's important to understand exactly the basis upon which the claim is made.

5

Telecommunications

Our global telecommunications network makes it possible for a person to pick up a telephone, dial a number, and speak to someone in almost any country on any continent in the world. The network also enables us to communicate with computers by voice (and other means) in most places throughout the world. Many events and complex processes take place in the completion of such calls. Often, the cooperative efforts of several companies and millions of dollars worth of switching, signaling, and transmission equipment and other facilities are combined to make the call possible. The seeds that gave rise to the worldwide telecommunications network we know today were planted more than a century ago.

Historical Perspective

By the year 1875, the Western Union Telegraph Company had already strung more than 175,000 miles of telegraph transmission wire across the United States. A code composed of combinations of short and long pulses had been developed by Samuel Morse for transmission of electrical messages through this network of wires. However, with the appearance of the telephone, Morse code would soon yield to voice as a communication vehicle. Once this new invention took root, a maze of interconnected wires and cables and machines sprouted up and spread like a net over the entire world. Telephone networks began their evolutionary growth in a Boston attic on June 2, 1875, when Alexander Graham Bell was hard at work in his shop. He was trying to find a way to send multiple messages on a single telegraph wire when he realized that the sound he heard from a vibrating metal reed in his receiving device was responding to a reed being plucked by his assistant in an adjoining room. He knew instantly that "sound" had been electrically transmitted through the length of wire connecting the two devices. Less than a year later, Bell was granted a patent on the electrical speaking telephone.

The Bell Telephone Company was founded in 1877 by Bell and two investors—one of whom was a patent attorney. The first telephone switchboard was installed in Boston that same year. It served six subscribers. When the first commercial telephone exchange, with only 21 subscribers, was installed in New Haven, Connecticut the following year, the monthly cost of telephone service was almost twice an average person's income for the same period. By 1880 there were 54,000 telephones in homes and offices, and a few years later people in Boston and New York could talk to each other by telephone. Switching was performed by young men and women manually pushing plugs into switchboards.

In 1889 a mechanical device was invented that lead to automatic switching and enabled subscribers in a community to carry on telephone conversations without the help of an operator. Dialing was primitive by today's standards. Nevertheless, 100 subscribers in LaPorte, Indiana, were able to conduct conversations using the very first automatic exchange. In 1893, Bell's original patent expired and opened the way for others to sell telephone equipment and service. Independent telephone companies abounded—at first in rural areas not serviced by Bell's companies, but later in the metropolitan areas as well. By 1895, more than 6,000 individual telephone companies were in operation in the United States alone. Of these, only about 1,800 existed before the patent expired. Most of the 6,000 companies had brief lifespans, and today, about 1,500 independent telephone companies remain.

By 1915, people in New York were talking by phone with people in San Francisco. In August of 1922, when Alexander Graham Bell died, almost 10 million telephones were served by the Bell System alone. The Federal Communications Act, passed in 1934 by the United States Congress, established the Federal Communications Commission (FCC), with responsibility for regulating rates and conditions of interstate, international, and marine communication. By this time, transmission technology had so improved that multiple conversations could be sent on the same medium. In 1936 the first coaxial-based transmission line was operational between New York and Philadelphia and, by 1941, a pair of coaxial tubes could carry 480 conversations. This number was soon expanded to 600. That same year there were about 24 million phones in the United States and 45 million in the world. In 1947, the first microwave radio system was put into operation, and by 1950 microwave transmission was becoming widespread. One year later, there were more than 13,000 route miles of private microwave systems in operation, and a single microwave system was capable of transmitting 600 simultaneous conversations on each of five links. Later in that same decade, improvements in antenna design doubled the transmission capacity of microwave systems.

By the year 1953, the capacity of a pair of coaxial tubes had grown to almost 2,000 voice channels, and the total number of miles spanned by microwave relay passed that of wire and cable spans together. Two submarine cables provided landline transmissions between countries. The first transatlantic cable, with 36 voice channels, was put in place in 1956 to link Newfoundland, Canada, and Scotland. That same year, to end an antitrust suit against them by the Justice Department, AT&T signed a consent decree that, among other things, required them to decline royalties on then-existing patents and to license all future patents at reasonable royalties. It's easy to see how this helped to promote growth in the telecommunications industry by making technology more broadly available. In the mid-1950s, digital computers made their appearance, but it would be a decade before computer-controlled switching would be put into operation.

In 1961 the United States had about 77 million of the world's 150 million phones. Digital transmission was introduced in 1962 with a system capable of multiplexing 24 voice-frequency (VF) channels on two paired cables. In 1963 a transpacific cable connected Canada, Australia, and New Zealand. Stored program switching control was introduced the following year, but the number of electromechanical switching installations continued to increase for a time. The development of solid-state semiconductor devices soon began a telecommunications explosion that has continued ever since. With the advent of semiconductor technology, the carrying capacity of a pair of coaxial tubes was increased to 3,600 VF channels (also called voice-band channels). A few years after the transpacific cable went into service, telephone conversations and data were being transmitted across continents and oceans by satellite microwave radio relay.

Meanwhile, groundwork for advancement outside the Bell System was being laid, and in 1968 the FCC ruled against AT&T and in favor of Carter Electronics of Texas by permitting direct electrical connection of third-party devices to the voice telephone network. To protect public networks from harm, such attachment required a special device available only from the telephone company—a protective coupling attachment (PCA) for voice lines or a direct-access arrangement (DAA) for nonvoice connections. The Carterfone Ruling, as it came to be called, was a boon to interconnect companies. Today there are thousands of companies manufacturing and selling telephone equipment for attachment to public networks.

By 1971, the Bell System alone was providing service to more than 100-million telephones in the United States—82 percent of all telephones in the country. In 1972 the International Telegraph and Telephone Consultative Committee (CCITT), an international committee established and supervised by the United Nations and working toward improvement of international communications, standardized PCM for digital networks and provided for a sampling rate of 8,000 samples per second and 8-bit encoding using either A-Law or μ-law companding. World telecommunications was going digital. While replacement of mechanical switching systems has continued since digital switching appeared in 1976, it will still be years before they disappear altogether. In 1980 CCITT recognized that substantial agreement had been reached in the industry concerning establishment of integrated digital networks and promulgated guidelines for studies that would lead to future establishment of Integrated Services Digital Networks (ISDN). Thus, that year, seeds were sown that would eventually lead to wideband digital networks and end-to-end connectivity supporting voice, data, sound, and video services. However, ISDN was for the future. Another antitrust suit against AT&T by the Justice Department ended in January of 1982 when the company agreed to a modification to the 1956 consent decree. The modification eased regulation on some activities and opened up a number of telecommunications markets that had formerly been denied to AT&T. More importantly, though, the 1982 ruling specified the breakup of the Bell System, effective January 1, 1984. On that date, AT&T divested nineteen Bell Operating Companies (BOCs) that were reorganized under seven independent Regional Bell Operating Companies (RBOCs). Today, RBOCs service about 80 percent of all telephone subscribers in the United States.

In 1984 there were about 21,000 public network switching facilities in the United States—about 14,000 of which were still mechanical. By the mid-1980s, one pair of coaxial tubes could carry 13,200 voice channels. Since then, high-capacity submarine cable systems have been developed, and satellite relay systems have become commonplace—as have fiber-optic transmission and digital coaxial systems. It's estimated that in 1991 there were more than 225 million telephones in the U.S. and more than half a billion worldwide. Digital transmission systems have evolved packet-switching and other techniques that provide high-quality data services to interactive and other users. Facsimile and video are both transmitted around the world. The popularity of the personal computer, which reached monumental proportions in the 1980s, has resulted in more intelligent telephone terminal equipment and has given rise to voice processing.

The following sections cover certain details concerned with telephone networks and include discussions of transmission facilities, switching systems, and signaling.

Telecommunications Networks

The worldwide telecommunications network is composed of numerous interconnected public and private networks throughout the world—each involving vast expanses of wire or other transmission media interconnected through numerous switching nodes. National networks are linked at gateway offices

Figure 5.1 Major Bell System transmission routes. *(Copyright (c), 1983, AT&T. Reprinted with permission.)*

by various switching and transmission means. Discussions in this chapter pertain primarily to the Public Switched Telephone Network (PSTN), which is most familiar because of its widespread and far-reaching influence in both our personal and business lives. Figure 5.1 illustrates the complexity of the PSTN in the United States. Many businesses use private networks for voice, data, facsimile and perhaps video communication between their various locations. Private networks use dedicated switching, transmission, and other equipment; otherwise, private networks are similar in operation to the PSTN.

The end points of a telephone network are the telephones and other terminals attached to it. In the present world environment, other devices besides telephones can provide termination points for a telephone network: modems, computers, facsimile machines, and other devices also connect to and use the PSTN. In addition, telephones can be either single-line or multi-line devices. All such telephones and other devices are referred to as *station equipment*. Station equipment must interface electrically to the network and must place signals on the network that are consistent with network protocols. Station equipment must also be able to interpret signals coming to it on the network. Telephones, for example, convert ringing signals to audible ringing (and sometimes to blinking lights). They also convert speech signals to audible speaking, and they convert input voice to speech signals and place them on the network. Telephones generate either pulse or tone digits on the network in response to rotary or keypad dialing. Other station equipment

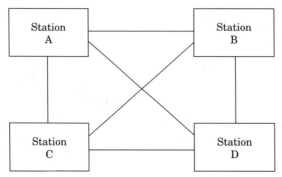

Figure 5.2 Directly connected network.

(such as a voice processing computer, for instance) detects and interprets Touch-Tone signals arriving on the network. Station equipment provides the user interface (either human or computer) to a telephone network.

The following paragraphs cover the general structure and operation of telecommunications networks.

Switched network

Millions of station devices can be attached to the PSTN at any given moment. The primary function of the network is to enable any of these devices to obtain and maintain a dedicated attachment to any other on demand and for an undetermined period of time. Any of a number of network arrangements could be established to accomplish this goal. For instance, every station could be connected to every other by a span of wire. A very small version of such a network is shown in Figure 5.2. The configuration requires six transmission wires and would not be very economical if the stations were widely separated. It certainly would not be economical for networks with a large number of stations. The advantage of including switching elements quickly becomes obvious when you consider networks involving millions (or even thousands) of stations. More switching systems can mean that fewer miles of transmission cable are required. On the other hand, switching equipment is expensive, so a trade-off between switching and transmission must be accomplished in the design of telecommunications networks.

Figure 5.3 shows a four-station network configuration in which connections between pairs of stations are accomplished by means of a switch. This arrangement is called a *star network*. The switch is able to interconnect any pair of stations and might even be able to simultaneously connect two pairs of stations. This arrangement has a large number of stations connected to a switch that is able, on demand, to interconnect pairs (or larger subsets) of stations and to disconnect them when communication is finished.

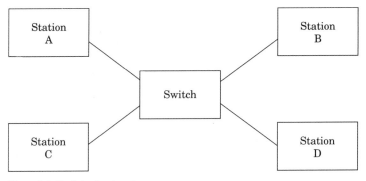

Figure 5.3 Switched network.

Central office (CO)

In a telephone network, a group of nearby stations are interconnected via switching systems located in a telephone company central office (CO), as shown in Figure 5.4. (Note the similarity between Figures 5.3 and 5.4.) The term *central office* doesn't imply a conventional office in the ordinary sense—rather, it refers to the building where the local switching system is located, to the local switching system itself, or to the switching system and associated equipment. It's also called a local central office, local exchange,

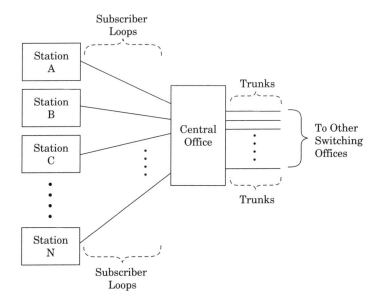

Figure 5.4 Telephone network central office.

or end office. A central office exists to accomplish switching between sets of local stations and to provide paths between them and stations attached to other central offices. Some communities have more than one central office to service the number of telephone stations required—large cities and communities typically have many central offices. Communication lines interconnecting switching systems are called *trunks*.

Connections between the central office and a customer station is generally accomplished with a pair of wires called a *subscriber loop*. The word *loop* refers to the fact that one wire extends out from the central office to the customer's station and the other loops back again. One subscriber loop is associated with one telephone line—and is dedicated to the station equipment to which it's attached. (I'll later discuss carrier systems that bundle groups of calls on a wire pair.) A call between stations connected to the same local exchange is referred to as a *local call* and is completed when the central office interconnects the two subscriber loops. The final four digits of a telephone number identify a given subscriber loop (sometimes five digits are used), so a typical central office can handle up to 10,000 subscriber loops—but some can have more. Three digits of a telephone number (but sometimes two) identify each exchange within an area. A subsequent section discusses calls to stations outside a local exchange.

Remote switch

If a group of stations are served by the same central office and located at a distance from it, it's sometimes more economical to install a smaller remote switching device to service the stations. Figures 5.5 and 5.6 illustrate this concept. Rather than routing many subscriber loops over a distance, calls are combined (multiplexed) and fewer transmission lines used. The cost of transmission is lessened at the expense of higher switching costs. The dia-

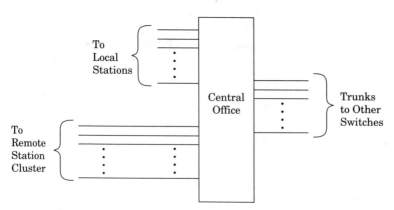

Figure 5.5 Central office directly serving remote stations.

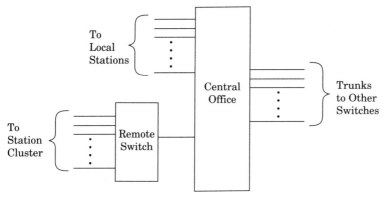

Figure 5.6 Remote switching from a central office.

gram of Figure 5.6 could represent attachment of a Private Branch Exchange (PBX) to the PSTN—in a very real sense, a PBX is a remote switch. PBXs are discussed in a later section in this chapter.

Toll office

Long-distance calls are routed from a subscriber's station through the local central office to a toll office (or offices) and on toward a distant central office for connection to one of its local stations. As with a central office, the toll office is not an office in a conventional sense. It might refer to the switching system that switches calls among other switching offices. A call that's switched through a toll office is referred to as a toll call and is differentiated from a local call. The network architecture for connecting distant central offices is shown in Figure 5.7. A toll office services numerous central offices and can connect with many other toll offices. A toll trunk (also called toll-connecting trunk) interconnects a central office with a toll office, and intertoll trunks connect toll offices to each other.

Tandem office

Nontoll calls within a large community can be routed from one central office to another. It's not practical to interconnect every nearby central office when large numbers of these are involved—so a local tandem office is interposed to switch calls between them. Tandem offices also play a role in switching between toll offices in the switching hierarchy discussed in the next section. As I mentioned with central offices and toll offices, a tandem office is not an office in the ordinary sense but refers essentially to switching equipment that interconnects other switching offices. Figure 5.8 illustrates the network architecture for a local tandem office whose function is to switch calls between nearby central offices.

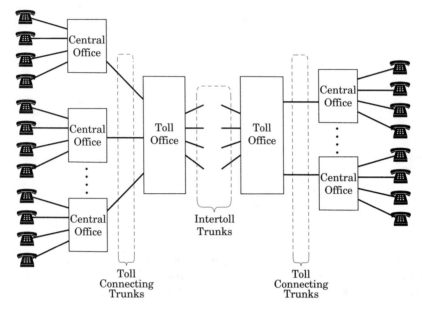

Figure 5.7 Telephone network with toll offices.

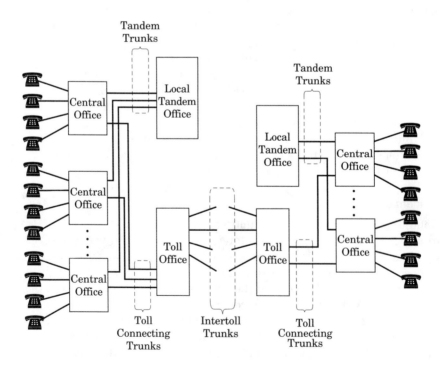

Figure 5.8 Telephone network with local tandem offices.

Toll network switching hierarchy

Long-distance calls in the PSTN, whether for voice or data transmission, are switched and accounted through a hierarchy of toll offices. *Direct distance dialing* (DDD—long distance calling without operator intervention) is available throughout most communities in the United States and many other countries. In England it's called *subscriber trunk dialing. Operator distance dialing* (ODD) has been used for intercontinental calling for many years, but calls between some countries, the United States and England for instance, can be dialed directly without intervention of an operator. Stations connected to one central office can dial (and be automatically connected) through toll offices to a distant central office and hence to one of its subscribers.

There are numerous paths a call might take on its route through various toll offices to the target central office. Two successive calls between the same two telephones might travel entirely different paths, perhaps through different cities miles apart—this is why most of us have at one time or another bothered to redial a call in hopes of getting a less noisy connection. A redundant network design like this results in more toll offices, but choices can be exercised concerning call routing so malfunctioning or busy trunks less often result in *blocked calls*. (A call is said to be blocked if it can't be routed through a switch or if there's no available transmission path for it.) The most direct trunks between two central offices are sometimes occupied or inoperative—so, more circuitous routes must be used. In the North American PSTN (which includes the United States and Canada) a five-level switching hierarchy defines alternate paths between toll offices. This concept is illustrated graphically in Figure 5.9.

Toll-office switching systems are established in four classes: regional, sectional, primary, and toll. Central offices are the fifth class in the hierarchy. Of the 20,000 or so switching offices in the PSTN, about 94 percent are class 5, less than 5 percent class 4, and the remainder represent about 1 percent. The toll network consists of those offices of class 4 and smaller. The United States is divided geographically into 10 regions—Canada is divided into 2. Each region is served by a regional toll center, and each is connected by a direct trunk group to each of the others. Each region is subdivided into sections and each section into primary areas and so forth. Switching systems serve each area and those at each higher level concentrate traffic from successively wider geographical areas.

Even though trunk groups interconnect various switching systems outside hierarchical levels, routing doctrine establishes the hierarchy within the network. In Figure 5.9, solid lines between centers define the hierarchy. An office at a lower level (higher class) is said to "home" on an office at the next higher level and a solid line drawn between them on the figure to signify the homing relationship. Though the figure doesn't show all such offices and paths, several central offices home into each toll office,

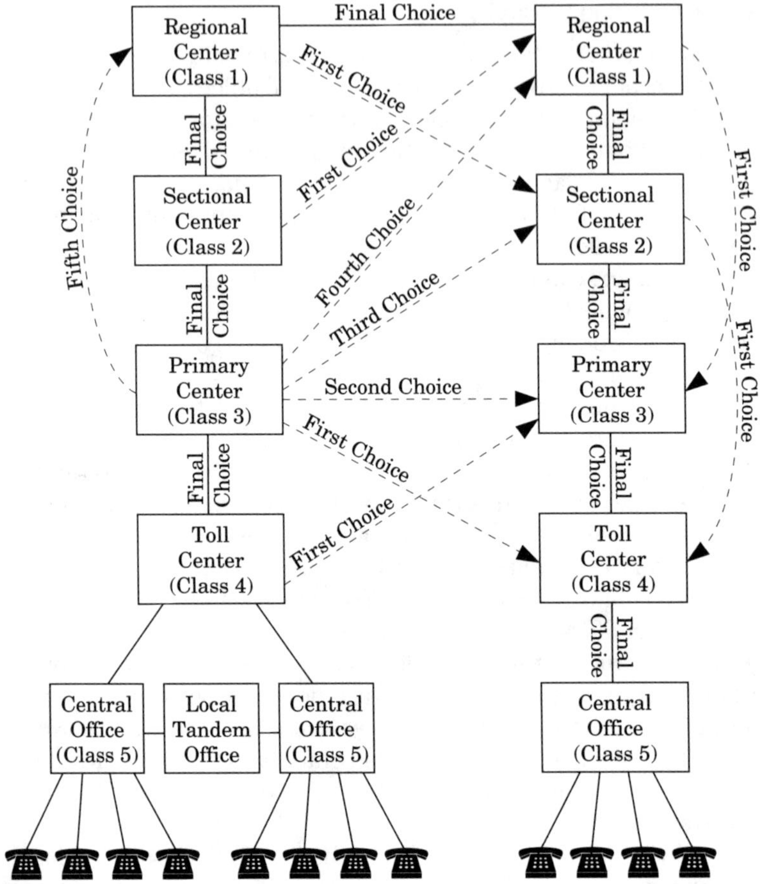

Figure 5.9 Toll office routing hierarchy.

several toll offices home into each primary center, and so on up the chain to form a treelike structure. Dashed lines between centers in Figure 5.9 indicate that a trunk group interconnects the two but that their relationship is not a homing one. Geographic or economic considerations might dictate that any two particular centers be connected, even though they exist at the same level or skip a level or two. This might happen when, for example, a primary center in one hierarchy is linked to a sectional center in another.

Network structure in the hierarchy is integrated in ways that are not obvious in the figure. Switching systems are able to perform route analysis and maintain billing records by means not possible with earlier equipment. Thus, integration of switching functions at various levels is possible within the same equipment—local tandem offices, toll centers, and central offices are often situated in the same system. In fact, in the North American PSTN, about five percent of central offices also perform toll-office switching, three percent include tandem and toll switching, and about one percent perform all three functions.

Figure 5.10 shows a rural branch of the North American PSTN. This branch covers about 20 counties in Mississippi and includes 46 central offices (end offices) that serve about 120,000 telephones. The figure illustrates that a string of distant central offices use common transmission facilities. In rural areas, where there are fewer calls in general but an even lower percentage of interoffice calls, trunks tend to be longer and fewer in number than in urban areas.

As a toll call is routed through the system, each switch attempts to find a trunk taking the most direct route to the destination central office. It often happens that all trunks on the most desirable route are busy, and an alternate route must be chosen. Doctrine dictates that priority be given to routes that take the call through the fewest switches and over the smallest number of trunks. If an interregion call were routed only along final paths, it would pass through ten switching systems before reaching its destination. On the average, though, a toll call in the PSTN uses only one or two intertoll trunks. Direct distance dialing has made this hierarchical approach viable—were it not for automatic switching, the setup time for such a call would be unacceptable. As was shown in Figure 5.9, if no first-choice trunks are available, second-choice trunks are sought, and so on. About one percent of the time, the final-choice trunk group must be used. Each switching system (except a regional center) homes on one at a higher level, and the trunk group for that pair is sized to handle a large number of calls because this path will be the last one available to many. If no idle trunk is found along the final-choice path, the call is blocked and a reorder tone is returned to the caller (who recognizes it as a fast busy signal—reorder and other signals are discussed in a later section in this chapter). A design objective of the PSTN is that no more than one percent of calls will be blocked, so these trunks are frequently implemented as high-capacity coaxial or microwave transmission lines.

Public versus private telephone networks

Large organizations with widespread telecommunication requirements can often meet their needs less expensively with a private network rather than relying exclusively on the PSTN. Many such networks employ leased lines and some use nonswitched facilities such as tie lines to interconnect distant PBXs. In any case, network facilities (or services) are guaranteed to the customer and are available for the sole use of that customer. Using private network facilities, employees might call each other in distant cities simply by dialing the other's extension. Companies can appear to have a local office

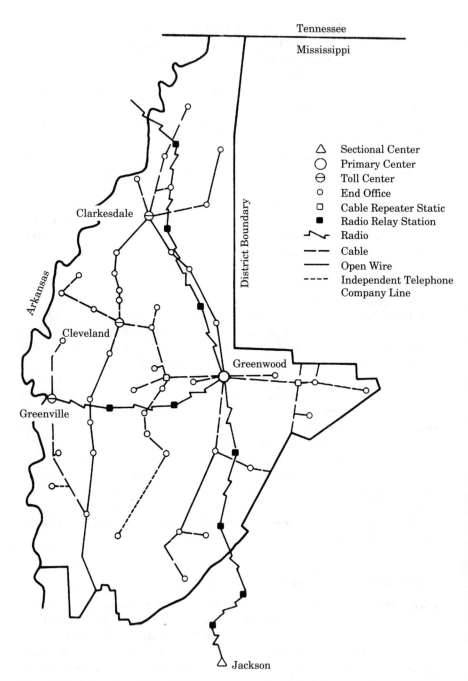

Figure 5.10 A rural interoffice facilities network—Greenwood District, Mississippi. *(Copyright (c) 1983, AT&T. Reprinted with permission.)*

when in fact they don't. Customers in one city, Los Angeles, for example, can dial a local phone number to speak with someone in the company's office in Philadelphia. The call is switched at a switching system in Los Angeles to private lines that carry the call to Philadelphia, where the phone is answered. FCC-regulated interstate private switched network services similar to those available on the PSTN can be purchased in the United States under either Common-Control Switching Arrangement (CCSA) or Enhanced Private Switched Communications Service (EPSCS). Both services offer a uniform seven-digit dialing plan and, for many companies, provide PSTN-compatible services at a lower cost.

EPSCS can provide communication services to facilities all across the United States. In many ways it appears to parallel the North American PSTN, using a two-level switching hierarchy similar to the PSTN's five-level scheme. The system includes specially modified switching systems and better-than-average transmission facilities to provide customers reliable, high-quality, long-distance voice and data communications. EPSCS switches are usually shared among customers because rarely does one customer have enough traffic to justify a dedicated switch. Trunks connecting switches to customer PBXs and to other switches are dedicated even though the transmission facilities on which these trunks are carried might be shared with other private network customers and with the public network. "Off-net" connections are made through various switching systems to provide access from the private net to the PSTN.

Analog versus digital networks

An *analog* system is one that accepts a band of frequencies, and a *digital* system is one that accepts a pulse stream (even though the pulses might be produced in an analog facility). The original telephone networks were based entirely on analog technology for both transmission and switching. However, in the mid-1960s, digital transmission facilities began replacing analog, and, about 10 years later, digital switching systems made their appearance. Most digital transmission systems have been designed to take advantage of already existing analog facilities. In spite of this, digital transmission and switching facilities offer cost and performance advantages over analog—and data is more naturally handled in digital facilities. Digital switching systems are less complex and consequently are considerably less expensive. Most networks today are best described as hybrid, containing both analog and digital elements. In the North American PSTN, traffic is frequently converted between analog and digital (or from digital to analog) as it moves through the network. A-to-D conversion is required whenever voice or data passes from an analog transmission facility to a digital switching system—or from an analog switch to a digital trunk. Likewise, D-to-A conversion takes place for calls moving in the opposite direction. Every time conversion is necessary, quality suffers a little. Furthermore, expensive equipment and its consequent maintenance is required at each conversion node.

The PSTN is constantly evolving, new facilities being added, and older ones being upgraded. There are about 1,500 independent telephone companies who replace, add, and upgrade switching and transmission facilities whenever they deem it economically advantageous to do so. The first transmission facilities to be replaced with digital were metropolitan, high-capacity, short-distance trunks. The first digital switching systems were installed in large toll offices and in small central offices. Other transmission and switching equipment is being upgraded to digital as it nears the end of its normal life cycle, but it will be many years yet before the PSTN is entirely digital.

Integrated services digital network (ISDN)

In 1980 the CCITT recommended that preliminary studies be conducted to establish standards for an international ISDN. The objective is an integrated digital services network that offers a full range of digital communications from low data-rate services (such as meter reading) to wideband services (such as television). Other services would include transmission of voice, data, music (and other sound), facsimile, and video—some of which would be offered as interactive services. It was envisioned that a simple transparent interface to all services would be provided at a reasonable cost by a single local serving office and that unified billing would be established. Customers would subscribe to only those services of interest to them.

Technical and implementation details differ from country to country. It was recognized that individual independent ISDNs based on existing digital network plans would evolve in each country, but international interfaces using standardized protocols should be defined. It seems natural that recommendations by CCITT would incorporate their earlier work by suggesting that ISDNs evolve from existing digital facilities. More recent CCITT studies have recommended three access levels by customers: basic, hybrid, and primary rate. Basic access would combine one 16 KB/sec link with from zero to two 64 KB/sec links carrying various combinations of voice and data. Hybrid access bundles one analog telephone line with a digital interface. Primary rate access provides for different configurations of digital voice and data links at rates of 1.544 MB/sec or 2.048 MB/sec.

ISDN is a worthy, long-range goal that provides a unifying direction for evolution of the world's telecommunications networks. Efforts toward ISDN are fragmentary and scattered, but the world is making progress in that direction. Studies and experiments are being conducted in North America (principally the United States and Canada), France, Japan, Germany (formerly West Germany), and Britain—but other countries are making progress as well. In some places progress entails little more than conversion and upgrade of existing networks from analog to digital—this is, however, a prerequisite to ISDN. In a number of countries wideband optical fiber transmission networks have been created to study techniques for delivering integrated services using this medium, and in one locality in France, a videotex directory service has been implemented on stand-alone terminals.

Transmission

The function of transmission systems is to convey information from one place to another. In the case of telecommunications, the information being transmitted is voice, data, facsimile, video, music or other sound, and it can be carried by wire, radio wave, or optical fiber. In the half-century before telephones were perfected, information was transmitted by telegraph. Operators at opposite ends of a cable strung on poles covering the miles between them would tap out codes on their telegraph keys. Depression and relaxation of the key would make and break the connection between a battery and the wire. The key at the other end would tap out the code in audible response. Repeaters were placed at intervals along the telegraph wire to regenerate and reshape the signal because electric current in a wire diminishes in strength the farther it travels. Messages were transmitted over this system as fast as an operator could tap the code on the key—a very slow rate of communication by today's standards. It was soon realized that communication cost could be reduced by finding a way to send simultaneous messages on the same wire. Indeed, it was in search of such a method that a technique for transmitting voice was discovered by Bell that day in 1875. From that time to this, research and development has been conducted into means for effectively, efficiently, and economically transmitting information over both short and long distances. The result has been that information is conveyed across broad distances very differently today than it was in the days of telegraphy and early telephony.

A basic element in telephone networks is the individual *voice channel,* the facility carrying a single telephone call. It's often referred to as a voice frequency channel, a VF channel, or a voice channel. It might also be called a voiceband channel, referring to the fact that each channel has a bandwidth of 4 kHz. The primary objective of transmission is to convey information from one place to another, but implicit in this goal is the intent that information carried in every VF channel, whether voice or data, should arrive nearly error-free. Naturally, more errors can be tolerated in some communications than in others. A noisy voice channel might be irritating or inconvenient but is probably not nearly so serious as a noisy data channel—one transmitting banking transactions, for instance. Today's telecommunication links are crowded and can be costly. There's ample incentive to optimize these facilities, so a primary goal in transmission engineering is to develop systems that are reliable, efficient, and inexpensive. In fact, in the

United States, the FCC requires that common carriers who offer microwave radio transmission services must provide a minimum number of voice channels in each microwave frequency band. (*Common carriers* are companies that provide transmission services.)

Transmission media

The wire, coaxial tube, atmospheric or space-borne radio wave, or light wave on which information travels is referred to as the *transmission medium*. Telephone transmissions can be placed on any of these media, and decisions as to which one is installed along a given route depends upon economic, physical, and technological factors. All of the media are used in various places and circumstances throughout the world. Transmission facilities using the media might be capable of *simplex operation* (transmission in only one direction), *half-duplex operation* (transmission in both directions but in only one direction at a time), or *full-duplex operation* (transmission in both directions simultaneously). Full-duplex is often used in transmission systems for no other reason than to eliminate or reduce the delay experienced when switching the direction of communication. For duplex transmission, paths in opposite directions might use separate physical media, or they might use the same medium but distinguish signals by frequency, wavelength, or time. In the following sections, I discuss the various transmission media.

Open-wire lines. Uninsulated wirepairs strung on poles are referred to as *open-wire*. They're usually mounted on large ceramic or glass insulators on crossarms and spaced a foot apart to minimize *crosstalk* and to eliminate shorting in high winds. (Crosstalk might occur when energy from a signal on one channel is induced on another nearby one). Open-wire is typically copper, copper-coated steel (the steel is for strength), or galvanized steel. Voiceband signals can be transmitted thirty or more miles on open-wire without amplification because it has low attenuation. However, when lines and insulators are wet or when temperatures are hot, attenuation increases. Repeaters in open-wire systems are typically located 30 or 40 (or more) miles apart. By multiplexing several signals (multiplexing is discussed later in this chapter), multiple VF channels can be carried in open-wire systems—but this means higher frequencies, higher attenuation, and more frequent repeaters. Except in some rural areas, open-wire has generally been replaced with paired cable.

Paired cable. Paired cable consists of many pairs of insulated wire twisted together in binder groups, several of which are twisted together and then wrapped in a sheath. Twisting reduces electromagnetic interference (crosstalk). In the binder groups, the twist rate is varied among wire-pair to further reduce crosstalk. Paired cable might contain only a handful of wire-pairs, or it might contain hundreds or thousands. It can be strung on poles, placed underground in conduit, or buried directly in the ground. Paired cable uses a smaller-gauge wire than open-wire cable, so attenuation is greater and more frequent use of repeaters required—every three or so miles. Multiple VF channels can be multiplexed and transmitted on paired cable, but this requires higher frequencies that can produce higher levels of crosstalk. With appropriate transmission facilities, a pair of low-capacitance cables can carry a hundred or so VF channels.

Coaxial cable. A coaxial tube is a pair of conductors arranged so that one of them completely surrounds the other. The inner conductor is a copper wire, and the outer is a grounded copper cylinder separated from the inner by some form of insulation. If the insulation is air, plastic spacers hold the two conductors apart. The term *coaxial* (sometimes called "coax" and pronounced as two words: "co ax") derives from the fact that the two conductors have the same axis. Coaxial tubes are bound together to form a cable containing multiple tubes. As many as twenty or more tubes can be bundled into a cable. Typically, a pair of coaxial tubes forms a full-duplex transmission path on which many VF channels are multiplexed.

The principal advantage of coax is that it's able to conduct many more multiplexed VF channels than either open-wire pairs or a twisted pair. Coaxial tubes can transmit much higher frequencies with much less attenuation than a twisted pair. The ability to handle higher frequencies means a greater bandwidth and the consequent improvement in the number of channels transmitted. Several factors contribute to the coax's minimal attenuation, even at moderately high frequencies. The grounded outer conductor acts as a shield, preventing radio frequency energy from either leaving or entering the tube. This results in an efficient conductor that's less subject to induced noise and practically immune to crosstalk—and shielding performance improves at higher frequencies. Coax is economically advantageous for high traffic, long haul routes between cities and is also used for undersea cables. A pair of coaxial tubes can carry thousands of full-duplex VF channels. For example, Bell's L5E L-Carrier system combines 13,200 voice channels on a coax pair. The coaxial cable, a bundle of 22 coaxial tubes, can thus carry 132,000 conversations.

Microwave. Terrestrial microwave systems transmit radio waves through the Earth's atmosphere. Theoretically, there's no maximum distance over which microwaves can be sent, but receivers and transmitters must be within sight of each other—the propagation path cannot be interdicted by buildings, mountains, or other obstacles. Nearby hills can cause reflection or scattering of microwave signals and reduce signal quality. Microwaves are focused into a beam by parabolic reflectors or antenna arrays to direct them from transmitter to receiver. A long-haul microwave radio link consists of a string of receivers and transmitters mounted on towers strung out across the landscape. The microwave signal is transmitted from an antenna and picked up by a receiver within line-of-sight, where it's retransmitted to the next antenna in the chain. Actual transmission distances depend upon transmitter power, quality of receivers and transmitters, and geography— typical distances between antennae average about 30 miles, and a coast-to-coast link in the United States includes only 100 or so towers.

Microwaves occupy the electromagnetic spectrum between about 3–100 GHz, and the Bell System employs microwave systems that operate in bands at about 4, 6, and 11 GHz (gigahertz—billion Hertz). These ultra and superhigh frequencies enable thousands of VF channels to be transmitted simultaneously along a single microwave path. The FCC has allocated a portion of the radio frequency (RF) band for use by common carriers and has subdivided this into radio channels. Because of the need to maximize the number of VF channels carried within the radio spectrum, the FCC has specified the number of VF channels that common carriers must establish in each radio channel. For example, the band from 10.7 to 11.7 GHz has been divided into twenty-five radio channels, each of which must carry at least 1,152 voice channels.

Microwave radio offers many advantages over other bulk transmission media. It requires no wires or cables along transmission paths; it easily spans bodies of water and difficult terrain. Because of directional focusing, microwave signals in the same frequency band on different microwave links can intersect and pass through each other without interference. Using repeater spacings of about 10 times that of coaxial cables, and with no requirement for underground or above-ground wires or cables, microwave is frequently used instead of coax for bulk telephone transmission. It's used for voice or data in both metropolitan and long-haul telephone routes and is popular for high-traffic private networks—particularly in densely populated areas where access to real estate along transmission routes is limited or expensive.

Fiber-optic cable. The concept of fiber-optic transmission is to produce a modulated beam of light (it varies in intensity in proportion to a signal), introduce it into a transparent strand or fiber, and trap it inside the strand so that it travels in the medium but doesn't escape it—thus, the optic fiber is a kind of pipe that carries light rather than fluid. The light source is a light-emitting diode (LED) or a laser, and the light travels in a glass or plastic fiber at a rate of about two-thirds of its speed in air. How can light be trapped inside a transparent fiber? It might seem that wherever the fiber bends, the light beam would simply pass out of the fiber and proceed in a straight line. But this is not what happens. Each time light traveling inside the fiber grazes the fiber's boundary at a shallow angle, it's reflected back into the fiber. Bends in the fiber are gradual to maintain a minimum angle of reflection inside the strand. In this way, light is propagated through the length of the flexible fiber with a very small loss in efficiency.

Optic fibers are very fine, and hundreds of them can be bundled into a flexible cable. Fibers are manufactured with three layers: a transparent core, a cladding layer (also transparent), and a light-absorbing protective jacket. The index of refraction of the core is greater than that of the cladding so that light propagated inside the core is reflected back into the core whenever it meets the core-cladding boundary.

Two kinds of fibers are used: single-mode and multimode. Single-mode fibers are fine enough that light is able to travel only one path. Multimode fibers have a larger diameter, and light travels various zig-zag paths through them. Signal fidelity of single-mode fibers is high, but they're harder to interconnect than multimode fibers. Light signals traveling in multimode fibers suffer modal dispersion. Some of the reflected routes traveled by the signal are longer and some are shorter, so there's a delay between their arrivals at the receiver; this results in blurring of the received signal. For this reason, repeaters are required more frequently with multimode fibers. Repeaters can be located at distances of about 25 miles apart with single-mode fibers, or about 15 miles apart for multimode fiber.

Practical considerations work to shorten the distances, however, which are dependent upon the grade of fiber and the number of cable splices. No insulation is required around the cable—electromagnetic induction doesn't occur with light transmission, so noise and crosstalk are practically nonexistent over optic portions of a link. Other kinds of interference can occur, however, and noise and crosstalk might be introduced in nonoptical facilities that interconnect with light facilities.

Fiber-optic transmission systems are cost-justified for some telecommunications applications, and many long distance trunks have been installed. The very wide bandwidth possible with fiber-optic telecommunications can result in exceptionally large numbers of VF channels transmitted by this medium. A thousand or more voice channels can be carried on a pair of very thin fibers. A bundle of hundreds of fibers can equate to hundreds of thousands of VF channels on a single optical cable.

Satellite. Telecommunications satellites and terrestrial systems use the same part of the spectrum for microwave communications. Because telecommunications satellites use microwave transmission, they also require line-of-sight between transmitters and receivers. A geosynchronous telecommunications satellite (one in "stationary orbit" above the Earth) is, therefore, the equivalent of a very high microwave antenna tower. Naturally, a satellite is not really stationary—it only appears that way relative to an observer on Earth. The satellite is placed in a circular orbit above the equator at a distance of 22,300 miles. At that altitude it travels about 6,900 miles per hour, so it orbits the Earth in exactly one day—just the time required for it to remain over the same point on the Earth's surface.

Three such satellites, each with transmitter and receiver look-angles of about 17 degrees, completely cover the Earth's surface. (The only uncovered areas are those within nine degrees of latitude from the poles.) Ground stations on the Earth's surface provide links to satellites from the world's tele-communications networks. Ground stations can be sited in any suitable location, and many are in existence. A ground station anywhere within sight of a satellite is able to communicate with any other that's within sight of the same satellite, and a single repeater is all that's used in the link. Fewer repeater stages means less signal degradation. Furthermore, only a small portion of the transmission path is subject to atmospheric disturbance—particularly for ground stations that pick up the satellite at a steep elevation angle. These advantages are, to some extent, offset by attenuation resulting from the distance the signal must travel (never less than 44,600 miles—one trip up and one trip down). Two-way conversations by satellite relay might be subject to annoying delays. It takes about a quarter second for a signal to travel from a ground station to the satellite and back to another ground station. In a two-way conversation, the turnaround delay, from one person's final utterance until a response is heard, is almost half a second. Additional delay is added if a relay from one satellite to another is required—as it certainly is in some intercontinental conversations. The delay is doubled if two ground-to-satellite links are used in making the connection. A half-second delay is just barely acceptable, but if delays are much longer than that, two-way conversations become trying.

Modulation

Modulation is the process of converting information to be transmitted from its original form to another that's more suited to the transmission medium. Essentially, modulation techniques are devised to pack information into a waveform that conforms to the characteristics of the media on which it will travel. Signals are degraded in various ways as they move along transmission media. Degradation increases in proportion to the distance traveled, but can be minimized by modulating the signal before transmission. A separate, higher-frequency sine-wave carrier signal is modulated to "carry," in a different form, the information contained in the signal to be transmitted. The modulated carrier is then transmitted rather than the original signal because its frequency spectrum enables it to be transmitted more effectively on the medium. The inverse process of demodulation is performed at the receiving terminal to derive the original information from the modulated signal. Much of the world's transmission network was designed to carry voiceband signals but, using various types and degrees of modulation, they can also be used to carry data. In fact, a modem is a device that modulates and demodulates digital data for transmission over analog circuits— even its name is a contraction of the terms modulate and demodulate.

Modulation schemes attempt to maximize the amount of data transmitted while minimizing the effects of distortions arising in the channel—these two goals must be traded off against each other.

A carrier signal's amplitude, frequency, or phase can be modulated to carry either voice or data information. All that's required is that one or more attributes of the carrier be modified in such a way that demodulation equipment can detect the changes and reconstruct the original information at the receiving terminal. Because telecommunications media generally have greater bandwidth than required for a single voice signal, several carriers of different wavelengths can be combined and transmitted together over the same medium (this packing process, called multiplexing, is discussed in the next section). Other efficiencies can be incorporated during a modulation process. Carrier frequencies can be shifted to bring them within FCC-allocated bands to achieve multiplexing or to permit use of less expensive repeaters along the transmission path. Furthermore, analog signals can be converted to digital during modulation to achieve higher-quality transmission for a given medium—or, digital signals can be converted to analog to take advantage of transmission facilities not suitable for digital waveforms. Modulation of a carrier's amplitude, frequency, and phase are discussed in the next sections.

Amplitude modulation (AM).   Figure 5.11 depicts an analog signal waveform (the information to be transmitted), a high-frequency sine wave carrier signal before modulation, and the carrier after *amplitude modulation* with the analog signal. In amplitude modulation, the information signal is superimposed on the carrier by modifying (modulating) the carrier's amplitude according to the amplitude of the information signal so that the modulated carrier's amplitude envelope mirrors the information signal. Frequency and phase remain constant.

The modulation process shown in Figure 5.11 is the type used in conventional AM radio broadcasting. A radio transmitter modulates a carrier wave in the studio and broadcasts it from an antenna. Any radio receiver within range can detect the transmitted signal and demodulate it (derive the information-bearing signal from the modulated carrier by measuring its envelope). Amplitude modulation schemes are used in telecommunications for both voice and data.

Figures 5.12a through 5.12d show two forms of amplitude modulation with digital data. Figure 5.12a represents the digital signal, and Figure 5.12b represents the carrier. Binary bits can be represented singly or in groups in the modulation process. Figure 5.12c gives the modulated waveform for 1-bit modulation, and 5.12d shows the waveform for 2-bit modulation. Depending upon the characteristics of the transmission media and other factors, higher data rates can be achieved using n-bit modulation—of course, a practical upper limit exists for the value of n.

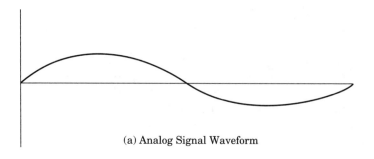

(a) Analog Signal Waveform

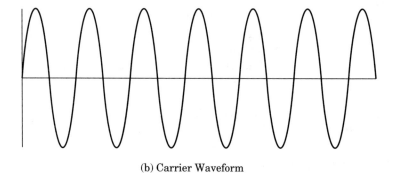

(b) Carrier Waveform

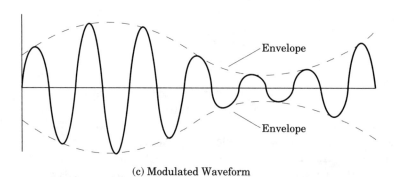

(c) Modulated Waveform

Figure 5.11 Amplitude modulation with analog signal.

The sine waves that are used as carriers are generated by an oscillator. Because no oscillator is perfectly stable, a carrier of frequency, f, contains energy (in diminishing amounts) in the frequency spectrum on either side of f. The frequency spectrum graph of an unmodulated carrier appears as a spike centered on frequency f. A carrier waveform that has been amplitude modulated by a band-limited signal (for example, let's assume a signal below d Hz) contains larger amounts of energy in the frequency bands on either side of f. These frequency bands are called *sidebands*; the one below f in the spectrum is the lower sideband, and the one higher in the spectrum is called the upper sideband. The lower sideband occupies the spectrum from $f-d$ Hz to f Hz, and the upper sideband goes from f Hz to $f+d$ Hz. This phenomenon is shown in Figure 5.13, the frequency spectrum of a modulated carrier. Information from the signal is contained within the sidebands. In fact, all of the information is contained within each sideband. Some modulation schemes take advantage of this redundancy and transmit only one of the sidebands in a process called *single-sideband transmission*. It has the advantage of using only half the bandwidth of standard amplitude modulation.

Frequency modulation. Just as AM radio broadcasting is an example of amplitude modulation, FM radio broadcasting is an example of frequency modulation. Instead of changing the amplitude of the carrier, as is done in amplitude modulation, frequency modulation varies the frequency of the carrier in accord with the information signal. Amplitude and phase remain constant. For analog signals, the frequency of the carrier is increased or decreased in proportion to increases and decreases in amplitude of the information signal. An FM demodulator at the other end senses frequency differences and reconstructs the original signal—or a close facsimile of it. For data signals, the frequency is varied among n distinct frequencies. FM was developed to replace AM because FM is less sensitive to distortions resulting from communication noise. Figures 5.14 and 5.15 show how a carrier is frequency modulated with analog and digital signals. The process of shifting back and forth between two frequencies as a digital signal is modulated, as shown in Figure 5.15, is called *frequency-shift keying (FSK)*. The term frequency-shift keying has roots in radiotelegraphy, and the process is fairly simple to implement. Frequency modulation and FSK produce sidebands in the modulated carrier's frequency spectrum whose bandwidths vary directly with the amplitude of the information signal. A compressor is sometimes used to limit the dynamic range of the signal— and to consequently limit sideband bandwidth.

Phase-shift modulation. The phase of a sine wave is measured in time relative to a reference sine wave of the same frequency. The position in time of a sine wave's amplitude maximums, zero-crossings, or minimums can be compared to a reference wave to determine the sine wave's phase relative to the reference wave. The reference wave is said to be "in-phase." To illustrate this concept, Figures 5.16a through 5.16d show four sine waves of the same amplitude and frequency. The wave shown in Figure 5.16a is "in-phase" and can be used as a reference against which the phase of the others is measured. The wave in Figure 5.16b is a quarter-wavelength out of

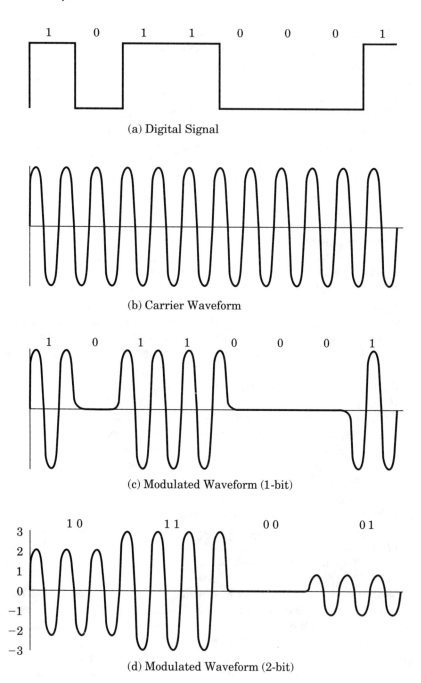

(a) Digital Signal

(b) Carrier Waveform

(c) Modulated Waveform (1-bit)

(d) Modulated Waveform (2-bit)

Figure 5.12 Amplitude modulation.

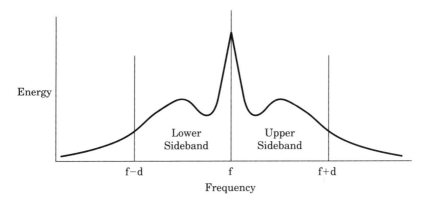

Figure 5.13 Frequency spectrum of carrier (f Hz) modulated with a low-pass, filtered (d Hz) signal.

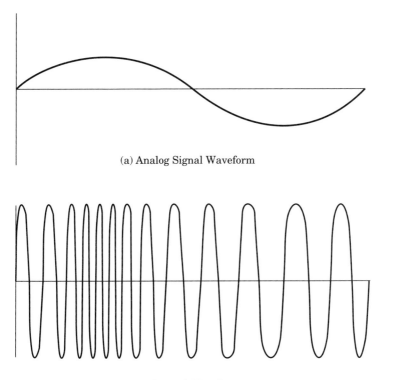

(a) Analog Signal Waveform

(b) Modulated Waveform

Figure 5.14 Frequency modulation with analog signal.

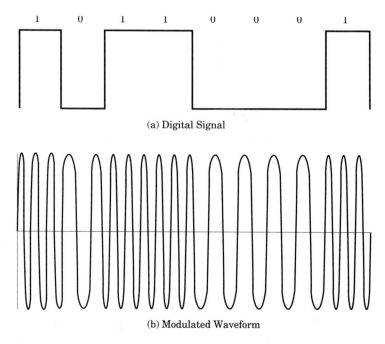

(a) Digital Signal

(b) Modulated Waveform

Figure 5.15 Frequency modulation with digital signal.

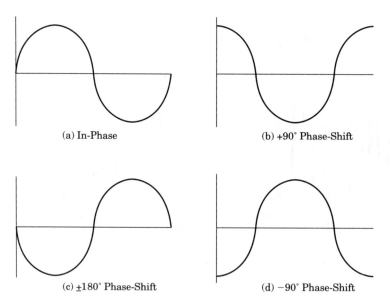

(a) In-Phase

(b) +90° Phase-Shift

(c) ±180° Phase-Shift

(d) −90° Phase-Shift

Figure 5.16 Phases of a sine wave.

phase. It is also +90 degrees out of phase or shifted in phase by +90 degrees. (One wavelength can describe the full 360 degree arc of a circle—or
one full turn of the armature of an electric generator.) The wave in Figure
5.16b is also said to be phase-shifted +90 degrees. Observe that a +90 degree shift is equivalent to a –270 degree shift in phase. The wave in Figure
5.16c is shifted 180 degrees in phase. A phase-shift of +180 degrees is indistinguishable from a phase-shift of –180 degrees. The wave in Figure
5.16d is –90 degrees (or +270 degrees) out of phase.

Phase-shift modulation is primarily used with digital data and is rarely
used with analog signals because of the difficulty in discriminating small
changes in phase. Figure 5.17 shows the result of phase-shift modulation in
which a carrier's phase is shifted +90 degrees in response to a binary transition from zero to one and is shifted –90 degrees (back to the original
phase) in response to a binary transition from one to zero. The modulated
waveform's frequency and amplitude are constant regardless of which of
the two phases is being generated. In Figure 5.17, the dashed lines trace the
constant-phase carrier waveform. Phase-shift modulation is also called
phase-shift keying (PSK) and can involve two or more distinct phases to

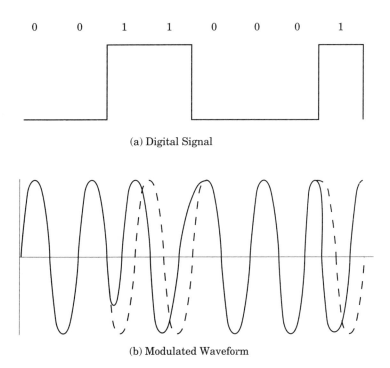

(a) Digital Signal

(b) Modulated Waveform

Figure 5.17 Phase-shift modulation.

accomplish 1-bit, 2-bit, or n-bit codings. PSK that uses only two phases is sometimes called *biphase-shift keying (BPSK); quadrature phase-shift keying (QPSK)* involves four distinct phases to represent two binary bits. *Eight-phase shift keying (8-PSK)* is used with 3-bit coding, and *sixteen-phase shift keying (16-PSK)* is used with 4-bit coding.

Multiplexing

Because of the cost of producing, installing, and maintaining transmission facilities, it was recognized, even before invention of the telephone, that the cost of telegraph transmission could be reduced if multiple messages could be sent at the same time on telegraph wires. I've mentioned before that Bell was searching for just such a technique when he happened upon the principle that enabled him to create the first telephone. The process of combining signals from two or more channels into a composite signal so they can be transmitted together is called *multiplexing.* When signals are multiplexed at one end of a transmission system, they're demultiplexed at the other to recover and separate the individual signals. The terms *MUX* and *DEMUX* are sometimes used to denote multiplex and demultiplex equipment. The decision as to whether or not there's a cost advantage to multiplexing involves a trade-off between higher terminal costs and lower transmission costs and thus depends upon the distance of transmission.

There are two means of multiplexing. One, *frequency-division multiplexing*, separates channels by frequency, and the other, *time-division multiplexing*, separates channels based on time. A third concept, *space division multiplexing* is used in the telecommunications industry when discussing large cables consisting of bundles of multiple wire pairs or coaxial cables.

Frequency-division multiplexing (FDM). Frequency division multiplexing combines individual signals into a waveform that can be transmitted on a single broadband path. Several signals are each modulated onto carriers of different frequencies, and a composite of all the modulated waveforms is transmitted. In the receiving terminal, filters separate the modulated carriers, which are then demodulated to reconstruct the original signals. Radio broadcasting is conducted in this way, and both AM and FM radio provide familiar examples of FDM. The FCC assigns each broadcast station a carrier frequency, which is modulated with a music or voice signal. The modulated waveforms from all stations in a locale are multiplexed when they're broadcast into the atmosphere. Radio receivers acquire all AM and FM signals within range and, by tuning their filters to pass only carriers of the desired frequency, eliminate unwanted stations. The selected carrier is demodulated, and the original signal is amplified and played through a speaker.

Like broadcast radio, frequency division multiplexing in telecommunications divides the transmission medium's bandwidth into slices, selects a distinct carrier frequency for each, and modulates a voiceband signal onto it.

Each slice of the medium's bandwidth is slightly wider than needed for a voice channel. Frequency-division multiplexing is also used to pack 24 telegraph channels into one voice channel. Inverse processes in the receiving terminal demultiplexes and demodulates individual channels. Telecommunications systems that multiplex multiple channels and transmit a composite are called *carrier systems*. Most transmission systems (though there are some exceptions) eliminate one of the two redundant sidebands, enabling a channel to occupy the smallest possible slice of the medium's bandwidth and packing more VF channels onto the medium. Single sideband transmission systems for voice circuits use a frequency band of about 4 kHz for channel spacing. When both sidebands are used, 8 kHz are required. In the United States, double-sideband transmission with 8-kHz spacing is in widespread use on short transmission routes. (Less expensive terminals can be used, and this offsets increased transmission costs.) In the Netherlands, 6-kHz spacing is common, but most of the rest of the world employs single-sideband with 4-kHz frequency slots.

Figure 5.18 illustrates how the broadband channel from 60 kHz to 108 kHz can be divided into 12 voice channels using FDM. Each voice channel (with

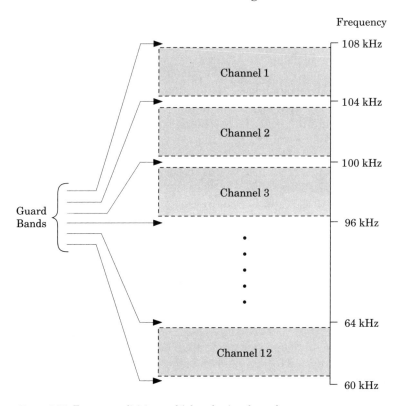

Figure 5.18 Frequency-division multiplexed voice channels.

one sideband removed) occupies the spectrum between 300 Hz and 3400 Hz—a single voice channel of 3100 Hz fits easily into a 4-kHz slot. The figure shows twelve 4-kHz bands, each with a voice channel modulated onto a carrier of the center frequency. Modulated carriers are filtered to limit their bandwidths to something less than 4 kHz. Filter cutoff frequencies are not perfectly sharp, so some small amount of energy outside the band gets through the pass filter, but a *guard band* between each pair of slots helps isolate each channel from the next. Without guard bands, energy from one channel could spill over to the next and result in crosstalk between adjacent channels. Technology would allow carrier systems to be engineered with fairly narrow guard bands, but the narrower the guard band, the more complex and costly the equipment required for multiplexing and demultiplexing.

Higher levels of multiplexing combine broadband signals into even wider bandwidths and result in thousands of channels being transmitted over a single path. A hierarchy of carrier systems that produce combinations in a range of bandwidths are discussed later in this chapter.

Time-division multiplexing (TDM). Like frequency-division multiplexing, the objective of TDM is to combine multiple signals for transmission over a single communication path. FDM separates signals by modulating them into distinct frequency bands. Time-division multiplexing separates signals into distinct time slots, assembling an instantaneous representation (sample) of each signal into a group called a *frame*. This effectively digitizes each signal. (Sampling and digitization was discussed in Chapter 3.) TDM samples each signal in turn, assembles them into a frame, then returns to the first to repeat the procedure *ad infinitum*. The composite result consists of a stream of frames at the sampling rate. In its most common forms, TDM interleaves PCM samples from multiple lower-bit-rate binary streams into a composite higher-rate stream. The process is the same for both digital voice and data. Figure 5.19 shows the TDM process for six VF channels. In the figure, time increases to the right. A frame consists of one sample in turn from each of the six voice signals. To reconstruct a signal, the demultiplexer assembles every sixth sample from the multiplexed input.

The example in Figure 5.19 does not allow for synchronization between the multiplexer and demultiplexer. A TDM signal consists of a stream of binary bits logically organized into frames; the receiving terminal must be able to determine which bit in the stream is the first in a frame. Because transmission systems are not perfect, a received digital signal can be expected to occasionally be out of synchronization. When this happens, the system must be able to regain synchronization quickly.

Various means are used to achieve and maintain synchronization. These means include use of a nationwide reference frequency-standard distribution network, a process called pulse stuffing, and detection of patterns of framing bits across many transmitted frames. The reference frequency-

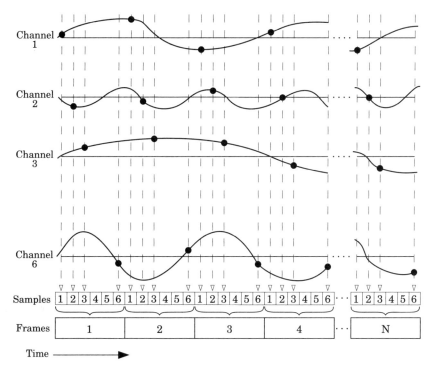

Figure 5.19 Time-division multiplexed voice channels.

standard provides timing information from a common source to enable nationwide synchronization. Pulse stuffing is used to raise the bit rate of a
multiplexed signal that is itself composed of signals produced using un-
synchronized clocks. The bit rate of the outgoing signal is intentionally established at a higher value than the sum of component signals—this
allows bits to be added to each of the signals to adjust them to the local
transmitter clock. The stuffed pulses encode no information; they're used
for place-filling only and are removed by receiving terminals. Framing bits
are added to frames and form a recognizable pattern over several frames.
When synchronization is lost, it can be regained by searching out the
known framing bit pattern.

Various digital packaging schemes can be used with TDM for transmission of digital voice and data; not only must they take into account the information to be transmitted, but they must also consider synchronization
and signaling. Both of these additional factors usually require extra bits to
be packed into each frame. Consider a TDM system that multiplexes 24
voice channels, each of which contains 8,000 8-bit PCM samples per second. The set of samples collected in each rotation through the source signals is organized into a frame, as shown in Figure 5.20. The frame is 193 bits

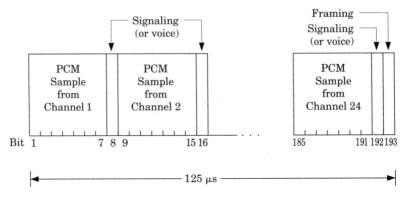

Figure 5.20 Time-division Multiplex frame (DS1 format).

in length. Data samples are eight bits in length, but in every sixth frame, each eighth bit is replaced by signaling and supervisory information. The small amount of signal resolution lost by appropriating the eighth bit in one frame out of six is not noticeable in the received transmission. The 193rd frame bit is used for synchronization. With this system, eight thousand 193-bit, 125 μsec frames are transmitted each second at a data rate of 1.544 million bits per second (Mbps).

Wavelength division multiplexing (WDM). Fiber-optic transmission media carry simultaneous multiple signals by the process of wavelength-division multiplexing. Fiber-optic-based signals are separated into light of different wavelengths and carried in the same fiber at the same time.

Packet switching. Packet-switching systems transmit data in small segments (about 2000 bits) over digital facilities. Each segment, called a *packet,* contains addressing and sequencing information so it can be routed, identified and delivered. A message to be transmitted is separated into many such packets, and, once sent, each packet might travel separately and by a different route than its neighbor. Packets arrive at their destination separately and not necessarily in the order they were transmitted. Packets are reassembled into the original message upon receipt, and missing packets can be retransmitted. Packet-switching systems are able to instantaneously take advantage of the best transmission routes available. Applications that benefit most from packet switching are those whose peak data transmission rates differ markedly from their average.

Carrier systems

Carrier systems combine either analog or digital signals (or both) into larger groups to achieve the economies of scale attendant to bulk transmission.

Individual channels are multiplexed, transmitted as a group over broadband transmission facilities, and demultiplexed at receiving terminals. Multiplexed data arrangements can be interleaved with other such inputs to produce signals at higher and higher bit rates. A range of both analog and digital multiplexed signals can be transmitted, and a hierarchy of facilities exist for multiplexing both forms, converting between forms, and demultiplexing either form. Multiplex/demultiplex devices exist to package or unpackage ever-larger numbers of channels for transmission over analog or digital facilities. Analog and digital hierarchies are discussed in the following.

Analog. Voice channels can be multiplexed in a cascade of analog multiplexers to combine more and more of them into a hierarchy of progressively wider broadband signals. The L-carrier, single-sideband, amplitude modulation system, which takes advantage of coaxial cable transmission technology, has been evolving since 1941 and has grown in terms of coaxial tube-pair capacity from 600 channels to more than 13,000. Parts of the L-carrier multiplex hierarchy are depicted in Figure 5.21. Each of the boxes in the figure represents one of a family of frequency-division multiplexers. The type of input signals to each of the multiplexers is indicated on the diagram. Notice that in moving from left to right, the bandwidth and the number of combined channels on each coaxial tube pair grows larger. Guard bands are inserted in various positions throughout L-carrier signals so that subgroups can be dropped or inserted without having to demultiplex and remultiplex an entire group.

An A-type channel bank multiplexes 12 VF channels and produces a signal called a basic group. The signal represented in Figure 5.18 is exactly that produced by the A-type channel bank. Five basic groups are multiplexed by a group bank and result in a basic supergroup, 10 of which are combined by a supergroup bank into a basic mastergroup. Three basic mastergroups are multiplexed to form the signal carried on a coaxial tube pair in the L3 system or six to become a basic jumbogroup in the L4 system. A jumbogroup multiplex combines three basic jumbogroups to produce a coaxial tube-pair signal for the L5 system. The L5E system, with 13,200 channels per tube pair, is not represented in the diagram. L-carrier system cables consist of different-sized bundles of coaxial tubes. The L4 system, for example, contains 20 tubes (of which 9 pair are used), and the L5 system contains 22 (10 pair used). Thus, the total bandwidth of an L-carrier system can be many times larger than shown in Figure 5.21. Furthermore, the multiplex hierarchy of the figure also represents a demultiplex train that moves through the system from right to left so that broadband signals can be broken down into their separate VF components.

Digital. A separate time-division multiplex hierarchy exists for T-carrier digital transmission systems. The North American system is described in the following paragraphs, but separate hierarchies exist in Europe and Japan. Recall that in the analog hierarchy (as illustrated in Figure 5.21), greater and greater bandwidth transmission facilities are used at each successive step up the hierarchy. With the digital transmission system, higher and higher bit-rate transmission facilities are used with each step up. Higher data rate signals are produced by multiplexing combinations of smaller data rate signals (as shown in Figure 5.22) and are transmitted on various media. Boxes in the figure labeled M12, M13, MX3, and M34 represent specific multiplexers. Parts of the North American digital transmission plan are summarized in Figure 5.22. The plan includes six transmission bit rates, from 0.064 Mbps (one PCM signal) through 274.176 Mbps (4032 PCM signals), as shown in Figure 5.23. These six bit-rates are also called levels, and each is assigned a label from DS0 through DS4. (DS means *digital stream.*) Other bit rates, usually multiples of those shown, are used in North America and other countries, but multiplexing concepts are the same. Similar designations such as T1, T2, and FT3 in Figures 5.22 and 5.23 refer to digital carrier systems and are discussed later in this section. As with analog transmission systems, individual digital transmission media are very often bundled, thus multiplying the number of VF channels carried along a single transmission path.

The D-type channel banks represented in Figure 5.22 are called primary pulse code multiplexers by the CCITT. They perform both D-to-A and A-to-D functions and TDM to form a composite digital signal (DS1) composed of 24 VF analog signals. A DS1 signal, which might also result from submultiplexing lower rate digital signals, is called a *digroup* (short for digital group) and is the basic building block of the hierarchy. Over the years there

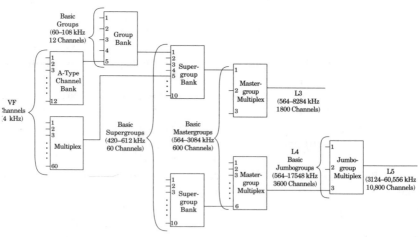

Figure 5.21 A frequency-division multiplex hierarchy. *(Copyright (c) 1983, AT&T. Reprinted with permission.)*

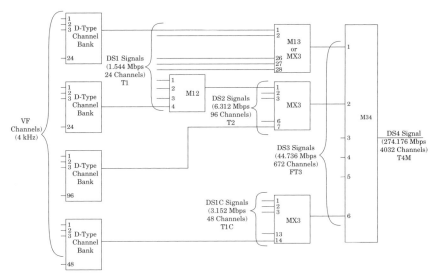

Figure 5.22 A time-division multiplex hierarchy. *(Copyright (c) 1983, AT&T. Reprinted with permission.)*

have been several versions of the D-type channel bank, with variations (and sometimes incompatibilities) between them.

VF channels digitized as 64 kHz PCM streams are referred to as DS0 signals. The box labelled M34 in Figure 5.22 is a multiplexer/demultiplexer that combines six DS3 signals to produce a DS4 format. It also demultiplexes six separate DS3 pulse streams out of a DS4 signal. Other channel banks and multiplexers accomplish various conversions and format exchanges between DS levels in the hierarchy. The DS1 frame layout (for a D3-type multiplexer) was shown in Figure 5.20. Various multiplexer configurations combine multiples of 24 voice channels to produce DS1, DS2, and other multiplexed signals. A variety of terminals including switches, facsimile machines, and call-processing equipment are designed to interface to DS1 trunks, and combinations of terminals might share a DS1 trunk.

The T1 digital carrier system was Bell's first digital transmission system used primarily for short-haul, intercity and interoffice transmission—distances of no greater than 50 miles. The T1 system transmits 24 voiceband channels (data or PCM voice) in a DS1, 1.544 Mbps bit stream, as indicated in Figures 5.20, 5.22 and 5.23. T1's DS1 signals are applied to two wire pairs, one for each direction, and might be used on subscriber loops. Repeaters are placed in transmission circuits about every mile to regenerate and reshape the digital signals. The T1 Outstate System (T1/OS) was later developed to increase T1 distances from 50 miles to about 150.

Improvements in technology have resulted in other digital transmission

Level	Bit Rate (Mbps)	Number of PCM Signals	Digital Facilities
DS0	0.064	1	–
DS1	1.544	24	T1*
DS1C	3.152	48	T1C*
DS2	6.312	96	T2
DS3	44.736	672	FT3*
DS4	274.176	4032	T4M

* and others

Figure 5.23 North-American digital transmission system levels. *(Copyright (c) 1983, AT&T. Reprinted with permission.)*

systems including the T1C (referenced in the figures) and T1D systems, which use different cable and achieve a bit rate more than double that of T1. T1C combines 48 VF channels into a 3.152 Mbps DS1C signal. (DS1C includes an extra 64 kbps component to accommodate pulse-stuffing synchronization between two DS1 signals.) T2 systems use a special cable in each direction to transmit DS2 digital pulse streams at a rate of 6.312 Mbps, combining four DS1 streams or 96 VF channels. T2 systems are used between cities and operate up to about 500 miles with repeaters located a little less than every three miles. FT3 is one of Bell's digital lightwave (fiber-optic) systems transmitting DS3 pulse streams at 44.736 Mbps over a pair of glass fibers and is primarily used between offices in cities. Later lightwave systems using the same fibers have even higher transmission rates than FT3. T4M is a 274.176 Mbps coaxial cable digital transmission system capable of operation up to 500 miles. Regenerators are placed at about one-mile intervals. The DS4 signal transmitted by the system carries 4032 VF channels.

Cellular systems

Cellular systems have become prevalent for mobile telephone communication. Geographical areas are divided into "cells," and a low-power radio transmission facility is placed in each cell. Transmission power is limited to prevent calls in one cell from interfering with calls in nearby but nonadjacent cells that are using the same frequency band. In this way, a limited number of RF frequencies can serve hundreds of thousands of users within a geographical area by reusing frequency bands in many cells. A large metropolitan community, for example, with only a hundred or so channels available for mobile communication can be subdivided into 15 cells to in effect have the equivalent of many times the 100 channels. A centralized computer and switching center keeps track of which channels are being used by whom in each cell and serves as a link to the PSTN and other telecommunications networks.

Small, inexpensive radio telephone terminals can be carried or installed in vehicles. Because of the low power requirements for such terminals, some are small enough to fit into a person's pocket. Slightly more powerful units are still small enough to be considered portable and are carried in a small hand case. Portable units are battery operated, but most provide a plug for a vehicle's cigarette lighter as an alternate power source. Calls are placed or received in the usual manner. If during a call, the caller moves from one cell into another, control is automatically transferred in a manner generally transparent to the caller. Cellular systems, however, are not available everywhere. As of this writing, most cells in the United States have been established in highly populated areas and in highway corridors following routes with high vehicle traffic.

Switching

As described earlier in this chapter, the PSTN and other networks include hierarchies of switches that are navigated to provide connections between telephone stations. Two stations, no matter how closely they might be located to each other, must go through at least one switch for interconnection. This section discusses technologies used to implement such switches.

The primary function of a telephone switch is to interconnect lines or trunks that might go to subscriber stations or to other switches. Switching facilities (or the personnel who operate them) must handle other duties besides switching: administrative duties such as signaling, route selection, and call accounting, for example. Since the establishment of the earliest telephone connections, three main switching technologies have been used: manual, electromechanical, and electronic. Furthermore, every switch requires some intelligent agent for management and control. In the case of manual switchboards, control is provided by the human operator. The two types of automatic control are called progressive control and common control. Each of these is covered in this section along with manual, electromechanical, and electronic switching.

Manual switching

The first telephone switches were manual. Connections were made by plugging patch cords (wires with plugs on each end) into sockets on a switchboard. The switchboard had sockets for a number of subscriber loops and some for connection to other switchboards, perhaps even to a long-distance switchboard. Figure 5.24 shows these interconnections. Each switchboard required a human operator who manually completed the required connections.

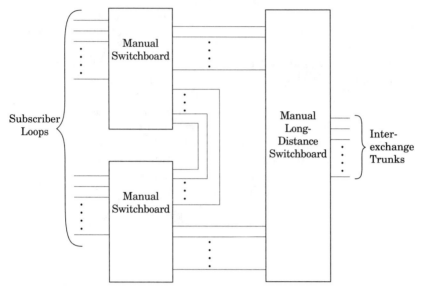

Figure 5.24 Manual switching.

Small line lamps near each socket came on to signal the operator that a sub-scriber had taken their phone offhook and required service. With the earliest systems, the subscriber turned a small hand crank on the telephone to gener-ate current to power the lamp. Upon seeing the lamp, the operator would con-nect a telephone headset into the subscriber's circuit and say something like "operator, number please," or perhaps "Hello Emma, this is Mable." The name or number of the party being called was obtained verbally by the operator.

If the called subscriber's loop terminated at the same switchboard as the calling subscriber, as it often did in the early days of telephone, the opera-tor would ring the line (sometimes by plugging a ring generator into the socket). If there were no answer, the calling party would be told verbally. If there were an answer, the calling and called parties were connected at the switchboard by plugging opposite ends of a patch cord into their two sock-ets. Often the called subscriber loop terminated in the same office but at a different switchboard. In such a case, the operator connected the near-end subscriber to the other's switchboard by plugging a patch cord into both the caller's socket and one for a trunk to the other switchboard—the operator of the second switchboard could then take over the call. If a call to another office was requested, the caller's line would be connected to a trunk run-ning to a long-distance switchboard operator who could connect to trunks leading to switchboards in other locations. When a call was completed and the parties had placed their phones back onhook, all patch cords were re-moved by the various operators.

Besides handling calls to as many as 10,000 subscribers (and sometimes more), operators were also required to obtain rate and route information and record calls for billing purposes. As the telephone industry grew, some metropolitan manual switching offices became very large and used long banks of manual switchboards. In some, supervisors responsible for many operators wore roller skates to enable them to glide more easily and more quickly along behind their operators, who sat in a line before the long switchboard banks. The number of operators employed in the Bell System hit a peak of more than 200,000 in about 1950. By 1990, it's estimated, there were still about 75,000 operators. However, switchboards have improved since the earliest days of patch cords. The first mechanization of operator stations replaced patch cords with pushbuttons and added numerical displays. Today, the most modern operator stations are computerized. Nevertheless, numerous manual switchboards are still in service, and many are used in private networks. Serious efforts to automate telephone switching have been underway since 1889. The first switching systems to replace manual switchboards were electromechanical.

Electromechanical switching

The first automatic switching element was invented in 1889 by an undertaker, Almon B. Strowger, in Kansas City. Strowger's device involved an electromagnet whose armature, connected to a pawl, drove a ratchet that turned a rotary switch. The ratchet moved one step for each pulse applied to the electromagnet—hence, it was called a step-by-step or *progressive* switch. The Strowger switch, in conjunction with rotary dialers (which emit pulses), enabled manual switching functions to be replaced with electromechanical ones. Installation of switches based on Strowger's device began in 1892, but, interestingly, the Bell System's first electromechanical switching system was acquired when they purchased an independent telephone company—Bell didn't install one on their own until 1919. Soon after that, under licensing arrangements, Bell began making improvements to Strowger's design and in a few more years produced their own stepping switch. Later developments produced other types of electromechanical switches, including the panel switch and the crossbar switch. Panel switches are no longer made, and those that were installed have been replaced, but crossbar switches had important advantages and soon became the switch of choice for many telephone companies.

Progressive switching. Switching systems that used Strowger's stepping switches and those using stepping devices that have evolved from Strowger's are called *step-by-step (SXS) switching systems*. They're also referred to as direct progressive control systems for reasons that will soon become apparent. Later designs for stepping switches enable a single device to provide connections for banks of about 100 trunks or lines. Switch contacts are arranged in semicircles, 10 to a level on 10 levels. Three wiper contacts mounted on a central shaft can be stepped to any level and rotated to meet any of the 10 contacts on that level. Two contacts (called *tip* and *ring*), are required for the voice path, and the third (called a *sleeve contact*), activates a holding circuit that also provides switch status information to other switching elements in the system. (Tip, ring, and sleeve originally referred to contacts on a phone plug.) In response to input pulses, the shaft is stepped vertically to one of 10 contact levels and can also be rotated in steps (also in response to input pulses) to select one of 10 contacts at each level. Three versions of this device are called a *line finder,* a *selector,* and a *connector.* Line finders are so called because their job is to hunt for, find and connect a subscriber loop that's requesting service. Line finders search both vertically and horizontally. Selector versions of the switching device are used in intermediate switching stages to search out an idle path and make connection to the next stage. Connector versions of the switch are employed in the final stage when connecting to the called party loop. Any SXS device taking part in a connection is dedicated to the connection for the duration of the call and can't be used for other calls until disconnected.

An SXS progressive control system employs banks of such stepping switches. When a subscriber takes a phone offhook, a line finder switch locates the loop and connects it to a selector switch that places a dial tone on the loop. On hearing the dial tone, the caller begins dialing, and the dial tone is removed. Subscribers dial using rotary dialers that emit pulses onto the loop, one pulse when the one digit is dialed, two pulses when the two digit is dialed, three pulses when the three digit is dialed, and so on.

Step-by-step switches are obsolete now, but they've had a very long service life and still provide an interesting means of understanding some basic telephone switching principles. For purposes of illustration only, let's assume a telephone exchange consists only of eight telephones and a step-by-step, progressive control switching system. For the example, let's invent switching elements that are two-level, step-by-step switches that can step vertically two levels then rotate horizontally two steps. Thus, they can connect one line to any of four possible lines. Because the switching elements in this example are two-level steppers, it's convenient to assign binary addresses to the eight telephone stations. Figure 5.25 represents the example system. In the figure, there are 10 two-level stepping switches (the shaded areas) organized as four line finders, two selectors, and four connectors. Each switch is shown with two levels (the semicircular lines) and two contacts on each level (the dots on each level).

In the figure, crossed lines don't make contact unless there's a dot at their intersection. Line finder switches search vertically and horizontally to contact a phone that's offhook. Selector switches accept one digit (as a series of pulses). If the selector switch is pulsed once, it elevates its wiper arm to

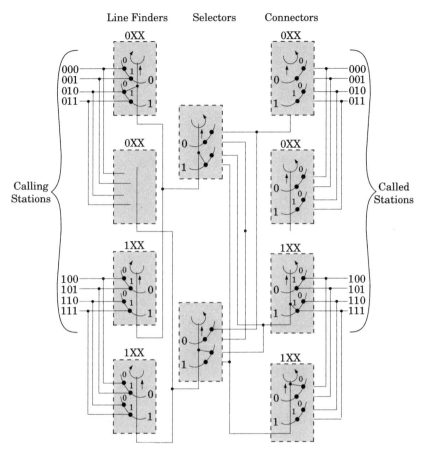

Figure 5.25 Example step-by-step switching system.

the first level (the "one" level). If it's pulsed twice, the arm is elevated to the second level ("zero" level). When it reaches a level, it rotates, searching horizontally for an idle path to the next stage. Notice that in these switches two pulses are required to reach the zero level. This is because on rotary telephone dialers, the "zero" digit follows the "nine" digit, so ten pulses are emitted when zero is dialed. In the binary analogy of our example, two pulses are emitted when zero is dialed. Connector switches accept two digits in succession, raising the wiper arm vertically when the first set of pulses is input and rotating horizontally to a specific contact on the second set, stepping the shaft once with each pulse in the digit.

As shown in the figure, two calls are in progress. In the first, a caller at line 010 has called someone at 100. When the phone went offhook at 010, the top line finder (being idle) found the offhook line and connected it to an idle selector (the top one), which returned a dial tone to the caller. After the caller dialed the first digit (remember, the called party is at 100), the selector received one pulse, stepped up to the first level, and searched for an idle connector in the 1xx bank. (In a larger network, a path through more selector stages would be needed before reaching the connectors.) The first idle connector switch it encountered was the bottom one in the 1xx bank, so the selector was connected to it. As the second digit of the phone number (a zero) was dialed, the connector switch received two pulses and elevated its wiper arm to the zero (second) level. On receiving two pulses from the third dialed digit (again a zero), the connector's shaft rotated two steps, completing a path to station 100 and placing a ring signal on the loop.

The second call in progress is from 001 to 111. Because the top line finder was busy, a second line finder was used to connect the calling party. In searching for a selector, the line finder found the top selector busy, so the line finder kept searching. It found the second selector idle and connected it. A dial tone was returned to 001. When the caller at 001 dialed the first digit, the bottom selector stepped to the first level and rotated its shaft one step searching for a path to the 1xx connector bank. That path was blocked because it led to the bottom connector, which was busy with the first call. Continuing its search, the selector rotated its shaft one step. This path, leading to the top connector in the 1xx bank, was idle, so the selector made the connection. The second dialed digit caused the wiper arm to step up to level one, and the third dialed digit produced a one step rotation to connect with station 111 and application of a ring signal.

In this example system, there are only two paths available between calling stations and called stations. Calls from either 000 or 011 will be blocked because all available line finders in the 0xx bank are busy. Even though the line finders for stations 100 through 111 are idle, attempts to call from those stations would be blocked because both selectors are busy. As soon as one of the existing calls is disconnected, a line finder, a selector, and a connector will be released and another call can be completed. Of course, other arrangements of switches in our example are possible. Each different arrangement would have its advantages and disadvantages. Additional switches could be designed into the system to allow more than two simultaneous calls. Furthermore, a real-world switching system would probably include access to trunks to other switching systems.

The example in Figure 5.25 also demonstrates the concepts of concentration, distribution, and expansion in a switching network. In the example there are eight telephones but only two paths. In that example, line finder switches concentrate loops onto two paths, and selector switches provide distribution of the two paths so that any of the eight phones can be reached through expansion by the connector switches. The line finders of the example have the effect of concentrating a greater number of subscriber lines into a smaller number of paths. The selector switches distribute calls to the connectors, which expand two paths to eight. In a community there could be 10,000 telephones, but not all of them would be in use at any given time. Thus, it would be wasteful to establish a switching path through the system for every telephone. Adequate service could be provided to all subscribers if there were perhaps only one path for each 10 telephones—that's 1,000 paths serving 10,000 subscribers. The ratio of paths to loops required to provide a given level of service would be different in each specific situation. Most large networks, regardless of whether they use step-by-step or other types of switching, are organized with concentration, distribution, and expansion stages. A network, such as this, one that doesn't provide a simultaneous path for every possible connection, is called a *blocking network* because, at times of high traffic, some calls might be blocked.

As shown by the example of Figure 5.25, control of a step-by-step switching system occurs in steps. Control is direct and progressive. A path through the network is not chosen in advance—it's selected piecemeal each step of the way as the caller dials. It occurs in steps and is paced by the caller. A digit is dialed, and that digit is used to find a next step in a link to the destination station. There's no way of searching for the "best" path or the "best" next move, the one that aims toward some optimum performance. A digit is dialed, and, as part of an irreversible process, an irrevocable next step is taken toward the goal. If it's later determined that step lies on a path that's blocked further downstream, then it's too late—the call will fail.

Step switching systems were the first electromechanical switching systems to be installed. They automated switching processes and offered numerous other advantages in telecommunications networks throughout the world. Fairly inexpensive, step switching systems were simple and could be operated in diverse climates. The nature of their operation made them reasonably fast—but, they required lots of space, power, and maintenance and were not adaptable for data transmission. Furthermore, additions such as Touch-Tone dialing and alternate route capability were quite expensive. In spite of these disadvantages, they have continued in operation at various places in the world for many years.

Common control. Common control was added to switching systems to solve problems that arise with SXS switching systems. Control of step-by-step systems such as those discussed above is progressive—a switching path is established in steps in direct response to successive digits dialed by a caller. Interexchange switching in such a system requires a separate trunk for each exchange. There's no way to concentrate calls to other exchanges on a few trunks because the call itself contains no addressing information. Once step-by-step switching is begun, addressing information is inherent in the state of the network and can be derived only by determining the state of each intermediate switching element through which the call passes. Furthermore, it's not always possible to pass dialing pulses from a progressive control switch to the next switch because incompatibilities or timing differences sometimes exist between the two switching systems. Thus, dial pulses, generated at the whim and dialing rate of a caller and traveling in trains on the network, can be missed by other switching systems down the line and result in incorrect connections.

A solution to all these problems is to send dialed digits along with a call as an unambiguous destination address so other switches can know how to handle the call. To implement this concept, dial registers are added to the switching system to accumulate and hold the number as it's dialed. Switching does not even begin until dialing is complete. With access to a call's destination address, an entire path, and alternative paths, can be examined before the first step in any path is committed. The dialed address is sent to other switching systems (by a device called a *sender*) when the call is sent. Each switch along the route registers the call's address and relays it to the next switch so that each switching system can make intelligent decisions about routing. Dial registers and senders exist as common equipment that is pooled and accessed by other equipment when and for as long as needed. These processes are part of the control scheme that's practiced in all modern switching systems and is known as *common control.*

Coordinate switching. *Coordinate switches* are organized with an X (horizontal) coordinate and a Y (vertical) coordinate. Switch connections are made at the intersection of these coordinates, so control of the switch is exercised by specifying an X-Y pair to be connected or disconnected. A square coordinate switch with eight horizontal connections and eight vertical connections is represented in Figure 5.26. Because contacts are mated at crosspoints (the points where horizontal and vertical coordinates meet), they are also called *crosspoint switches.* Multiple crosspoints can be connected in a single switching device, and a "make" at a single crosspoint might actually connect one, two, three, six, or more circuits. Coordinate

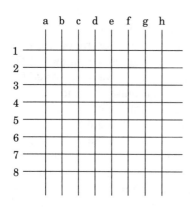

Figure 5.26 Non-blocking, 8×8 coordinate (crosspoint) switch.

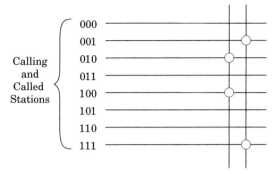

Figure 5.27   Blocking, 8×2 coordinate (crosspoint) switch.

switches can be configured in a rectangle rather than a square, there being a greater or smaller number of output (vertical) lines than input (horizontal). Whenever there are fewer outputs than inputs, a coordinate switch is said to be a blocking switch because, once all outputs are connected, the remaining inputs are blocked from making contact anywhere. Square coordinate switches are nonblocking.

Figure 5.27 shows an 8×2 switch that satisfies the requirements of the example telephone network previously discussed with Figure 5.25. Telephone stations are once again numbered in binary to facilitate comparison of the two examples. There are eight telephone stations in the network, but only two conversations can take place simultaneously. In Figure 5.27, the same two telephone connections have been established, as in the earlier example of Figure 5.25 (the circled crosspoints in Figure 5.27 have been made). A caller at 010 is talking to someone at 100, and a caller at 001 is speaking with a person at 111. Anyone else attempting a call will be blocked because the only two paths are already in use. Notice, by comparison of Figures 5.25 and 5.27, the difference in complexity of two separate implementations of the same network.

Coordinate switches are used in exchanges handling thousands of telephone stations. The number of crosspoints required in a nonblocking network approximates the square of the number of subscriber loops in the network (it's slightly less because a subscriber does not phone himself or herself). Thus, as the number of subscriber loops grows, the number of crosspoints grows approximately with the square—a 10,000-subscriber nonblocking exchange would require 99,990,000 crosspoints. For this reason, blocking-switching networks are created, and the number of required crosspoints is reduced to a more reasonable number. Recall that blocking switching systems can be created by designing concentration, distribution, and expansion stages. Figure 5.28 provides such an example using coordi-

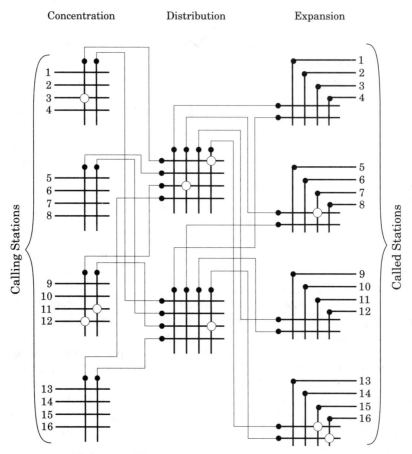

Figure 5.28 A blocking coordinate switching network.

nate switches. There are 96 crosspoints in the system shown, whereas a square nonblocking matrix handling the same number of subscribers would require 240 crosspoints. Figure 5.28 represents a network of 16 telephones and a coordinate switching system that allows eight simultaneous conversations. However, because of the blocking inherent in the design, some connections might be blocked even if there are only two calls in progress. If we consider the circled crosspoints to have been made, three conversations are in progress: line 3 is connected to 15, 11 to 16, and 12 to 7. Another five connections are possible, but lines 9 and 10 are blocked, and any calls to lines 13 or 14 will be blocked even though those phones are onhook. In this switching system, any two lines in any of the four groups of four can be connected. Attempts to connect a third phone in one of the groups will be blocked. Coordinate switching systems also include paths to trunks, so calls can be routed to other switching systems in the network.

Common control techniques are applied to coordinate switching systems so that an entire path through the system can be planned before any of the connections are made. Thus, if a call from line 7 to line 14 were requested while those shown in Figure 5.28 were still in progress, common control functions would attempt to plan the path. Before any crosspoints were made, the common control functions would realize that line 14 is blocked, and a busy signal would be returned to the caller.

Coordinate switches were initially implemented as *crossbar switches*— so called because a predominant feature of these devices is a series of movable horizontal and vertical crossbars. When one horizontal and one vertical bar are selected and moved, the set of contacts at their intersection are made. Crossbar switches created for use in the former Bell System have five horizontal bars and either 19 or 20 vertical bars. The horizontal bars can be rotated either up or down so that each can make contacts for either of two horizontal rows. Each horizontal row and each vertical column has 10 sets of contacts. Thus, there are crossbar switch implementations with 100 crosspoints and those with 200 crosspoints. When a crosspoint is made, it's latched with a holding circuit and maintained until the call is finished. Other crosspoints in the same crossbar device can be made so that up to 10 or 20 simultaneous connections can be established—one for each vertical bar. The first crossbar system, called the No. 1 Crossbar System, was able to select and make a crosspoint in less than a tenth of a second and could usually set up a complete path through the system and be ready for the next call in about a second.

Crossbar switches were conceptualized by Bell employees as early as 1913, but the first installation was in Sweden in a non-Bell System telephone company. It wasn't until 1938 that Bell installed a crossbar switch. Later coordinate switching systems used dry-reed switches at the crosspoints. These devices, which maintained contact from the time a first pulse was received until a second one was applied, consisted of two magnetic reed contacts sealed in glass. Subsequent coordinate crosspoint switch designs have featured newer, solid-state electronic technologies and have included silicon-controlled rectifiers, diodes, transistors, and integrated circuits. As new generations of coordinate switches have been developed, each has had greater switching capacity and been more reliable, faster, smaller, and more economical in both power consumption and maintenance.

Digital switching

The analog switches previously discussed can be described as *space-division switches* because telecommunications paths through a switch are separated in space. By contrast, switching systems discussed in this and the following sections are *time-division switches* with paths separated in time. Time-division switching, like time-division multiplexing, is based on digital technology and has been brought about through the evolution of electronics. Digital time-division switching has created a revolution in switching networks. In 1959 Bell Telephone Laboratories conducted an experiment with digital switching and digital transmission using the best solid-state technology available at the time. It was not until 15 years later that a wholesale replacement of analog switches by digital began. That process is still underway and can be expected to continue for many years before all the world's analog switches are finally replaced.

Advances in digital technology have come rapidly in the past several decades and have brought integrated circuits and inexpensive general-purpose and special-purpose computers. Computers have been used with space-division switching systems to implement common control, accounting, and other functions. However, many other advantages accrue beyond these when the actual switching elements are implemented with digital technology as well. Digital switches are many times faster and many times less expensive than electromechanical devices. Digital switches require significantly less power, space, manpower, and maintenance—and they switch data circuits as easily as voice circuits. Furthermore, when used in conjunction with digital transmission systems, considerable expense for analog-to-digital and digital-to-analog conversion equipment is avoided. The trade-off is balanced in favor of digital in spite of the fact that digital switching systems require synchronization not needed in analog networks. Modern switching systems based upon integrated circuits and general purpose computer technology have made possible a variety of service offerings that would have been expensive beyond imagination with older analog switches. Features such as call-forwarding, conferencing, call-waiting, speed-dialing, and others are all software-based. Changes or upgrades of new switching features or options can be added easily. Hundreds or thousands of switching systems can all be upgraded simultaneously by simply installing new software versions.

Time-division multiplexing figures importantly in digital switching. In Figure 5.20, we showed a TDM frame, the basic element of organization in TDM. Essentially, switching occurs when time-slots are interchanged within or among TDM frames. Digital transmission systems and digital switching systems manipulate TDM trains as a normal part of their operation. Transmission systems send them (in the form of bit-streams) from location to location. Switching systems assemble and store or forward them—or retrieve and disassemble them. Switching functions can be performed anywhere a train of TDM frames is available to a digital processor. Figures 5.29 through 5.34 illustrate the TDM switching process called time-slot interchange (TSI). In Figure 5.29, a train of TDM frames (labeled f and f') are processed through a TSI in a digital processor. Frames labelled with f' designations have been switched, and those labelled with f have not.

A switching control block provides instructions to the processor regarding which time-slots in the TDM frames are to be switched. Every frame is

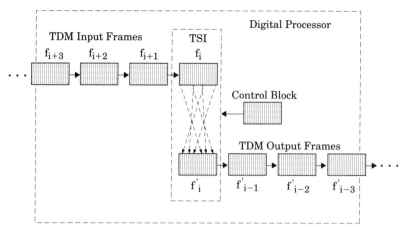

Figure 5.29 TDM frame-train with time-slot interchange.

treated the same, in accord with the control block, until the control block is changed to reflect a different switching strategy.

Figure 5.30 shows, in a simplified way, how interchanging time-slots in TDM frames results in switching signals among various lines. The figure assumes digital switching for analog transmission facilities so that signals are converted to digital before switching and converted back to analog after switching. In Figure 5.31, a CODEC is a device that can perform both A-to-D (A/D) and D-to-A conversions. Figure 5.31 more accurately shows the form that such a system would take, but Figure 5.30 is more illustrative of the concept and will be used in the following example.

A/D devices input analog signals from n telephone lines, and each produces an 8-bit PCM sample 8,000 times per second. The time-division multiplexer (TDM MUX) inputs a PCM sample from each A/D converter and assembles them into corresponding time-slots in the current TDM frame. It outputs an unswitched frame 8,000 times per second. The TSI module receives TDM frames and performs switching by rearranging PCM samples in frame time-slots according to instructions it obtains from a control block in memory. It does this identically for each and every frame and operates at a rate of 8,000 frames per second. A delay is introduced into the multiplexed stream because the accumulation of n samples in memory requires waiting n/8000 seconds for all the samples to arrive—during that time, none of the samples are forwarded. The TDM demultiplexer (TDM DEMUX) inputs switched TDM frames and disassembles them, passing the sample from each time-slot to its corresponding A/D converter at the rate of 8,000 samples per second. Each of n A/D converters outputs an analog signal onto a telephone line.

Figure 5.32 illustrates a digital processor implementation of a time-slot interchange in greater detail. A control block gives information about which

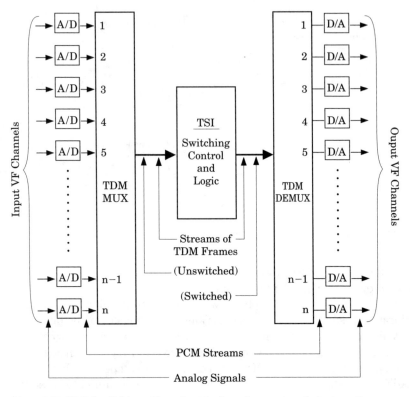

Figure 5.30 Digital switching with analog telephone lines—expanded schematic.

time-slots are to be rearranged. In the example, there are n time-slots in each frame, and every slot contains a PCM sample (labelled s). Both the control block and the current frame are stored in memory. The control block is relatively constant and is changed only infrequently when a call is originated or terminated—or when other control decisions have been taken by the processor and necessitate a switching change. TDM frames move through the system at a rate of 8,000 per second. They're placed in memory, their contents rearranged, and they're sent along. As each frame is accessed by the processor, the first entry in the control block is consulted. Its contents tell to which time-slot the first sample should be moved. In the example, the sample in time-slot five must be removed before the sample in time-slot one is stored there. So, sample five is placed in a temporary register (let's call it register A), and sample one is moved to time-slot five. The processor then consults entry five in the control block and finds that sample five (now in register A) is to be moved to time-slot six. So, the contents of register A (the sample from time-slot five) are moved to register B, and the contents of time-slot six are moved to the now-empty register A. Now, sample five in register B can be placed in time-slot six. The processor now consults entry six in the control block to find where it is to go. So the process continues in round-robin fashion until all samples to be switched have been processed.

Most TDM systems are four-wire systems because telephone signals are carried separately in each direction on a wire-pair. In fact, Figure 5.29 depicted only one TDM stream. Actually, separate TDM streams travel in each direction, so the situation is more correctly depicted in Figure 5.33. Likewise, the time-slot interchange shown in Figure 5.32 has its corresponding interchange taking place for the stream moving in the reverse direction. That process (already discussed) is illustrated in Figure 5.34. Time-slot interchanges for both the forward and reverse directions might take place in a time-shared fashion in the same processor. Switching of other TDM streams can also be time-shared in the same processor if its input/output, storage, and processing capacities are sufficiently sized. Large digital switching networks are able to switch VF channels within and among multiple TDM streams. Any time-slot in any time-division multiplexed stream can be exchanged with any time-slot in the same or other time-division multiplexed stream. This is typically accomplished by constructing a

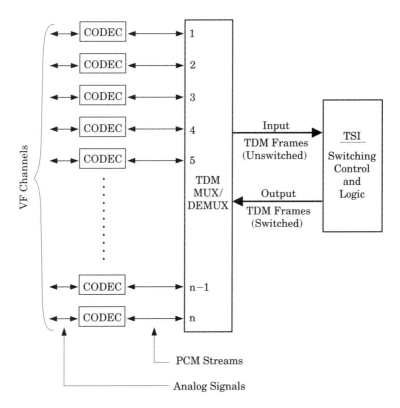

Figure 5.31 Digital switching with analog telephone lines.

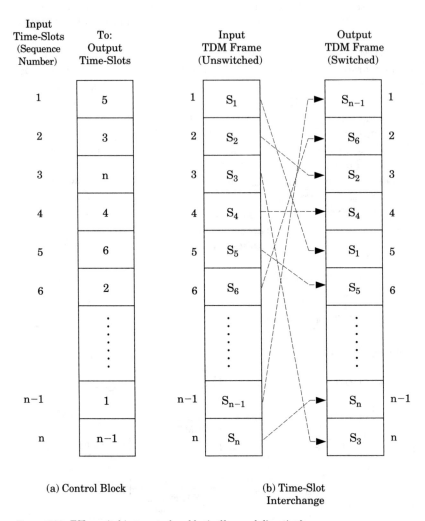

Input Time-Slots (Sequence Number)	To: Output Time-Slots		Input TDM Frame (Unswitched)		Output TDM Frame (Switched)	
1	5	1	S_1		S_{n-1}	1
2	3	2	S_2		S_6	2
3	n	3	S_3		S_2	3
4	4	4	S_4		S_4	4
5	6	5	S_5		S_1	5
6	2	6	S_6		S_5	6
⋮	⋮	⋮	⋮		⋮	
n−1	1	n−1	S_{n-1}		S_n	n−1
n	n−1	n	S_n		S_3	n

(a) Control Block   (b) Time-Slot Interchange

Figure 5.32 TSI—switching control and logic (forward direction).

time-multiplexed switch (TMS) in multiple stages using TSIs and one or more space-division switches. The TMS used most often in what was formerly the Bell System consists of a TSI stage feeding a space-division switching stage that, in turn, feeds a final TSI stage. Such a TMS is labelled a TST switch (meaning *time-space-time*). Other combinations of three and more stages are possible. STS, TSST, and other switches have been implemented. As with any switching system, blocking will occur if there are not enough paths available to meet demand. In TDM switching, blocking might result if too few time-slots are available at some stage.

Figure 5.35 illustrates the 3-stage TST time-multiplexed switching concept. TDM streams from n TSIs are input to a space-division switch whose interconnections are varied from time-slot to time-slot. The TST consists of three stages: two time-division (T) stages and a center space-division switch stage (S). Let's assume each TDM frame contains s time-slots and that the sampling rate is 8,000 samples per second. Binary bits are clocked into the space-division switch's input ports in serial, but the input streams are logically grouped into frames and time-slots within frames. Input ports are time-synchronized. The purpose of the S-stage switch is to interchange samples between TDM streams. The space-division switch performs identical switching for each frame, but, within frames, changes its switching arrangement each time a new time-slot appears at its input ports—it changes switching arrangements s times for each input frame (8,000 input frames appear each second). When a frame has been processed and a new one appears, the S-stage switch starts over and begins its switching cycle again. It goes through a complete switching cycle 8,000 times each second. Thus, in the S-stage, a sample in any time-slot in any input stream can be moved to the same time-slot in any other stream before output. The 3-stage TST switch, therefore, is able to move any sample from any of s time-slots in any TDM stream to any of the s time-slots in any other stream. The TSIs rearrange the time-slots prior to input to the center-stage space-division switch and also after output from it, so that, through the entire TMS, any VF channel can be switched with any other. As mentioned, such communication channels operate in two directions, so every time-slot switched has its associated, mirror-image reverse-direction time-slot that's also switched.

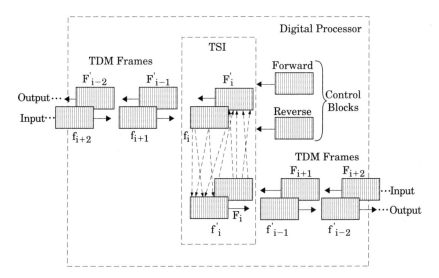

Figure 5.33 Bidirectional TDM frame-trains with time-slot interchange.

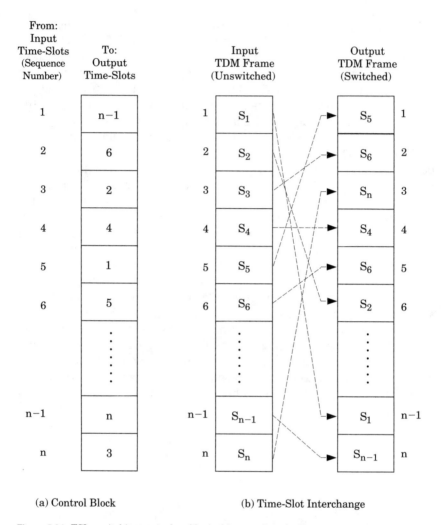

(a) Control Block   (b) Time-Slot Interchange

Figure 5.34 TSI—switching control and logic (reverse direction).

To help understand how the space-division switch in a TMS might accomplish its tasks, Figures 5.36 and 5.37 illustrate one such scheme. There are n TDM streams, and all frames have s time-slots. Figures 5.36 and 5.37 show four space-switching arrangements, one for each of four different input time-slots. Interchange logic is given in n×n coordinate switching notation in Figure 5.36. It might be helpful to keep in mind that each time-slot in each TDM stream represents a separate VF channel, and a different TDM stream is input at each of the n input ports. Each of the four diagrams, (a) through (d), in Figure 5.36 represents the time-slot moves to be made at

each of four different slot times (1, t, $t+1$, and s), and the circled inter-
sections represent interchanges. The purpose of Figure 5.36 is to demonstrate that time-slot interchanges can be different for each time-slot (any
set of slot times could have been chosen for the example). For each frame
in every TDM input stream, Figure 5.37 shows the time-slot moves resulting from interchanges specified in Figure 5.36 (time-slots are shown within
frames in Figure 5.37 as though bits are moving from left to right, so those
time-slots indicated to the left in a frame actually occur later in time).

Private branch exchange (PBX)

PBXs are switching systems used by companies and other organizations to
provide switching among a number of company telephone stations and to
provide access to the PSTN. In essence, a PBX is a remote branch of the local central office, and it offers similar functions and features. It handles normal calls in much the same way that a central office does. For example, a
PBX generates a dial tone when a connected phone is taken offhook. It accepts dialed digits and determines how to route calls. It rings and connects
to other extensions for intercom calls or obtains a trunk to the central office

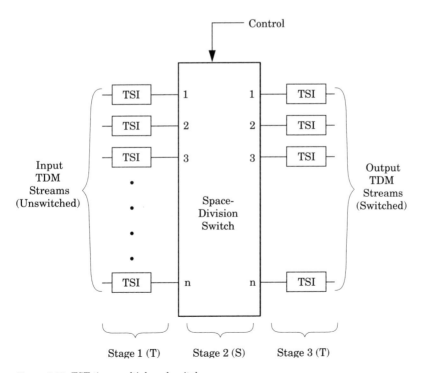

Figure 5.35 TST time-multiplexed switch.

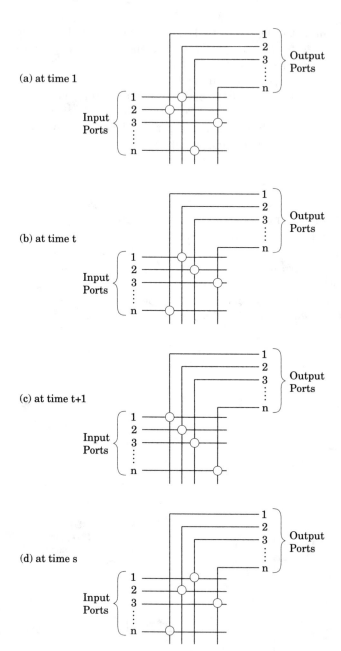

(a) at time 1

(b) at time t

(c) at time t+1

(d) at time s

Figure 5.36 TST space-division switching stage for one frame.

for outside calls. It produces appropriate audible signals similar to those callers have come to expect when using the PSTN. Furthermore, modern PBXs are computer-based (hence, they're sometimes referred to by the term *PABX*—private automatic branch exchange), and they offer hundreds of special features such as call hold, music-on-hold, call waiting, call forwarding, conferencing, automatic callback, redial, speed dialing, paging, dictation, voice mail, and interactive voice response. They also perform automatic route selection, maintain call accounting records, and produce a variety of management reports dealing with every aspect of the telecommunications they handle. Some of the features and functions of modern PBXs are provided directly from the telephone company's central office switch under a service called Centrex.

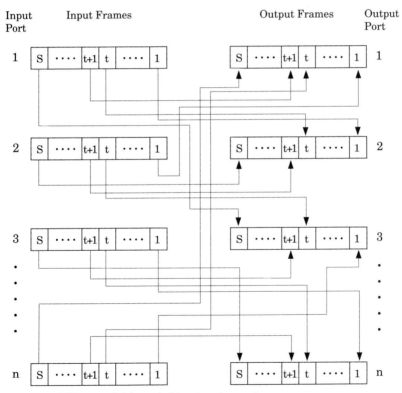

Figure 5.37 TST space-division switching stage for one frame.

In the early days of private branch switching, PBXs were miniversions of central office switches, so much of what has been said about telephone switching earlier in this chapter applies to PBXs. The first PBXs were manual switchboards very like those used in central offices; they handled only a small number of telephone switching functions—primarily local calling and connection to the central office. The first dial PBX was introduced in the late 1920s and used progressive switches just as telephone company automatic switching offices did—often these systems also interfaced to a switchboard. PBXs of the 1950s and 1960s featured improved step-by-step switching devices and replaced the switchboard with an operator console. They sometimes included such features as Touch-Tone dialing and direct-inward-dialing (DID—described later in this chapter, under Signaling). Coordinate switching found its way into PBXs about the same time that it became available at telephone company offices. As with the larger crossbar switches, crossbar-based PBXs were quieter and required less space. These advantages were particularly attractive in office environments where space was often limited and noisy equipment not practical. In 1974, the Bell System introduced a time-division multiplexed PBX using a digital computer designed especially for telephone switching. Computer control and digital processing have provided the base from which hundreds of customer features available in today's PBXs have evolved.

Modern PBXs can be configured for a few or thousands of lines and from a handful to hundreds of trunks. Blocking, when it occurs, results when all possible connections are already in use, but integrated circuits and modular technology simplifies expansion. Within limits, more lines, more trunks, more consoles, a greater number of connections, and enhanced processing capacity can be added by plugging in additional hardware modules. Reconfiguration for additional ports, attachments, features, or users is readily accomplished in software.

Signaling

The term *signaling* refers to the movement of control information through a telephone network, information that's required to make decisions concerning management of the network. When a caller lifts or replaces the telephone to place or end a call, the central office is signaled. When a caller dials a phone number, the dialed digits are passed along to the central office, which might forward the information to other offices. When a call is blocked or a called line is offhook, a busy signal is returned to the caller. These and many other actions are part of signaling.

Signaling in a telephone network is conducted for one of three purposes. It occurs to originate or terminate a call, to forward destination address information to switches along a call's route, or to monitor a call's progress as it proceeds along its path. In early telephone networks, signaling information was generated manually or verbally. A subscriber whirled a crank on the side of the telephone a few turns to light a lamp or ring a bell at the local office. This signaled an operator who obtained destination address information verbally. At first, exchanges were quite small, so subscriber John Jones, for instance, could spin the crank and say "Hello Mable. Please connect me with the Johnson's." Mable would oblige by ringing the Johnson's phone. When someone answered, she would tell them John Jones was calling then complete the connection by plugging opposite ends of a cable into the jacks for Jones and Johnson.

The need for signal information exists not only in the communication path between subscriber stations and the central office but between switching offices as well. Until recently, this information was also exchanged verbally between operators. Even though we could dial local calls directly, many of us remember having to dial zero to make a long distance call. The long distance operator would come on the line and say "long distance," or "number please." We would say the name of the city and the number in that city we wished to call—then we would hear "just a minute please." We could hear some clicks on the line then the number repeated to another operator in the distant city, who would make the final connection.

Signaling information was originally transmitted on the same facilities as the call it concerned. Mutual interference between the call and signaling was avoided by separating signals and voice in either time or frequency. Today, such means are still used, but, in addition, some signals are transmitted on separate facilities and sometimes along a different route from that taken by the call. With computers controlling such processes, more complex signaling features can be provided by telephone companies. Three examples are *direct inward dial* (DID), *automatic number identification* (ANI), and *dialed number identification* service (DNIS). DID allows a PBX to interconnect any of a few incoming trunks to any of a larger number of local stations because the station's address is passed to the PBX with the incoming call.

When a call comes in on a trunk, the dialed number is transmitted first so the PBX can direct the call to the appropriate station. With ANI, the local office first sends the number of the calling party so the called organization might learn who is calling (and perhaps search for pertinent database information) before coming on the line. In another application of ANI, the calling party's phone number appears on the called customer's phone bill. With DNIS, the telephone company sends the digits of a dialed 800 number ahead of the call so the called customer can discern which number has been dialed. This is particularly useful in ACD applications where 800 calls coming in on a bank of lines are routed to a pool of operators.

Signaling techniques have evolved over the years to accommodate improvements in transmission and switching methods so that today different means exist for exchanging signals throughout a telephone network. Among others, these include DC (direct current), SF (single frequency), MF (multi-

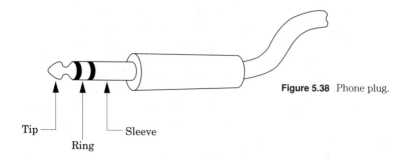

Figure 5.38 Phone plug.

Tip ——┐   ┌—— Sleeve
       └── Ring ──┘

ple frequency), DTMF (dual-tone multifrequency), digital carrier, and CCIS (common channel interoffice signaling). The signaling methods familiar to most of us are those we commonly hear in our own telephone calls.

DC signaling modifies the amplitude or direction of flow of direct current to convey information and is used both in subscriber loops and in trunks. *SF signaling* employs a single tone to convey information. Its presence or absence indicates one of two states such as busy/idle or ringing/not ringing. *MF signaling* involves various combinations of tone-pairs to send address information between switching offices on normal VF circuits—but only at a time when there's no voice signal being transmitted. DTMF is commonly known by the name Touch-Tone (an AT&T Company registered service mark). DTMF is similar to MF signaling, except that DTMF uses frequency pairs that are unlikely to be inadvertently produced by callers during a telephone conversation (an event known as *talkoff*). Digital carrier systems multiplex digital signal information with voice or data for transmission together as a composite. CCIS (and a similar international common channel signaling standard known as CCITT System No. 6) use a separate digital packet-switched transmission link for signaling information.

SF, MF, and DTMF are known as *in-band signaling methods* because they share VF channels with voice and transmit signals within the voice-frequency bandwidth. As such, all are susceptible to talkoff, but can be used with any facility that provides a VF channel—including digital carriers. They can be transmitted through a voice network without regard to transmission facilities or switches. Rarely applied, *out-of-band signaling* uses tones at frequencies above voice but below 4 kHz (between about 3.5 and 4 kHz).

Before continuing with a description of signaling means and methods, let's review the events and processes that occur in a typical phone call.

A typical call

A phone call begins when a caller (or automatic machine) takes a line offhook to request telephone service. However, even before that, a local switch has been monitoring the line for just such an event. (This process is referred to as *supervision*.) When the central office is aware that a subscriber is requesting service, it searches for an idle digit receiver (a register) to connect to the calling line. When the register is attached, a dial tone is applied to the line to signal the caller to proceed with dialing. As the number is dialed, it's recorded in the digit register. When dialing is complete, the stored number is analyzed to determine if the destination line can be reached without access to another switching office. If it can't, an idle direct trunk to the called exchange is sought. If no direct trunk is available, an idle trunk that advances the call toward its destination will be selected, probably to an office higher in the switching hierarchy. The selected trunk is seized, sending a request for a digit register to the far-end switching office. When a digit register is available, the far-end office returns a *wink* signal (an offhook signal of short duration—interoffice trunks can be thought of as being onhook when they're idle and offhook when busy). The wink signals the originating office to commence transmitting address digits. If at any step along the way there are no trunks available to advance the call—or if the call is blocked in a switch—a *reorder tone* (fast busy tone) is returned to the caller. Otherwise, by some route, the call is switched to the far-end local exchange, where the destination line is examined for idle status. If it's already offhook, a busy tone is returned to the calling party; when the originating station is back onhook, all intermediate links are disconnected. If the destination line is idle, a ringing signal is connected to it, and an audible ringing signal is returned to the caller. When the called party lifts the telephone handset to accept the call, both ringing signals are removed and a connection completed between the two parties. Both the originating and terminating central offices continue to supervise their respective lines, monitoring for call completion. When one or both callers go back onhook, all links are disconnected and idle line supervision resumes until the next request for service.

Subscriber loop signaling

Signaling between the subscriber loop and the central office involves supervisory, address, and call-progress signals—and, for most subscriber loops, takes place over a pair of metallic wires. One of the wires is called the *tip connection* and the other the *ring connection*. These names derive from connections appearing on manual switchboard phone plugs (as shown in Figure 5.38). When station equipment is connected through a customer's carrier terminal, loop signaling occurs between the station and the customer terminal and between the CO and its own carrier terminal. Other signaling means are employed between customer and CO terminals. Supervision involves monitoring the loop for changes in idle and busy status. Supervision determines when a phone has gone offhook or onhook. Two methods are commonly used for loop supervision: loop-start and ground-start. Destination address signals are sent when dialed digits are applied to the loop at the subscriber end by rotary pulse dialers or by DTMF dialers. Call-progress signals are returned to a calling party in the form of recognizable audible tone patterns that indicate ringing of the called party's line, blocking somewhere in the network, or a busy called party line. Let's consider the two methods of subscriber loop supervision.

Loop-start. A subscriber loop consists of two metallic conductors (tip and ring) between the CO (or a customer terminal) and a customer's station. The negative side of a DC power supply (usually –48 volts) is attached to the ring conductor at the central office. When the phone is onhook, tip and ring conductors are open. A loop is formed and current flows in a loop-start circuit when the phone is taken offhook, causing the tip and ring conductors to be connected. The CO senses current flow, interprets that as a request for service, and, when ready to receive digits, sends a dial tone. During a call, the loop is monitored at the CO. When the phone is placed onhook, again opening the circuit, current flow stops, and this is the CO's signal to disconnect all links in support of the call. To signal an incoming call, the CO applies a ringing signal to the ring conductor. When the phone is taken offhook, the ringing signal is removed.

Loop-start circuits are subject to seizure simultaneously by both the CO and the station. Perhaps you've had the experience of picking up the phone to call someone, only to find that, even though the phone has not rung, someone is on the line who has just dialed your number. That was the result of simultaneous seizure. Loop-start circuits are most susceptible to this event during an initial four-second silent portion of a ringing signal—ringing has not yet been heard despite of the fact that an incoming call is waiting to be answered. Another important disadvantage to loop-start lines, particularly for voice processing applications, is that automated terminal equipment attached to the line has no immediate indication when the far-end party has disconnected.

Ground-start. With ground-start circuits, the CO maintains a negative DC voltage (generally –48 volts) on the ring conductor, and a negative DC voltage (usually –48 volts) is maintained on the tip conductor at the terminal side. While the loop is idle, the tip conductor is open at the CO. To request service from the CO, subscriber terminal or station equipment momentarily grounds the ring conductor, causing current to flow. The CO senses current in the ring side and, when ready to receive dialed digits, grounds the tip and at the same time sends a dial tone. Having detected the grounded tip, the terminal connects the ring side of the loop. The CO completes the loop by closing the tip side of the circuit. The subscriber equipment then sends address digits to the CO. To end a call, both ends revert to idle condition: the subscriber equipment opens the ring conductor and the CO responds by opening the tip conductor and disconnecting any other links. To signal the station equipment that a call is incoming, the CO grounds the tip lead and places a ringing signal on the ring connector. On answer, the loop circuit is made at both ends for the duration of the call.

Ground-start circuits don't require tone detectors because the CO's removal of the tip conductor ground can be used as a dial signal. Furthermore, ground-start circuits are less prone to being seized simultaneously by both the station and the CO. This is because seizure by the CO is immediately signaled by a grounded tip lead that persists throughout the entire ringing cycle, and seizure by the station end is signaled by a grounded ring lead. Another advantage of ground-start loops is that when the far-end party goes back onhook, the CO gives the subscriber's equipment a definite signal of that fact when it opens the tip lead—a feature of significant importance to automatic terminal equipment.

Rotary dialers. The layout of a rotary dial is shown in Figure 5.39. To dial a number, a person places a finger in the appropriate hole in the dial. (Each hole corresponds to a digit to be dialed.) The dial is rotated clockwise until the finger reaches the stop and the dial released. The spring-loaded dial returns to its at-rest position. In so doing, the loop is opened and closed a number of times, equal to the digit dialed. (The zero digit is an exception, producing ten pulses when dialed.) If the three digit is dialed, for example, the loop is opened and closed three times in succession. The loop circuit is opened for about 60 ms for each pulse. A dialed address of ten digits appears as a stream of pulses on the loop in digit groups. This means of dialing is compatible with step-by-step switching, but pulses are carried no further than the local central office, where the digits they represent are recorded in registers for use in setting up a call. As of this writing, a reasonably large percentage of subscribers throughout the world still use rotary dialers—particularly in rural areas and in less-developed areas of the world.

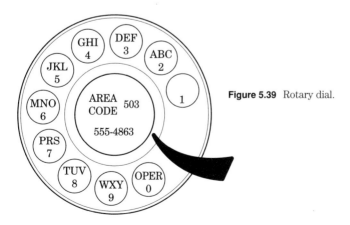

Figure 5.39 Rotary dial.

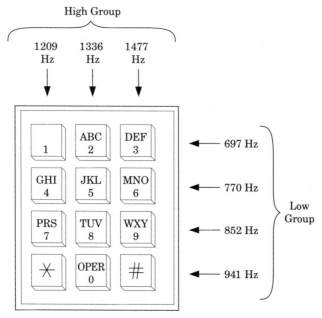

Figure 5.40 DTMF keypad.

DTMF dialers. *DTMF (dual-tone multifrequency) dialers* are also called Touch-Tone dialers. They produce inband signals designed not to interfere with (or be interfered with by) voice signals. DTMF signals are tones composed of pairs of frequencies that have been selected so as to be unlikely to be inadvertently produced during a telephone conversation. Two groups of frequencies have been chosen: a low-frequency group and a high-frequency group. One DTMF digit consists of a tone of one frequency from each group. Figure 5.40 shows a DTMF keypad and indicates which frequency pairs are combined for each key. Because DTMF signals are inband, they're transmitted from end to end through a telephone network. They can be propagated simultaneously with voice, usually without interference, and can be carried in either analog or digital carrier systems. Because of these features, DTMF signals are particularly useful with voice processing systems for control and numerical data entry.

Call progress. A group of audible tones is produced in the network as a call progresses from an originating station to its destination. These signals are recognizable by both the human ear and by voice processing systems designed to perform call-progress analysis. There is no change in call progress

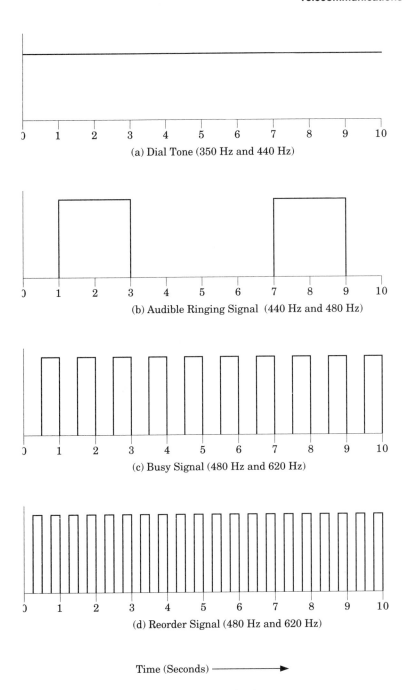

(a) Dial Tone (350 Hz and 440 Hz)

(b) Audible Ringing Signal (440 Hz and 480 Hz)

(c) Busy Signal (480 Hz and 620 Hz)

(d) Reorder Signal (480 Hz and 620 Hz)

Time (Seconds) ⟶

Figure 5.41 Call progress signal frequencies and cadences.

signals as they pass from trunks to subscriber loops. They're transmitted along the entire path of a call—usually from the farthest reach of the call back to the calling party. Many call-progress signals are used in telephone networks, but those of primary concern to callers include the following. The dial tone applied by a local central office can be considered the first of several to be heard by a caller. Another is the audible ringing signal returned from the far-end central office when the called party's station is being rung. If the called party's station is busy, the far-end central office places a busy signal on the circuit. If, as the call is progressing toward its destination, no interoffice trunks are available to advance the call, it's blocked, and a reorder signal is placed on the line. Likewise, if the call is blocked in a switching system, a reorder signal is returned.

Call-progress signals are composed of pairs of frequencies with recognizably different cadences. Details of the four call-progress signals of importance to call originators (human or machine) are shown in Figure 5.41. Several other events occur in the process of placing calls, and the detection of these events is of interest to developers of voice processing systems. These include answer by human, answer by answering machine, and answer by modem or FAX. Another possibility is that, while waiting for someone (or some machine) to answer a call, nothing happens. No sound is heard, and, no matter how long a caller waits, the line is silent. This is sometimes referred to as a *high-and-dry*. To guard against taking a line out of action indefinitely due to a high-and-dry, call-progress detection software usually includes timeouts. Detection of talking by voice processing machines is standard today but is not perfectly accurate. Detection of answer by answering machines can be accomplished by timing the verbal response after the called station goes offhook. This technique might also be used to distinguish between calls that are answered at a business rather than at a household because businesses usually respond by stating the name of the business, while households usually just say, "Hello." Both modems and FAX machines generally place an immediate carrier signal on the line, and these are easily detected by call-progress analysis software.

Interoffice signaling

Signaling between switching offices has traditionally been conducted along the same path, on the same trunks, using the same facilities and carrier systems as the calls with which the transmitted signals are associated.

This path-sharing approach is called *per-trunk signaling* (probably because trunks were added to a call path one at a time) and uses either of two interfaces for supervisory functions: loop-reverse-battery or E&M lead. Per-trunk signaling is still used, but an alternate signaling approach called *common channel interoffice signaling (CCIS)* was introduced in 1976. CCIS employs separate, dedicated links for digital transmission of signaling information for a group of trunks.

Loop-reverse-battery. The purpose of loop-reverse-battery is to enable offices at opposite ends of trunks to communicate with each other regarding trunk seizure. When loop-reverse-battery is used, trunk seizure can occur from only one end of the trunk. In the idle condition, the originating end maintains an open circuit between tip and ring. A direct current of –48 volts DC is maintained on the ring conductor at the terminating end, and the tip conductor is grounded. Even though there is no actual switchhook for trunks, as there is for subscriber loops, an idle trunk is considered onhook and, when seized, a trunk is considered offhook. To seize the trunk, the originating office closes the loop by connecting tip and ring. In response to the flowing current in the pair, the terminating end reverses polarity of tip and ring, grounding the ring and putting –48 volts DC on the tip.

E&M lead. The E&M lead is a supervisory interface. As distinguished from loop-reverse-battery, E&M lead is symmetric in that it appears the same from either end of a trunk, and either switching office can seize the trunk. The term E&M lead actually refers to designations of the pair of wires used in original E&M lead implementations, but it might be helpful to think of the analogy with mouth (M-lead) and ear (E-lead) because of the way the E&M lead system operates. Facilities at each end of a trunk manage the signaling operation and accomplish conversions so that the M lead at one end drives the E lead at the other—and vise versa. These devices interface between a switching office and transmission facilities, placing onhook and offhook signals on a trunk and converting such signals that appear on the trunk to E&M lead conventions. An idle condition is signaled from the switch by grounding the M-lead. Offhook is signaled by placing –48 volts DC on the M-lead. These signals appear at the other end of the trunk on the E-lead, onhook by an open and offhook by a ground.

Common channel interoffice signaling (CCIS). With the advent of common control, digital switching, digital transmission, and many other advances taking place in telecommunication networks, the need for more flexible network management and faster signaling arose. In 1976, CCIS was introduced in the Bell System to answer these needs. Other implementations of the CCIS approach have appeared—including CCITT System No. 6, which differs only in detail from CCIS.

CCIS sends signaling information pertaining to a group of trunks over separate digital links. One data link supports signaling for many trunk groups, and these links are not necessarily parallel to transmission routes. Instead, a separate digital network has been established. CCIS messages contain trunk and trunk-group identifying information, destination address, error correction bits, and other data. The CCIS messages are packet switched through nodes in the CCIS network called *signal transfer points (STP)*. At an STP, destination information is interpreted and a packet advanced toward its destination. Signals often reach destination switching offices before the call transmission path to that office is established. Formerly, with older signaling systems, a signal's arrival over a trunk assured the viability of that trunk. With CCIS, signaling information does not travel via the trunks that will carry the call, so these must be quickly tested immediately before being switched into a circuit. Failure of a CCIS link could mean serious service disruptions because so many trunks are handled by each one. To avoid such problems, redundancy has been designed into the CCIS system; duplicate paths, alternate routes, and backup facilities are featured.

CCIS brings numerous advantages to high-traffic network management. For example, busy signals can be returned from the near-end central office rather than being transmitted through the network from the far end. This makes intermediate trunks available to other calls much sooner. Simultaneous seizure of trunks is called *glare*—switches at each end of a trunk have both seized it and are "glaring" at each other from opposite ends of the trunk, each waiting for something to happen. With CCIS signaling, problems of glare are easier to avoid—and easier to solve when they do occur. Furthermore, call tracing is faster and simpler. In general, much greater control over the network is obtained through CCIS.

6

Requirements and Features

Despite the proliferation of computers, many people are still intimidated by machines. Computer literacy classes are working to correct this situation, and, in time, the problem will be further lessened as more and more people are exposed to voice processing's telephone-computer applications. Nevertheless, designers of voice processing systems must plan for access by people with various levels of skill and experience. Even those who are not intimidated by machines can easily become confused or frustrated by poorly designed applications—this is especially true for voice processing applications whose only interface with users is aural. The inability to see written instructions, the need to remember several prompts, the short periods of silence, the brevity of information, and the complexity of data entry can easily lead to confusion. Errors and frustration can be caused by menus that are too long or that occur too frequently. Prompts that are wordy or repetitious or that rush the caller can also create frustration. If people become confused or exasperated, they might tune out and stop using the system. Some will even find a way to defeat it. Others will go to great lengths to convince their co-workers and bosses that the system is not worthy and should be removed. If too many users feel they've had a negative experience with a voice processing application, the system will fail to accomplish its goal.

Some people resist new ways of doing things. Others will try a new idea unless it somehow turns out to be unreasonably difficult or frustrating. Anything that can be done by system designers to enhance the friendliness of the voice processing system will increase the probability of its acceptance. Any positive steps taken to include those features that tend to make a system nonthreatening and nonjudgmental will go furthest toward winning users.

Other factors not within control of system developers can intervene to destroy a voice processing system's viability. When users are distant from the computer and the only connection is via the public, switched telephone network, occurrences common to the network can cause the system to appear to malfunction; these events should be anticipated. The telephone connection might be a poor or noisy one, the equipment might be busy and inaccessible, a sudden disconnect might occur in midsentence, or Touch-Tone digits can be mistransmitted. Such eventualities will degrade the system's operation and must be accommodated with some form of graceful degradation. These troubling events will not be catastrophic if a voice processing system is able to recover automatically when they occur.

Design suggestions that appear later in this chapter will be useful to those designing, developing, or buying voice processing systems. It doesn't matter whether the system under consideration is a voice-response system, a voice-messaging system, or a call-processing system. The collection of features has evolved over a period of years; it has resulted from the development of several versions of a handful of voice processing systems. Some of the suggestions might seem obvious. The reasons for others might seem obscure, and you might disagree as to their value. Some of the techniques are difficult to implement—others are not so difficult. Some might be more important than others, but they should all be considered during the design phases of any implementation or during the acquisition phase for any off-the-shelf system. Callers will accept and use a system if it makes their life easier. A poorly conceived user interface will turn callers away. The quality of the interface will be judged by many things, including the hardware, the features implemented, the expertise applied to vocabulary production, even the quality of the telephone network. In designing any modern computer system, especially in the field of voice processing where users are constrained to communicate by telephone and keypad, it's crucial that designers and those who implement the system achieve the most enlightened user interface possible.

Requirements

This section explores requirements for multiline voice processing systems. It discusses a variety of functions and features that might be employed in such systems. A thorough understanding of the various elements that might be required in a voice processing system are a necessary foundation for later chapters.

Basic capabilities

Certain capabilities are found in almost every multiline voice processing system. The major ones are covered in this section.

Multitasking. The need to conduct simultaneous telephone conversations between multiple callers and the computer necessitates multitasking. On personal computers, OS/2 and UNIX-based operating systems provide multitasking services, but some of the most popular operating systems for personal computers don't. Many voice processing systems are developed on OS/2 or UNIX-based systems, but many more are developed using DOS or MS-DOS, which don't support multitasking. These nonmultitasking operating systems can still be used in multitasking environments—techniques for accomplishing this are discussed in chapter 8.

Status display. A status screen showing every telephone channel and its status is a standard part of most voice processing systems. Various items of information can be displayed on the screen, including current date/time, operation presently being performed on each channel, date/time of previous call, number of calls inbound and outbound, and others. The screen can be displayed by pressing a hotkey or by selection from a menu. Figure 6.1 shows an example status screen. Standard operations that might be displayed in such a screen include: waiting for ring, busy signal, speaking, no answer, waiting for DTMF, speaking, timeout waiting for DTMF, and so on. Status screens customized for specific applications can display their own informative status information like the following: "speaking greeting," "entering PIN," "waiting for account number," "requesting credit authorization," "invalid client number," etc.

Automatic restart on early disconnect. Any number of occurrences can result in a premature disconnect. Whether the caller hangs up unexpectedly or a network fault or hardware malfunction occurs, a voice processing sys-

```
                  A U T O M A T E D    B I N D I N G    S Y S T E M
                           ABC Insurance Services
                       T E L E P H O N E    S T A T U S
```

TELEPHONE		CONDITION SINCE		CALL COUNTS		CURRENT ACTIVITY			
LN	NUMBER	CND	TIME	DATE	IN	OUT	DIR	ELAPSED	TONES	STATUS
1	283-0231	ok	1823	06-04-92	3367	442		1		Ready
2	283-0232	ok	1823	06-04-92	3201	338	in	3	13221*2	Waiting DTMF
3	283-0233	ok	1824	06-04-92	2127	343	in	3	2231**1	Speaking
4	283-0234	ok	1826	06-04-92	2326	258	out	0		Waiting Ansr
5	283-0235	ok	1832	06-04-92	1986	112	in	3	43425#22	Waiting DTMF
6	283-0236	ok	1840	06-04-92	1289	62	in	2	21*33241	Recording
7	283-0237	ok	1857	06-04-92	774	51	out	0		Dialing
8	283-0238	ok	1940	06-04-92	472	36	in	1	331	Speaking
9	283-0239	ok	2129	06-04-92	298	29		1		Ready
10	283-0240	ok	2352	06-04-92	204	21	in	2	282#1121	Speaking
11	283-0241	ok	0136	06-05-92	143	14		2:23		Ready
12	283-0242	ok	0307	06-05-92	87	9		2:58		Ready

Line 1: Program 1, Binder

`<Esc>` or `<Alt-T>` to toggle display. `<F10>` for funcs.   Fri 06-05-92 6:24pm

Figure 6.1 Telephone status screen.

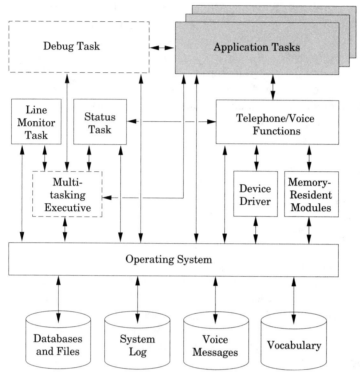

Figure 6.2 Software structure at runtime.

tem must be able to recover without degrading service on other lines. Various line-monitoring techniques can be implemented to enable programs to recover in an orderly fashion when a line is unexpectedly disconnected. This is often accomplished through cooperation between hardware and software. A disconnect causes a change in loop current. Hardware detects this and issues an interrupt notifying a user program to abort and resume waiting for calls.

Multiple applications.   A single voice processing system can assign different applications to different sets of phone lines. Figure 6.2 shows a combination physical and logical runtime architecture for a voice processing system. The components labelled "Telephone/Voice Functions" represent library telephone and speaking functions. User programs are inherently represented in the boxes labelled "Application Tasks." Application tasks are logical entities defined for a multitasker—there's usually at least one task for each telephone line. Tasks are not themselves programs but are each associated with a program located in memory. A program can be associated with more than one task and can, therefore, handle multiple telephone lines. If a program is re-entrant, only one copy is needed in memory, regardless of how many tasks it supports.

Tasks can be assigned to programs in many different ways. A separate program might be assigned to each task or the same program assigned to every task—or something in between. Any task can be associated with any program. For example, suppose a single voice processing system with 16 telephone lines was developed to run three different applications: voice mail, account inquiry, and order entry. There would be three user programs: one for each of the applications. There would be at least 16 tasks: one for each telephone line (and a few others). Then, for example, at any given time, lines 1–7 could be assigned to voice mail, 8–10 to account inquiry, and 11–16 to order entry. At another time, lines 1–4 might be handling voice mail, lines 6–8 executing account inquiry, 11–15 doing order entry, and lines 5, 9, 10, and 16 unassigned. Any arrangement of lines and application can be accomplished—and changed anytime.

Miscellaneous capabilities

The following features might be found in any voice processing system.

Configuration file.   Many features of a system's runtime operation are variable and can be specified at runtime by the values of control variables. One method of setting and maintaining control parameters is through a text configuration file loaded at the start of a run. The configuration file is easy to create and maintain with any text editor. Figure 6.3 is a listing of just such a file. Notice how simply parameters are specified. A keyword appears in the first column and is followed by one or more parameters. In this example some keywords are required (e.g., to define the hardware interrupt level), and others are optional. In some cases a keyword might appear more than once—as with "vocab," which defines vocabulary files. Entries are not ordered within this example file, so keywords might appear on any line and lines in any order. A line on which the first word is not a keyword is considered a comment line. This feature makes possible the inclusion of headers and other descriptive text, renders the file more readable, and facilitates later revision and update.

Some parameters that might be specified in a configuration file or like device are: hardware interrupt level, software interrupt levels for memory resident modules, digitization rate, application programs to be loaded (and stack size for tasks using them), number of telephone lines with phone numbers and applicable program, utterance number ranges for indexed vocabulary files, numbers of special utterances (e.g., numbers, days of month, etc.), number of seconds before aborting a line in case of no DTMF input, display mode (normal or reversed video), key to be used as status display hotkey, and others. Most of these can be seen in Figure 6.3. A configuration

```
CONFIGURATION FILE for: USER                            June 16, 1989

HARDWARE INTERRUPT LEVEL:
hwint          5                Hardware interrupt level 5 (2 is default)

SOFTWARE INTERRUPT LEVEL:
bdswint        109              Board Software interrupt level 109 (0x6d)
mtswint        110              Multitasking Exec. s/w interrupt level 110 (0x6e)

SAMPLES PER SECOND FOR RECORDING AND PLAYBACK:
samprate     6053               Default is 6053 samples/second

USER PROGRAMS AND STACK: .
   PROGRAM   BYTES IN           NAME (1 word of less than 16 chars)
    NUMBER    STACK
prog    1     1500             Telephone_Lines
prog    2     2000             Non_telephone

LOCAL TELEPHONE LINE:
local   1                       Local line is on port 1

TELEPHONE LINE TASKS:   (program number must be defined above as "prog")
                        PHONE     PROGRAM
          LINE          NUMBER    NUMBER
line    02             283-2122     1
line    03             283-2123     1
line    04             283-2124     1
line    05             283-2125     1
line    06             283-2126     1
line    07             283-2127     1
line    08             283-2128     1
line    09             283-2129     1

NON-TELEPHONE LINE TASKS:   (Other tasks to be spawned)
         PROGRAM     (program number must be defined above as "prog")
          NUMBER
task      2          This program will control the display and keyboard

VOCABULARY:        (Vocabulary files with utterance number ranges)
                   FILENAME  FIRST  LAST   DESCRIPTION
vocab              asnummid      1    31   Numbers
vocab              asnumend     51    81   Numbers
vocab              asckin      101   125   Test utterances
vocab              asckin2     151   170   Test utterances
vocab              tones       201   218   Tones utterances
vocab              asstd       301   318   Standard utterances
vocab              asstatus    351   369   Telephone status vocabulary
vocab              asclock     401   410   Clock and Time vocabulary
vocab              silence     901   904   Silence utterances
vocab              askeys     1001  1030   Touch-tone key utterances
vocab              asrecord  10001 10033   Record utterances -- part 1
vocab              asrec2    10051 10061   Record utterances -- part 2
vocab              asalert   10151 10179   Alert utterances
vocab              asclback  10201 10202   Callback utterances
vocab              assup     10251 10254   Supervisor utterances

NUMERIC UTTERANCES: (Starting utterance numbers)
          NUM                   DESCRIPTION
numbers     1                   First number with normal intonation
dnumbers   51                   First number with downgoing intonation
dom       305                   First number of day-of-month
minus     304                   Number of "minus"

TOUCHTONE INTERLOCK SECS:  Line will abort in this many secs if DTMF
interlock  60                              is requested but none is input

TELEPHONE STATUS DISPLAY MODE:  (normal, reverse, or omit)
status    normal                Status display in normal video

TELEPHONE STATUS HOTKEY:   (hex -- key to toggle status and user displays)
hotkey   1400                    Hotkey is Alt-T

NUMBER OF TELEPHONE/VOICE BOARDS INSTALLED: (0 for none)
boards     3                     There are 3 boards installed
END
```

Figure 6.3 Configuration file listing.

```
┌─────────────────────────────────────────────────────────────────────────┐
│               SSTS -- Security Officer Checkin System (V1.1)              │
│                                                                           │
│           T E L E P H O N E     L I N E     C O N F I G U R A T O R        │
├──────────┬─────┬──────────┬───────────────────────────────────────────────┤
│ Voice    │Port │Telephone │                                               │
│ Hardware │ Num │ Number   │                                               │
│          │     │          │                                               │
│ Board 1  │  1  │Local Line│ INSTRUCTIONS:                                 │
│   "      │  2  │254-1002  │                                               │
│   "      │  3  │254-1003  │   Enter the phone number for each line that is│
│   "      │  4  │254-1004  │   connected. Every phone number entered will  │
│ Board 2  │  5  │254-2115  │   cause the system to assume that the line is  │
│   "      │  6  │254-2116  │   connected. If a line is NOT connected, blank │
│   "      │  7  │254-1143  │   out its telephone number.                   │
│   "      │  8  │254-1144  │                                               │
│ Board 3  │  9  │254-1145  │   Press <Esc> when done.                      │
│   "      │ 10  │254-8779  │                                               │
│   "      │ 11  │          │                                               │
│   "      │ 12  │254-3611  │                                               │
└──────────┴─────┴──────────┴───────────────────────────────────────────────┘
```

Figure 6.4   Configuration file line number entry screen.

file data entry program can be used to further facilitate creation and maintenance of a configuration file and to diminish the possibility of introducing erroneous parameter values. Figure 6.4 shows an example screen as it might appear in such a program for entry of line and telephone numbers to a configuration file.

Application displays.   There might be application-specific screens available to an online user. For example, an application that refers to and updates a local database might have database access screens for online reference and updating. A main menu that can be customized facilitates switching between application and system screens.

Hotkey to display status screen.   Some systems feature a hotkey to enable online users to immediately extinguish any screen and display a telephone-line status screen rather than backing down screen-by-screen to a menu. The hotkey can be specified in the configuration file. Depressing the hotkey while viewing the status screen will extinguish it and redisplay the original screen. Thus, the hotkey becomes a toggle switch for the status display.

Indexed vocabulary files.   It's not unusual for voice processing systems to require a large number of utterances to be instantly available to applications. However, other system requirements don't always permit time to be spent opening a vocabulary file each time the file's speech data is needed. Furthermore, to accommodate memory buffer limitations, operating systems limit the number of files that can be open at any time, and this is frequently not a large enough number to accommodate many applications using files containing only a single utterance. Operating system maximums can usually be overridden, often with difficulty and always with the disad-

```
            V O I C E     W O R K S T A T I O N   (Vers 3.1.2)
                         Pelton Systems, Inc.
                         U T T E R A N C E S

FILE:   C:\CHECKIN\DB\ASNUMMID.VAP
```

UTT NUM	LENGTH SECS	BYTES	DESCRIPTION
1	0.4	1444	Zero
2	0.4	1444	One
3	0.4	1292	Two
4	0.3	1064	Three
5	0.3	1064	Four
6	0.5	1520	Five
7	0.3	1140	Six
8	0.3	1140	Seven
9	0.3	912	Eight
10	0.4	1444	Nine
11	0.3	988	Ten
12	0.4	1368	Eleven
13	0.4	1444	Twelve
14	0.5	1520	Thirteen
15	0.5	1748	Fourteen
16	0.5	1748	Fifteen
17	0.6	1900	Sixteen
18	0.7	2128	Seventeen
19	0.5	1672	Eighteen
20	0.6	1900	Nineteen
21	0.4	1292	Twenty
22	0.4	1216	Thirty
23	0.4	1292	Forty
24	0.4	1292	Fifty
25	0.5	1520	Sixty
26	0.5	1520	Seventy
27	0.4	1216	Eighty
28	0.4	1368	Ninety
29	0.4	1292	Hundred
30	0.5	1520	Thousand
31	0.5	1596	Million

Figure 6.5 Speech editor output showing contents of indexed file.

vantageous use of more memory. Many systems support use of RAM disks for vocabulary storage, and this, to a large extent, gets around both problems. Use of RAM disks can be inconvenient or expensive but can often be avoided by employing indexed vocabulary files. Indexed files contain multiple prompts, phrases, and other utterances in a single disk file, and their use can result in smoother and more natural concatenation of sentence segments. Their use certainly facilitates vocabulary distribution and maintenance. Figure 6.5 shows the contents of an indexed vocabulary file designed for use with applications that speak numbers. The figure was produced as hard-copy output from a speech editor. (Speech editors are discussed in chapter 8.)

Statistical reports. It's not unusual for system sponsors to collect statistical information regarding caller's interests, system performance, and telephone calls handled by their systems. They might wish to know, for instance, how many inbound and outbound calls have occurred in a period. They might be interested in how many callers selected a particular item in a menu, or how many times a given caller returned to a particular portion of the program. Some of this information is desired as a distribution by time of day, day of week, or day of month. The ability of a system to discriminate, save, and report required information significantly affects its usefulness.

Error handling. Callers don't have a screen to look at when they're communicating with a voice processing system. They must be guided by the computer via an aural interface. Many system malfunctions inhibit the system's ability to speak to the caller. Nevertheless, if avoidable, it's unacceptable for the caller to be suddenly cut off without some explanation. It's incumbent upon the voice processing system to prevent this by detecting and handling errors automatically whenever possible. Whenever it's possible to do so, a voice processing system should gracefully degrade service and inform the caller if there's some problem that's preventing continuation of the call.

Event logging. Debugging of multitasked applications is different than for normal applications because task interleaving makes it exceedingly difficult to track program flow and to know which process was executing at any given time. Multiple executions of one or many programs occur in tiny time slices, one following upon the other in an often obscure sequence. Special tools are needed to unravel the execution threads during debugging. Among other tools, an event log or trace facility is useful. The resulting log can be thought of as a trace of important processing events. *System events*, those detected by system or library modules, are logged automatically without any action required by the user—user events are chronologically merged with them. One of the main advantages of a logging feature with multiline voice processing systems is its chronological record of all events for all running tasks. It helps to pinpoint complicated errors whose effects might not be immediately observed. This might include situations in which operations occurring in one task interfere with or otherwise affect another—for example, situations in which a task is suspended by the multi-tasker or might not be reinvoked as expected.

Programs that log events (e.g., such as receipt of a DTMF digit, commencement of speaking, an error return from a function call, and many others) can do so by calling a function that enters the event's code and other pertinent information into a disk file established for the purpose. Naturally, the process is a FIFO one, logged information going into the file in chronological order, usually in some compressed form to conserve file space. Circular log files can be used to limit file length, but older material is replaced each time new information is logged. Depending upon the length of the file, the degree of logging, and the amount of information compression achieved, this loss of information need not be serious. Event logging can be turned on or off to suit the needs of the tester.

```
                    MT/y -- Pelton Sytstems, Inc.

                      E V E N T      L O G

 DATE  | TIME     | KEY   | LN | T | INFORMATION
 Jun 04 1823:21            2       ANSWER: Ready for incoming call
 Jun 04 1823:22            2       Line ready to be answered -- waiting for ring
 Jun 04 1823:22            3       LOADVARS: var1<-con1, var2<-con2, var3<-con3
 Jun 04 1823:22            4       UNLOCKDB: Database 8 unlocked
 Jun 04 1823:22            3       ANSWER: Ready for incoming call
 Jun 04 1823:22            3       Line ready to be answered -- waiting for ring
 Jun 04 1823:22            4       OPENDB: database 9 opened
 Jun 04 1823:22            4       OPENDB: database 10 opened
 Jun 04 1823:22            4       * OPENDB: Error, ret 1 from d4buf_unit()
 Jun 04 1823:22            4       LOADVARS: var1<-con1, var2<-con2, var3<-con3
 Jun 04 1823:22            4       ANSWER: Ready for incoming call
 Jun 04 1823:22            4       Line ready to be answered -- waiting for ring
 Jun 04 1824:08  enter            1c0d - Displaying phone status screen
 Jun 04 1825:13  esc              011b - Displaying Main Menu

Cursor keys to page or scroll. <F10> for functions. <ESC> to quit.
```

Figure 6.6 Scrollable screen from log-parsing utility.

A special parsing program should be available to expand event codes and other logged information into understandable statements and display or print logged information. Figure 6.6 shows a portion of a screen from such a log-parsing program. Text statements associated with logged codes are often maintained in an ASCII file so they can be created or changed easily using a text editor. The column labelled "KEY" in the figure contains every keyboard keystroke, the column "LN" shows the telephone line to which the event applies, and the column labelled "T" is used to log both inbound and outbound DTMF tones (digits). Note in the field labelled "INFORMATION" that system events, keyboard events, and telephone events are merged and appear in order of occurrence regardless of which line they support. The example log time-stamps every event. An actual log generated at runtime is coded to minimize recorded data—comment, information and other fields can be added later when the log is viewed via an offline log-parsing program.

Interface to local database. Numerous voice processing systems access and update information stored in local databases. Database references are usually in support of applications, but might sometimes involve system functions—for instance, event logging and reporting features might use local databases.

Outbound calling. The most familiar applications are inbound applications, those in which a caller dials a telephone number that's answered by a voice processing system. However, there are also outbound applications—where the system places calls. Telephone solicitations are perhaps the best-known outbound applications—and probably the most annoying. However, outbound calling is used in many other cases. For example, employee scheduling applications place outbound calls to inform employees of changes in work schedules. Security guard systems call remote posts to check on security or call supervisors to report irregularities.

Voice messaging. It's common practice to combine voice messaging with voice-response applications. Some establish voice mail on specific lines with other applications on remaining lines. Many systems integrate voice messaging capabilities into an otherwise nonvoice-mail application. The employee scheduling and security guard applications previously mentioned, for instance, might feature a voice messaging option in their main menus to enable callers to record messages for each other.

Access from rotary phones. While Touch-Tone telephones are common in most metropolitan areas, there's still a very high proportion of rotary phones throughout the world. Hardware is available to enable voice processing systems to recognize rotary pulses. Nevertheless, most voice processing systems either ignore rotary telephones altogether or connect to a live operator who services callers without Touch-Tone telephones.

Application upgrades at runtime. Systems that must be on the air continuously might require software or vocabulary upgrades to be installed without interruption to operations. This can be done by installing new software or vocabulary in parallel with the old. As individual lines become idle, they can be switched to use the new versions—when all lines have been upgraded, old versions can be removed. It's even possible for upgrades to be applied remotely over a telephone line, and some systems allow new vocabulary to be recorded while applications are running.

Multiple languages. Because vocabulary is stored in files, identical prompts, phrases and other utterances can be provided in more than one language. One set of files might be recorded in English, for example, with another in Spanish. As many duplicate sets in as many languages as required can be recorded. Files can be swapped at startup or chosen by callers to feature identical applications in different languages. However, if input or stored data is interpreted vocally, phrasing might require alteration from language to language.

Remote diagnostics. Some voice processing systems are located at a distance and must be maintained remotely. This is frequently the case for off-the-shelf systems. Various copies of a system might be operating in locations around the world, far from the technical staff. Remote maintenance usually involves uploading and downloading data and files for analysis or upgrade. Fortunately, systems created to operate with telephone lines can conveniently transmit statistics, data, or files over telephone lines and can be designed to install programs and vocabulary under remote control.

External interfaces

Voice processing systems interface to the switched telephone network to make themselves accessible by telephone. Some systems link to other computers, making those computers' processes and data available to callers. These interfaces are briefly discussed in the next sections.

Switched telephone network. Not every voice processing system is connected to the switched telephone network—but most are. That connection might take any of several forms. Some voice processing systems interface directly to a telephone company's central office, others attach inboard to a PBX, and still others interface through a telephone key system. Those connecting to a PBX or key system are able to exercise features inherent to that equipment. They can, for example, switch outside calls between inside extensions. They can switch any call to a live operator—or, calls can be answered by a live operator who can decide to switch the call to the voice processing system (usually a voice mail system). Also, calls placed directly to an extension can be automatically switched to the voice mail system if there's no answer.

Telephone companies offer several special services that are sometimes integrated into a voice processing application. One of these is Automatic Number Identification (ANI), which passes a caller's phone number to the called party along with the call. ANI and other telephone services are discussed in chapter 5.

External computers. Many voice processing applications interface with external computers to accomplish transactions with applications running there. Interfaces could be established to enter orders, access inventory records, verify credit, inquire about account status, or to accomplish any of a large number of other transactions. Interface between the external computer and a voice processing system might be by local channel, network, modem, or remote controller. Depending upon the type of interface implemented, connection to a remote computer could require installation of interfacing hardware in the voice processing computer. Perhaps the most common interfacing approach is by terminal emulation—the voice processing system attaches via a port on the host's remote controller, appearing to the host as another of its terminals.

Optional installed hardware

Interfacing voice processing systems with external computers, as previously discussed, often requires special hardware and driver software. Other features also require installation of dedicated hardware and handler software. The major ones are covered in this section.

Speech recognition. Recognition can be integrated with voice processing systems to eliminate or reduce the use of Touch-Tone keys for menu selections and data input. In general, recognition over telephone lines is more rigorous because of the restricted bandwidth of the switched telephone network. Nevertheless, hardware add-in boards are available for telephone speech recognition. Even so, most developers approach this technology cautiously. They establish only modest recognition tasks—for instance, recognition of the spoken digits from zero to nine plus a few commands like "yes," "no," "repeat," and so on. Some of the techniques suggested later in this chapter should be used with recognition to reduce input errors.

Text-to-speech. Because text-to-speech voices are significantly inferior to stored voices, most systems employ text-to-speech only when use of stored speech is impossible or clearly impractical. Sometimes, a combination of stored speech and text-to-speech offers advantages—particularly for applications that must say names or other items that are so numerous that not all instances can be stored. When saying names of persons, cities, or streets, or when speaking text fields or files whose contents can vary widely, text-to-speech could be the only answer. Normal prompts and phrases are spoken with recorded stored voice, and text-to-speech is used only for special utterances. The following example demonstrates how smoothly a combination of voices can be integrated. In recorded voice the system says, "The computer will read your address as it appears in our files." Then in a text-to-speech voice, the system continues. "123 Rodeo Drive, Beverly Hills, California."Again in recorded speech: "If the address is correct, press one. If not, press two. To repeat the address, press three." and so on.

Facsimile. Integration of FAX with voice processing has become a popular capability. A FAX add-in board is installed in the computer with a driver and other support software, creating increased possibilities for written information dissemination and multimedia communication. Such integrations are able to reduce both personnel costs and delivery response time for many kinds of information, including product data sheets, drawings, brochures, publications, receipts, product documentation, price lists, and almost any other type of written or graphic information. In a typical application, a voice processing system might first send a document catalog or list to a caller by FAX on demand. From then on, the caller can request documents via the system, identifying each item ordered by entering its catalog number on the Touch-Tone keypad. Documents are then automatically transmitted to the caller by FAX.

Design Features

Implementation of voice processing capabilities is a process similar in many ways to interfacing any piece of computer hardware into new or existing products or applications. Voice processing applications, however, require their own user interfacing techniques. Computers that talk to people over the phone and respond to Touch-Tone inputs differ greatly from systems that interface with users via keyboard and display screen. New techniques have had to be developed to support the new technology; the old techniques, which are so well known for presenting information and choices visually in a two-dimensional format, don't easily adapt to the sequential aural interface required over the telephone.

Let's consider some of the differences. Please note that devices such as a mouse or touchscreen are not specifically mentioned because, for our purposes, they can be considered keyboard substitutes.

Screen and keyboard versus telephone

The screen interface is a visual one and presents a large amount of information all at once, much of which the human eye and brain can assimilate at a single glance. Even if the user must study the screen, scanning up and down and across, the user accesses the information randomly. A telephone interface, on the other hand, is an aural one and presents information serially, one thought at a time. To scan the information, the caller must first listen to and memorize all of it—then scan mentally. If the caller forgets the details of a particular prompt, he or she must cause the menu to be repeated from the top and listen to everything until the forgotten prompt is spoken again. If, by that time, the caller has not forgotten the other prompts, he or she might be able to perform the mental scan. Scanning information in an aural interface is at best an awkward and unwieldy procedure.

Whereas a display-based system always has a screen for the user to look at—usually for as long as the user wishes—a voice processing system has frequent periods of silence, periods during which there's no information being communicated from computer to user. That dead time is not always totally wasted, however. Silence is important to a voice processing system because callers need a moment to assimilate the previous message, time to decide which key to press, or time to recall a prompt. Nevertheless, silence is often perceived as a "blank screen." How many systems are you familiar with where a blank screen would be acceptable? An information screen might remain static on the display indefinitely while the user thinks, gets a cup of coffee, makes notes, chats with a friend, or leaves for the night. On the telephone, once the message is spoken, nothing remains except in the caller's memory while the system waits for the caller's response. A system timeout might occur after a short period, but for a few seconds the system is quiet—and well it should be. During these moments, the user's mind might wander. Perhaps the user has some other business that's distracting. Once refocused on the task at hand, the user might have lost his or her place. If the user were looking at a screen, the user would be reminded of what the system expects at this point. On the telephone, for a brief period (which might seem like a very long time) only silence is heard—there is no reminder.

A computer's keyboard has a full set of keys representing letters, numbers, punctuation, and special characters. In fact, many computer keyboards have more than 100 keys. Voice processing systems that communicate over the telephone must usually get by with the 12 keys found on a Touch-Tone keypad. These include only the numbers from zero through nine, and the keys * and #. Making choices or entering numeric values can be easy enough on the keypad, but entering alphabetic information is complicated and could frustrate the most patient of human beings. This is so even though some keypads are marked with letters. On such keypads the two-key is marked ABC, the three-key, DEF, and so on. The use of letters with telephone dialing dates back more than a few years to a time when telephone exchanges were addressed by name. When I was a child, our phone number was Trinidad three four three seven (written as TR-3437). There are no keys for the letters Q and Z. A telephone keypad layout is shown in Figure 6.7. Multiple-key methods have been designed for entering letters, but these are all complex, hard to explain (especially aurally), and not easy for callers to remember.

Finally, in conventional computer systems, software and hardware failures will more frequently result in some anomaly that can be observed visually. When there's something wrong, the user might be able to reboot the system or power it down and start again. From a distant telephone, if any failure occurs, there will most likely not be much indication to the caller that things have gone awry. There will almost certainly be no way the caller can reboot or power down the system.

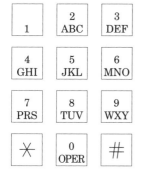

Figure 6.7 Telephone keypad.

Systemwide features

The following concepts apply to every voice processing system and should be considered in both acquisitions and new designs.

Create a polite, patient system. Machines can be intimidating devices to those who don't use them frequently. Designers and those who implement systems have a responsibility to be sensitive to this fact. An expert in any field can be intimidating if speaking harshly to a neophyte. Likewise, voice processing systems should not speak harshly to their users. Vocabulary for these systems must be designed with sensitivity and should emphasize the positive, not the negative. The system must never sound like it's scolding or judging. Tone of voice can imply disapproval, but the words themselves might also. For example, if an incorrect key is entered, the system might say, "Invalid. Enter another key." For most people it will sound less threatening to hear, "The key you entered is not valid. Please try again." Or, a system might say "The account number is wrong. Start over." Wouldn't you rather hear something like "We're unable to find that account number. Please enter it again." Or, "We don't have that account number. Please reenter." In fact, either of these responses would probably be a more correct explanation of the situation than the first one.

Interrupt speaking on key input. As users become accustomed to a system, they increasingly need to hear less and less of any given prompt. For those who have greater familiarity with computers, this phase could begin within the first few sessions. For others, it might never occur. The system should be planned to accommodate both groups, as well as all intermediate ones. A useful approach in doing this is to design prompts for users who need the most information, but couple this with the capability to stop a prompt when any Touch-Tone key is pressed. This allows those who want to hear the entire menu to do so but also satisfies those who want to skip or interrupt prompts to move things along faster.

Assign key for backup to previous message. A user looking at a display screen in a well-designed conventional system is able to easily navigate through the system from screen to screen, either forward or backward. In the most thoughtfully designed systems, there's a single key, often the Esc key, that's used to back up to the previous screen or logical operation. Thus, a user can return to the main menu by repeatedly pressing the key. Likewise, in a well-designed voice processing system, there could be a Touch-Tone key, active anytime the system is expecting Touch-Tone input, that will reactivate the previous menu, prompt, or message. If the caller loses his place, he or she can always find the way back to something familiar—if need be, the user can go all the way back to the main menu. It might also be helpful to add a menu function or define a standard key whose function is to return directly to the main menu.

Repeat message on timeout. The silence that occurs in a voice processing system is unavoidable, but it can contribute to the caller losing his or her place. Callers have nothing to look at to remind them of the next required action. However, the prompt can be spoken automatically again after a period of time. If a caller doesn't enter a key within, say, 12 or 15 seconds after a prompt, the system should timeout, repeat the prompt, and start the wait period again. If four or five timeouts occur in succession, it's reasonable for the system to assume the caller has abandoned the call and hang up.

Identify the main menu. In most conventional keyboard and screen systems, there's a central place, a hub, from which all system capabilities can be accessed. In most well-designed screen and keyboard systems, the main menu is the hub and is usually instantly recognizable. Voice processing systems also have a main menu. However, a spoken main menu is not always easily recognized. It can be useful to make the main menu's prompts distinctive, to make them different in some way from all other prompts. Try using a different voice for the main menu, or precede the main menu with an identifiable sound such as a tone or a pair of tones.

Assign standard keys. Minimize the length of spoken menus to avoid burdening callers with too many prompts to remember. However, balance this goal against the need to provide clear and complete prompts—it's much more important that prompts be stated in a meaningful way than that they be brief. A better balance can be achieved by assigning standard keys to systemwide functions that appear in every or nearly every menu—functions such as Backup to Previous Message, Return to Main Menu, End-of-Input, etc. High-quality designs are possible in which such standard operations need not be spoken in every menu but instead are stated once at the beginning or in help prompts.

Planning for data input

Data entry via Touch-Tone keypad is tricky due to lack of visual feedback and because of the small number of keys. Some data entry is complex and quite prone to error, particularly if it involves alphabetical material. Some of the following suggestions can help to avoid data entry errors.

Confirmation of critical data inputs. Decoding of Touch-Tone inputs that arrive via the public switched telephone network is an imperfect science and can easily produce an erroneous digit. Touch-Tone signals might travel through many miles of wire and be processed through many pieces of equipment before reaching their destination. Weather, equipment malfunction, and other conditions beyond human control work against the orderly transmission of such signals and often result in their distortion. Furthermore, it's not unusual for people to simply press the wrong key. The voice processing system can and should be designed to detect such occurrences and eliminate the problems that could result. For example, critical Touch-Tone inputs, after being read by the system, can be repeated verbally by the system so the caller knows exactly how the input was received. The caller can be asked to either reenter the input or to press a confirmation key. Consider the following exchange. The system says, "Please enter your personal identification number now." The caller presses four keys: one, two, three, and four. The caller then hears, "One, two, three, four. To confirm your entry, press the poundkey, or you may reenter." A more sophisticated approach is given by the following scenario. A caller has made several Touch-Tone entries as prompted by the system. The caller hears, "You wish to transfer seventy dollars from savings to checking. To complete the transfer, press one. To start over, press two." In either case, an input error or a transmission distortion would be caught and corrected before any action were taken.

Handling complicated data input schemes. A telephone Touch-Tone keypad generally has only twelve keys. It's basically a numeric keypad, even though many implementations divide most of the alphabet into groups of three letters (Q and Z are omitted) and print these letter-groups on the keys. Techniques for entering alphabetic information have been devised. For example, a two-key sequence can be used for each letter (with the 6 key assumed to contain Q and PRS and the 9 key assumed to represent Z and TUV—just where they occur in the alphabet). To enter the letter A, a caller presses the 2 key (for ABC), then the 1 key to indicate the first letter in the group. Entry of F would require depression of the 3 key twice. Another technique that avoids multiple keys for letters works very well for a specific class of applications but requires sophisticated software. This approach is particularly useful for entering names where the set of names has been enrolled (i.e., is known to the system). A caller sequentially presses the keys corresponding to the letters in the name he or she desires to enter. Because each key represents more than one letter, the input sequence is subject to redundant interpretation. However, for small name-sets, few actual redundancies will occur. When they do, they can be resolved by indicating the choices to the caller and asking the caller to select the correct one. Naturally, as the number of names in the set grows, so will the probability of redundancy and the quantity of time and system resources expended to complete the transaction.

Other schemes for entering complex data are possible, but the problem of communicating over the phone using the keypad is already difficult without further burdening the caller with an unusual combination of keys for data input. It might be possible to structure an application so that alphabetic and other complicated data inputs are not required. If that can't be done, portable extended Touch-Tone keypads can be incorporated into the design. Of course, it would be an inconvenience to have to carry an extra device, but, for some applications, that might be the most efficient solution.

Miscellaneous ideas

The following paragraphs present some additional ideas that can be employed to improve system usability.

User profiles control interface features.   Another idea is to store user profiles and use them to customize the interface for each caller. The level, number and speed of prompts, and perhaps other features can be adjusted to each caller's personal preference.

Documentation supplements for users.   Use of a caller reference guide, wallet card, and Touch-Tone template should be considered as aids to callers navigating voice processing applications via a Touch-Tone keypad. Figure 6.8 shows the front and back of a wallet card used with a scheduling application. Two different approaches to caller reference guides are given in appendix A and appendix B. The guide in appendix B is for the same voice processing system as the wallet card of Figure 6.8.

Verbal help.   Just as some conventional keyboard and screen applications offer help screens, a voice processing system can provide verbal help on demand. Concepts and features can be explained progressively in as much detail as desired. Spoken help messages can be structured in many ways, and, except for being verbal and requiring more detail, can follow approaches taken with conventional systems.

Script Design

Think of the voice processing application's vocabulary as one side of a human dialogue. A conversation can sound courteous or rude, sensitive or insensitive, harsh or mild, intimidating or considerate, happy or angry, and so on. In fact, one person in a conversation can be motivated by one emotion while the other person is feeling something quite different. So it can be with a computer dialogue: the application's voice can seem like the other half of a human dialogue—particularly if the caller is feeling intimidated or even just a little uncertain. The most effective voice processing applications tend to put a caller at ease rather than exacerbating his or her lack of confidence. Our creations, the machines we build, should not speak harshly to their

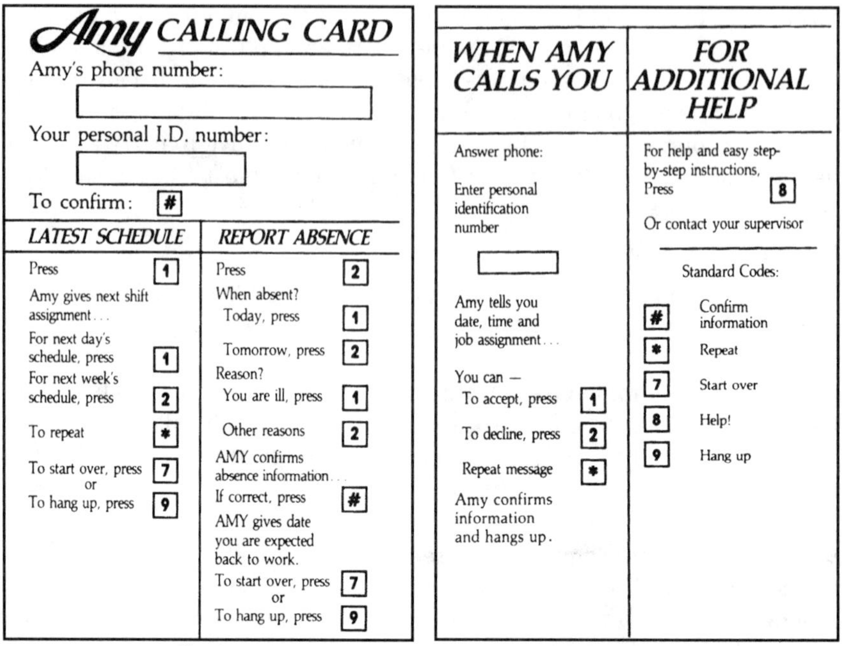

Amy CALLING CARD

Amy's phone number:

Your personal I.D. number:

To confirm: [#]

LATEST SCHEDULE	REPORT ABSENCE
Press [1]	Press [2]
Amy gives next shift assignment...	When absent?
For next day's schedule, press [1]	Today, press [1]
For next week's schedule, press [2]	Tomorrow, press [2]
To repeat [*]	Reason? You are ill, press [1]
To start over, press [7] or To hang up, press [9]	Other reasons [2]
	AMY confirms absence information.. If correct, press [#]
	AMY gives date you are expected back to work.
	To start over, press [7] or To hang up, press [9]

WHEN AMY CALLS YOU	FOR ADDITIONAL HELP
Answer phone:	For help and easy step-by-step instructions, Press [8]
Enter personal identification number	Or contact your supervisor
[ ]	Standard Codes:
Amy tells you date, time and job assignment...	[#] Confirm information
You can — To accept, press [1]	[*] Repeat
To decline, press [2]	[7] Start over
Repeat message [*]	[8] Help!
Amy confirms information and hangs up.	[9] Hang up

Front · Back

Figure 6.8 Wallet card.

users. Vocabulary for voice processing systems must be designed with sensitivity and should emphasize the positive, not the negative. The system must never sound like it's scolding or judging. As much is conveyed in the tone as in what's said. As they approach their respective parts in a project, it's essential for system developers, particularly script writers and announcers, to attain an attitude of sensitivity, caring, and respect for potential users.

A few people will resist anything new. Others will cooperate and try out a new idea until it succeeds or until they somehow become frustrated in the attempt. Probably nothing much can be done to change the minds of the people at the first extreme, but anything that can be done to enhance the friendliness of a user interface will increase the probability of its acceptance by all the others. Any extra effort to make an application sound nonthreatening, nonjudgmental, pleasant, patient, respectful, and friendly will help the users and be worth the investment. The most obvious place to begin is with design and production of that part of the system that will stand foremost in the ears and minds of users. The following sections present ideas that will help accomplish this goal—ideas concerning the design and creation of vocabulary.

Scenarios

The sound and "feel" of an application can't be entirely experienced until the application is operated on the computer and telephone. However, during design stages, development of application scenarios can give a sense of the dialogue and how it plays in given situations. Scenarios also give a feeling of an application's flow. They provide a sort of paper version of the application. Appendix C and appendix D provide examples of two different approaches to designing system scenarios. Both are real-life examples.

Prompt and menu design

Prompts and menus (lists of prompts) guide callers through the logic of an application. In a human-machine dialogue conducted over the telephone, there's no display screen to help users find their bearings once they've lost their place. From script design through final editing, prompts and menus must be carefully considered and well crafted. It's important to keep in mind during design and development that the computer's side of the dialogue must always be coherent and clearly stated. Even the least important prompt must be unambiguous. The computer, after all, is expected to be the leader, the one in charge of the process. Many details have to be considered in the accomplishment of that objective. None should be taken lightly. Comprehensive testing with prototype vocabulary should be conducted with a variety of users to test the effectiveness of script and menu design. Make changes and test again and again. When permanent vocabulary finally replaces prototype vocabulary, test the permanent vocabulary too. Also remember that permanent vocabulary is not really permanent—it can and should be changed whenever a problem with existing vocabulary is discovered.

Several ideas and features that bear on prompt and menu design are discussed in the following. All of these ideas have helped to improve the effectiveness of the systems in which they were used.

State the function before the key. Each prompt generally contains two pieces of information: the function to be performed and the Touch-Tone key for activation. If the key is stated before the function, the caller must remember that number while waiting for the rest of the prompt. For instance, consider the prompt: "Press three to hear your account balance." By the time callers comprehend the full meaning of the prompt, they might have forgotten which key to use. If callers are thinking about how to invoke a given function, they might not really hear the word "three." It's better to rephrase the prompt to read, "To hear your account balance, press three." If callers have been waiting to find out how to get their account balance, they will focus on the rest of the prompt once they hear the words "account balance."

Abbreviate prompts or speak them faster. Frequent users of an application will quickly become conversant with its scripts. They will quickly get a "feel" for the interface and might soon become frustrated with its "wordiness." Of course, they can stop the system's voice and move on at any time by typing ahead. However, at times, even the most advanced users must hear an entire prompt or two—enough to remind them what the system expects of them. Some users will find themselves wishing the system would talk faster, or move along faster. Sometimes it's appropriate to switch to abbreviated versions of prompts. With some voice hardware it's possible to articulate the vocabulary faster by filtering out some of the vocabulary data. Either approach can be used to give the impression of a faster-moving system. Consider employing a user profile record (one that can be changed by the user). Each user's competence level can be recorded here and used by the system to adapt prompts. You might think of many improvements to the idea—such as measuring the speed of responses to prompts, the frequency of type-aheads, frequency of use, elapsed time since the previous session, and so on. This information can be used to determine when to play full prompts, short prompts, or something in between.

Paraphrase prompts.   Frequent users not only become conversant with the script, they become bored with it. When people have ongoing dealings with each other, even if our day-to-day conversations remain essentially the same, we vary the words and sentences we use. It's helpful to create that same effect in voice processing systems by alternating among several differently worded versions of each prompt. This example illustrates the idea: "For your work schedule, press three," "To hear your schedule, press three," "To learn when you work, press three," and so on. It requires the production of additional vocabulary, but the payoff will be worth it.

Clearly signify the moment for user response.   We all try to create prompts that are unambiguous. However, nobody is perfect. Prompts that require a response from the caller, whether a voice or a Touch-Tone response, should clearly signal the moment at which the response is expected. It's inefficient and can be disconcerting to callers if they must discern the end of a string of prompts from nothing more than the span of silence that inevitably occurs there. That can cause users to feel that they've been left hanging. The prompt can easily be worded in a way that leaves no doubt. The following are examples: "Please enter your identification number now," and "Enter the amount now." Another idea is to sound a soft tone at the end of prompts that request user input. This is not a new idea. It's precisely what's done with telephone answering machines. Those expect only voice input, but the same concept has been extended to include Touch-Tones and has been used effectively in voice processing systems.

Limit menus to three items.   In spite of the fact that voice menus can be interrupted by typing ahead, users new to the application must hear the whole menu. Often, several prompts must be remembered before one can be selected. It's rare that a caller has a pencil and paper to write down the choices—nor should the user have to do so. It's possible to remember each component of a short menu, so those containing no more than three prompts are ideal. Occasionally it's necessary to include more choices, but this should be avoided whenever possible. Design the application with more short menus rather than a few long ones.

List most frequently used items first.   Callers typically press a Touch-Tone key to interrupt a menu when they hear the item of interest. To optimize the efficiency of the system, determine which menu items will be used most frequently and list them at the top of menus. Thus, users can move through the call faster. Not only will they find the experience more satisfying, but calls will be shorter on the average and fewer telephone lines will be needed.

Avoid repetitive form.   It's a natural tendency to use identical forms for each of the prompts in a menu. Consider the following menu. "To hear your schedule, press one. To enter your availability, press two. To report an absence, press three." It helps the caller distinguish among items when the form is varied slightly. Suppose you rephrase the menu as follows. "For your latest schedule, press one. Entering availability? Press two. If you'll miss your shift, press three." Which would you prefer to hear?

Refer to keys by number, not by letter.   It's prudent to assign Touch-Tone keys in some easy-to-remember fashion. A number of schemes will come to mind for any given menu. For instance, you could always assign the Touch-Tone key associated with the first letter of the main verb in the prompt. Accordingly, you would pick the PRS/7 key for a REPEAT function, the MNO/6 key for NO, and the ABC/2 key for an ACCOUNT BALANCE function. There are two serious problems with this idea. First, not all telephones have letters printed on or near the keys. Even when letters do appear, they're often so small that they're unreadable without lots of light (and perhaps glasses)—two items that can easily be missing during a phone call. The second problem is even more crucial. No matter how high the fidelity of the vocabulary encoding technology, no matter how well the words are enunciated, no matter how noise-free the telephone connection, it's almost impossible over the telephone for anyone to distinguish any single-syllable word that rhymes with "bee," and there are a lot of those—one-third of the English alphabet consists of such letters. Both problems are avoided if prompts refer to Touch-Tone keys by their number rather than by an alphabetic letter.

7

Hardware

This chapter introduces and discusses some of the major hardware components used in voice processing. The chapter is confined in scope to equipment or devices most often used with personal computers to create voice processing systems. My intent is to convey a top-level understanding, a broad sense of the building blocks from which voice processing systems are assembled. Because ample information on personal computers and PBXs is readily available in numerous other sources, PBXs are not discussed here.

Most PC-based voice processing systems are implemented with add-in boards that extend the computer's functions into telephonics, facsimile, speech recognition, text-to-speech, and other voice processing areas. Combinations of personal computers and boards become either general voice processing platforms or dedicated application systems, depending on what software is loaded—almost any voice processing application can be created with the software development products described in chapter 8.

Add-in boards for personal computers are created with a variety of microcircuits—chips of every description, from the most common to the very specialized. The following section introduces a few specialized microcircuits that are used most frequently in voice processing systems.

Microcircuits

As semiconductor technology advances, the space required for each transistor, gate, amplifier, and bit in memory decreases—making it possible to include in a single microcircuit more and more specialized functions. The process of miniaturization has already progressed to the point where a single chip can perform functions once requiring hundreds and thousands of components. General-purpose integrated circuits are used by the millions in today's computers, cars, VCRs, washing machines, and other intelligent consumer products. Voice processing systems also use these and dozens of special-purpose microcircuits. In most cases, the cost of voice processing products would be prohibitive were it not for a handful of specialized microcircuits that perform particular telephone and speech processing functions. Some of the more interesting of these microcircuits are discussed in the following sections.

Telecommunications

Voice processing systems include both analog and digital circuitry designed for connection to the public, switched telephone network. As could be expected, many microcircuits have become available to help with the task of interfacing to both the networks. Examples of microcircuits for these functions include incoming ring signal detectors, DTMF and pulse decoders and dialers, DTMF encoders, subscriber line control circuits, and others. Complete modems are also available as a microcircuit.

Signal processing

In an earlier chapter I described the digitization, quantization, and compression/decompression operations used in speech signal processing. Analog circuitry might be needed to interface these functions with the telephone network, but digital-to-analog and analog-to-digital conversion can be handled with microcircuits. CODECs implementing either μ-Law or A-Law companding are available, as are filters to limit the bandwidth of incoming signals. Furthermore, a number of time domain and frequency domain speech compression algorithms have been implemented in dedicated microcircuits that are used in computer add-in boards. For example, chips are available for LPC, DM, ADPCM, subband coding, and others. Of these, several different ADPCM implementations have become popular because of the advantages the technique brings to speech compression. Naturally, boards created with dedicated compression/decompression chips lack flexibility—they're unable to take advantage of improved algorithms and can't switch between compression and other signal processing functions for which they were not designed. Because of this, newer products are being designed to employ digital signal processors (DSPs) in place of dedicated compression/decompression chips. Products created with DSPs achieve greatly enhanced functionality and can be upgraded with DSP software to benefit from new technologies or improved algorithms.

Digital signal processors (DSP)

Digital signal processors are microprocessors designed to be especially efficient when executing algorithms common to realtime signal processing—and this includes the processing of speech signals. DSPs are designed to efficiently handle high-precision, high-throughput arithmetic operations that must be executed in typical signal processing algorithms such as digital filtering, fast Fourier transforms, spectrum analysis, and others. DSPs might appear to some as standard microprocessors—they usually include a generalized system interface and can be used to implement many standard applications—but they incorporate a handful of features that optimize their performance for arithmetic-intensive algorithms. They are orders of magnitude faster than normal microprocessors—especially when executing arithmetic operations.

DSPs feature very fast cycle times, a high degree of parallelism, and sophisticated arithmetic units that execute, in a single machine cycle, instructions that would require multiple cycles in a standard microprocessor. Exceptionally fast floating-point DSPs have been implemented, and some DSP chips overlap execution of several instructions, performing their operations at the same time. Instruction overlap can be particularly helpful with floating-point operations. Multiplication, crucial to sum-of-products algorithms executed frequently in signal-processing algorithms, is given special attention and occupies an extraordinary percentage of DSP chip area to assure that high-precision products can be obtained in no more than one machine cycle. Most DSPs use a Harvard architecture featuring separate buses for data and instructions. This enables them to simultaneously fetch data operands and instructions—which reside in separate address spaces. Some DSPs have as many as eight separate buses to permit an even higher degree of fetch overlapping. In addition to multiple internal buses, some chips feature eight or more registers or accumulators and multiple input/output ports. High precision is obtained through the use of wide registers and wide buses—32-bit operands leading to 64-bit results are not uncommon today and can be expected to increase in later DSP designs. These high-precision results are especially important in recursive calculations where round-off errors accumulate with each iteration.

Specialized instructions are also used to optimize signal processing operations. For instance, at least one DSP design implements a single cycle compound instruction that loads an operand for multiplication, shifts it to a second location in memory, and performs the multiplication. This combination of operations is used often in numerical solutions of differential equations. Another special instruction sets an overflow mode that results in a register being set to its maximum value on numeric overflow instead of changing the register's sign-bit (which is the usual course of action and produces a register value inordinately different from the expected result). Some overflows can thus be ignored, and those that can't still might not require recalculation.

There are numerous examples of improvements in signal processing that are directly attributable to DSPs. Call progress analysis can reach levels of sophistication that were unachievable in the past. Comprehensive DTMF detection programs have been developed that make DSPs vastly superior to dedicated chips for detection and discrimination of incoming DTMF signals over noisy channels and during outgoing speech production. Switching and conferencing is much more easily performed by DSPs processing digital signals for multiple telephone channels: bit streams for affected calls are simply rearranged or replicated. DSP-based add-in boards can alternately perform as compression/decompression devices, data modems, facsimile machines, and others. Programs can be loaded from ROM or downloaded from external RAM to instantaneously carry out changes in the chip's function. This feature brings a very powerful advantage to DSP-based add-in boards. Programs, for example, for DTMF generation, ADPCM compression, call-progress monitoring, DTMF detection, text-to-speech, speaker verification, delta modulation compression, or any of a number of other speech-processing tasks can be loaded whenever needed—and replaced an instant later if necessary. A board can be a speech decompression engine one instant and execute voice recognition the next. Speech-processing boards designed with one or more DSPs achieve a flexibility of operation not even considered only a few years ago.

Portable, special-purpose speech DSP

Text-to-speech and other speech technologies are used in a number of consumer products, including toys, automobiles, and calculators. Handheld dictionaries, language translators, games, and palm-top computers also feature text-to-speech. Many of these products operate on battery power and so must be designed with lightweight devices that are low-cost, have reduced cubic-volume, and don't consume much power. Conventional DSP chips don't conform to these requirements—they are met, however, by a special-purpose DSP chip optimized for LPC speech processing. As with all DSPs, the chip is capable of high-speed, high-precision multiplication, but the design has been streamlined. Features and functions not crucial to LPC algorithms have been eliminated. The special chip implements a vocal tract model (it converts LPC-compressed speech to digital waveforms) and is used in a variety of products. The chip offers the same quality synthetic voice output as full-featured DSPs and is also capable of producing LPC-compressed speech from prerecorded human voice data stored off-chip.

Text-to-speech applications employ a separate conventional processor (whose software resides in ROM) for conversion of text to parameters. The vocal tract model is implemented with the LPC-optimized DSP. Text-to-speech in different languages is obtained by changing ROMs. For LPC recorded human voice, a separate ROM can be used. Text-to-speech ROMs are available for English, Spanish, French, and other languages.

Figure 7.1 shows an example speech system using the special-purpose, LPC-specific DSP. The figure could represent any battery-powered pocket

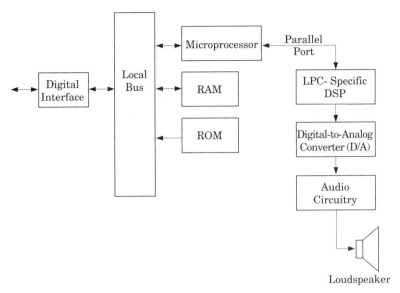

Figure 7.1 Voice processing system with LPC-specific DSP.

translator or dictionary with a digital interface for keypad input and LED display output. The ROM contains appropriate software for either text-to-parameter processing or for selecting and transmitting stored LPC speech parameters to the custom DSP. Choice of ROM determines whether text-to-speech or LPC-compressed human speech is used and which natural language is supported. The same diagram can represent other systems. Consider, for instance, a vehicle's on-board annunciator communicating by radio transmitter or satellite downlink. In this example, the audio circuitry and speaker in the figure might be replaced by the vehicle's own radio.

Personal Computer Add-in Boards

Voice processing systems based in personal computers are composed of the computer with one or more add-in boards installed in the computer's bus. These components extend the computer's operation into most of the disciplines collectively known as telecommunications. The add-in boards enable the computer to interface with telephone networks, digitize and compress speech signals, detect and decode rotary and DTMF digits, decompress speech data, convert text to speech signals, recognize spoken utterances, transmit and receive facsimile data, and other functions. A variety of software is available to support individual add-in boards and systems assembled from them. The boards most commonly used in voice processing are discussed in the following section.

Telephone/voice boards

Add-in boards designed for speech applications that connect to telephone networks are variously called voice processing systems, voice cards, audio boards, audio adapters, audio voice adapters, voice communications systems, communications cards, voice processing platforms, or simply circuit cards. In this book, all such add-in boards are referred to as *telephone/voice boards* or *telephone/voice cards*. All are designed to be installed in a computer bus and to interface to analog or digital telephone networks (either directly or via other add-in cards). Telephone/voice boards are available from numerous manufacturers and vary somewhat in capability. Some use dedicated compression/decompression chips; others employ digital signal processors. All feature at least one on-board control processor. Some might attach only to the analog telephone network, others only to the digital network. Still others connect to either one through appropriate interface boards. Some handle only one telephone line (or channel), while others handle dozens. Board makers offer selections from single channel cards up through products capable of interfacing several dozen channels. Boards from a single manufacturer are usually upwardly compatible so that software developed for fewer lines can be easily adapted to run on cards with more lines. Most boards can be installed in a computer in multiples to extend the number of lines serviced—the total being dependent upon the complexity of the application, the power (speed) of the computer's processor, the size and speed of the disk subsystem, and the number of bus slots available.

Most telephone/voice boards are registered with the Federal Communications Commission (FCC) because they might produce radio frequency emissions and might interfere with radio and television reception. Such interference, however, is almost never a problem if the system is located at an appropriate distance from radio and television sets. General discussions concerning the functionality, interfaces, and architecture of telephone/voice boards follow.

Functions. Telephone/voice cards install in a computer bus and, when used with a driver and other support software, enable the computer to manage one or more telephone lines (sometimes as many as 24 or more). Most systems support multiple boards. Telephone/voice cards thus provide real-time control for dozens of lines from the telephone company central office or from a PBX or key system. These cards can invoke many functions. Telephone/voice boards also digitize and compress speech and other signals. Compressed data are passed to the computer for storage in memory or on disk. Likewise, telephone/voice boards decompress speech data and place resulting signals on a telephone line. They also handle telephony functions such as ring detect, pulse dialing, tone dialing, offhook or onhook, DTMF encoding and detection, and call progress monitoring. Some multi-

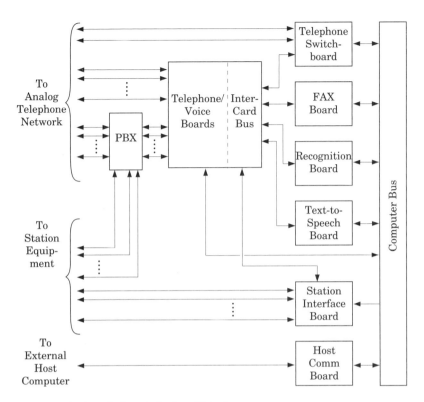

Figure 7.2 Analog telephone/voice board interfaces.

function telephone/voice cards also perform voice recognition tasks and might include text-to-speech, FAX, and data modem capability. Many boards that don't themselves possess these additional capabilities are able to cooperate with other special-function cards that do.

Figures 7.2 and 7.3 depict voice processing system configurations with telephone/voice cards and other telephone devices. The figures are meant to be representative only, and many other configurations are possible. Activities of systems composed of a telephone/voice card and other special function boards are coordinated by software. Communication between the telephone/voice board and specialty boards might be via software and the computer's bus, but some boards also feature a board-to-board digital bus for control and communication.

Operational overview. When a voice processing system is booted, application software initializes all installed telephone/voice boards. During operations, a ring on any line is detected by the board and causes a hardware interrupt to the computer. Code in the board's computer-resident driver is

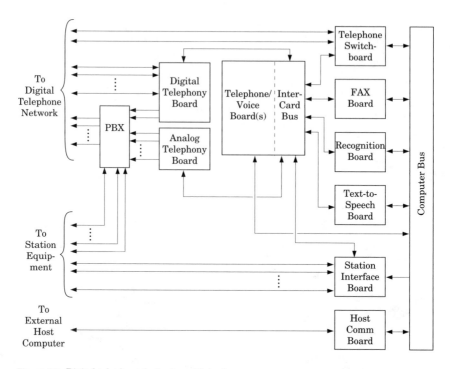

Figure 7.3 Digital telephone/voice board interfaces.

alerted and determines the cause of the interrupt by reading status registers on the board. The driver places an appropriate notification in an event queue. When a telephone line is idle, the computer's application software pays no attention to it other than to periodically poll the event queue to see if the line needs attention (e.g., an incoming ring has occurred or the application requires a line for an outbound call). When a ring occurs, for instance, the hardware interrupt leads to execution of a program that takes the line offhook, determines whether the call comes from a person, and speaks a greeting to the caller.

Typically, a voice processing application, after speaking its greeting, asks the caller to select a system function from a menu of choices. While waiting for a key to be pressed, the software goes about its tasks, handling other lines, monitoring the online keyboard, or just repeatedly polling the event queue. Certain events occurring on the board (e.g., DTMF digits received, incoming ring detected, speaking finished, recording finished, line onhook, line offhook, etc.) cause FIFO entries in the event queue. While speaking, the computer passes speech data buffers to the board as needed, usually alternating between a pair of memory buffers, filling one while the other is accessed by the board. The reverse is true when recording. A pair of buffers are alternately filled by the board and moved into RAM or written to disk by the computer. These processes might take place on all lines simultaneously and are driven by board-generated hardware interrupts that occur whenever a buffer is emptied during speaking or filled during recording. In this way, all boards' processes can continue asynchronously in an apparently simultaneous fashion.

Interfaces. A telephone/voice board communicates with the computer in which it's installed, the telephone network, and perhaps with other add-in boards. At installation or at startup, certain options must be defined for each board. For example, hardware and software interrupts must be specified. Shared memory addresses and buffer lengths are required by support software. Some boards also require certain telephony defaults to be selected (e.g., whether loop start or ground start is to be used and whether lines are put onhook or taken offhook at power-up). These and other parameter settings might be determined by DIP switch or jumper settings on the board or, in some cases, specified to the board's driver software at startup.

Information exchange between the computer and the card takes place in response to hardware interrupts via the computer's bus (which also supplies power to the card). The bus carries data and control information that might be organized as input/output exchanges or as DMA or shared memory accesses. A telephone/voice board might include dual-ported RAM that's accessible via the bus by both the computer and the card. Either can write to or read from the shared RAM. When either device writes to this memory, an interrupt is issued to the other. In this way communication via the bus can be conducted asynchronously by either computer or telephone/voice board. Support code in the computer, for example, might instruct the card to playback, record, dial an outbound call, or go onhook or offhook. Likewise, the board can notify the computer when it needs service. It might tell the computer that a buffer is empty or full, that DTMF digits have been received, or that dialing is complete. It can signify that recording or playback is finished, ringing is detected, and whether or not loop current is present (e.g., whether a caller is still on the line). It can also notify the computer of changes in hook status or call progress status.

Some vendors provide means of communicating between the various boards in their own product lines; interboard telephone communications are also possible with selected products from different makers. Both digital and analog intercard communications have been implemented. A digital interface called MultiVendor Integration Protocol (MVIP) has been defined for telephone-related devices using IBM-PC/AT compatible buses. MVIP is hoped by some to become a standard for interchange of telephone information between products from different vendors.

MVIP specifies sixteen 2.048 Mbps serial data streams. Each stream can carry 32 channels at 64 Kbps for a total of 512 separate 64 Kbps channels.

A 40-conductor ribbon cable interconnects devices on the bus and is totally contained within the computer's enclosure. The MVIP specification also requires call switching elements to be distributed among various MVIP-capable devices—with switching control centralized in software that resides in the computer. MVIP is supported by numerous manufacturers and is able to interconnect telephone/voice systems, FAX, speech recognition, T1, and other telephony-related boards. MVIP and similar protocols enable integrators to bring diverse products from individual suppliers together in a single system; they enable economical integrated solutions to voice processing requirements. In the figures of this chapter, MVIP and similar buses are labeled "InterCard Bus."

Telephone/voice boards connect to the public switched telephone network. Part of their function involves controlling or monitoring signaling and switching activities taking place on these lines. Attachment might be to the analog network, or it might be to the digital network. Boards with 12 or more telephone ports might require auxiliary boards for interface to a telephone network, and attachment details differ for analog and digital. Early telephone/voice boards are designed exclusively for the analog network, with each board able to handle only a few lines. Circuitry allowing attachment directly to the phone network or to a PBX or phone system is contained on the board. Later boards, however, provide circuitry for many more lines, so telephone interface circuitry might have been omitted. If so, these boards require an external telephony interface; separate boards are available for analog, T1, European CEPT, and U.S. and European ISDN primary rate interfaces. An advantage is gained with such boards because, with separate interface cards, a single telephone/voice board can service either voiceband or any of the various digital services.

Architecture. Telephone/voice boards are manufactured by several different vendors. Almost every manufacturer offers a product line that includes boards for connection to the analog telephone network. Some also have products for interconnection to the digital telephone network and also offer a host of accessory products that support their telephone/voice board offerings. Furthermore, each item in a product line is designed with a specific form factor (e.g., for a specific computer bus). Those designed with a PC/AT form factor will not work in a microchannel machine, and vice versa. Some of the earlier boards are designed for a single line. Four-line analog boards are used in hundreds of systems. Telephone/voice boards designed for the digital network typically support a dozen or so lines but require separate boards for connection to the telephone network (telephony interface cards are described later in this chapter).

Figure 7.4 shows the structure of a typical telephone/voice board for connection to the analog switched telephone network. The board that's depicted features three or more telephone channels and one dedicated com-

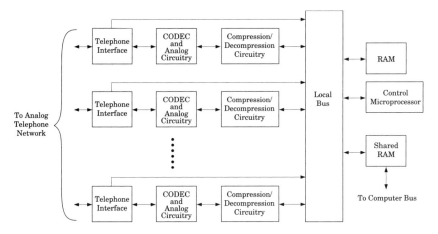

Figure 7.4 Telephone/voice board with analog telephone interface.

pression microcircuit per channel. The telephone interface circuitry for each line connects to voiceband telephone circuits from a central office, PBX, or other telephone system. Telephone interfaces generally provide transient protection, isolation of RFI (radio frequency interference), ring detection, loop current detection, and other features. Input signals are digitized and compressed before storage in the shared RAM, where they can be accessed over the computer's bus. The card's on-board microprocessor supervises interleaved movement, storage, and distribution of digital data. It also handles most communication with the computer. Some boards have a similar architecture but substitute audio output in place of connection to telephone circuits. These boards are designed for nontelephone applications—for instance, educational or training applications that record or recognize speech input via local microphone and that speak through a loudspeaker.

Figure 7.5 shows the major functions and components of analog telephone/voice boards in which the functions of dedicated compression/decompression chips (as used in the system shown in Figure 7.4) are handled instead by one or more DSPs. There are many advantages to this architecture, but the principal one is the flexibility it achieves. The system is able to alter its operation simply by changing DSP programs. Such architectures (or variations of them) are capable of performing typical telephone/voice board functions but might also execute speech recognition, text-to-speech conversion, or facsimile operations. These architectures might also function as data modems. A multiplexer, whose job is to interleave digital data from multiple bit-streams, might not be required. Some implementations of this architecture dedicate a separate DSP to each telephone line, which can each run its own private speech-processing algorithms.

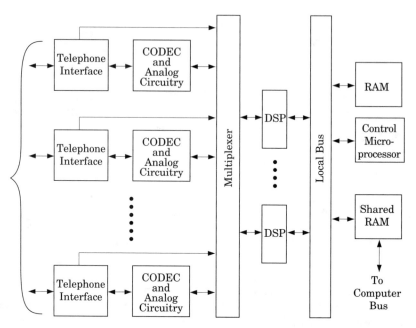

Figure 7.5 Telephone/voice board with DSPs and analog telephone interface.

As the number of lines handled by a telephone/voice board increases, more and more board real estate is required for telephony circuitry—and there are economic advantages that go with systems with more lines. Microcomputers have a limited number of slots for add-in boards, so board makers try to maximize the number of lines per slot handled by their boards. An approach taken by several board designers is to isolate telephone interfaces from signal processing functions by placing the former on separate boards. This architecture has the added benefit of permitting boards with many processing channels to be front-ended by different telephony interface cards—one for analog and one for digital, for example. Figure 7.6 gives an architecture for telephone/voice boards adopting this approach. Notice that telephony might conveniently interface via an intercard bus (such as MVIP discussed previously). The number of telephone channels supported by such an architecture depends on a number of factors: the capacities of the intercard and local buses, number of DSPs, speed of the on-board microprocessor, transfer rate of the computer's disk system, speed of the computer's processor, complexity of voice processing applications being supported, and a multitude of software factors. Products exist that support from one to several dozen lines using this architecture. Telephony interfaces for these products are discussed in the following sections.

Telephony interfaces

A variety of telephony interface functions might be packaged as add-in boards (or even as daughterboards on add-in boards). Some interface functions that have been implemented include direct-inward-dialing, multifrequency signaling (in support of automatic number identification an called-party number identification), rotary-to-DTMF conversion, conference bridging, and others. However, of greatest interest are those add-in cards used with a telephone/voice board's intercard bus to provide connection to analog and digital telephone networks. These and other devices are covered in the following.

Analog network interface. Telephone/voice boards like that depicted in Figure 7.6 are intended primarily for interface to the digital telephone network. They typically support a large number of telephone channels. Boards of this type from some manufacturers can also be connected to the analog network by means of a special card like the Analog Telephony Interface board diagrammed in Figure 7.7. Telephone inputs from multiple analog voiceband channels are digitized, and the PCM data is multiplexed and formatted on an intercard bus where they're routed to telephone/voice boards via ribbon ca-

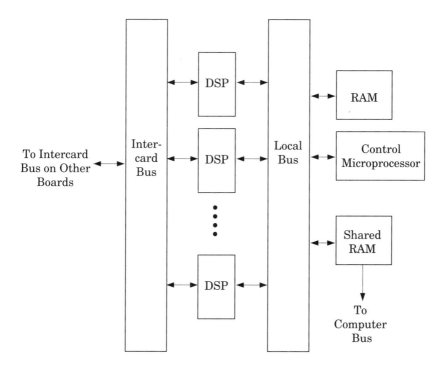

Figure 7.6 Telephone/voice board with digital telephone interface.

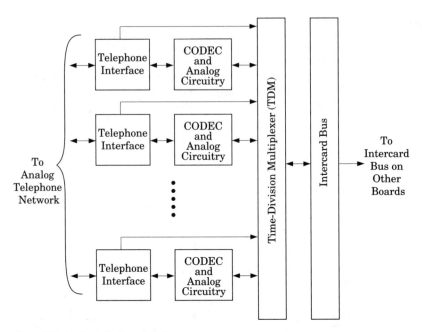

Figure 7.7 Analog telephony interface.

ble. Outbound calls can also be processed. Analog telephony boards can be configured for attachment to a dozen or more trunks and can offer a selection of physical line connections. Although these cards are installed in the computer, they might require only power from the computer's bus.

Digital network interface. Telephone/voice boards whose telephony interface terminates in an intercard bus (like those depicted in Figure 7.6) can be connected to the digital telephone network. A special card, a digital telephony interface (Figure 7.8) can be used to interconnect a telephone/voice board to the digital network through their respective intercard bus connectors. Typically, the digital connection is structured for T1 digital trunks, but boards are also available with E1 (European CEPT) or ISDN primary or basic rate interfaces. Sometimes the digital interface card takes the place of a channel bank. Some perform the functions of a channel service unit. A logic array on the board formats the bit streams from digital channels, demultiplexing and multiplexing them for insertion onto the intercard bus. Reverse processes are performed for outgoing calls. Power for these devices is taken from the computer's bus.

Digital-to-analog telephone/voice boards. Figure 7.9 shows a card configured as a digital network interface to telephone/voice boards (of the type shown in Figure 7.4). The card in Figure 7.9 is intended to interface analog circuits to the digital network. Digital telephone formats are demultiplexed to split off individual calls. These are converted to analog in the CODEC and passed on to analog ports on telephone/voice boards. These conversions are reversed for outbound calls. Composite boards composed of combinations of interfaces have also been implemented. For example, features of interfaces shown in Figures 7.8 and 7.9 can be combined to support drop and insert applications where calls on a digital network can be transparently tapped off to analog telephone/voice boards while also being passed on to separate digital interfaces.

Station interfaces. Figure 7.10 shows a card designed to interface multiple telephone stations to systems using an intercard bus. For example, the MVIP bus mentioned earlier for PC-AT form-factor computers carries digital data for as many as 256 calls. Boards such as those represented by Figure 7.10 could route any of those 256 conversations to any of its stations. Conversely, calls originating on any of the station sets can be distributed onto any of the MVIP's 256 call positions. An external dc power source might be required for station interface boards.

Switches and conference bridges. Many of the boards described above are capable of call switching and conferencing—particularly those that deal with calls on a digital intercard bus that multiplexes data streams for multiple calls (sometimes hundreds of them). Switching or conferencing can be performed by rearranging or duplicating data streams as they're inserted or

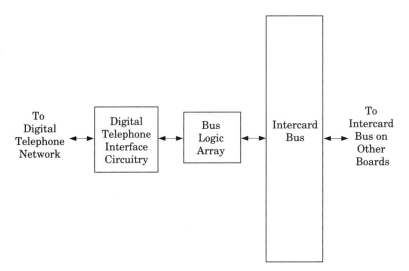

Figure 7.8 Digital telephony interface.

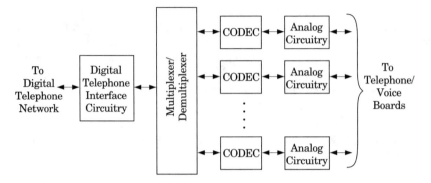

Figure 7.9 Digital-to-analog telephony interface.

removed during multiplexing or demultiplexing. Refer again to Figures 7.7 and 7.9 and try to imagine how these devices can be used for call switching and conferencing. Other implementations are available for switching or conferencing audio signals between the analog network and a collection of analog devices.

Speech recognition

Many interesting nontelephone speech recognition applications have been developed: voice-activated typewriters (VAT), dictation machines, PC application voice-command devices, and other computer keyboard alternatives. Some speech recognition hardware products are sold as computer external devices, while others are intended for installation in a PC; all provide voice input by microphone. Dictation applications, such as VAT, are available with PC add-in speech-to-text cards as speaker-dependent, isolated-word systems with active vocabularies that can range beyond 30,000 words and phrases. These systems are based on hardware dedicated to recognition tasks and require a high-performance PC with a large hard disk and a lot of RAM.

Telephone-based recognition. Our primary interest, though, is recognition hardware intended for use with voice mail, interactive voice response, and other telephone-based voice processing systems. In these contexts, speech recognition can extend system services to rotary telephone users and enhance Touch-Tone interfaces. These products have all been expressly designed for telephone use where speech arrives as a narrowband signal after being transmitted over an oftentimes noisy channel. As discussed in an earlier chapter, recognition of speech from signals received under these circumstances requires more rigorous processing algorithms. Those restrictions notwithstanding, a number of acceptable products have appeared in the marketplace. Some of them are not hardware products at all but, rather, are implemented as software added to existing DSP-based telephone/voice boards. When such boards also support an intercard bus (such as MVIP), they can be connected to and used as a speech recognition resource with other telephone/voice cards.

Either speaker-dependent or speaker-independent recognition can be implemented, and some recognizers even feature realtime speaker adaption. Structured to take the place of DTMF inputs in voice-processing systems, telephone-based recognizers handle continuous digits from zero through nine in addition to a collection of discreetly spoken commands such as "yes," "no," "cancel," "start," "stop," etc. With some products, as many as 50 isolated words or phrases can be recognized at a single prompt—this compares well with the three or four Touch-Tone selections recommended at each prompt for DTMF input. Because continuous recognition means more demanding algorithms, restrictions (such as fewer channels of recognition) might be imposed with continuous digit software. User-defined commands can be recognized in conjunction with standard ones provided by the manufacturer. Some recognizers are field-trainable, and others are speaker-adaptable. Preparation of speaker-independent recognition data requires that hundreds of individuals of both sexes with di-

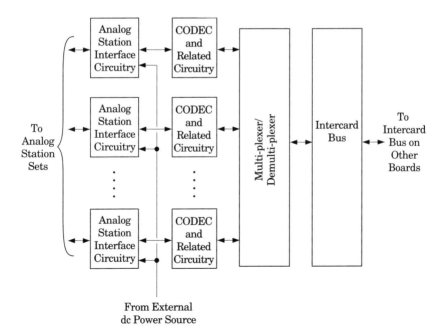

Figure 7.10 Station interface.

verse regional dialects record individual training utterances over the telephone in a balanced number of local and long-distance calls. Recorded materials are processed to produce recognition data that's made available to the recognizer at runtime. Standard vocabularies are provided by manufacturers (often in different regional dialects) for many languages, including English, French, Spanish, German, Japanese, and others. Dedicated off-the-shelf vocabularies are sold by vendors for voice-mail commands, colors, clothing sizes, and dates. Many variations of standard vocabularies in any language are possible.

Hardware configurations. Dedicated hardware recognition products tend to be self-contained, requiring very little from the computer other than downloading software and commands necessary for operation and control. A memory-resident driver is usually installed for using applications and system software. Via the driver, system parameters (such as audio gain or timeout periods) can be changed. Many channels of speaker-dependent or speaker-independent recognition can be available on a single board— though often daughterboards must be added. Most vendors support the use of multiple boards in a system, and a typical configuration might allow a ratio of one recognition channel for each four telephone lines—the recognition channels being shared as needed and released when not needed. Depending on computer specifications, thousands of users can be enrolled for a speaker-dependent system. Communication between recognition cards and telephone/voice boards might be by intercard bus, but some cards feature an audio interface.

Operation. A voice processing system substituting recognition in place of some or all Touch-Tone inputs first delivers its prompt (e.g., "Please enter your personal identification number now.") then instantly, seamlessly, and transparently switches to recognition. Switching can be accomplished between hardware devices or by invoking different software in a board's DSP. If training and/or enrollment of subscribers is required (as for speaker-dependent recognizers), that will be accomplished beforehand. The recognition system continuously monitors the input signal until speech (or other audio activity) is present. When recognition occurs, control is returned to the using application (which chooses its next step based upon the caller's response). With some products, after an utterance is recognized, more than one candidate result (with rankings or confidence factors) are output, and the application is called upon to resolve ambiguous results. Most recognizers interrupt their outgoing prompts the moment something is said by a caller. Some products actually perform recognition while outgoing prompts are being spoken, but others only determine that inbound speech is present without understanding what's said.

Performance of recognizers varies widely and depends upon many factors: vocabulary, hardware, telephone network, makeup of the user group, and others. Not all of these factors are within control of system developers.

Speaker verification. Many experts agree that each person possesses a personal voice "signature" that can be recognized by analysis of the person's *voice-print* (a sample signal produced from speech). The process of analyzing speech signals to verify that a person is who he or she claims to be is called *speaker verification* and, with some systems, it can be accomplished simultaneously with recognition over the telephone. The speech signature of a caller who is asked to say a personal identification number (PIN) or other digit string can be checked against the speech signature stored at prior enrollment. Not only can the PIN be tested for validity, but the caller's own voice can be tested as well. Not all recognition boards are able to perform verification, but those that can require an enrollment session in which the person speaks a digit string or other identifying phrase several times. Claims have been made by designers of these systems that instances of both authorized user rejection and casual impostor acceptance occur less than two percent of the time.

Facsimile (FAX)

FAX add-in boards can be purchased for use with other voice processing functions. Integration of facsimile hardware and software with voice processing systems makes possible a host of automatic, multiline, hard-copy store-and-forward and delivery services. Hard-copy images can be stored in databases and transmitted to FAX machines or other FAX-capable computers automatically or on command. Images in a FAX database might be computer-generated text or graphics; computer-stored images can be input from a FAX or other scanner or might be transmitted from other computers. Once stored in a voice processing system, images can be reformatted and communicated via the public switched telephone network to other computers or to FAX machines anywhere in the world. Transmissions can be scheduled in advance to occur at a later time, or they can be requested to be sent immediately. Calls to a busy FAX machine can be redirected to a voice processing system for storage and later forwarding of images.

Callers to an integrated system can identify by Touch-Tone (or voice) input the documents they wish sent to their FAX machines. Documents can be broadcast to many FAX machines (or FAX-capable computers); distribution lists can be input online or by phone. FAX mailboxes that operate in a similar manner to voice mailboxes can be established for users. Documents in a FAX mailbox can be retrieved by phone—either directly in that call or by transmission to another FAX phone number. Furthermore, documents in FAX mailboxes can be protected by system security features like those used in voice-mail systems. In fact, through integrated services, FAX and voice mailboxes can be logically related so that a caller requesting delivery (by FAX) of documents already in his or her FAX mailbox, might also hear annotated voice messages. Or, the caller might receive notification in his or her voice mailbox of the arrival of documents in his or her FAX mailbox. Users might also receive a voice message (or FAX message) confirming delivery of an outgoing FAX or voice message.

Add-in FAX cards for popular computer buses are readily available from numerous manufacturers—some of these are also capable of operation as a data modem. With these products, FAX images and data can be transmitted at various rates up to 9,600 baud. Multiple FAX boards can be installed to create systems capable of handling FAX on many lines simultaneously, and FAX operations can occur at the same time as voice processing functions on other lines. Connection of telephone lines to the FAX board might be by RJ-11 connector, and often a spare jack enables use of a local telephone. Or, on some boards, calls might be routed on an intercard bus. Basic FAX functions are similar for all FAX add-in boards, although options and extras vary. Some DSP-based telephone/voice boards are available with optional FAX DSP software—saving the cost of a dedicated FAX board and freeing one bus slot for other uses.

FAX boards, like all other special hardware, require support software and are delivered with, at minimum, a memory-resident driver. Development toolkits and application generators might also support particular FAX equipment. FAX software runs as a background process, allowing normal operations to proceed simultaneously. Software features include automatic dialing, redial of busy numbers, and scheduling of transmissions. Software might also support maintenance of distribution lists, broadcast dialing, management and status reports, and the ability to edit images before or after transmission.

Text-to-speech

Today, most systems that are capable of text-to-speech are created by porting software to a DSP-based telephone/voice board, rather than requiring dedicated add-in boards. In the following section, I consider both dedicated text-to-speech boards and text-to-speech software running on off-the-shelf telephone/voice boards.

Telephone/voice boards with text-to-speech software. Most of the work done by text-to-speech synthesizers is accomplished by software. Hardware is required, of course, as in all computer-based processes. In fact, text-to-speech software can be run on almost any PC, provided it has sufficient RAM and meets other minimal requirements—but to talk, digital speech parameters produced by those software algorithms must be processed through hardware implementing a vocal-tract model. Most DSP-based telephone/ voice boards can be used to implement a vocal-tract model and so can be used to implement software-based text-to-speech functions. Board manufacturers who wish to include this capability in their products must license software from one of the few text-to-speech software developers.

Several open-architecture, multiline telephone/voice boards are available with text-to-speech. Those that also feature an intercard bus can be used either as an integrated voice processing utility or as a dedicated text-to-speech device under control of another telephone/voice board. Some products offer integrated voice processing functions such as recorded-voice, FAX, speech recognition, data communications, and text-to-speech.

Dedicated text-to-speech boards. There are only a handful of dedicated text-to-speech add-in card products available—software-based systems being the preferred approach. One offering, though, is a single channel card that receives text from a computer via a serial interface, converts it to voice, and outputs it on a telephone line. The card performs standard telephone interface functions such as auto-answer and DTMF generation and detection. It's also capable of outbound calling.

Multiple, simultaneous text-to-speech channels are possible on a single PC card. Figure 7.11 is a diagram of a product with three 20-MHz microprocessors that convert text to ADPCM in realtime on 16 channels. The control processor performs bookkeeping and text-to-parameter processing for all 16 channels. Results are passed in shared RAM to two DSP processors, where the vocal tract models for eight channels each are implemented. Compressed waveforms are passed back to the PC in RAM buffers

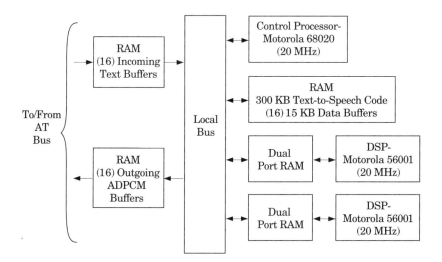

Figure 7.11 AT form-factor board for 16 channels of text-to-speech.

(8 KB each—two seconds of ADPCM speech). The control processor runs under a multitasking system, so text-to-speech code in the local RAM is re-entrant. Each text-to-speech task maintains a dedicated 15 KB data buffer in local RAM. With faster components, this design is able to handle more channels of text-to-speech in realtime. Such a board can be used in multi-line voice processing systems with text-to-speech channels either dedicated on a per-line basis or shared among many lines.

Common features.   Regardless of whether text-to-speech is implemented on a dedicated, single function card or as software downloaded to a general-purpose telephone/voice board, regardless of whether the implementation features human diphone concatenation or 100 percent synthesized voice, text-to-speech features available to users for control of voices don't differ much. Some of the most important features are discussed in the following.

All implementations use an exception dictionary that allows any word to be given a custom pronunciation. Users are able to add any word or abbreviation to the exception dictionary along with its preferred phonemic transcription. The dictionary is searched for each word and, if found, its phonemic transcription is taken from the dictionary instead of being algorithmically derived from the text. The system is thus able to force an interpretation and pronunciation on any input.

Speech delivery can be affected by inserting control characters into the input text stream. Some default parameters can be set or changed in this way. Among these are *gain* (loudness) and speaking rate. Some systems even permit gain of unvoiced speech to be increased or decreased relative to voiced speech. Faster or slower speaking rates can be an advantage in some applications. For example, when scanning a passage of text, a FAX or E-mail message might not need to be understood in its entirety, and a faster speaking rate could be a convenience. When the portions of interest are located, a slower, more comfortable rate of speech can be selected.

Other options can be selected. Punctuation in text cues the processor to insert pauses in spoken output. The length of such pauses can be adjusted to suit personal taste. A spelling mode can be invoked, causing each letter of every word to be spoken individually. In the same vein, every digit can be spoken individually rather than being formatted and said as a dollar amount, day of the month, or numerical value. The system can be set to speak all punctuation marks, including tabs, spaces, and carriage returns. A further feature allows expansion of arithmetic equations so that, for example, a string of the form "12*123/2" would be spoken as "twelve times one hundred and twenty three divided by two." Another feature enables acronyms to be pronounced as though they were a word—normal operation is to spell acronyms appearing as capital letters. This optional feature, for instance, would force the construct "ASCII" to be pronounced "ass-key" rather than being spelled out.

Some features are particularly valuable during system debugging but others can be used to improve (or correct) pronunciation. *Homographs* (words whose meaning is changed with pronunciation even though they have the same spelling) such as bow, wind, read, minute, project, entrance and duplicate are ordinarily pronounced according to their most common usage. This default can be overridden and the word's least common form used instead. Pauses can be inserted anywhere in a text, and stress can be increased or decreased to give certain words or syllables greater or less emphasis.

Some of the variations that can be controlled affect the sound and quality of the voice produced. Obviously, text-to-speech implementations that employ segments of human recorded speech exhibit the general character and sound of the original human speaker—even so, some characteristics can be varied. Fully synthetic speech can be controlled to a greater extent. The speaker's sex can be chosen and either male or female voices produced. Voices can be made to whisper or to speak with special effects. Average pitch of a voice can be moved up or down and its dynamic range expanded or contracted. The size of a speaker's head affects the way the voice sounds, and some implementations offer options to define that feature.

Text-to-speech boards, either dedicated or general telephone/voice cards, can be used with a variety of natural languages. The language spoken usually depends on software and stored data, so different languages can be easily swapped. Most of the following languages can be spoken by products that are easily obtainable in the marketplace: American English, British English, French, Belgian, Flemish, Dutch, German, Spanish, Korean, Japanese, Malay, Thai, Cantonese, and Mandarin.

Peripheral Text-to-Speech Products

Some applications for speech synthesis are most properly addressed with *peripheral devices*, external equipment that attaches to a computer and has its own power but is not independently programmable. Some manufacturers offer systems composed of one or more text-to-speech boards. These are rack-mounted or packaged in an enclosure with its own power supply and are interfaced to a computer via serial communications. Controls for the product are sent via the RS-232 communication link. These peripherals might either attach to a telephone line (or lines) or might operate as an annunciator (output speech through a loudspeaker). In general, the features and controls applicable with these synthesis products are the same or similar to those with text-to-speech add-in boards.

System-Level Products

Thousands of operational voice processing systems have been developed with the equipment and products covered in this chapter. Collectively, these systems answer or initiate thousands upon thousands of calls every hour. Many of them run single-purpose applications, but many others integrate various voice processing functions—some even participate as nodes in local area networks. An assemblage of hardware components doesn't make a system—it must be complemented with software before it can accomplish anything useful. Development projects using the equipment described in this chapter are aided and enhanced with an impressive array of software development products. (Development software is covered in chapter 8.)

With the advent of DSP-based boards, powerful development tools, and comprehensive support software, a developer can easily include speech recognition, speaker verification, voice output, text-to-speech, facsimile, data communication, and other technologies in a single system. Furthermore, voice input and output can be conducted with a choice of compression rates to adjust to differing circumstances—and, it's possible for all this to be provided in a single add-in board. As a result, multimedia applications are no longer uncommon. Integrated systems incorporate interactive voice response, voice mail, FAX, and even E-mail into a single platform; such systems offer powerful capabilities and appear to be broadly welcomed in the marketplace.

8

Development Software

In this chapter, I'll discuss software that's used by system developers to create voice processing applications. I'll cover both runtime modules and software development tools that are specific to the voice processing industry. I'll discuss voice processing device drivers, multitasking executives, development toolkits, application generators, and speech editors. Because use of the personal computer as a platform for voice processing systems has become prevalent, I'll target my discussions to software that's intended for the microcomputer. Except for matters of scale, most of the ideas and concepts covered here are applicable in a general way to implementations on larger computer systems.

There are only a limited number of ways to produce the software for a voice processing application. Conventional methods of software development, assembly and higher-level languages, are always available to experienced programmers—but, as I'll explain in this chapter, those approaches are probably not the most effective ones for voice processing applications. The crucial topics covered in this chapter are those pertaining to voice processing development toolkits and to application generators. However, before either of these can be applied, other software must be available to the developer. Hardware devices such as telephone/voice boards, FAX boards, text-to-speech boards, and other devices typically employ support software as the interface between user programs and their hardware. These software packages simplify invocation of hardware capabilities by an application program. Such software is almost always provided with the hardware by the manufacturer and is called a *device driver* or *handler*. In this chapter, I'll discuss drivers for voice/telephone boards and the higher-level language support libraries that usually accompany the driver.

Multitasking is required in any voice processing system using more than one line—and in one-line systems using the display and keyboard. Multitasking can be handled by an operating system that supports multitasking, one such as OS/2 or UNIX. However, nonmultitasking operating systems (DOS on the IBM-compatible PC, for example) can also be used if a cooperating multitasking module is present. In later sections, I'll discuss the details of multitasking executives and how they operate and relate to nonmultitasking operating systems.

All voice processing systems, no matter what tools are used in their development, contain similar runtime software components: a suite of modules that differ somewhat from nonvoice processing applications. This makes possible the creation of comprehensive, full-featured development toolkits and application generators that go a long way toward automating voice processing system creation. Development toolkits augment conventional software production tools such as assemblers, compilers, and special function libraries (also called toolkits). They provide a set of capabilities including a library of voice processing functions for use with higher-level language compilers. The better toolkits relieve the developer of many of the unique considerations and concerns that are crucial to development of voice processing applications. Development toolkits are powerful tools and will be thoroughly discussed in this chapter.

Most voice processing applications can be created using an application generator (also referred to as an APGEN), often allowing programming at a higher level than with either assembly or compiler languages. It would be wonderful if APGENs allowed the system designer or software engineer to simply provide a statement of requirements or even a specification for the application. However, as you shall see, more than this is required.

Speech editors are software support packages that are used to record and edit speech. Speech editors are sometimes called prompt editors and are an important tool for production and management of an application's voice files. The actual speech production process is covered in only a cursory way in this chapter and only when it's important to the understanding of other software tools being discussed. A thorough treatment of the subject of vocabulary production is presented in chapter 9. (The term *vocabulary* is used to collectively denote voice prompts, phrases, and other utterances composing a system's speech repertoire.)

Device Drivers

Every hardware device installed in the computer is associated with a suite of software functions used by application programs in their interface with the device. This software suite is usually called a device driver or handler and is provided by the hardware manufacturer. Without a device driver, users would have to concern themselves with many intricate details re-

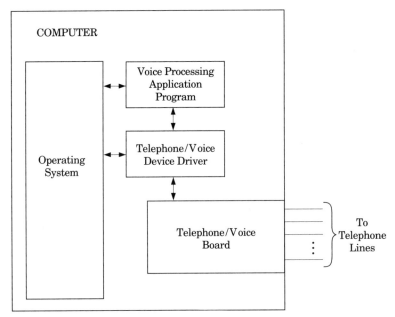

Figure 8.1 Relationship of telephone/voice driver and other software.

quired for control of a device and would have to develop a driver or its equivalent before employing the device. The telephone/voice boards in voice processing systems require a device driver that uses operating system services in the execution of its own duties. For example, when recording a voice message from a telephone line to a file, the driver uses the operating system's file creation and writing functions. Figure 8.1 shows the relationship between the driver, the operating system, and the other voice processing modules in a computer.

The following sections cover a number of features and capabilities relating to telephone/voice board device drivers.

Multiline requirements

The purpose of a driver is to simplify the interface between application programs and telephone/voice hardware while supporting implementation of all system requirements. For multiline voice processing applications, the driver must enable multitasking and must handle multiple boards. These requirements are discussed in the following.

Multitasking. Some systems support dozens of telephone lines. Speaking or recording, for example, can occur on many lines at the same time; the driver's speak or record function is entered once for each line. This fact leads to the requirement that device driver code be re-entrant. Each line must be handled by application software as though it were the only one, and device drivers are designed to facilitate this process. Most use at least two techniques pursuant to this requirement. First, when a driver function is called and it requires a period of time to complete, the function doesn't retain control of the central processor during the entire execution. Rather, the function initiates its operation then returns to the calling program. The initialized function proceeds asynchronously, driver code being executed as needed when triggered by appropriate hardware interrupts. For example, when an application calls a driver function to produce speaking on a telephone line, the driver acquires the line number and a speech data pointer then initializes a pair of speech buffers. Control is returned to the calling program by the driver as the board begins speaking. Soon, a speech data buffer empties, causing a hardware interrupt to be issued. Whereupon, the driver regains control, refills the buffer, handles any required scheduling or bookkeeping, and again returns control to the calling program. When the next buffer empties, another interrupt is issued to return control temporarily to the driver. The process continues until all speech data has been processed (spoken) by the hardware. In this way, driver code is executed only when necessary. Application programs are not monopolized by a single telephone line—they're free to proceed with their support of other lines and other tasks.

The second technique used by the device driver in support of multitasking is used to notify application programs of the occurrence of events requiring their attention—for instance, when a ring signal is detected or when DTMF input is received. When such an event occurs, the driver puts a coded notation (with the phone line number) into a FIFO queue. Application programs are responsible for frequently checking and removing notations from the queue. The queue might contain notations for many events, including the following: speaking finished, recording finished, DTMF digit received, DTMF string received, phone line ring detected, onhook complete, offhook complete, dialing complete, operating system error, and a host of others. Some drivers optionally offer a polling mode—instead of reading an event queue, application programs poll the driver to learn the status of a prior function invocation. Application code can handle processing for each event in the queue anytime after it occurs, but processing must keep pace to prevent queue overflow. User processing must proceed rapidly enough to handle simultaneous calls in an orderly manner and to prevent discontinuities in caller dialogues.

The driver is responsible, among other things, for providing voice data to the hardware and for storing voice data during recording. It must do this at a rate fast enough that data is not exhausted during speaking and that buffers don't overrun during recording. If the driver is operating with a non-multitasking operating system, one whose code is not re-entrant, it can't perform file operations when entered via a hardware interrupt because any file function might itself have been interrupted. Because of this, drivers typically wait and perform file operations only when they're entered via software interrupts (generated by application programs). Application programs, therefore, must call the driver frequently to enable it to keep up with its file processing tasks. Some drivers provide a special scheduling function that can be entered at any time for this purpose.

Multiple voice boards. Because most individual telephone/voice cards can support only a few telephone lines, most manufacturers support the installation of multiple cards in a single personal computer. The device driver must be able to assign a set of logical numbers to each card and to assign a set of numbers sequentially across several boards. Because the telephone/voice cards are not always associated with the same physical lines from the central office or PBX, it's more convenient to refer to the interconnection between software and telephone/voice cards as an assignment of logical numbers to the hardware's channels rather than to the physical lines. It's this channel number that the driver subsequently uses in all its communication with application code to identify where things are happening in the outside world.

Special features

Besides its primary responsibility to provide an interface between application programs and the telephone/voice devices, most drivers contain special functions and features that enhance use of the hardware they support. Some of the more important features are covered in the following paragraphs.

Override of setup parameters. Every telephone/voice card and its driver include numerous features whose operations are controlled by values set into parameters in memory. For example, two such features are:

1. The minimum time that DTMF must be present on a line to be detected.
2. The delay time after dialing is complete before a drop in loop current will be recognized as a connect.

There are many more whose operation is variable and dependent upon the value set into a control parameter. Usually, the whole set of parameters are automatically set by default upon loading and startup of the driver, but these can be overridden by an application.

High-level and low-level programming. Many drivers provide functions for either of two levels of programming. High-level functions enable users to interface with the driver as you would expect of a higher-level programming language. For example, a function that records a caller's voice and creates a speech file would be considered a higher-level function. Some drivers additionally provide, as an alternative, lower-level programming functions to give the user more control. An example would be a function that records a caller's voice data to a pair of buffers specified by the user. With low-level functions like this one, application code would be responsible for managing the buffers but would be notified by the driver of key events such as when a buffer is nearly full or when it's nearly empty. Use of low-level functions requires attention to much more detail on the part of the application program, but it permits greater flexibility. For instance, implementation of a speech cut-and-paste function, which requires speech data in buffers to be moved about, can't be accomplished with the high-level functions of most drivers.

Hardware and software interrupt default override. Normally, a single hardware interrupt is used by all telephone/voice boards to signal the computer that it needs attention. A jumper or switch is set on each card to specify which interrupt is employed, and the driver must know how the switch is set. Boards come from the manufacturer preset for a default interrupt; the driver is set for the same default. Likewise, a default software interrupt is defined for use by application programs. Because conflict with other hardware and software must be avoided, drivers provide some means of changing both software and hardware interrupt levels.

Buffer location and length. To provide the most efficient use, memory allocations are usually under control of application programs. Information regarding speech data buffer locations and sizes are usually provided to the driver in a command line when the driver is loaded. This approach enables users to make crucial memory allocation decisions at runtime.

Support for other options. Either or both the computer and the telephone/voice boards can offer optional features that are supported by the driver. For example, extended or expanded memory options can be offered with the computer. These are frequently important to voice processing applications, which often require large amounts of code and very large speech data buffers. Except for the possible need to handle hardware malfunction, support by the driver for extra memory is transparent to the user. Another optional feature that can be supported by the driver involves telephone-line switching hardware. In this case, the driver includes functions for making, breaking, or masking connections in the switching matrix.

Call progress monitoring. If the telephone/voice board has the capability to perform outbound calling, its driver will offer *call progress monitoring*—sometimes called call progress analysis. Call progress monitoring enables application programs to monitor outbound calls as they progress through the several stages between dialing and connection with the called party. Many different resources become involved in placing a telephone call, and many events occur in the process. Some of those that can be detected by the human ear include dial tone, dialing, ringback, busy, and several intercept signals. Of course, talking can be detected, but there's nothing inherent in the information received from talking that indicates whether it emanates from a recording or a person (timing the length of the response might provide an indication). If, during an outbound call, enough of the many expected events don't occur, if enough resources are already busy or otherwise not available, the call will not connect. There are numerous ways an outbound call can end; most don't result in the desired connection. Some of the possible results include: no dial tone, network busy, called-party phone busy, high-and-dry, no answer, and others. Furthermore, the phone can be answered by a machine—a modem, a computer, a FAX, or an answering machine. Each of these results might require a different reaction, and the driver should enable an application to discriminate between them.

The analysis required to perform call progress monitoring is complex. It's made more complex by the many environments to which the computer's telephone lines can be attached. Because each produces different call progress signals, it's not possible for one set of parameters to control call progress analysis in every environment. Many different sets are required, depending upon the country of operation, the area within the country, whether attached to a trunk or PBX, the vintage of equipment at the central office, which PBX is used, and other factors. There are utility programs available from board manufacturers that help determine an appropriate set of call progress parameters for any particular setup.

User interface

Drivers are memory-resident, and their functions are invoked by software interrupt. Values and pointers needed by the driver's functions are provided by loading them into the computer's registers before the interrupt is invoked. Likewise, any information returned by the driver to the calling program is passed in registers. The following paragraphs provide several examples to illustrate this process.

To speak on a telephone line, the telephone/voice hardware must be provided with a set of speech data. That data could reside in memory, in a single disk file, or in several disk files. The device driver includes several speaking functions or various versions of the same one to handle the differences. One function drives the hardware's speech circuitry with data it finds in a single disk file. Another speaks with data it obtains by alternating between a pair of memory buffers. Yet another function collects speech data from several disk files. If these functions are respectively called SPEAK_FILE, SPEAK_BUF, and SPEAK_TABLE, then Figure 8.2 gives an

REGISTER			
A	B	C	D
Function Code	Channel Number	Pointer To:	Return Code
SPEAK_FILE 1		n	File Read/ Write Block	—
SPEAK_BUF 2		n	Buffer Table	—
SPEAK_TABLE 3		n	Table of Files	—

Figure 8.2 Register-loading for device-driver calls.

example of the contents of registers as they must be loaded for each of these functions before calls to the device driver. The registers in the figure are labelled A, B, C, and D. The function code is placed in one, and the registers and the channel number are loaded to another. The driver needs different information depending on which function is desired. For the three functions, that difference is represented in register C. To execute the SPEAK_FILE function, the driver must be told which file to access, how much speech data to use, and the offset within the file of the first datum. This information could be placed in memory in a formal structure called a file read/write block. The buffer table referred to in Figure 8.2 for the function SPEAK_BUF might be the same read/write block structure. For this function, though, the buffer table contains the location and length of memory speech buffers. The example function, SPEAK_TABLE, requires a table specifying a sequence of files, the starting offset within each file, and the number of data bytes to be used from each file.

Once the registers are loaded for a given function, the driver interrupt can be invoked and the function executed. One register referred to in the figure will contain a return code when control is returned by the driver. This register is used to inform calling programs of results. Naturally, for those functions that initiate but don't execute their action upon being called, it's not possible to return complete status. That will eventually be returned in the event queue. Codes representing the following outcomes are typical of what might be expected in the return register: invalid function code, channel busy, invalid channel number, insufficient memory, buffer empty, successful initiation, or function completed successfully.

Function libraries for higher-level languages

To facilitate use of the device driver from programs that are written in higher-level languages, board manufacturers frequently supply function libraries especially for popular compiler languages. These libraries contain object code functions that correspond to the functions of the device drivers. Driver function calls are made to the corresponding library function in the language's own syntax. Thus, the tasks of loading registers with call parameters and invoking the software interrupt are removed from the application program. This facilitates development of voice processing applications in two ways. First, it promotes development in higher-level languages. Second, it greatly reduces the chance of programming error by using standard, debugged code for the often tricky task of loading the computer's registers and invoking a software interrupt.

Multitasking Systems

Multitasking describes the mode of operating a computer that makes it seem to be executing many processing tasks at the same time. In the strictest sense, it's actually executing only one tiny slice of each at a time, sequentially interleaving them so the tasks appear to be simultaneous. Unless a computer is designed with parallel processors, it executes central processor instructions sequentially, one at a time. Memory accesses, various input/output operations, and central processor operations are commonly overlapped. Nevertheless, most voice processing applications are developed on computers whose processors operate sequentially. Furthermore, voice processing typically deals with telephone applications that handle multiple simultaneous telephone dialogues. In most voice processing applications, one processor must not only respond to a console operator but also, at the same time, respond to the needs of dozens of callers. It was for exactly this type of application that the concept of multitasking arose.

Requirements

What's needed to make a computer appear to be processing many tasks at the same time? What does it mean for a computer to be multitasking? In answering these questions, you can't simply think of the computer's memory as being divided into separate areas, one per task, each containing all elements necessary to its execution. Rather, you might think of the computer's time resource as being allocated more or less equally among all tasks—a little bit of time spent executing code for one task, then a little spent on another, and another, and so on in round-robin fashion. The same program in memory might be executed for all tasks—or at least for more than one of them. Memory might contain one program to be used for every task, it might contain a separate program for each task, or something in between. The system must know of the presence of each task and be aware of the location in memory at which that task will next execute. The system must establish a stack for each defined task and be able to divide time into small segments that can be successively allocated to each task in turn. It must be able to switch its attention from one task to the next at the end of each time division. It must save the operating environment (registers, flags, and stack location) for a task when its time is up, and it must restore that environment when the task is next executed. In many applications there's a need to synchronize tasks or to exchange information between them. These notions lead to the requirement for intertask communication. Finally, code that's to be executed by more than one task and that can be interrupted must be re-entrant. If the software meets these requirements, a multitasking operation can be established.

Voice processing systems

In a voice processing system, an individual task is associated with each telephone line (or with each telephone/voice board channel). Whenever processing occurs for a given line, it's accomplished by a program in memory but under the auspices of the task assigned to that line. There is usually not a one-to-one correspondence between tasks and programs—in fact, all tasks might be executing the same program. An example in Figure 8.3 shows the relationship between tasks and programs in a multitasking voice processing system. Some programs reside in memory, as do a number of individual stacks, one for each task. Programs and stacks actually take up space in memory, but tasks are a logical concept resulting in logical entities rather than physical ones (except for its stack in memory and some administrative information). A task is said to be executing whenever any program whatsoever is executing using that task's stack. When a task is created, a program is assigned to it (although this assignment could be changed during processing). That same program might also be assigned to other tasks. When a task is executed, the associated program executes using that task's stack. The same program in a different time-slice might be executing under the auspices of another task using the other's stack.

In any multitasking environment, tasks possess similar properties to each other. For voice processing systems, they exhibit most of the following. A task can be created or extinguished at any time during an execution. One task can create (spawn) another. A task might extinguish itself. Tasks can be "turned off" temporarily without being extinguished, and they can subsequently be turned back on—these processes are conveniently thought of as putting a task to sleep and awakening a sleeping task. Any task can send a message to any other.

Multitasking is ordinarily thought of as an operating system function, and some common operating systems for personal computers do include multitasking capabilities. Both OS/2 and UNIX-based systems feature multitask-

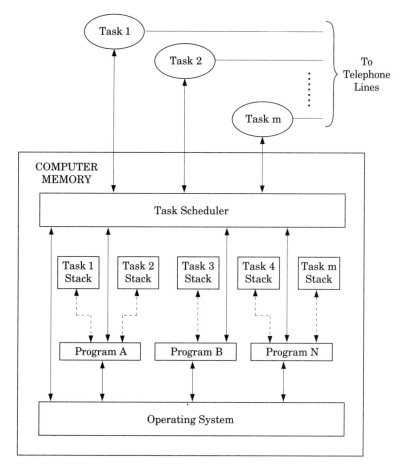

Figure 8.3 Multitasking in a voice processing system.

ing. IBM's DOS and Microsoft's MS-DOS don't. Even though these operating systems lack multitasking, many voice processing systems are developed on IBM compatible personal computers with either DOS or MS-DOS. Such implementations get around the lack by either embedding multitasking within their application programs or by employing a multitasking executive that works with and supplements the operating system. These two approaches are discussed in the following sections.

Embedded multitasking

Device driver support for multitasking was discussed earlier in this chapter. The device driver for the telephone/voice board provides a mechanism for queuing telephone, speech, and other events generated by the hardware and

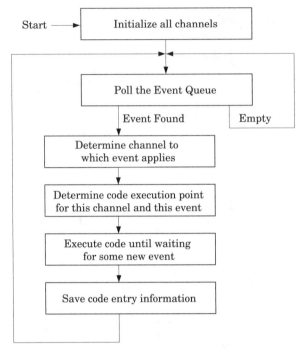

Figure 8.4 Flow of an application with embedded multitasking.

by the device driver. The queue includes such events as: speech buffer empty, DTMF digit received, recording buffer full, onhook complete, timeout waiting for DTMF, and many more. Figure 8.4 depicts the general flow of an application built with embedded multitasking. Applications of the form represented by the figure continuously poll the event queue. If it's empty, they simply poll it again (they might poll the keyboard buffer once in a while also to allow an online user to control or interrupt the application). When an event's occurrence is detected in the FIFO queue, the application breaks out of the polling loop to handle the situation. In addition to a notation of the event, the queue contains a parameter indicating to which hardware channel (i.e., to which telephone line) the event applies. Using state tables or other means, an appropriate execution address is determined, based on the event and channel. Processing proceeds for the channel from that address until the processor must wait for some new event. At that point, polling of the event queue is resumed. Other events might already be queued (if not, one soon will be), so processing might proceed for some other channel.

When developing applications with embedded multitasking, care must be taken to assure that not too much continuous time is spent on any one channel. Every caller dialogue must proceed smoothly and continuously, without interruption, so applications are required to service each channel's needs promptly. If the polling loop is not entered frequently, some channel might be neglected and cause speaking or recording to be interrupted. The event queue could even overflow, causing a serious interruption to one or all of the calls in progress.

A disadvantage of embedded multitasking is that it must be re-created for every application and involves much programming that can be avoided. It results in more code that must also be debugged. Fortunately, there are easier ways to produce multiline applications with nonmultitasking operating systems. The following section describes multitasking executives.

Multitasking executives

A multitasking executive is a software module that works with an operating system to enable applications to include multitasking. A program module containing only a handful of functions that operates in conjunction with a telephone/voice device driver is all it takes to create a simple multitasking executive. Only a few capabilities are needed to accomplish the objective. New tasks are created when they're spawned by another task. A task, once spawned, might be put out of existence by itself or by any other task. A task might put itself to sleep—a sleeping task will not execute again until it's awakened. Any task might wake another and might send a message to any other. This meager collection of capabilities composes a simple multitasking executive suitable for most voice processing applications developed for a personal computer. The multitasking executive can be linked with application programs or, more appropriately, might be memory-resident, callable via a software interrupt from programs written in any language. The functions described below compose a multitasking executive and can be implemented in a reasonably short time.

Spawn function. This function creates a task and tells the executive about it (e.g., makes appropriate table entries). Several parameters must be passed with the function. Each spawned task has its private stack space in memory, so the stack's location and length must be indicated when the task is spawned. The first executable address of the program to be associated with the task must also be passed when the spawn function is called. On each successive execution of the task, the next execution address will have been saved in the task's stack, so no further information regarding execution addresses need be passed. When the spawn function is called, a sequence number is assigned to the task, and all the appropriate system tables are updated to bring the new task into existence and awake.

Extinguish function. A call to the extinguish function passes a task number and causes the specified task to cease to exist.

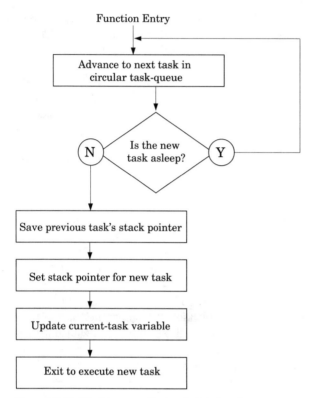

Function Entry

Figure 8.5 Multitasking executive's schedule function.

Schedule function. The schedule function swaps tasks. Whenever the schedule function is called, the next task in rotation is executed if it's awake. Figure 8.5 shows a flow chart for the function. A table containing pointers to every task's current stack address is updated, as is a variable specifying the current task.

Sleep function. When the sleep function is called, the currently executing task is put to sleep, and the schedule function is called to pass control to another task. The sleeping task will not execute again until it's awakened by some other task.

Wake function. When the wake function is called with the number of a task to be awakened, the status of the task will be changed from asleep to awake.

Communicate function. The communicate function enables messages to be passed from one task to another. Several means can be employed in such communication, but it will suffice to pass the task number of the message recipient and a pointer to a data area containing the message. Some implementations might also pass the task number of the sender.

Pollqueue function. The pollqueue function is actually implemented as a task that polls the telephone/voice device driver's event queue. Figure 8.6 shows the flow of this function (note the similarities between Figures 8.4 and 8.6). If there's nothing in the queue, the scheduling function is called so other tasks can execute. If an event is found in the queue, then the function consults a system table to obtain the task number for the event's channel and wakes the task. Pollqueue then calls the scheduler. Note that on return from the scheduler, the polling loop is re-entered.

Startup function. The startup function is actually a task that spawns a task for each channel (or telephone line) defined for this invocation of the application. The startup function calls the spawn function once for each channel, constructs a table of channel versus task number (which is accessible to other functions), then extinguishes itself.

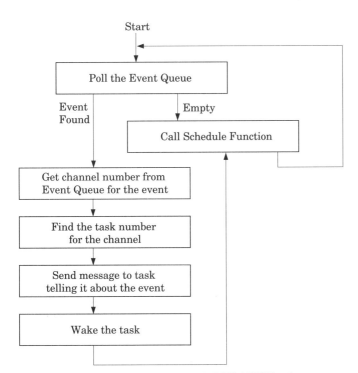

Figure 8.6 Flow of multitasking executive's POLLQUEUE task.

Scheduling in a multitasking executive. The schedule function must be called frequently to give each task a chance to execute for a brief time-slice. A common way to assure that these calls are placed regularly is to tie them to a clock or timer interrupt. The schedule function can be called on every clock or timer interrupt or at some multiple of them. Either way, each task is given its turn to execute in regular rotation. There is, however, a drawback to this approach. A nonmultitasking operating system's functions are not re-entrant. This is the case with both IBM's DOS and Microsoft's MS-DOS for IBM-compatible personal computers. This fact prevents tasks from calling any operating system service function because the one called might have been interrupted itself and, since it's not re-entrant, will not operate properly when re-entered. This situation, if not remedied, would be a fatal flaw. One successful approach is to pass all calls to operating system services through a sort of gatekeeper, a sentinel that resolves conflicts and makes sure an interrupted function is not re-entered. While the gatekeeper technique can be implemented, it's a complex and very difficult job fraught with many opportunities for error. Fortunately, developers can avoid having to deal with these problems because multitasking executives for DOS and other operating systems are available commercially.

For those who do wish to develop their own multitasking executive, there's another solution. It requires that every user program regularly call the schedule function—so the resulting multitasking system must be dedicated, and doesn't permit running foreign programs such as off-the-shelf word processors or spreadsheets while the voice processing application is executing. The discipline has great advantages. Because all application programs are under control of the developer, it's possible to enforce the following regimen. The scheduler is called by system and user programs:

1. Any time the program must wait for some external event.

2. Immediately after any time-consuming operating system call.

3. One or more times in every long loop.

If loops are nested, the scheduler calls would be placed in the inner loop or in all loops. Every library function in support of voice processing cooperates by calling the scheduler at strategic points. As a practical matter, the scheduler can be called anytime and anywhere within programs. No one program should monopolize the processor too long before voluntarily relinquishing control by calling the scheduler. The idea is to be neighborly and share the processor's time among all running tasks. Task swapping occurs only between operating system calls because operating system functions never call the scheduler, and they're never interrupted to swap tasks. The operating system re-entry concern becomes a nonissue.

The concept is that each task runs until it voluntarily yields control. The scheduling strategy is nonpreemptive—every task has the same priority as any other, and control is not taken away from any task involuntarily. Thus, each task (or program) must cooperate with the overall objectives of the system and yield control frequently. Imagine, for example, that the telephone/voice board is producing outgoing speech on channel one. The task handling that channel is asleep. Suppose some other task neglects to yield. Speaking will continue uninterrupted on channel one as long as executing tasks make occasional calls to the device driver. However, if one program fails to yield, no other task gets to run. When speaking ends on channel one, that line goes dead because there's no program checking the event queue to wake channel one's task. Even if it's wakened, it never runs because the scheduler is no longer being called. Notice, too, that if the event queue polling task is ever put to sleep (or extinguished), nothing more can happen on any telephone line because each task will eventually put itself to sleep and none can ever be awakened.

Once a task calls the scheduler, there's no return to that task until the scheduler has given control once in rotation to every other nonsleeping task and the original calling task's turn comes around again. When finally that task's turn comes again, the scheduler swaps stacks and hands control back by emulating a return from the schedule function call. It appears to the calling task that there has been no interruption, that processing for the task has been continuous and the schedule function has simply been called, done its job, and is now returning control. The original calling task has no knowledge or sense of other tasks having executed—it probably doesn't even know they exist. It appears to any task that its own stream of consciousness (if I might use that term) is continuous and the only one in existence. Except for the event queue polling task, every other task operates as if it were the only running task. This fact makes it possible for developers to create multitasked programs without concern for multitasking, as if they were single-thread programs (of course, the scheduler must be called, but this poses no particular complication).

Developing with a multitasking executive. Programs to be run under a multitasking executive like the ones described in this chapter can be programmed as single-thread programs, without consideration for multitasking other than calls to the scheduler. Programs can be developed as though each program is the only one to be run. This is a considerable advantage because it relieves the developer of many details. There are, however, a few issues with which developers must be concerned when using such a multitasking executive. Some compilers generate object code that checks the stack for overflow every time a function is called. Because the multitasking executive redefines stacks for each task, these checking functions will register an error, believing the stack has overflowed when it has not. Stack checking features must be disabled. Another concern is that if any one task exits to the operating system, whether intentional or through a fault, the system stops running. After development, some programs might need tuning to adjust frequency of scheduler calls, but this is a small price to pay. Also, the voluntary scheduling approach means that standard off-the-shelf programs, such as word processors and spreadsheets, can't be run concurrently with the application. As already noted, if the queue polling task is put to sleep, all telephone tasks will soon find themselves in a fatal sleep. Care must be taken to avoid these circumstances.

Development Toolkits

A voice processing toolkit is an integrated package of software development and runtime tools that facilitate creation of multiline voice processing systems. A toolkit might include each of the following:

1. A library of higher-level language voice processing functions.

2. A multitasking executive.

3. A runtime shell.

4. A speech editor.

All of these software components cooperate with the device driver for a telephone/voice board, might be dependent on a specific programming language, and might require a particular assembler or compiler. The function library contains object code modules (and might include source code) for controlling telephone equipment, recording voice messages, converting variables to spoken representations of the variable (e.g., dollars and cents, date and time, etc.), accessing local databases, communicating with an external host, and more. The runtime module might support not only actual operations but also debugging and testing activities. Some toolkits come as a null voice processing system, a complete shell into which the programmer need only specify, in a higher-level standard programming language, the processing details of an application—all the standard system capabilities are already there for free.

Voice processing system development with a toolkit and a standard programming language has many advantages. Off-the-shelf compilers provide a powerful development environment, and toolkits extend their scope to include voice processing. This is a capability that should not be overlooked by anyone contemplating such a project. Standard higher-level language compilers provide development features that have been fine-tuned over the years; it has taken many years to create these capabilities, and it would take as many or more to re-create them. It's doubtful whether any development environment that doesn't allow inclusion of modules developed with these compilers will be able to match their flexibility and power for many years to come.

One of the most important advantages of development toolkits, especially those that include a runtime shell, is that most of the system has already been developed and debugged by the toolkit developers—the remaining application programming can be a small portion of the total system, and that can be done in a standard, higher-level language, taking advantage of all the inherent power and capability.

Use of a toolkit can relieve the developer from most concerns regarding multitasking. The function library and runtime module have been designed to work together and to cooperate with the operating system (and multitasking executive, if one is included). If the user creates only re-entrant code for the application and meets all other requirements, he or she can program as though the application will run as a single-thread process without further concern for multitasking. Timeouts and error handling features are built into the toolkit, so only a minimal amount of programming is required in these areas. Toolkit features might also be available for customizing runtime status and statistics screens. All in all, use of a function toolkit can provide many advantages to a voice processing application developer because much of the job is already done.

The relationships between toolkit components and other development tools and modules is shown in Figure 8.7. Toolkit applications are programmed in much the same way as conventional applications. Calls are made to operating system functions, to toolkit functions, or to functions that might be memory-resident at runtime. These latter include device driver functions, text-to-speech, FAX, or voice recognition functions. Toolkit libraries might exist as either source code or object modules to be combined at link-time. The developer creates application programs and links their compiled versions with other toolkit components such as a runtime shell to create an integrated runtime package.

Features

Toolkits include functions and features designed to provide maximum power to developers. An integrated toolkit will have optional support for almost all special voice processing capabilities such as local database access, external host communications, speech recognition, interactive FAX, and text-to-speech. An integrated toolkit will also support use of configuration files, indexed vocabulary files, event logging, automatic restart, and others. If a status screen or a telephone line statistics screen are incorporated into an application, there must be some means to invoke them. Most voice processing applications use the display and keyboard for application-specific information exchange between the system and an online user. This can be facilitated by allowing developers to customize a main menu screen from

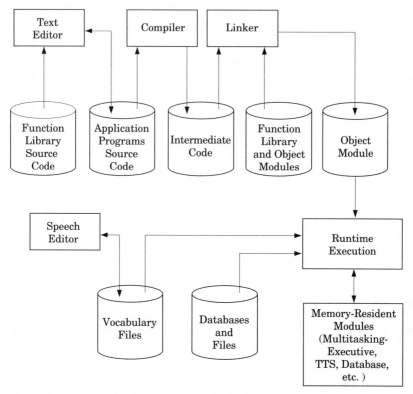

Figure 8.7 Development toolkit software relationships.

which online users can select the screens they desire. Figure 8.8 portrays an example menu that includes a status screen, a telephone line statistics screen, and an item leading to a subsidiary set of application screens.

Components

Figure 8.7, mentioned earlier, showed the major components of a voice processing development toolkit. Perhaps the most obvious element is the function library because that's most often associated with the term "toolkit." In the case of voice processing systems, however, it's possible to provide, in addition to a function library, an entire suite of development modules. Elements that might be present are the function library, a runtime module, a speech editor, documentation, and optional memory-resident modules. The latter might include a multitasking module if the target operating system does not support multitasking. There might also be memory-resident modules that support text-to-speech, local database operations, host communications, voice-recognition, FAX, logging, reporting, and others.

One of the more important components is the runtime module, an operating (but null) runtime system. It's referred to as "null" because, even though it does run, it has no application programs to guide it, so it doesn't know what to do when the phone rings, and it can't perform any meaningful voice processing functions. Even so, it multitasks, logs system events, is ready to automatically handle errors, can switch between telephone status and telephone statistics screens, and to all appearances looks like an operating voice processing system. It's a shell consisting of everything except the application programs to be provided by the developer. A complete voice processing system can be created simply by linking an application program to the runtime module. The major components of a voice processing development toolkit are discussed in the following sections.

Function library. Use of a toolkit's function library is probably already familiar to experienced programmers. Just as a developer might employ a database function library to get a head-start on development of database-oriented applications, the function library packaged with a voice processing function toolkit provides a head start in that area. For example, the library will contain several functions that convert DTMF input strings to different variable types. It will contain functions that permit a single variable, say the value 12345 to be interpreted and spoken in a number of different ways. The variable, for instance, can be spoken as "one, two, three, four, five." Or it can be said as "twelve thousand, three hundred forty-five," "one hundred twenty-three dollars and forty-five cents," or "January twenty-third, nineteen forty-five."

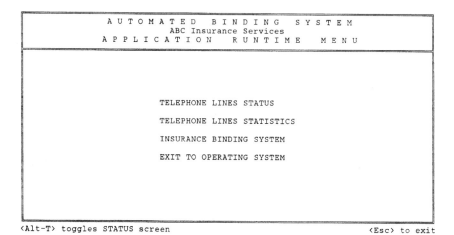

Figure 8.8 Customizable main menu screen.

There are still other formats in which a variable can be spoken. The function library can be quite diverse, containing functions of a variety of types. In addition to converting variables into spoken values, the library will contain functions to initialize and shut down the hardware, control telephone functions, record and store inbound messages, speak on the telephone line, perform math and logic on variables, etc. The library can contain literally any function imaginable. Some go beyond the requirements of voice processing applications in an attempt to make the toolkit more general (for example, by including functions that produce displays or that access local databases). These are, in a sense, redundant because function libraries are already commercially available for these extra functions.

A given version of a toolkit supports a specific programming language for a particular telephone/voice hardware product; the version might require a particular compiler or assembler for the language. Toolkits seem to be most popular for C language compilers. Typically, the function library can be used with operating system functions and with toolkits for database, mathematical, or general operations. The function library requires and calls functions in the hardware's device driver. The library is provided in object form and can be combined with user programs when linked with other toolkit modules. Source code, if provided, facilitates upgrading and adding new functions—particularly those that can be composed of or from existing ones.

The library will contain functions for initializing and shutting down the telephone/voice board. One of the functions will be used to determine if the required hardware is present, and another function will run diagnostics on the hardware. It's important to make such tests when the system first comes up and to provide an appropriate message to the user if these tests fail for any reason. Other functions are used to set default parameters such as DTMF timeout, interlock delay, line restart procedure, etc. Toolkit functions attempt to handle unusual situations and errors automatically. Thus, for instance, a DTMF input function measures the time it waits for a key to be pressed. If the caller fails to enter a DTMF key within the given time, an exception handling program can be entered. Some toolkits include interlock protection that will timeout if a call is abandoned by the caller or is unexpectedly disconnected for any reason (some telephone equipment either doesn't report or doesn't detect a drop in loop current when disconnect occurs). When an early disconnect occurs, the line must be reset and processing restarted. The toolkit will include a function for specifying the restart procedure. System initialization might also include a function for assigning lines to applications if this task is not handled at startup.

Many telephone control functions are available in a toolkit's library. One, an "answer" or "wait-for-ring" function, will wait for the phone to ring, then go offhook. This function, like many others that must wait for an event to occur, cooperates with multitasking operations by initiating the process, suspending (putting to sleep) the task handling that line, and lying dormant until the event occurs. Then, when a ring does occur on the line, the task will be awakened by another task (whose job it is to watch for such things) so it can complete its operation. Any function required to wait for some event to occur cooperates with multitasking. There are many of these: reading DTMF inputs from the telephone line, placing speech on the line, dialing, hook-flashing, or monitoring call progress. Even the functions for going onhook and offhook must operate in that fashion. Onhook and offhook operations require setting a mechanical switch, a matter of milliseconds, but long enough that the computer must not be monopolized while waiting. A delay function is often included in the toolkit's library. When programming telephone applications, many situations arise where a delay of a tenth of a second or half a second are required (e.g., to make dialogue seem natural). Because a delay must wait for an event (a period of time to expire), it too must initiate then sleep until the delay period has passed.

Some of the functions that demonstrate the real power of a toolkit involve converting variables to particular speech formats. For example, in voice response systems designed for employee scheduling or bank account access, passages like the following are used. "Your next shift is on Thursday January twenty-fourth at four-thirty PM," or "Your Maximizer Account balance is five-thousand, two-hundred seventy-three dollars and six cents." The toolkit library contains functions that cause a variable to be interpreted and spoken as a date, time, day of month, year, dollar amount, etc. In computer memory a variable is dimensionless. Information about a variable's dimension is usually inherent in the application program. When developing with a toolkit, this information exists, among other ways, in the form of calls to these toolkit functions. There should also be an ample supply of functions to update both the telephone status screen and the telephone statistics display. As calls arrive or are placed, counted events might be updated automatically by the system, but application-specific events and statistics must be defined and maintained by the application programs using calls to library functions. Examples of C programs using a voice processing toolkit are given in appendix E.

Many toolkit functions are higher-level implementations of collections of other toolkit functions. Users might combine existing functions to add functions of their own. Imagine three toolkit functions SPEAK, SPEAKNUMBERS, and SPEAKMONEY. The function SPEAK is called with the line number and the index number of a prompt, phrase, or other utterance, and it causes the utterance to be spoken on the specified telephone line. SPEAKNUMBERS, when passed a telephone line number and a variable, causes the contents of the variable to be spoken as a number (i.e., "one hundred twenty-four thousand, six hundred ninety-one)." The function SPEAKMONEY, when called with a line number and a variable, causes the contents of the variable to be spoken as a dollars and cents value (i.e., "three hundred eighty-nine dollars and forty-two cents)." Clearly, SPEAKNUMBERS can

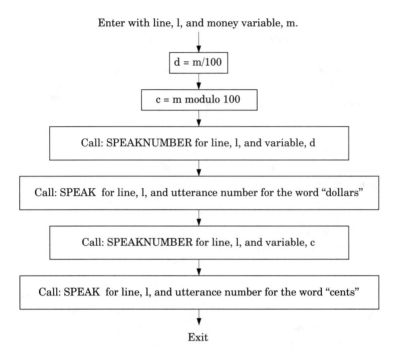

Figure 8.9 Flow of Speech toolkit function SPEAKMONEY.

use SPEAK in its implementation, and SPEAKMONEY can use both the others. Figure 8.9 shows an implementation of SPEAKMONEY. It demonstrates how simply that function can be constructed from the other two. Figure 8.10 lists the C source code for a similar toolkit function.

Runtime module. A group of runtime capabilities required for voice processing systems includes everything that's not application-dependent. These are packaged in a runtime module. Some have already been discussed in an earlier chapter: event logging, telephone status and telephone statistics screens, a reporting module, a configuration setup feature, and standard prototype vocabulary. The runtime module consists of all components of an operational voice processing system except application code, permanent vocabulary, and databases that are to be provided by the system developer.

Optional runtime support packages are implemented as memory-resident modules that can be piled one upon the other as they're added to the system. Any optional collection of functions can be packaged as a memory-resident module that might or might not be present at runtime. A multitasking executive can fall into this category. Other examples include software support for FAX, text-to-speech, voice-recognition, local database support, and host-communication modules. Access to each of these is via interrupt with parameters passed in registers. A small executive can be loaded to provide common access to all modules, enabling them to be accessed by the same interrupt level rather than by separate ones.

Most system sponsors want to collect operational results in the form of printed reports. The toolkit might support production of such reports with a report utility and a set of library functions designed to simplify collection of desired data and information. Some support conditional logging and reporting that can be dependent upon the occurrence of an event or set of events. In some cases, reporting information is accumulated in a local database. Off-the-shelf database utilities offer flexible report generation capabilities. Some toolkits write report data to dual files, thereby decreasing the probability of lost results. Some permit reporting directly to a system printer.

Many voice processing systems contain vocabularies with standard language, words such as "January," "Wednesday," "twenty-third," "o'clock," "PM," "and," and "or." Additionally, spoken variables use words like "dol-

```
/* SAY_HR_MIN_SEC():    Given a variable containing seconds and a telephone */
/*                      line number on which to speak, resolve the seconds  */
/*                      into hrs, mins and secs and speak them as:          */
/*                      "H hour(s), M minute(s), and S second(s)".          */

say_hr_min_sec( line, seconds )
int line;                       /* phone line on which to speak             */
SECS seconds;                   /* seconds to resolve to hrs, mins, & secs  */
{
    SECS hrs; SECS mins; SECS secs;  SECS temp;

    temp = seconds%x360;
    hrs  = seconds/x360;   mins = temp/x60;    secs = temp%x60;

    if( hrs )                          /* if hrs is non-zero                */
    {
        speaknumbers( line, hrs );     /*    say number in hrs              */
        if( hrs == 1 )                 /*    if hrs is singular             */
            speak( line, v_hour );     /*      say "hour"                   */
        else                           /*    else, if hrs is zero or plural */
            speak( line, v_hours );    /*      say "hours"                  */
    }

    if(( hrs ) || ( mins ))            /* if hrs or mins is non-zero        */
    {
        speaknumbers( line, mins );    /*    say number in mins             */
        if( mins == 1 )                /*    if mins is singular            */
            speak( line, v_minute );   /*      say "minute"                 */
        else                           /*    else, if mins is zero or plural */
            speak( line, v_minutes );  /*      say "minutes"                */

        speak( line, v_and );          /*    say "and"                      */
    }

    speaknumbers( line, secs );        /* say number in secs                */
    if( secs == 1 )                    /* if secs is singular               */
        speak( line, v_second );       /*    say "second"                   */
    else                               /* else, if secs is zero or plural   */
        speak( line, v_seconds );      /*    say "seconds"                  */
}
```

Figure 8.10 Example speech toolkit function in C language.

lars," "thousand," and "million." Other examples include sets of numbers, months, days of the week, and silences of various lengths. Furthermore, the sets might include versions with different intonations. Standard words are produced by toolkit developers and distributed with their products to be used as either prototype or final vocabulary. Prototype vocabulary is temporary speech that can be produced inexpensively. It's used only during system development and is replaced by permanent vocabulary soon before or soon after beta testing. Prototype vocabulary is discussed in greater detail in chapter 9.

Speech editor. A comprehensive speech editor is a key toolkit component that's crucial to the production and management of an application's vocabulary. Speech can be quickly recorded using a local telephone, but this doesn't result in the highest-quality voice. Vocabulary production can be contracted to a professional recording studio at an exceptionally high cost—in this case possession of the speech editor is in the hands of studio professionals. However, many experienced developers produce high-quality voice right in their own offices. For these developers, a comprehensive speech editor is a must. Speech editors are discussed in detail later in this chapter. Vocabulary production is covered extensively in chapter 9.

Documentation. As with all development tools, clear, complete documentation must be available. Because the toolkit contains not only development tools but also a runtime package, documentation in both categories is included: an overview of the toolkit summarizing its content and use, operating instructions for the runtime shell, comprehensive descriptions of every library function, instructions for operating every utility, and perhaps source listings (or source code) for library functions.

Application Generators

Overview

Application generators, often called APGENs, simplify the process and reduce the cost of developing voice processing applications—even beyond that achieved with development toolkits. APGENs have evolved from our efforts to automate software development. To understand how development of the least complex applications can be automated, consider those that are diagrammed as hierarchical structures similar to that shown in Figure 8.11. These are characterized by a set of prompt-and-response processes organized in a tree structure. Each branch starts with a spoken prompt menu (e.g., "To speak with someone in Sales, press one. For Accounting, press two," etc.). The caller enters a response by selecting an item from the menu and pressing the corresponding Touch-Tone key.

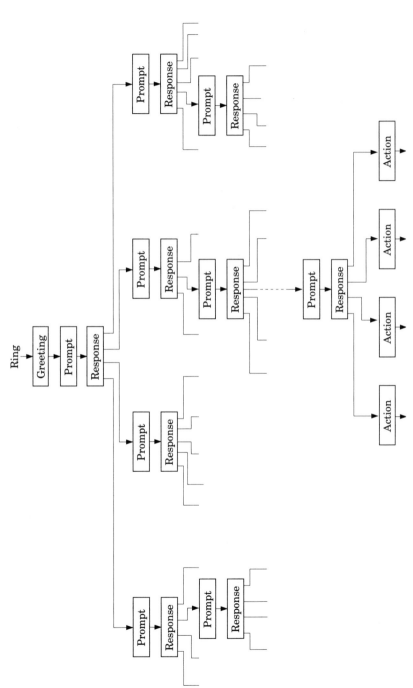

Figure 8.11 Voice processing application tree structure.

Depending on which key was input, a different branch is followed, and each leads to another prompt menu at the next level in the tree. Eventually, working through the tree, a level is reached at which some action is taken—presumably, a different action for each branch: someone's phone is rung, an information message is read to the caller, or a voice message is recorded. Until the action level is reached, prompt-and-response operations are identical in form with those at all other levels in the tree. Operations of each branch within a level are also identical in form.

It's natural to attempt to automate implementation of applications with this redundant hierarchical structure—these are the most simple ones. However, APGENs successfully support development of a much wider range of applications—applications with complex structures. APGENs routinely deal with applications involving most of the typical voice processing system features and requirements: local database access, communications with remote hosts, voice messaging, FAX processing, text-to-speech conversion, and speech recognition. To handle processing situations not normally covered by its standard capabilities, most application generators facilitate execution of custom user-code.

The fondest aim of application generator developers would be to produce a tool capable of creating viable voice processing systems without programming. The ideal would be a system that correctly executes an application from nothing more than a statement of its requirements. Of course, requirements can be stated in a variety of ways and at many levels. The ultimate application generator would create a working program (or programs) from an application's highest-level definition—which must provide enough detail to allow complete and correct execution. No programming would be required, only a formal statement of requirements would be input. While many companies claim their APGENs have attained this goal, in reality, except for the simplest applications, most fall far short. The process required by all of them for communicating the necessary detail must unavoidably be called programming. This is not to say that those application generators are not effective development tools. On the contrary, they're almost all exceptionally powerful and have contributed to a manifold reduction in the cost of voice processing application development.

Numerous techniques are used by application generators to implement voice processing systems, but all start with a high-level system definition, description, or specification produced by the application developer. This description is called a *source description*. The source description is compiled (or otherwise converted) to an intermediate representation that, depending upon the style of the APGEN, is either linked to produce executable object code or used as input to a runtime interpreter. Some application generators resemble the standard compilers and differ only in that their languages are designed specifically for voice processing applications and support particular telephone/voice hardware. Most application generators, however, approach the task in an entirely different manner, operating as interpreters rather than compilers. (A comprehensive development toolkit provides a very solid foundation for an application generator, and a later section contains a discussion of the process of creating an APGEN from a toolkit.) All of these approaches rely upon runtime code that's already tested and known to be correct—code produced and tested earlier as the APGENs runtime module or compiled by the APGENs compiler, which is assumed to generate correct object code if given logically correct source. Hence, an accurately defined application can run error-free almost the moment it's input. APGENs enable the development of a voice processing system in considerably less time than other development approaches.

In an earlier chapter I discussed characteristics inherent in any voice processing system. The most powerful APGENs are able to generate systems combining many of those characteristics, including host communication, local database access, text-to-speech, FAX, voice recognition, and so on. However, because APGENs are each different and because system requirements vary, not every application generator is optimum for every application. If you think of every application as belonging to a class depending upon its complexity, then a given APGEN is suitable for a subset of those classes. Most are not perfectly appropriate for every class. Voice processing application generator technology is still fairly young. As it matures, you'll see application generators that are more nearly universal.

All APGENs, regardless of how they accomplish it, attempt to incorporate large bodies of both syntactic and semantic knowledge and thus remove a large burden from developers and eliminate many sources of error. Syntactic knowledge is concerned with the details of a programming language, such as how to construct a well-formed statement in the language, which functions are available, and so on. Semantic knowledge is that pertaining to concepts—such as how a binary search operates. Normal programming activities require programmers to remember large amounts of both syntactic and semantic knowledge. APGEN developers try to build syntactic knowledge into the generation module and as much semantic knowledge as possible into the runtime module. Application generators with a custom editor might go to great lengths to remove sources of syntactic error. Those that permit application definition with fewer (though more comprehensive) steps go furthest toward eliminating sources of semantic error, but at the expense of more greatly limiting the application classes to which they apply. Figure 8.12 depicts this trade-off graphically. APGEN developers are working diligently to reduce the class of applications for which their products are not an obvious choice.

A key to a successful APGEN is its user interface, language, protocol, or other discipline designed for communicating application requirements to the generator. Some APGENs include sophisticated front-end editors to facilitate production of an application's definition. A variety of interfacing

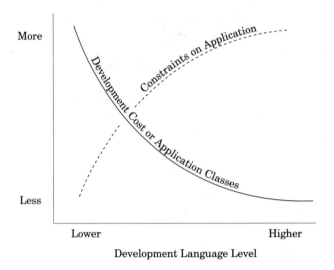

Figure 8.12 Application generator cost/suitability trade-off.

styles have been implemented: displayed forms to be filled in, menus of specification items, higher-level procedural languages, and simple CAD-like graphic displays. Two examples of higher-level languages are given in appendix F and appendix G. Voice processing programming languages like those in the appendices are called *scripting languages*. I've included scripting languages in the category with application generators because many in the industry have become accustomed to thinking of them that way. Scripting languages are, nevertheless, more closely related to standard programming languages. Figure 8.13 shows an example of a fill-in form displayed in a screen window (fields to be filled in are highlighted). Menus and forms are often combined. While filling in a field, context-sensitive APGEN editors can display a menu of choices. The field is filled in automatically when the user selects from the menu. A graphics approach to user interfacing employs on-screen flow charting to define an application's structure. APGEN editor approaches are discussed in more detail later in this chapter.

Every voice processing application must have vocabulary (the application's voice—prompts, phrases, and other utterances that it speaks). There's little an APGEN can do to reduce vocabulary production cost because the process required for creation of high-quality voice is the same no matter what application development tools are used. Nevertheless, an application generator can manage the process. It has knowledge of an application's structure and knows which vocabulary segments are required, which are associated with each element, and which have and have not been recorded. Maintaining status of prompts, phrases, and utterances, an AP-

GEN can apprise developers of every inconsistency. It can even track vocabulary versions, storing information on completed utterances and those still in prototype form awaiting rerecording. Some automation of vocabulary development is even possible. For example, tracts of silence can be automatically trimmed from the start and end of speech data.

Implementation with an APGEN imposes limitations that are not apparent when developing with a toolkit. Restrictions arise primarily from the structured nature of APGENs but might also result with APGENs that lack richness. Those applications that can be implemented with an APGEN, however, benefit from significantly shorter development cycles and reduced maintenance costs. In general, limitations are far outweighed by the numerous advantages. An APGEN automatically handles multitasking, timeouts, error recovery, variable parsing and formatting, transaction logging, status updating, and many other details that might otherwise concern programmers. An APGEN application can more easily be modified, updated, or expanded to meet new or changing requirements, and its source and derivatives therefrom often provide the only documentation needed. Using an application generator, voice processing applications can more often be implemented by nonprogramming developers without recourse to contractors. This places control of the project totally in-house and saves the huge fees often incurred in such undertakings. APGENs can be powerful system prototyping tools. For projects where more efficient implementation is desired, an application generator can be used to get a demonstration or prototype version on the air quickly and inexpensively. Once the system design has solidified, the prototype version can be replaced with more permanent code—an approach to software engineering that has been proven to shorten development cycles and reduce costs.

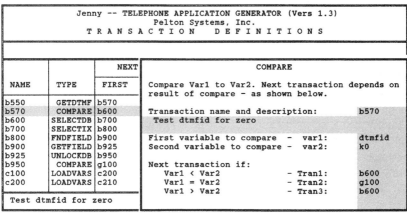

Figure 8.13 Highlighted fill-in form in pop-up window.

Some of the more important features of application generators are discussed in the following sections.

Features

You expect to see features in application generators that enable them to produce systems meeting most if not all the general requirements for voice processing systems. Furthermore, because development toolkits and APGENs are but two solutions to the same problem, and because many application generators are actually constructed on the foundation of a toolkit, you should not be surprised to see similar features in both tools. This is particularly true as it applies to runtime modules for both APGENs and tool-kits. One difference, though, is that APGENs integrate features in a way that makes them automatic and transparent, while toolkits might require special attention by the application developer. There are, however, features that apply only to application generators, features that are meaningless or inappropriate for development toolkits. Exits to user code, for example, is an APGEN feature that broadens applicability. Others involve features found in APGEN custom editors, features such as context-sensitive help and windowing. Comprehensive static testing, which can be performed by APGEN editors, is discussed in a later section in this chapter.

Some application generators implement logical constructs such as register, timers, and counters that might or might not have correlative devices in hardware. Logical devices such as these are usually referenced symbolically—as are variables, prompts, phrases, and other utterances. Features often found in compilers can also be implemented in APGENs: arrays, pointers, and lookup tables. Scripting languages can be graded for feature richness in much the same way as the higher-level compiler languages, to which scripting languages are so comparable.

An application generator's runtime module can enable invocation of an application based on time-of-day or elapsed time. Or it can allow an application servicing any line to cause another to be loaded and run. Both these runtime features provide flexibility in structuring applications and enhance their adjustability to changing circumstances. A runtime debug mode can be a powerful feature. Emulation of telephone functions such as ring and DTMF input, initiated at the keyboard, makes it possible to conduct active testing without actually connecting to a telephone network. Other convenient debug facilities include switching event logging on and off, single stepping, break points, and the ability to display and set variables, timers, counters and registers. Some APGENs even allow application or vocabulary redefinition, update, and modification while running, and some enable this to be accomplished remotely over the telephone.

Software architecture

To better understand the architecture of voice processing application generators, it's helpful to first consider the runtime structure of such systems. The runtime structure of a voice processing system was discussed in chapter 6. Regardless of what development tools are used to implement a multiline application, its runtime structure will be similar to that shown in Figure 6.2. The component labelled "Application Tasks" in that figure represents those tasks managing telephone lines. Application tasks are associated with a collection of application programs that contain application-specific intelligence, programs embodying the essence of an application. These application programs provide knowledge about what the system must speak in given situations, how it should respond to particular inputs, when it must update status displays, what information to collect for reports, what information it will obtain or provide to databases, when and what data it must communicate with an external host, and the like. Let's consider in more detail application programs produced with an APGEN.

First, one class of application generator compiles the developer's source input and produces object or runtime modules, as do standard compilers and assemblers. Runtime modules are executed directly by the computer, so the application programs for this class of generator are very similar to those produced with a toolkit and compiler. I refer to this class of APGENs as the object class. All other APGENs fall into the one remaining class whose members execute as interpreters. I call this class the interpreter class. Its members execute preprepared system code as guided by their interpretation of application-specific instructions (either the developer's source input or a coded or tokenized form derived from it). The actual source representation can be interpreted directly, but execution is more efficient from a compressed or abbreviated form. Application programs are more complex for interpreter class generators than for those in the object class. This is true because in addition to code for all functions, interpreters must also include code that parses and interprets an application's definition and executes the pre-existing telephone/voice functions in the sequence required by the application.

Let's consider the software architecture of each APGEN class separately. Figure 8.14 diagrams the architecture of APGENs in the interpreter class, and Figure 8.15 diagrams those of the object class. Notice how closely Figure 8.15 follows a standard language development procedure—differing in only two respects:

1. In accommodating vocabulary.

2. In using a custom editor.

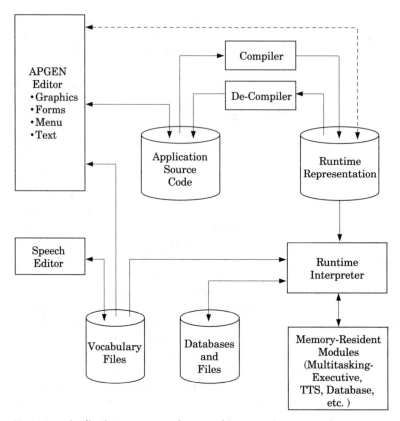

Figure 8.14 Application generator software architecture—interpreter class.

Custom APGEN editors are discussed in the next section. Were it not for these two exceptions, you could be looking at a diagram of any application developed in a standard compiler language. Observe the similarity between Figure 8.15 and the earlier Figure 8.7, which describes the architecture of a system developed using a toolkit. The similarity suggests that the existence of a custom editor qualifies a member of the object class as an application generator. It implies that systems featuring a voice processing language and a standard text editor would perhaps not be considered an application generator. If such is the case, a custom APGEN editor must be a powerful development tool indeed. In the next section I'll explain why this can be so.

APGEN editors. Editors are used to communicate application requirements to an APGEN. Sometimes a standard text editor, familiar to every programmer, can be used. Text editors are intended for general use, even though some are quite sophisticated and might even recognize what language is being programmed. However, it's their very generality that limits their power as a system development aid for use with application generators. A custom APGEN editor, on the other hand, is designed for a specific application generator. It embodies considerable syntactic knowledge and is thus able to participate in and contribute to the development process by providing computer-aided system engineering features to voice processing application developers. There are many examples of features not available in standard text editors. A custom editor, for instance, might allow symbolic reference to utterances, timers, registers, variables and other resources. When a fill-in form is displayed by the APGEN editor, a menu of allowable entries can be popped up in a window for selection. This is not possible with general text editors, but it enhances the applica-

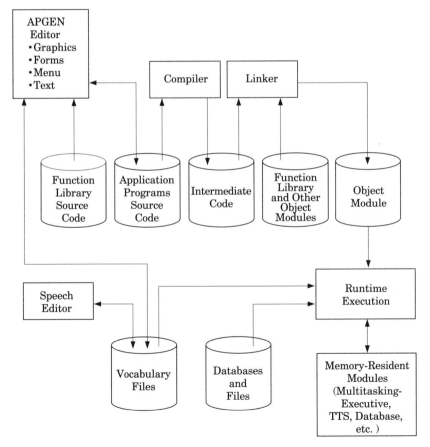

Figure 8.15 Application generator software architecture—object module class.

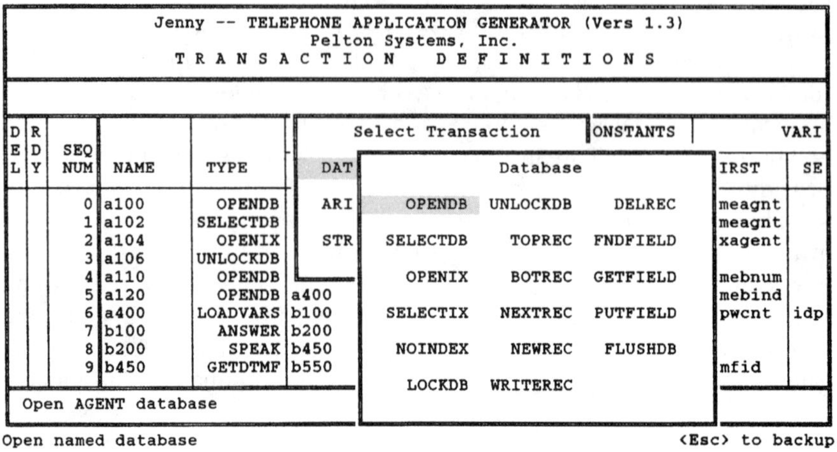

```
                Jenny -- TELEPHONE APPLICATION GENERATOR (Vers 1.3)
                            Pelton Systems, Inc.
                 T R A N S A C T I O N     D E F I N I T I O N S


  D R                                  Select Transaction    ONSTANTS         VARI
  E D  SEQ                           |
  L Y  NUM  NAME       TYPE      DAT |             Database           IRST      SE
        0  a100       OPENDB     ARI |  OPENDB   UNLOCKDB    DELREC    meagnt
        1  a102       SELECTDB       |                                meagnt
        2  a104       OPENIX     STR |  SELECTDB  TOPREC     FNDFIELD  xagent
        3  a106       UNLOCKDB       |
        4  a110       OPENDB         |  OPENIX    BOTREC     GETFIELD  mebnum
        5  a120       OPENDB    a400 |                                mebind
        6  a400       LOADVARS  b100 |  SELECTIX  NEXTREC    PUTFIELD  pwcnt   idp
        7  b100       ANSWER    b200 |
        8  b200       SPEAK     b450 |  NOINDEX   NEWREC     FLUSHDB
        9  b450       GETDTMF   b550 |                                mfid
                                     |  LOCKDB    WRITEREC
   Open AGENT database

  Open named database                                              <Esc> to backup
```

Figure 8.16 Menus in layered windows.

tion generator by eliminating the need to type an input. It greatly reduces erroneous entries. APGEN editors can check syntax during editing and perform other static tests. They could recognize context and present a set of features that are optimum for the situation. APGEN editors can be aware of the status of prompts, phrases, and other utterances and make this information available on-screen. Or, they might raise an on-screen warning if crucial information is missing from an application's specification. Illegal constructs can be disallowed and alternate ones suggested. The extent to which such editors can further the development process depends upon the features of the particular APGEN, but the possibilities seem limitless.

As mentioned earlier, APGEN editors use a variety of techniques to input application descriptions. They can be only slightly more complicated than a text editor or as complex as a CAD graphic interface. Some use a combination of menus and displayed fill-in forms. Figure 8.13, mentioned earlier, depicts a form displayed in a screen window. Items to be entered in the form are highlighted. Many context-sensitive, forms-based editors pop-up a menu of applicable entries for fields in which the allowable entries are limited and known in advance. The user moves a cursor over the menu and selects the appropriate item, which is then automatically entered into the field. This method of input is fast and efficient. Typing errors and incorrect entries are avoided. Figure 8.16 shows a screen on which two menu levels have been overlaid in windows.

A particularly interesting type of APGEN editor uses graphics to define an application's structure. Imagine a graphic editor that allows an application's top-level flow chart to be composed of about 12 different node types. Consider, for instance, a graphics editor composed of the following node types: ANSWER, KEY, HANGUP, DIAL, PLAY, RECORD, DO, HOST, FILE,

SPEAK, GOTO, and SWITCH. ANSWER waits for a ring signal on a line, then takes the phone offhook. KEY waits for and accepts DTMF inputs and HANGUP places the phone onhook. DIAL sends DTMF signals out on a line. PLAY is used for speaking voice messages and RECORD for recording them. DO exits to user programs, and HOST specifies operations involving communication with an external host computer. The FILE operation is used for any function accessing local databases or files. SPEAK is used to speak voice prompts, and GOTO enables program flow to be transferred to another flow chart. The SWITCH node checks a variable and goes to one of a set of other nodes, depending on its value. Mouse or cursor keys are used to place these constructs on the screen and to interconnect them. Application details are provided in pop-up forms for each individual node. An application might consist of multiple flow charts that are each entered as appropriate to the application.

Figure 8.17 is an example top-level flow chart as it might appear after

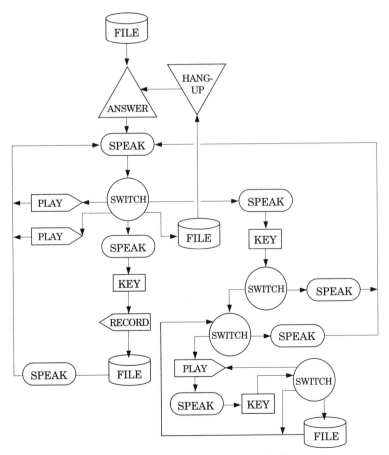

Figure 8.17 Top-level program flow from graphics APGEN editor.

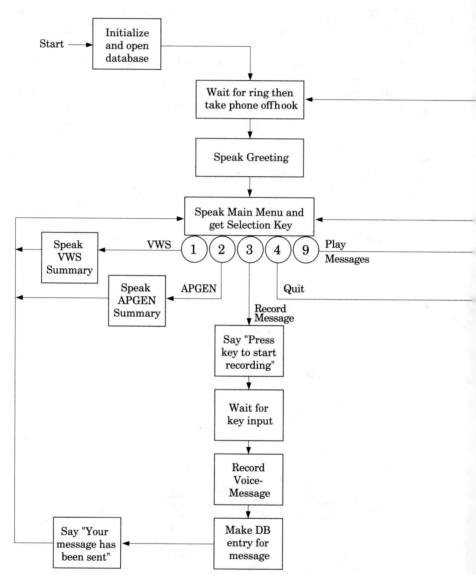

Figure 8.18 Flow of example application (Smart Answering Machine).

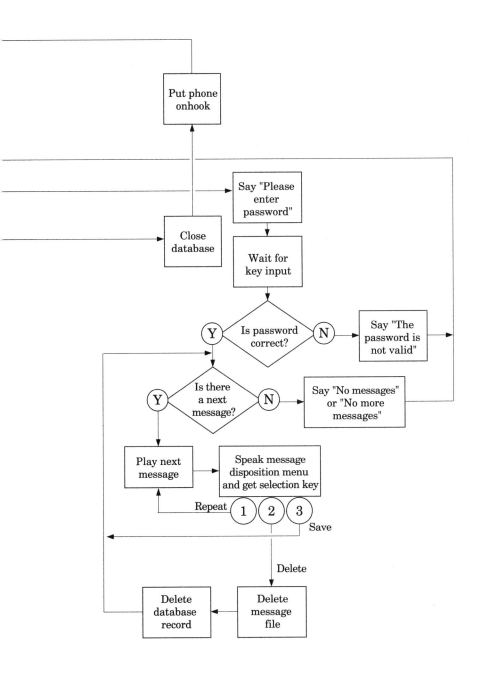

preparation with this editor. Of course, many details must yet be specified for the application it represents. A flow chart with as many nodes as that of the figure would have to be scrolled in two dimensions across the display because it could not be displayed in its entirety on most computer monitors. Figure 8.18 shows the same application in more detail in a nonautomated flow chart.

A special editing case arises for APGENs that support host communications. The host and voice processing system exchange data pertaining to the application. An application might be required to parse and speak values for instances of data in a host's database, or it might enter values that have been input via Touch-Tone to a host's database. Pertinent database fields must be defined and specified for use by the application generator. A typical approach is to download and display a copy of the host computer's access screen containing the field of interest. Under control of the APGEN editor, the application developer moves a cursor across the screen to highlight the field so it can be located in the screen. Its location is stored for later use. At runtime, a data stream representing the screen is transmitted from the host to the voice processor. The field value is either extracted from this data stream, or, for transmissions to the host, inserted into the data stream before the field value is retransmitted back to the host.

The capabilities of an application generator's editor—including its flexibility and ease of use—significantly affect its perceived value. Application generators deemed most powerful are those featuring a comprehensive and innovative custom editor. Not every application generator has one. Text editors are used by some voice processing development systems claimed by their developers to be application generators. You're justified in asking whether such systems are APGENs or just specialized higher-level programming languages.

Regardless of the approach used in an APGEN editor, its purpose is always to produce a machine-readable representation of an application. Application representations and related concepts are discussed in the following sections.

Application source representation. An application's *source representation* is the defining information and data that's produced and stored by an APGEN's editor. There are as many forms of source representation as there are application generators, and they vary from script languages to tables and relational databases containing various constructs. Perhaps the easiest to comprehend, because of their similarity to standard programming languages, are those represented as a succession of program statements in a scripting language. A simple application programmed in an example scripting language appears in appendix G. A flowchart of this application is shown in Figure 8.18. More obscure source representations involve sets of tables. Many custom APGEN editors, including the graphics-oriented ones, express and store an application as a set of tables or their database equivalents.

Let's examine the set of source tables required for definition of a voice processing application. This can best be done by considering a simple application and an example APGEN. Figure 8.18, just mentioned, depicts program flow for a smart answering machine. The application is intended to run asynchronously on multiple lines. When a line rings, it is taken offhook and a greeting and a prompt menu are spoken. The caller is offered an opportunity to hear either of two product summaries or to record a message. A local database contains the file name of each voice message. A system user can obtain his messages by telephone after correctly entering a fixed password. For purposes of this discussion, assume that this application has been implemented with an interpreter-class APGEN that produces its source representation in the form of tables.

Figure 8.19 lists the commands available in this example. The source rep-

EXAMPLE APPLICATION GENERATOR COMMANDS		
CODE	COMMAND	DESCRIPTION
1	ANSWER	Wait for x rings, go off hook, initiate call statistics
2	HANGUP	Go on hook, complete call statistics
3	SPEAK	Speak a prompt, phrase, or other utterance
4	GETDTMF	Wait for x DTMF digits to be entered
5	COMPARE	Compare two variables, jump if =>, =, or <=
6	MENU	Speak prompts, wait for 1 DTMF, jump based on selection
7	SWITCH	Compare variable to range set, jump based on result
8	INCRTEST	Increment a variable by one and jump based on result
9	INCR	Increment a variable by one
10	COPYVAR	Copy up to three variables to other variables
11	LOADVARS	Initalize up to three variables (from constants)
12	GETTIME	Put system time into a variable
13	GETDATE	Put system date into a variable
14	SELECTDB	Select a database and make its status "current"
15	SELECTIX	Select a database index and make its status "current"
16	NOINDEX	Set database mode for use with no index
17	FLUSHDB	Write all current database records to database
18	FNDFIELD	Make specified database field "current"
19	GETFIELD	Place contecurrent database field in variable
20	PUTFIELD	Place contents of variable into current database field
21	TOPREC	Make current database's first record "current"
22	BOTREC	Make current database's final record "current"
23	NEXTREC	Make next database record after current one "current"
24	NEWREC	Create a new database record
25	WRITEREC	Write the current database record to current database
26	MOVE	Move characters within a variable to another variable
27	PACK	Pack constant characters into a variable
28	RESETVAR	Reset a variable to its default value
29	NOOP	No operation
30	OPENDB	Open a database
31	OPENIX	Open a database index
32	LOCKDB	Lock a database so other tasks may not access it
33	UNLOCKDB	Unlock a database an make it available to all tasks
34	TINTON	Enable interrupt of speaking based on DTMF input
35	TINTOFF	Disable interrupt of speaking based on DTMF input
36	RECMSG	Record a voice message
37	CLRDTMF	Empty the DTMF buffer
38	PLAYMSG	Play a voice message
39	DELMSG	Delete a voice message
40	DELREC	Delete a database record
41	SETABORT	Establish restart location in case of early disconnect

Figure 8.19 Application generator commands.

Pelton Systems, Inc.
TELEPHONE/VOICE APPLICATION GENERATOR (Vers 1.3)
C O M M A N D   D E F I N I T I O N S

SEQ NUM	NAME	COMMAND TYPE	NEXT COMMAND FIRST	SECOND	THIRD	CONSTANTS 1	2	3	VARIABLES FIRST	SECOND	THIRD	DESCRIPTION
1	Begin	OPENDB							vmdbname			Good password – Open messsages.dbf
2	Restart	SELECTDB							vmdbname			Select messages database
3		SETABORT		Restart								Set next command for restart
4		FLUSHDB							filename			Flush database buffer
5		UNLOCKDB	Answer									Unlock database
6	Answer	ANSWER				1						Answer on 1st ring
7		SPEAK										Speak Greeting
8		SPEAK										Speak Main Menu
9	Waiting	GETDTMF		End_call		1	9	7	mainmenu			Get one key for Main menu selection
10	Switch_1	SWITCH	Waitring				9	7	mainmenu			Go to selected Main Menu function
11	Rec_msg	RECMSG				3	5	90	filename			Record voice message
12		SPEAK										Say "Your message has been sent"
13		LOCKDB										Lock database (WRITEREC unlocks)
14		NEWREC										Create new database record
15		PUTFIELD							filename	fldname		Put filename into record
16		WRITEREC	Waitring									Write record to database and unlock
17	Say_VWS	SPEAK	Endsumm									Say VWS Summary messages
18	Say_APG	SPEAK										Say APGEN Summary messages
19	Endsumm	CLRDTMF										Get rid of any keys
20		SPEAK	Waitring									Say end of both summaries
21	End_call	SPEAK										Speak farewell message
22		HANGUP	Answer									Hangup and wait for next call
23	Password	SPEAK										Ask for password
24		GETDTMF	Waitring	End_call		5	8	8	pwdtmf			Get 5-digit password from caller
25		COMPARE	Waitring	DB_top	Waitring				pwdtmf	pwfixed		Verify password
26	DB_top	TOPREC	Filename	No_msg					filename			Make first record current
27	Filename	GETFIELD	Repeat						filename	fldname		Get filename from database
28	Repeat	PLAYMSG							filename			Play current voice-message
29		SPEAK										Speak Playback Menu
30		GETDTMF		End_call		1	8	8	playkey			Get Playback Menu selection key
31	Switch_2	SWITCH	Repeat						playkey			Go to selected function
32	Delete	DELMSG							filename			Erase message file
33		DELREC										Erase database entry
34		NEXTREC	Filename	No_more								Get next message
35	No_msg	SPEAK	Waitring									Say "no messages"
36	No_more	SPEAK	Waitring									Say "no more messages"

Figure 8.20 Command definitions source table.

```
                        Pelton Systems, Inc.
             TELEPHONE/VOICE APPLICATION GENERATOR (Vers 1.3)
                 V A R I A B L E S    D E F I N I T I O N S

                                   PRIVATE
  SEQ                                 or
  NUM    NAME       TYPE            PUBLIC     VALUE     DESCRIPTION

    1  filename  CHARACTER          PRIVATE              Filename will be deposited here
    2  fldname   CHARACTER          PUBLIC   filename    Name of MESSAGES.DBF field for filename
    3  k-1       NUMERIC            PUBLIC   1           Constant: 1
    4  k-2       NUMERIC            PUBLIC   2           Constant: 2
    5  k-3       NUMERIC            PUBLIC   3           constant: 3
    6  k-4       NUMERIC            PUBLIC   4           Constant: 4
    7  k-9       NUMERIC            PUBLIC   9           constant: 9
    8  mainmenu  NUMERIC            PRIVATE  0           Key input for Main Menu selection
    9  playkey   NUMERIC            PRIVATE  0           Selection from playback menu
   10  pwdtmf    NUMERIC            PRIVATE  0           Password input from dtmf
   11  pwfixed   NUMERIC            PRIVATE  82633       Password - must be entered to get voice-messages
   12  vmdbname  CHARACTER          PUBLIC   messages    Name of Voice-Messages Database
```

Figure 8.21 Variable definitions source table.

resentation of an application consists of a set of tables, as shown in Figures 8.20 through 8.25. To express an application in this example APGEN, commands are grouped sequentially, as shown in Figure 8.20. The figure shows an APGEN editor access screen for the command table. The information in the table can't be viewed completely in one screen, so it can be scrolled in both dimensions on the screen display. Variables are defined for use by certain commands. These are specified in the variables table, whose scrollable access screen is given in Figure 8.21. To define an application's vocabulary, the utterance table (Figure 8.22) contains information pertaining to prompts, phrases, utterances, and their speech files. Sequences of utterances are attached to various speaking commands—these are referenced and spoken sequentially at runtime. Strings of prompts, phrases, and other utterances attached to a command appear in a table like the one shown in Figure 8.23. The SWITCH command tests the contents of a variable and, depending on its contents, jumps to a next command in the command table. Information regarding variable ranges and jump locations are contained in a switch range table like the one whose scrollable access screen is given in Figure 8.24. Finally, to enable each line to be associated with its own application, a telephone line table (Figure 8.25) specifies the starting command for each line. It's important to bear in mind that the commands and tables shown in the figures represent but one implementation of an APGEN. Many thousands are possible.

Source representation might occur in other forms, but tables are most natural for use with both relational databases and interpreters. Source tables can be stored in files or in a database and can be loaded to memory during application generation or accessed directly from disk during the generation process. In the example, the application generator's custom editor enables creation of the tables and displays their contents for review or editing. Each command will be interpreted in turn at runtime, causing appropriate code to be executed to accomplish the command's intent. Notice

```
                    Pelton Systems, Inc.
       TELEPHONE/VOICE APPLICATION GENERATOR (Vers 1.3)
          U T T E R A N C E   D E F I N I T I O N S
```

SEQ NUM	NAME or FILENAME	TYPE	REFERS to VARIABLE	DELAY (0.1 SECS)	DESCRIPTION	RECORDED FILE			
						DATE	TIME	BYTES	SECS	READY
1	2end	RECORDED		3	Press any key to end recording	05 Feb 91	19:59:02	8436	3	No
2	2erase	RECORDED		3	To erase and continue, press 2	05 Feb 91	19:50:04	7676	3	No
3	2quit	RECORDED		3	To return to main menu, press 9	06 Feb 91	12:02:48	6612	2	Yes
4	2recmsg	RECORDED		0	To record a voice message, press 1	05 Feb 91	20:03:50	6156	2	No
5	2repeat	RECORDED		3	To repeat, press 1	05 Feb 91	19:52:20	11020	4	Yes
6	2save	RECORDED		3	To save and continue, press 3	06 Feb 91	11:58:38	18544	6	No
7	2start	RECORDED		0	Press any key to start recording	06 Feb 91	12:07:12	12996	4	No
8	4apgsumm	RECORDED		3	For APGEN Summary, press 3	06 Feb 91	12:09:26	8588	3	No
9	4vwssumm	RECORDED		3	For VWS Summary, press 2	28 Jan 91	12:03:58	101308	33	Yes
10	apg001	RECORDED		3	APGEN Summary 1 of 8	28 Jan 91	12:06:58	34732	11	Yes
11	apg002	RECORDED		5	APGEN Summary 2 of 8	28 Jan 91	12:34:34	36328	12	Yes
12	apg003	RECORDED		5	APGEN Summary 3 of 8	28 Jan 91	12:09:56	54340	18	No
13	apg004	RECORDED		5	APGEN Summary 4 of 8	28 Jan 91	12:12:52	31616	10	No
14	apg005	RECORDED		5	APGEN Summary 5 of 8	28 Jan 91	12:29:38	65512	22	No
15	apg006	RECORDED		5	APGEN Summary 6 of 8	28 Jan 91	12:31:58	68476	23	No
16	apg007	RECORDED		5	APGEN Summary 7 of 8	25 Jan 91	15:24:44	83752	28	No
17	apg008	RECORDED		5	APGEN Summary 8 of 8	06 Feb 91	12:25:48	27968	9	Yes
18	both001	RECORDED		7	Introduce VWS and APGEN Summaries	25 Jan 91	14:49:26	83220	27	Yes
19	both081	RECORDED		0	Play this on tail end of both vws and apgen summ	06 Feb 91	12:32:04	70148	23	No
20	both091	RECORDED		0	Play this after both VWS and APGEN Summaries	28 Jan 91	12:58:02	9044	3	Yes
21	farewell	RECORDED		0	Thankyou for calling XYZ Company. Goodbye.	06 Feb 91	12:35:18	6080	2	No
22	greeting	RECORDED		3	Hello. This is XYZ Company......	06 Feb 91	13:16:38	6308	2	No
23	ifdone	RECORDED		0	If you are finished, press four.	05 Feb 91	19:53:18	4864	2	Yes
24	inputpw	RECORDED		0	Enter your password	06 Feb 91	18:06:44	4560	2	Yes
25	msgsent	RECORDED		0	Your message has been sent	05 Feb 91	19:54:20	4332	1	No
26	nomore	RECORDED		0	No more messages	05 Feb 91	19:55:16	3648	1	No
27	nomsgs	RECORDED		0	No messages					No
28	promo	RECORDED		0	Promotion message					No
29	reclimit	RECORDED		0	Your message may be 90 seconds in length	24 Jan 91	09:00:00	4636	2	No
30	tone	RECORDED		3	<Tone>	19 Feb 91	18:51:38	2053	1	Yes
31	vws001	RECORDED		3	VWS Summary 1 of 4	25 Jan 91	14:43:06	152912	51	No
32	vws002	RECORDED		5	VWS Summary 2 of 4	25 Jan 91	14:35:30	135584	45	Yes
33	vws003	RECORDED		5	VWS Summary 3 of 4	25 Jan 91	14:41:26	60268	20	Yes
34	vws004	RECORDED		5	VWS Summary 4 of 4	25 Jan 91	14:46:10	136420	45	No

Figure 8.22 Utterance definitions source table.

Pelton Systems, Inc.
TELEPHONE/VOICE APPLICATION GENERATOR (Vers 1.3)
C O M M A N D ' S   U T T E R A N C E S

COMMAND: Say_VWS   Say the VWS summary messages

SEQ NUM	NAME or FILENAME	TYPE	REFERS TO VARIABLE	DELAY (0.1 SECS)	DESCRIPTION	RECORDED FILE				READY
						DATE	TIME	BYTES	SECS	
1	both001	RECORDED		0	Introduce VWS and APGEN summaries	06 Feb 91	12:25:48	27968	9	Yes
2	vws001	RECORDED		3	VWS Summary 1 of 4	25 Jan 91	14:43:06	152912	51	No
3	vws002	RECORDED		5	VWS Summary 2 of 4	25 Jan 91	14:35:30	135584	45	Yes
4	vws003	RECORDED		5	VWS Summary 3 of 4	25 Jan 91	14:41:26	60268	20	Yes
5	vws004	RECORDED		5	VWS Summary 4 of 4	25 Jan 91	14:46:10	136420	45	No
6	both081	RECORDED		7	Play this at end of both VWS and APGEN Summ	25 Jan 91	14:49:26	83220	27	Yes

Figure 8.23 Utterance source table (command 17 Say_VWS).

```
                            Pelton Systems, Inc.
                TELEPHONE/VOICE APPLICATION GENERATOR (Vers 1.3)
                S W I T C H    R A N G E    D E F I N I T I O N S
```

COMMAND: Switch_1	Go to the selected Main Menu function

VARIABLE RANGE		NEXT	
FROM VAR	TO VAR	CMD	DESCRIPTION
k-1	k-1	Rec_msg	Key [1]
k-2	k-2	Say_VWS	Key [2]
k-3	k-3	Say_APG	Key [3]
k-4	k-4	End_call	Key [4]
k-9	k-9	Password	Key [9]

Figure 8.24 Switch ranges source table (Command 10 Switch_1).

```
                            Pelton Systems, Inc.
                TELEPHONE/VOICE APPLICATION GENERATOR (Vers 1.3)
                T E L E P H O N E    L I N E    D E F I N I T I O N S
```

LINE NUM	TELEPHONE NUMBER	STARTING COMMAND	PHONE LINE DESCRIPTION
1	283-0232	Begin	Local and test line
2	283-0233		Not used
3	283-0234	Begin	Live telephone line for inbound calls
4	283-0235	Begin	Live telephone line for inbound calls

Figure 8.25 Telephone line source table.

in the table that any command can be addressed symbolically by giving it a name. This example APGEN uses a command structure that permits specifying any of four commands to be executed after the current one. The next command depends on the results of the current command's execution. Not all commands use all four possibilities—only one is required. The ANSWER command (and many others) has only one possible next command, the one immediately succeeding it in the table. Many commands proceed to the next command in the table on normal completion but go to the first, second, or third "next command" on an error or abnormal completion. For others, the next command depends on computations. For example, the COMPARE command compares the contents of two variables. If they're equal, the second "next command" (as shown in the table) is executed. Otherwise, the first or third "next command" is executed, depending on which variable is larger.

The example application generator also allows each command to specify up to three constants and up to three variables. As with "next command," constants and variables might or might not be used by any particular command. COMPARE, for example, uses only two variables (the ones being compared) and RECMSG (record a voice-message) uses three constants and one variable. The final column in the command table contains a comment or description for use of the developer. A string of prompts, phrases, and other utterances to be spoken in sequence can be attached to a command—so either simple or compound utterances can be spoken.

Variables are referenced by either commands or utterances. For example, a command might specify that a variable be changed to contain the sum of two other variables, or an utterance entry in the table might specify a variable and ask that it be spoken as a dollar amount. Variables are defined in the variables table. Each row in the table represents one variable. Notice that variables are typed and, further, can be either private or public. There's only one instance of public variables, but there are separate instances of private variables—one for each telephone line. Variables are initialized with the values shown in the "values" column. A separate table, a value table, contains the current contents of each instance of every variable.

Prompts, phrases, and other utterances used by the application are defined in the utterance table. Each line in the table represents one utterance file, and each can be addressed by a symbolic name or filename. The example uses only recorded utterances, but there are provisions for other types (e.g., those that parse and speak a variable in a specific format such as a date or dollar amount). A "delay" column specifies a period of silence to be inserted ahead of the spoken utterance. This feature enables developers to adjust the rhythm of speaking for concatenated prompts and phrases. If an utterance has been recorded, its file information is given in four columns on the display—this information need not appear in the database because it's easily available from the operating system. A final column can be used to indicate whether the recorded file contains prototype or finished vocabulary. Subsets of this table are linked to individual commands in the command table and appear in a command's utterances table.

Some features of this APGEN are not apparent in the tables. SPEAK commands in the command table are each linked to a subset of the utterance table, and SWITCH commands are linked to a switch range table. Speaking commands concatenate in sequence the files appearing in the speaking commands' individual utterance tables. The tables contain as many entries as needed, and any utterance can appear in any subset more than once. Switch range tables define ranges of variable values. SWITCH commands specify a variable to be tested against these ranges to determine the next command to be executed. A telephone line definition table is used to define telephone lines for the application and to specify each line's starting command in the command definitions table. Thus, different programs can be run for different lines. The telephone line table of Figure 8.25 shows only four lines for purposes of illustration, but, it could have 24, 48, or any other number.

A quick study reveals that the source tables contain all the information necessary to completely specify the application. To aid developers, the source representation also contains ancillary information such as command descriptions, symbolic names, and file dates. Processing source representations at runtime would entail significant inefficiencies attendant to moving and parsing larger amounts of information. In the next section I'll discuss more concise runtime representations that can be derived from source representations.

Runtime representation. Object class APGENs, by definition, use a standard runtime module format for their runtime representation. For interpreter class APGENs, on the other hand, runtime representation might take any of many forms. Source and runtime representations can be one and the same. There's a trade-off, however, between the need for source to be human-readable and descriptive and the need for runtime representations to be compressed for efficiency. Source forms are most useful when they include ample amounts of ancillary reference material. Runtime representations are most effective when they contain absolutely nothing more than what's sufficient to define the application—this means no extraneous or redundant information. These objectives are diametrically opposed. It follows that using a source representation at runtime places severe demands on the system, which must spend more time accessing, parsing, and understanding its instructions. The extra demand ultimately results in restrictions on the number of telephone calls handled simultaneously. To conserve storage space and minimize access times, source tables are translated either into object code, a set of abbreviated tables, or some representation most efficient for use at runtime. Naturally, if encoding is part of the compression process, savings in access time might be squandered on decoding the material before it can be used. Most interpreter-class APGENs employ a table structure at runtime. Tables lend themselves well to the structural requirements of a voice processing application and are natural for use with relational databases. Runtime tables can be saved in files or databases to be loaded and run from memory, or they can be interpreted directly from disk.

An interpretive application generator that can execute an application without an intermediate compilation or conversion of source data offers advantages. Nevertheless, these are not great enough to compensate for loss of runtime efficiency. The conversion step might be called conversion, compilation, or translation—but, no matter how its labeled, its main purpose is to remove redundant and extraneous information such as descriptions from source representations. It might also convert ASCII fields to binary, or tokenize the source, exchanging symbols or numbers for text commands. Consider the Figures 8.26 through 8.31. These are runtime tables derived from source for the example application previously discussed. In memory or on disk, they would probably be stored in a binary format to reduce storage to an absolute minimum. As presented in this chapter, some of the fig-

		NEXT CMD			CONSTANTS			VARIABLES			ATTACHED	
SEQ NUM	CMD	1st	2nd	3rd	1st	2nd	3rd	1st	2nd	3rd	UTTS	RANGE
1	30							12				
2	14							12				
3	41		2									
4	17							1				
5	33	6										
6	1				1							
7	3										1	
8	3										5	
9	4		21		1	9	7	8				
10	7	9				9	7	8				6
11	36				3	5	90	1				
12	3										11	
13	32											
14	24											
15	20							1	2			
16	25	9										
17	3	19									12	
18	3										23	
19	37											
20	3	9									15	
21	3										17	
22	2	6										
23	3										29	
24	4		21		5	8	8	10				
25	5	9	26	9				10	11			
26	21	27	35									
27	19	28						1	2			
28	38							1				
29	3										26	
30	4		21		1	8	8	9				
31	7	28						9				1
32	39							1				
33	40											
34	23	27	36									
35	3	9									31	
36	3	9									28	

COMMAND

Runtime Table

Figure 8.26 Command Runtime table.

ures include a sequence number or line number for our convenience. These are not really part of the stored table—they're implicitly derived at runtime from an item's position in the table. Segments for a command's utterances or switch ranges attached to the command runtime table are referenced by their sequence or index numbers. In both cases, command utterances and switch ranges, the tables consist of a segment for each speaking or switch command, even though the figures show segments for only one command each.

Comparison of each source table with its corresponding runtime table reveals how much memory space is reduced. Sequence numbers, line numbers, and ASCII descriptions have been deleted. Symbolic reference points such as command table names, variable names, and utterance names have been replaced with index numbers or pointers to their corresponding items in the various tables. Command symbolics have been replaced by command

VARIABLES			
Runtime Table			
SEQ NUM	TYPE	PRIV or PUBL	VALUE
1	0	0	
2	0	1	filename
3	1	1	1
4	1	1	2
5	1	1	3
6	1	1	4
7	1	1	9
8	1	0	0
9	1	0	0
10	1	0	0
11	1	0	82633
12	0	1	messages

Figure 8.27 Variable runtime table.

codes. Variable and utterance types and a variable's private/public designations have been binary coded. Almost all parameters can be stored in binary
form for compactness. A significant reduction in memory has been accomplished by changes of this type. The result is that source tables might contain as much extraneous descriptive information as desired, while runtime
tables are trimmed to a minimum for efficient access and processing.

The script program of appendix G and the source tables of Figures 8.20
through 8.25 are both implementations of the Smart Answering Machine
application, whose flowchart was shown in Figure 8.18. It's easy to imagine
how the source tables could have been derived from the script language
program. It's also easy to imagine an inclusive application generator that:

1. Implements such a script language.

2. Includes a compiler to produce source tables from script code.

3. Features a custom APGEN editor for source tables.

4. Translates source tables to runtime tables.

Such powerful multisource application generators do exist.

In many cases, a de-translator can be designed to convert from runtime

		REFERS to VARIABLE	DELAY (0.1 SECS)	
UTTERANCE Runtime Table				
SEQ NUM	TYPE	REFERS to VARIABLE	DELAY (0.1 SECS)	READY
1	2		3	0
2	2		3	0
3	2		3	1
4	2		0	1
5	2		0	0
6	2		3	1
7	2		0	0
8	2		3	0
9	2		3	0
10	2		3	1
11	2		5	1
12	2		5	1
13	2		5	0
14	2		5	0
15	2		5	0
16	2		5	0
17	2		5	1
18	2		0	1
19	2		7	1
20	2		0	1
21	2		0	1
22	2		0	0
23	2		3	0
24	2		0	1
25	2		0	1
26	2		0	0
27	2		0	0
28	2		0	0
29	2		3	0
30	2		0	1
31	2		3	0
32	2		5	1
33	2		5	1
34	2		5	0

Figure 8.28 Utterance runtime table.

COMMAND 17's UTTERANCE Runtime Table
UTTERANCE INDEX
18
31
32
33
34
19

Figure 8.29 Utterance runtime table (Command 17 Say_VWS).

SWITCH RANGES for COMMAND 10 Runtime Table		
VARIABLE RANGE		NEXT CMD
FROM VAR	TO VAR	
3	3	11
4	4	17
5	5	18
6	6	21
7	7	23

Figure 8.30 Switch ranges runtime table (Command 10 Switch_1).

TELEPHONE LINE Runtime Table		
LINE NUM	PHONE NUMBER	STARTING COMMAND
1	2830232	1
2	2830233	1
3	2830234	1
4	2830235	1

Figure 8.31 Telephone line runtime table.

back to source representations. In the case of the example, output from the de-compiler or de-translator could be either script code, source tables, or other. In most cases, the value of this conversion is small for two reasons. First, most application generators preserve source code for later upgrades or editing. Second, even if such a de-translation were desired, all human-readable information will have been lost in translating from source to run-time representation. This information can never be regenerated in its original form from only the runtime representation. Descriptions and meaningful symbolics for commands, variables, and utterances can't be recovered. The best that can be produced are sterile, machine-generated symbolics.

Memory-resident modules. As in the case of toolkits, APGENs might feature optional runtime support packages implemented as memory-resident modules. If the operating system doesn't support multitasking, a memory-resident multitasking executive would be included as part of the application generator. FAX, text-to-speech, voice-recognition, local database support, and host communication can be implemented as optional memory-resident modules. Some APGEN developers also treat special variable-parsing and speaking functions, transaction logging, and voice messaging features as optional and offer them as memory-resident packages.

Runtime interpreter. The interpreter module serves as an intermediary between an application's runtime representation and runtime code in memory, implementing the various voice processing functions. The interpreter runs as a task (or tasks) under multitasking, accesses a runtime representation from memory or database, parses it, and assembles a sequence of calls to appropriate executable code functions.

The structure of an interpreter can be quite simple. An example is shown in Figure 8.32, which depicts the highest-level flowchart for an interpreter. Such an interpreter might be programmed in a higher-level language like C with surprisingly few statements. Except for a number of administrative details, it can be accomplished in one main loop that decodes and parses each command in turn and passes control to a separate command execution module depending on the command. The loop is entered once for each command executed. Variables, utterances, and other definitions are accessed as needed. Command decoding can be common to a point, but each command-type must have its own execution module because execution of each differs in some respect from all others. Adding a new command to the application generator involves only two steps:

1. Installing object code for the command.
2. Entering the command's execution address into a table.

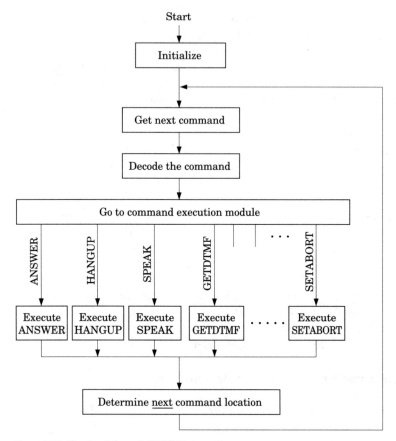

Figure 8.32 Top-level flow of APGEN interpreter.

Vocabulary files. Vocabulary files consist of the prompts, phrases, and other utterances that compose an application's voice. They can be packed many into a single file, or each can reside in their own file. Complex applications use more utterances and can result in a very large file if all are squeezed into a single file. While there are advantages to having only one vocabulary file, large files are more difficult to maintain and harder to move from system to system. Vocabulary for an application can be distributed among several files. This approach allows for logical grouping that can be more conveniently maintained. It also facilitates moving vocabulary items between applications. In a multiline system, a large number of lines could be using vocabulary at the same time, placing enormous demands on the file system. For this reason, a very fast hard disk is often used. In many systems, particularly those supporting many telephone lines, vocabulary data might reside in memory, perhaps on a RAM disk, and be loaded from files at runtime.

Debugging. An application generator, given a logically correct application definition, should result in a bug-free runtime system. For complex applications, however, it's not likely that the application can be flawlessly defined without testing. While APGEN makers often claim their tools enable users to create complete running systems without programming, the process of producing voice processing systems with an application generator can definitely be called programming. All but the most uncomplicated computer programs require some debugging. With an application generator, though, debugging means finding logical inconsistencies in a collection of constructs that form the application's source representation. If the source is a scripting language, debugging is essentially the same as for conventional applications.

APGENs provide numerous features to aid in debugging: event logging, transaction logging (not necessarily intended for debugging, but it can help), runtime displays, and more. Debugging APGEN-developed systems is usually not a daunting task because application generators typically allow programming at a high level. They rely to a very large extent on execution of code that has been previously developed and should be viable. An application can often be debugged intuitively by running it and observing its operation. The relationship between the application's source and its operation is usually so direct that the nature of an observed malfunction easily suggests that part of the application's definition that is in error.

Vocabulary production

Vocabulary files, an application's voice, are created either offline with a speech editor or under the auspices of the APGEN editor. High-quality voice can be produced in a simple but adequate facility with a rudimentary speech editor if proper measures are taken. However, many application generators provide little support for this crucial development task—support that does not often result in the best vocabulary possible. Furthermore, documentation accompanying some APGENs tends to minimize the task, furthering the mistaken notion that developers need exercise only minimal care when producing vocabulary for their applications. It's best, even when developing applications with an APGEN, to produce finished vocabulary in a more controlled manner and to consider that created with the application generator's editor to be only prototype vocabulary. A comprehensive APGEN editor has knowledge of what prompts, phrases, and utterances are required for an application. They can thus be of important service in managing the vocabulary production process. Chapter 9 discusses vocabulary production methods and requirements for creating high-quality speech.

Application documentation

An application generator has information concerning all components, procedures, processes, and relationships pertaining to its applications. Thus, as an integrated system with full knowledge of all aspects of an application, it can supply developers with more thorough documentation. It's able to produce not only archival materials but also documentation that furthers the development process, including one-dimensional listings of defined elements and cross-reference listings relating an application's logical segments, commands, variables, and vocabulary items. It can include source listings, reporting and communication specifications, as well as variable, vocabulary, and screen definitions. It might include specifications giving a quasi-English language description of an application's functional flow. A description of the system's configuration details can also be produced, showing assignment of telephone lines, communication channel arrangements, default parameter settings, and the like. Application documentation at this level can shorten development cycles and significantly reduce the cost of maintenance and later upgrades.

Creating an APGEN from a toolkit

Given a voice processing toolkit, a simple APGEN featuring original and derived toolkit functions can be produced by an experienced programmer. Naturally, the toolkit must support multitasking either through the operating system or a multitasking module. Any of the APGEN architectures previously discussed could be implemented from a toolkit. However, as an example, let's consider construction of a simple scripting language, table-based, interpreter-class APGEN. Elaborate scripting languages are possible, but for this example, let's support only features and commands existing in the toolkit or derived from them. This restriction enables creation of an APGEN with the least effort. First, a scripting language must be defined— one that follows the functions and capabilities of the toolkit. The new scripting language could be used to create the program of appendix G. Any text editor can be used to produce source, so you're not concerned with developing a custom editor. A compiler must be developed that reads source script and produces, as an alternate source representation, a set of tables similar to those of Figures 8.20 through 8.25. Tables will be implemented as a set of relational databases that include a command database that lists script commands and information pertinent to their execution, an utterance database defining voice prompts and phrases, and a variables database composing a table of variables used by applications. A telephone-line database containing a table of applications to be associated with lines at runtime, a switch-range database, and a variable's values database containing current values of variables will also be needed. The line database will be constructed and managed in a separate, simple process (that must also be developed), so it can be changed anytime without recourse to the compiler.

If scripting language commands correspond to those of the toolkit, or are derived from them, creation of an interpreter (like that of Figure 8.32) is easily accomplished by experienced programmers. The interpreter's command execution modules already exist in the toolkit's function library. Development of the interpreter will be an easier task than development of the language compiler, which must parse source script statements and construct appropriate entries in the databases. Of course, it's possible to load an application's tables to memory, but this technique would unnecessarily limit the size of applications. An off-the-shelf speech editor can be used to produce vocabulary. However, a simple vocabulary recording utility that references the utterance database could be developed for use, making it difficult to overlook production of any utterance. Prototype vocabulary can be replaced later.

Speech Editors

A speech editor is a software utility that helps developers create, modify, and manage prompts, phrases and other utterances that compose an application's voice. Besides providing many editing features, speech editors enable developers to create, record, edit, move, copy, rename, or delete any utterance or file. Speech editors simplify and enhance creation of professional-level speech. Editing is done on scrollable, full-screen graphic displays of an utterance's energy. Most editors are designed for a specific telephone/voice board and, to some extent, editor features are dependent on its compression algorithm. As mentioned in an earlier chapter, frequency domain encoding techniques differ from time domain techniques. Their respective output data streams contain different speech parameters—some of which lend themselves more naturally to changes that can be edited. Such editing leads to a direct and predictable speech result. For example, LPC includes an energy parameter that can be increased or decreased to cause the speech to be spoken louder or softer. No such parameter exists in ADPCM, delta modulation, nor in many other encoding schemes.

Vocabulary for voice processing systems is organized into well-defined segments that are used individually or concatenated to form longer segments. Prompts, phrases and other speech segments are stored in either single utterance files or indexed files containing multiple speech segments. Indexed speech files include a directory relating every utterance to its starting offset in the file, its length in bytes, and the offset of its text description. Not all editors support descriptions, and some record them in a separate file. Single utterance files contain speech data for only one utterance (which might also be associated with a text description in another file). Some speech editors handle either type of file, and some feature full file-management capabilities, allowing files and utterances to be copied, deleted or renamed.

The most convenient speech editors allow visual editing on full-screen displays on either monochrome or graphic monitors. Both graph an utterance's energy versus time and can also feature zooming. Speech editing features are discussed later.

Hardware requirements

It would theoretically be possible for an editor to prepare voice data in any compression algorithm using a general signal processor, but most editors use the same computer and telephone/voice hardware required by the target voice processing system. Except for speaking and recording, editor features should be operational even when the telephone/voice board or its software driver are not installed. File management functions don't need the hardware, and some editing features can be performed without it. Typically, editors don't require multitasking unless editing takes place while a voice processing system is up and running. Speech editors might require more expensive graphic displays, but those that display energy graphs on any monitor from monochrome on up are available. A telephone handset, microphone, or recorder is required for inputting voice to the board for digitization, compression, and disk storage. An amplifier with speaker or headphones is required to monitor stored speech data. Many boards require a special adapter to drive these audio devices. Some audio adapters operate on battery power and suffer from inconsistent operation associated with frequent battery failure.

Speech file management

Voice processing applications can use large numbers of prompts, phrases, and other utterances. Many require hundreds, each of which is either installed in its own file or grouped, several dozen to an indexed file. Either way, numerous files must be maintained because during the life of an application, utterances undergo changes. They're created, replaced, deleted, moved, and copied. The speech editor is the logical tool for handling these tasks. It must, therefore, display pertinent information regarding vocabulary files and their utterances. As an example, Figure 8.33 shows a scrollable screen that lists files containing one utterance. Notice that most columns display standard information readily available from the operating

```
         V O I C E      W O R K S T A T I O N   (Vers 3.1.2)
                        Pelton Systems, Inc.
            S I N G L E      U T T E R A N C E      F I L E S

FILES:   C:\MS\RUN\*.apg
```

	VERSION		LENGTH					SAMPLES PER
FILENAME	DATE	TIME	SECS	BYTES	ATTR			SECOND
1MOMENT	01-15-91	12:22:56	1	3192	.a..			6053
ANNOUNCE	03-14-91	10:38:00	66	199196	.a..			6053
BINDER	01-15-91	10:50:40	3	8512	.a..			6053
CUSTSVC	01-15-91	10:55:30	4	10944	.a..			6053
ENTER	01-15-91	10:57:34	7	20596	.a..			6053
ENTERPIN	01-15-91	10:48:26	6	19380	.a..			6053
FAREWELL	01-15-91	11:02:04	2	5852	.a..			6053
GREETING	01-15-91	11:04:30	5	16188	.a..			6053
MENU	03-11-91	09:38:23	13	39976	.a..			6053
MESSAGE	03-14-91	10:57:24	45	135508	.a..			6053
PROMO	01-15-91	11:16:30	12	35036	.a..			6053
TRAINING	03-11-91	10:54:02	57	170544	.a..			6053

```
<Cursor keys> Select Item      <Esc> Previous Menu      <F10> Function Menu
```

Figure 8.33 Scrollable display listing single-utterance files.

system—including the column labelled ATTR, which shows four DOS file attributes. A column displaying speaking time is derived from file length in bytes.

Figure 8.34 gives an example of a scrollable screen for multiple-utterance files. This example also lists standard file information and gives cumulative speaking time for all utterances, maximum number of utterances the file can contain, number actually installed in the file, and the recording sample rate. The number of possible utterances for a file is limited only by current index (or directory) size—which can be increased. Individual utterances within an indexed file can be copied to a single file or can replace an utterance in the same or another indexed file. Any utterance in any file can be deleted or rerecorded.

Figure 8.35 represents an expansion of one of the files (ASSTD.VAP) of Figure 8.34. Figure 8.35 lists, in a scrollable display, each of the utterances in the file. This screen shows utterance length in both speaking time and bytes. It also provides a description—which might be a verbatim record of the utterance. Some editors allow deleting, replacing, rerecording, or copying of utterances (and description editing) directly from such screens. A variety of file management (and other) functions are typically available from screens like those shown in Figures 8.33 through 8.35. Figure 8.36 gives an example of one of the screens, with a pop-up window listing applicable functions. Any single utterance file can be played, rerecorded, graphed, copied, deleted, or renamed. Most of these functions are discussed later in this section. Each of the three example screens would feature its own set of functions. A multiple-utterance screen, for instance,

```
┌─────────────────────────────────────────────────────────────────────────────┐
│          V O I C E    W O R K S T A T I O N  (Vers 3.1.2)                     │
│                      Pelton Systems, Inc.                                     │
│          M U L T I P L E      U T T E R A N C E    F I L E S                  │
├─────────────────────────────────────────────────────────────────────────────┤
│ FILES:   C:\MS\RUN\*.vap                                                      │
├────────────┬──────────────────────┬──────────────────┬──────┬──────┬──────┬────────┤
```

FILENAME	VERSION		LENGTH		ATTR	MAX NUM UTTS	NUM UTTS USED	SAMPLES PER SECOND
	DATE	TIME	SECS	BYTES				
CLOCK	03-23-90	12:06:00	5	15200	....	10	10	6053
DATES	02-03-90	16:34:02	10	34521	....	20	19	6053
NUMS_DN	01-25-90	02:14:22	17	51376	....	40	31	6053
NUMS_MID	01-23-90	12:03:46	15	44004	....	40	31	6053
NUMS_UP	01-25-90	04:34:56	18	54398	....	40	31	6053
STANDARD	05-22-90	11:25:30	28	84512	.a..	20	18	6053
TONES	05-18-89	09:30:04	13	39494	.a..	13	13	6053

```
<Cursor keys> Select Item        <Esc> Previous Menu        <F10> Function Menu
```

Figure 8.34 Scrollable display listing multiple-utterance files.

```
┌─────────────────────────────────────────────────────────────────────────────┐
│          V O I C E    W O R K S T A T I O N  (Vers 3.1.2)                     │
│                      Pelton Systems, Inc.                                     │
│                      U T T E R A N C E S                                      │
├─────────────────────────────────────────────────────────────────────────────┤
│ FILE:   C:\MS\RUN\ASSTD.VAP                                                   │
├──────┬──────────────┬──────────────────────────────────────────────────────────┤
```

UTT NUM	LENGTH		DESCRIPTION
	SECS	BYTES	
1	0.5	1672	Thankyou.
2	0.7	2204	I'm sorry.
3	0.8	2660	Please reenter.
4	1.9	5776	We are having technical difficulties.
5	2.0	6308	Please call back in 15 minutes.
6	2.1	6460	Please call back in about 30 minutes.
7	2.7	8436	System is being taken offline temporarily.
8	1.1	3344	Please try again.
9	0.8	2432	When you're done.
10	0.7	2128	Otherwise,
11	1.9	5852	Thankyou for calling. Goodbye.
12	1.9	5776	We'll Be seeing you. Goodbye.
13	0.6	1824	Goodbye.

```
<Cursor keys> Select Item        <Esc> Previous Menu        <F10> Function Menu
```

Figure 8.35 Scrollable display listing utterances in an indexed file.

would not have a GRAPH function but would require an EXPAND function to list a file's utterances.

Recording

New prompts, phrases and other utterances are created when voice signals are input to the telephone/voice board for recording. A speech editor manages the recording process. Signals can be patched in from magnetic tape or digital recorders, or input live via microphone or local telephone handset. Speech data for recorded utterances might be appended to a file, placed in a new file, or might replace existing data. When recording a series of speech items, it's convenient for each to be automatically placed in a separate file. This way, developers can concentrate on recording—they need not be distracted by editing or file management details that can be put off until later. These can be addressed after all new utterances have been input.

Some editors even provide an on-screen VU meter to aid in setting audio record levels. Figure 8.37 illustrates an on-screen pop-up VU meter. Some telephone/voice boards have an AGC (automatic gain control) and don't support adjustable record levels on the board. With such equipment, the VU meter is used to set external gain.

Visual editing

Characteristics inherent in speech can be exploited visually to enhance editing. Patterns formed on an energy-versus-time graph are convenient and, in a general way, can be related to the speech sounds they represent. Most speech sounds result in patterns that you can quickly learn to discriminate. For instance, vowels, spoken with articulators open, are produced with high energy. By contrast, consonants are spoken with constrictions in the articulators— they form irregular patterns and don't occur with high energy. Unvoiced sounds form a low-energy pattern that's regular in appearance.

Speech editing is enhanced by energy displays such as those depicted in Figures 8.38 and 8.39. These screens can be scrolled or paged forward or backward, so, even for long utterances, all speech can be viewed. Displays

```
         V O I C E    W O R K S T A T I O N   (Vers 3.1.2)
                     Pelton Systems, Inc.
         S I N G L E    U T T E R A N C E    F I L E S

 FILES:  C:\MS\RUN\*.apg

              VERSION          LENGTH                         SAMPLES
                                                                PER
  FILENAME    DATE     TIME    SECS    BYTES    ATTR           SECOND

 1MOMENT    01-15-91  12:22:56                                  6053
 ANNOUNCE   03-14-91  10:38:00  ┌──────── FUNCTIONS ────────┐   6053
 BINDER     01-15-91  10:50:40  │                           │   6053
 CUSTSVC    01-15-91  10:55:30  │ FILE PLAY                 │   6053
 ENTER      01-15-91  10:57:34  │ RECORD NEW FILE           │   6053
 ENTERPIN   01-15-91  10:48:26  │ VU METER                  │   6053
 FAREWELL   01-15-91  11:02:04  │ GRAPH (LOW RESOLUTION)    │   6053
 GREETING   01-15-91  11:04:30  │ COPY FILE                 │   6053
 MENU       03-11-91  09:38:23  │ NAME FILE (RENAME)        │   6053
 MESSAGE    03-14-91  10:57:24  │ DELETE FILE               │   6053
 PROMO      01-15-91  11:16:30  │ PRINT RECORDED UTTS LIST  │   6053
 TRAINING   03-11-91  10:54:02  └───────────────────────────┘   6053

 Place cursor on function and <Enter> to execute      <Esc> To backup
```

Figure 8.36 Files screen with pop-up function window.

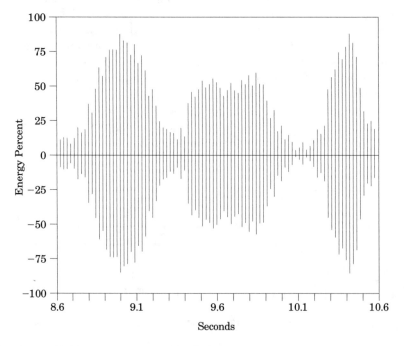

FILENAME	VERSION DATE	TIME	LENGTH SECS	BYTES	ATTR		SAMPLES PER SECOND

```
              V O I C E     W O R K S T A T I O N   (Vers 3.1.2)
                           Pelton Systems, Inc.
                S I N G L E      U T T E R A N C E      F I L E S

  FILES:   C:\MS\RUN\*.apg

                     VERSION             LENGTH                         SAMPLES
                                                                          PER
   FILENAME     DATE        TIME      SECS    BYTES    ATTR              SECOND

   1MOMENT   01-15-91 | 12:22:56 |    1  |   3192  | .a..              6053
   ANNOUNCE  03-14-                                                    6053
   BINDER    01-15-              VU METER                              6053
   CUSTSVC   01-15-                                                    6053
   ENTER     01-15-    0     25      50      75     100%               6053
   ENTERPIN  01-15-                                                    6053
   FAREWELL  01-15-                                                    6053
   GREETING  01-15-         5   10   15   20   25  30                  6053
   MENU      03-11-    0                                               6053
   MESSAGE   03-14-                                                    6053
   PROMO     01-15-                                                    6053
   TRAINING  03-11-91 | 10:54:02 |   57  | 170544  | .a..             6053

  Turn on recording source before adjusting gain. Press any key when done.
```

Figure 8.37 On-screen pop-up VU meter.

Figure 8.38 Energy screen on graphics display.

like that of Figure 8.38 require graphics controllers and monitors. Figure 8.39, on the other hand, represents speech data the way it appears graphed on monochrome monitors. Notice that data displayed in Figure 8.38 is redundant about the horizontal axis. In Figure 8.39, redundancy has been re-

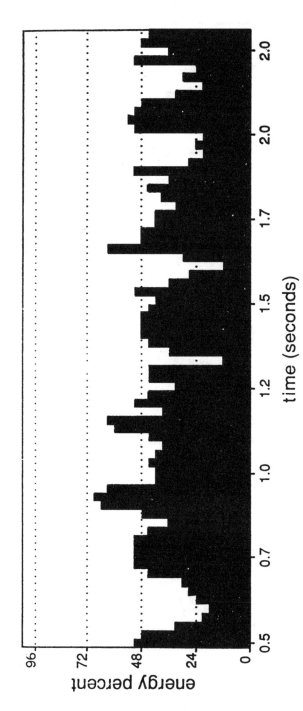

Figure 8.39 High-resolution energy screen on monochrome monitor.

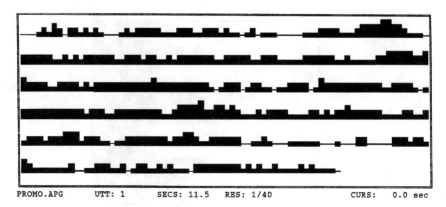

PROMO.APG   UTT: 1   SECS: 11.5   RES: 1/40   CURS: 0.0 sec

Figure 8.40 Low-resolution energy screen on monochrome monitor.

moved and vertical (energy) resolution doubled by displaying only that portion occurring above the horizontal axis. Energy scale is represented as percent of full range. It might seem that greater horizontal (time) resolution
can be obtained on a screen like the one in Figure 8.38, but, in reality, either
format is able to resolve time down to a single data point. Most editing, however, uses no more than two to four seconds of summary speech information displayed across the screen. Longer segments can be displayed on a
single screen by reducing vertical resolution, as shown in Figure 8.40. In
this screen, created on an IBM-compatible personal computer with a monochrome monitor, energy is resolved to only five levels, enabling eight times
as much speech to be seen on a screen. While editing features such as play,
zoom, trim, delete, cut/paste, quiet and other effects can be performed on
either high-resolution or low-resolution displays, lower resolutions are used
primarily for navigation, for locating particular segments. Once located,
zooming produces a finer time resolution.

The best editors make changes only in a buffer and don't apply edited
changes to actual data in files until specifically instructed to do so. Editing
steps or changes are noted on the screen whenever edited speech data is
displayed. Thus, various changes can be tested but backed out if they don't
produce desired effects. Only acceptable ones are retained. Some additional editing features often found in speech editors are discussed below.

Playing (speaking). Playing occurs when the editor passes speech data to
the telephone/voice board so it can speak. Some editors synchronize the
cursor when speaking, tracking it across the screen in time with the data
being played so displayed patterns can be matched with the sounds they
represent. Various forms of playing are possible. Speech data can be played
in its original form as it exists in the file. It can be played as currently edited,

as it appears in an edit buffer, or it can be played with special effects. For instance, some editors allow dwelling on a small section of speech data during speaking to aid in navigating through a long utterance. When speaking reaches a point of interest on the screen pattern, it's allowed to dwell there for about one second. Dwelling is accomplished by replaying the same short tract of speech data until the dwell time has elapsed. The aural distortion produced by the dwell clearly pinpoints a place in the utterance and unambiguously establishes correspondence between a pattern on the screen and the sound it represents.

Trimming. Before editing there's usually a short burst of silence at the front and back of a recorded utterance. *Trimming* is the process of removing this silence. If editing with an energy graph, trimming can be as simple as pinpointing the first rise and last decline in energy to identify the exact beginning and end of the utterance. Trimming is one of the few editing operations that are easily automated, and some telephone/voice boards and some editors do offer automatic trimming.

Deleting. There can be many reasons for deleting sections of speech. An imperfection in recording can often be removed by deletion without marring understandability—particularly if the imperfection occurs in a vowel (actually, that's the least likely place for such problems to occur). Utterances can be segmented by deleting, and unwanted portions can be erased. Entire utterances can be shortened so speaking takes less time. Large portions of vowels can almost always be safely removed by deletion without creating distortion, but great care should be exercised when deleting portions of other speech segments.

Quieting. *Quieting* modifies speech data so no sound is produced when it's played. Any speech data can be converted to a set of values that produce silence. Breathing and ambient noise often show up in recordings at places where silence is desired. These and other noises can be removed through quieting. A combination of deleting and quieting is sometimes used to adjust interword or interphrase timing (which can also be expanded by inserting silence).

Compressing. An utterance's dynamic range, the swing in energy level, can be compressed through adjustment of energy parameters. Compression can be performed on a proportional basis, or it can be biased according to some mathematical formula. Compression might result in smoother sound, but it doesn't always improve an utterance. So, as with other editing operations, compression is usually not applied to source data until after it has been audited and deemed an acceptable change.

```
┌─────────────────────────────────────────────────────────────────────┐
│         V O I C E    W O R K S T A T I O N   (Vers 3.1.2)             │
│                    Pelton Systems, Inc.                               │
│                   SETUP CONTROL PARAMETERS                            │
├─────────────────────────────────────────────────────────────────────┤
│                                                                       │
│      GENERAL:                                            VALUES       │
│        File extension for single utterance files        *.apg        │
│        File extension for multiple utterance files      *.vap        │
│        Dialogic channel for monitoring and recording     1           │
│        Number of cursor positions/second for graphs      40          │
│        Scroll low-res graph during speaking? (y/n)       N           │
│                                                                       │
│      RECORDING:                                                       │
│        Sample rate for recording                         6053        │
│        Seconds of silence that terminates recording      5           │
│        Maximum length of recording (seconds)             120         │
│                                                                       │
│      INTERRUPTS:                                                      │
│        Dialogic Driver hardware interrupt level          5           │
│        Dialogic Driver software interrupt level          06d         │
│                                                                       │
│  Up/down arrows to select. Enter to change. Esc when done.           │
└─────────────────────────────────────────────────────────────────────┘
```

Figure 8.41 Parameter setup screen.

Cutting and pasting. Many editing situations require insertion of a portion of one utterance into another. The process begins by specifying a segment of speech to be *cut*. The cut segment is not necessarily deleted from the original—it's most often copied to a cut buffer where it's held until replaced. *Pasting* is the process of inserting the contents of a cut buffer into an utterance. There might be multiple cut buffers, and they can be saved beyond editing sessions. Cut and paste usually allows portions of utterances to be moved between files, enabling diverse words, syllables, phonemes, and other speech segments to be concatenated. Using this feature, entirely new utterances can be created in an individual's voice if an adequate collection of their speech is available. Achievement of these kinds of natural-sounding manufactured utterances is time-consuming because speech segments with correct energy, stress, and intonation must be found and fitted together.

Special effects. Some editors offer a set of special effects such as echo, fade-in, and fade-out. While these effects can be interesting, they're rarely used in voice processing systems and seem more theatrical than creative.

Recovering deleted, quieted, or inserted speech data. When sections of speech are deleted, they're simply marked in their buffer as "deleted." No data is destroyed. Likewise, when a section is converted to silence, it's simply marked as "quiet." When a speech segment is inserted from a cut buffer, no data is really inserted. Rather, the edit buffer is marked for the insertion. Thus, original data can be restored at any time by "unmarking" these edits. The actual edits are not applied to the speech data file until specifically commanded or until the memory edit buffer is written to a disk file. Modern text editors thus allow hundreds of editing steps to be backed out—but only those made since the file was last written to disk. Speech editors, similarly, permit undoing deletions, quiets, or insertions made since the most recent file update.

System setup. As with all computer programs, system parameters control certain editor operations. Most editors begin with default values for control parameters—these might never need to be changed. Nevertheless, provisions are made for overriding system defaults. Some editor control parameters include software and hardware interrupts, vocabulary file extensions, graph resolutions, recording sample rate, and others. Figure 8.41 shows an example editor setup screen in which current parameter values are displayed and can be changed at any time.

9

Vocabulary Production

Vocabulary is the voice processing system's voice—commands and instructions spoken by the system to prompt a user through an application. Some voice processing systems use text-to-speech vocabulary; its preparation is as easy as typing a line of text. However, production of recorded speech is the subject of this chapter, so text-to-speech will not be considered further.

Vocabulary resides in digital files on disk or in the computer's memory. I distinguish vocabulary files from files that contain user voice messages, whose contents are unknown to the computer. Vocabulary can consist of either or both of two types: permanent and changeable. *Changeable vocabulary* consists of those voice prompts and commands that are designed to be changed by a user or application manager—perhaps even over the telephone. *Permanent vocabulary* (sometimes called fixed vocabulary) is composed of voice prompts, phrases, and other spoken utterances that remain fixed and are not designed to be modified. Of course, like everything else in a system, even fixed vocabulary can be changed. The remainder of this chapter concerns the design and production of permanent vocabulary, with sections covering the equipment and facilities necessary for production.

Design and production of fixed vocabulary is a new and unfamiliar task, one that must be accomplished in addition to those already common for developers of conventional applications. For many, this means learning new disciplines—disciplines whose importance is all too often underestimated. Fixed vocabulary is the voice processing system's principal connection with its callers, who don't see the well-crafted, multicolored, many-layered screens displayed for the online user. A caller can't wrap a fist around the mouse and click on the screen's dozen or so suggestive icons displayed there. A caller is able only to listen to what's spoken by the system.

It takes energy to participate in a conversation. Just picking out enunciated sounds, emphasized syllables, and inflection in another's voice can be stressful—especially if conditions are not perfect. This is doubly true when conversation takes place over telephones. Understanding what's meant by the words even when another's voice is clearly heard also requires concentration, focus, and energy. Many of us have experienced the frustration of trying to comprehend instructions that were not spoken clearly, or were delivered in a poor listening environment. When the speaker is a computer, the medium is a telephone network, and the caller is unfamiliar with either computers or the application, the situation is greatly exacerbated. So, to avoid confusing, frustrating, or even angering callers, the voice processing system should speak with a voice that's pleasing, intelligible, and natural. As a member of a technological society, you've come to expect the highest quality in audio recording. Wherever you are—at home, at the beach, riding in your car—you can slip a tiny cassette or compact disc into an inexpensive machine and be immediately surrounded by faithful, flawless, high-quality sound reproductions. When a voice processing system has an inferior voice, callers know it. The perception of a technological failing is created, and the user's confidence is diminished. It's the developer's responsibility to create a system that leaves only positive impressions in the mind of the user. That means, among other things, producing the highest-quality vocabulary that technology allows.

Permanent Vocabulary Production

When recorded vocabulary is digitized, any one of a variety of compression algorithms can be used, each different, each with its own requirements for optimum performance. Unwanted sounds and audio distortions detract from the intelligibility of the finished vocabulary, defeat the compression analysis, and result in suboptimum voice. Such sounds can emanate from outside the recording facility or from within. They can radiate through walls, seep around doors and windows, find their way in through ducts and electrical outlets, or be introduced by faulty or poorly maintained audio equipment. Extraneous sound energy should be eliminated as completely as possible, even if not audible. Sometimes the greatest planning and the most precise care must be exercised to eliminate these errant sound

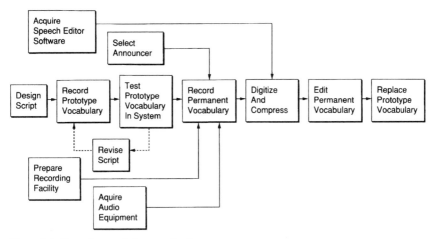

Figure 9.1 Steps for vocabulary production.

sources and distortions and to assure that none are introduced during processing—but the effort will be keenly repaid.

Figure 9.1 shows the steps involved in vocabulary production. Before production can begin, an adequate auditioning and recording facility must be available. The facility need not be a professional recording studio, but it must at least be isolated from ambient noise and must include basic audio recording equipment, including a microphone, tape recorder, amplifier, and perhaps other audio-conditioning devices. A computer with appropriate voice hardware must also be available—although not necessarily within the studio proper. A full-featured speech editor designed for use with the voice hardware is important for editing and voice file management. From an initial tentative script, prototype vocabulary can be easily and inexpensively prepared as needed for alpha and beta tests. Prototype vocabulary is temporary vocabulary, inexpensively recorded in the easiest manner. It's installed and used only during test to give the "feel" of the system. It's modified often and will finally be replaced by permanent vocabulary after testing, when scripts are frozen. However, preliminary work towards permanent vocabulary can proceed in parallel with other development and testing tasks. Early in development, the announcer who will record permanent vocabulary is auditioned, selected, and hired for the project. Of course, this happens only after issues such as age and sex of the announcer have been thoroughly discussed and decided upon. Based on experience gained during tests, script revisions are finalized and recording sessions are scheduled. As system testing nears completion, permanent, finished vocabulary is produced and quietly substituted in place of prototype vocabulary files.

The steps required for production of high-quality vocabulary are discussed in the following sections. Each function must be accomplished with care; each contributes to the end product, which will be only as good as the least of these steps.

The Recording Facility

Vocabulary production for voice processing systems can be subcontracted to professionals. However, it need not be. With care and a little study, high-quality speech can be produced in a home or office. A room or other facility will be needed for recording. Speech production for use with computers involves considerations that don't occur in audio production for records or film. Nevertheless, basic acoustic principles apply and must be considered when selecting or preparing the room in which to record.

Some principles of audio

The following paragraphs present some important fundamentals of audio. Before embarking on a vocabulary development project, it's important to acquire a basic understanding of these principles.

Sound transmission.   Sound is propagated in all directions from its source. You normally think of sound being transmitted in air, but sound travels in other media as well—including gases, liquids, and solids—as waves of alternately compressed then rarefied molecules. The distance from one compressed crest to the next is the *wavelength; frequency,* expressed in Hertz (cycles per second), is the number of compressed crests passing a given point in a second. The velocity of sound in air is about 770 miles per hour (1,130 feet per second) and is constant, regardless of atmospheric pressure. The velocity of sound varies directly with temperature, increasing as the temperature rises. Sound travels in other media besides air. In fact, its speed of travel varies according to the material. It travels, for example, at about 1,130 feet per second (fps) in air but at about 12,500 fps in brick and 16,500 fps in steel. The intensity or *amplitude* of sound in a medium is measured as the sound pressure level (SPL). Sound intensity is damped with distance, dissipating and becoming weaker the further it travels from the source—it varies inversely with the square of distance. If it travels far enough, SPL drops almost to zero, and the sound can no longer be heard. The rate of decay is frequency-dependent, with the energy at higher frequencies dissipating sooner. Lower frequencies lose less energy over the same distances than higher frequencies.

When a sound wave traveling in air encounters an object, say a wall, part of its energy is reflected from the wall (as depicted in Figure 9.2), with the remainder either being absorbed by the wall or transmitted through it. The

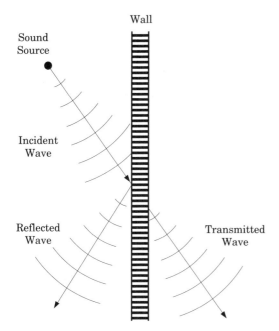

Wall

Sound
Source

Incident
Wave

Reflected
Wave

Transmitted
Wave

Figure 9.2 Effect of sound
waves meeting an object.

original wave is called an *incident wave,* the portion reflected is referred to
as the *reflected wave*, and that portion passing through the object is called
a *transmitted wave*. The proportions of each depend upon the density and
elasticity of the material encountered. Softer materials absorb more and reflect less, while harder materials, such as concrete, absorb less and reflect
more. If the surface of the object is smooth, the reflected wave will glance off
the surface at the same angle from which the incident wave approached—it
bounces off the surface in about the same way a thrown ball would. The
sound energy absorbed into the wall is actually refracted and transmitted
through the wall (dissipating on its way)—the sound has transferred from
one medium to another. On the other side of the wall another transfer takes
place, this time from the solid material back to air, where the wave is again
refracted before being transmitted outward from the wall. To an observer,
the wave appears to pass through the wall, reducing in intensity as it does.

Energy in a wave striking an object is resolved into three components: reflected, absorbed, and transmitted. If E_i represents energy in an incident
wave, E_r represents energy of the reflected wave, E_t represents energy in
the transmitted wave, and E_a represents absorbed energy (which dissipates
in the object), then the principle of conservation of energy assures us that
the following equation holds.

$$E_i = E_r + E_t + E_a$$

The sum of reflected, transmitted, and dissipated energy is equivalent to energy in the incident wave. The proportion of each depends, among other things, upon the material of the object encountered.

In a studio, you should have walls that neither reflect nor transmit too much energy. The studio should be acoustically correct inside and reasonably isolated from outside sounds. Thus, it's important to consider the materials from which the studio is constructed. Different materials act differently on sound waves and are rated on their ability to impede transmission of sound. The more dense a material is, the better it attenuates sound energy—the more mass a material has, the less energy it transmits. Materials attenuate high frequencies more than low frequencies. Thus, a material that adequately blocks the sound of a siren might not adequately attenuate the low frequency rumble of the fire truck itself. The ratio of energy in a transmitted wave to that in the incident wave (for a given frequency), E_t/E_i, is called the *transmission coefficient.* This gives a measure of the extent to which a material transmits sound at that frequency—the larger the coefficient, the poorer the attenuation of the material. Figure 9.3 shows an example of the relationship between the transmission coefficient and frequency for a typical material.

The inverse of the transmission coefficient is *transmission loss.* The equation

$$TL = 10 \log (E_i/E_t)$$

yields transmission loss, *TL*, in decibels (dB) at a given frequency. If, for example, you construct a studio in which 20 percent of an incident wave at a given frequency is transmitted through the walls, then sound outside the studio at that frequency will be attenuated at about 7 dB. If ambient noise

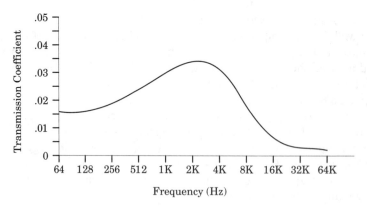

Figure 9.3 Relationship between frequency and transmission coefficient for a typical material.

outside the studio is measured as 40 dB at that frequency, then it will be 33 dB inside.

Reverberation. Sound energy bouncing off an object, a wall, for instance, creates an echo. The echo, in turn, might also bounce off an object to create its own echo. In a closed room, energy from a sound source travels around the room, bouncing off the walls, dissipating in strength with each impact and with each foot it travels. Of course, sound travels in all directions from its source, so there's not just one path from which reflections occur in a closed room; the sound takes many paths. A room or studio can be rated by the time it takes for a sound to diminish to one millionth of its original energy after the source has stopped producing sound—this is called *reverberation time.* This is about the same as the time it takes the sound energy to decrease by 60 dB. Reverberation time is dependent upon the volume of the room and its absorption characteristics. If reverberation time is too long, echoes persist, bouncing about the room and distorting recordings, which will sound fuzzy or smeared. If reverberation time is too short, the room will be "dead" and recordings will not sound natural. A recording studio should not be *anechoic* (almost totally dead), although it should tend toward deadness—a reverberation time of about 0.5 second will accomplish this.

Standing waves. Standing waves resonate in a room and cause tonal imbalance and distorted recordings. Standing waves are so named because, rather than dying away, they tend to persist. As depicted in Figure 9.4, wave trains of certain frequencies moving in the same direction become phase-locked and travel along together, reinforcing each other. Crests of an incident wave and all its reflections arrive at the same point at the same time. Standing waves occur at each fundamental resonant frequency and its harmonics; fortunately, these are predictable frequencies. Standing waves with the most energy are those whose wavelengths are twice the distance between pairs of parallel walls. In a room whose dimensions are 30 ft.× 20 ft. × 10 ft., these frequencies are 18.8 Hz, 28.3 Hz, and 56.5 Hz. The further removed a harmonic is from its fundamental, the less energy it contains—so, standing waves at harmonics of a resonant frequency tend to be less serious. Standing waves take different paths around the room, rather than always traveling directly between two opposing walls. Waves that glance off four walls and those that reflect from all six walls before returning to reinforce themselves also result in standing waves. Naturally, the more reflections that occur and the longer the distance taken, the weaker the returning wave. So, most troublesome are standing waves resulting from a pair of opposing walls.

Placement of furniture and people in a room changes the dynamics a bit,

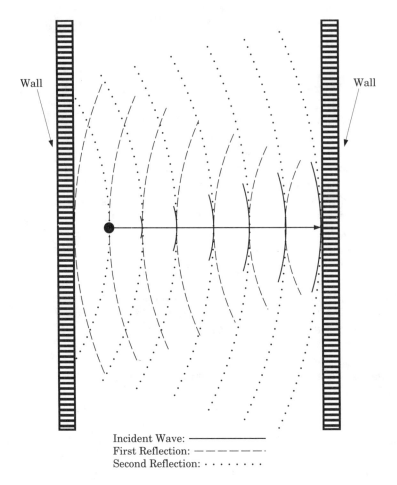

Wall

Wall

Incident Wave: ——————
First Reflection: — — — — — —·
Second Reflection: · · · · · · · ·

Figure 9.4 Reinforcing wave trains in a standing wave.

as does increased sound absorption or splayed walls. The adverse effects of standing waves can also be reduced by distributing them through the frequency spectrum. This is achieved through careful selection of room proportions. The 30 ft.×20 ft.×10 ft. studio dimensions in the previous example should be avoided because too many resonant frequencies are common to all pairs of parallel walls. Resonances resulting from the 10 ft. dimension, for instance, are boosted by resonances in both the 20 ft. and the 30 ft. dimensions. Recording rooms should be sized to avoid bunching resonances too closely. In this way, almost every frequency will benefit from resonance boost—providing the room is large enough to include resonances for the lowest frequency components present. The idea is to boost all frequencies, including the low ones, about equally. For this reason, small talk booths, popular at one time, have been found to be inadequate for voice recording. As a rule, it's easier to distribute speech resonances through the spectrum with larger studios. Long waves in a small, 4 ft.×4 ft.×8 ft. studio would not produce much resonant energy. Speech below 40 Hz contains little energy, so it's usually adequate to plan for frequencies of 40 Hz and above (a 40 Hz component has a wavelength of 28.25 ft.). Studios with a volume of at least 1500 cubic feet have been found to be best for speech applications.

Echoes. Larger studios can be susceptible to echo. An echo occurs when the time delay between the source sound and its reflection is large enough to be perceptible, about ⅟₂₅ of a second. Sound travels slightly more than 45 feet in that time, so any studio with a wall about 23 or more feet from the microphone can suffer an echo. *Flutter echo*, a string of echoes caused by parallel walls, can be even more serious than a single echo. Geometric diffusers, splayed walls, and splayed observation windows are used to deflect sound waves and reduce the effects of echo. Many diffusers (such as convoluted foam) are also sound absorbent (usually at the higher frequencies) and serve not only to control echo but also to reduce reverberation time. Many smaller patches, rather than a few large areas of absorptive or diffusive materials, is a more effective approach—particularly in corners of a room. It's also wise to cover hard surfaces such as windows and desks with soft materials. Pillows or blankets serve adequately if more conventional acoustic materials are not readily available.

The professional studio

Concern over these acoustical considerations can be avoided by using a professional recording studio—which can be rented in most cities with or without an audio engineer. Many audio engineers have little or no experience producing recordings for digital speech, so it's wise to exercise caution here. High-quality speech recordings can be produced, however, without a professional studio or engineer.

Recording studio at home or office

An office or other quiet room can be used as a temporary studio if care is taken in its selection and preparation. If the temporary studio is planned before the room is constructed, an audio professional can be consulted for advice on eliminating extraneous noise sources—both within the studio and without. The following paragraphs cover some of the basic considerations that most seriously affect production of high-quality vocabulary.

Exclude external noise. Sounds of any frequency are more effectively attenuated by walls with large mass than by lighter ones. Cement walls, for example, are better at excluding external sounds than those constructed of wood or plaster. A normal room cannot be padded enough to exclude high-amplitude sounds. Most low-frequency energy present in rumbling noises will pass easily through normal walls, even those that are heavily padded. The simplest way to exclude noise originating outside the studio, noise that could potentially contaminate recordings, is to select a room where the external noise level is low at the times you'll be recording. With many applications, the time required to record vocabulary is small, so a studio might not be needed all hours of the day or all days of the week. It might be possible to record evenings or weekends. Some locations are much more quiet during nonbusiness hours. A studio whose use is limited can take advantage of such circumstances and can be constructed much less expensively. No matter how massive the walls of a studio, unwanted sounds might enter via heating ducts, air conditioning vents, and through openings made for electrical sockets. These should be sealed to minimize the problem.

Eliminate internal noise. Extraneous noises generated within a room contaminate recordings as easily as external ones. The room should not contain motors or electrical equipment—even if its sounds are inaudible. The room should be free of hard surfaces such as glass, metal, and plastic, which reflect most energy in sound waves, promote reverberation, and reduce intelligibility. Use of diffusive materials and nonparallel surfaces within the room helps to disperse reflections and prevent standing waves. If possible, a room with carpets and acoustic ceiling should be selected. Pillows, cushions and other soft materials that absorb high-frequency sound waves can be placed throughout the room prior to recording to improve attenuation of reflected waves. Glass and other hard surfaces can be covered with egg-carton foam pads, thick blankets, or pillows. Low-frequency sound waves are not easily attenuated, and their effects can be disastrous if the dimensions and other characteristics of the room are such that it resonates at one of these frequencies. The best solutions for this problem involve splayed walls and careful selection of room dimensions—but no amount of planning can completely eliminate all adverse effects.

Hardware for Vocabulary Production

The means for recording vocabulary are often provided with voice processing development systems, but such means usually involve recording directly to the voice hardware through a local telephone or over the public switched telephone network. Often these systems don't even include speech editor software. When producing vocabulary in this way, the announcer's voice is input in realtime directly to the digitization process, and, for several reasons, results in inferior vocabulary. First, the recording session can easily be conducted casually in an office setting, rather than in a quiet environment under competent direction, as a professional recording session should be. Second, microphones in telephone handsets are of very poor quality. Finally, speech transmitted over the switched telephone network easily becomes distorted. Because the process is made to seem simple in the manufacturer's advertising and sales materials, you're misled into thinking that quality control is unimportant. Once efficacy of the input has been compromised, digitization, compression and editing can't be expected to correct the earlier deficiencies and produce optimum output. It's vital to start with and maintain the highest-quality recordings all the way through the speech production process. The only way to assure this is to record under near-studio conditions using the best voice available, a competent director, a high-quality microphone, and good audio equipment. The following sections discuss the crucial equipment requirements relating to vocabulary production.

Microphone characteristics

The microphone is the first piece of equipment used to record speech, and, perhaps because of its easy availability, is often given least consideration. Every item of equipment in the audio chain is equally important. Inexpensive, poor-quality microphones that are inappropriate for voice proc-essing applications are numerous and seem so handy. Because there are so many different types of microphones, considerable space is devoted to them in this chapter. The following sections describe the various types of microphones, basic principles of their operation, and the features and characteristics that are most important to consider when selecting a microphone.

A microphone (mike) is a *transducer*. It converts energy from one form to another—in this case, from sound to electricity. A microphone senses the air pressure wave resulting from sound and outputs an electrical analog of the wave. There are many ways to convert sound pressure level to an electrical voltage. Not surprisingly, there are as many different types of microphones—each with its own advantages and disadvantages. Some familiar names are given to microphone categories: carbon, condenser, dynamic, ribbon, electret, crystal, ceramic, and others; the major ones are discussed shortly. First, though, it will be helpful to consider a few characteristics that differentiate microphones.

Sensitivity. Microphone *sensitivity* refers to the ratio between sound pressure level and output voltage. One mike is more sensitive than another if its output voltage is higher for the same sound at the same distance. Sensitivity, the ratio of signal output to sound input is also known as response coefficient and can be given in millivolts or in decibels. Conditions under which response coefficients are measured should be taken into account when comparing microphones. Furthermore, it's not necessarily true that the higher the output sensitivity the better the mike because mike output that's too high might overdrive the amplifier and cause distortion on louder passages.

Transient response. *Transients* are steep vertical excursions, either up or down, on a graph of sound pressure versus time. Transients are rapid changes in sound pressure level, moments when sound changes in loudness very quickly. The ability of a microphone to respond rapidly to transients is referred to as its *transient response* and is a measure of how well the mike's output voltage matches input sound pressure during sudden changes in loudness. The microphone's diaphragm (and perhaps other mechanical parts) must move in response to sound. Small, lightweight moving parts are better able to overcome inertia than larger ones of greater mass. So, lightweight parts respond more crisply to transients.

Internal (self) noise. There's almost always a flow of electrons in a microphone's circuitry, even when no sound is produced to excite the device. This flow, experienced as a small output voltage, is known as internal or self-noise and can be tested by measuring the output when no sound is present. Naturally, a high level of internal noise is undesirable and, due to its effect on signal-to-noise ratio, can be especially troublesome if sensitivity is low.

Directional response. Some microphones are intended to be more sensitive to sound coming from a certain direction relative to the mike. These are called *directional* or *cardioid* mikes (for reasons that will soon become apparent). Other mikes are almost equally sensitive to sounds coming from any direction, and these are called *omnidirectional* or simply *omni* mikes. There are several directional sensitivity patterns that relate to microphones; polar response diagrams are commonly used to describe them. Figure 9.5 gives polar response diagrams for both directional and omnidirectional mikes. Imagine that the polar response diagram represents a two-dimensional space with the microphone oriented at the center of that space—the position of the microphone corresponds to the center of the diagram. Notice that the circumference of the diagram is marked in degrees from zero through 360—these provide a directional reference and assign a specific orientation to the microphone. By convention, the base or shaft of the mike points toward the back, toward 180 degrees. Concentric circles of the diagram are marked with dB levels (negative dB levels). These circles indicate in decibels the amount of sensitivity loss. The sensitivity loss experienced for sound arriving from every direction relative to the mike is shown by a heavy tracing that continues around the entire circle.

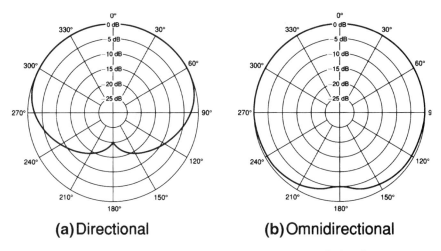

(a) Directional   **(b) Omnidirectional**

Figure 9.5 Polar response diagrams for directional and omnidirectional microphones.

Notice in Figure 9.5 that the directional mike shows a sensitivity loss of about 20 dB for sounds coming from directly behind the mike (along the shaft). The directional mike has a polar response pattern resembling a heart shape—hence the name cardioid. Cardioid mikes are often used in noisy environments to concentrate on a single sound source in front of the mike and eliminate spurious sounds coming from other directions. Cardioid patterns are particularly good when recording a speaker in less than ideal recording environments.

Polar response diagrams are two-dimensional. To portray the situation accurately, a third dimension would be needed. Sounds arrive at a microphone from above and below as well as from the front, back and sides. Most manufacturers, however, provide only two-dimensional diagrams, but it's usually safe to assume that the pattern shown can be rotated about the front-back axis (e.g., the response is the same no matter how the microphone is rotated about the axis running through its shaft). Microphone response varies with frequency, so the diagrams of Figure 9.5 represent only one specific frequency. Polar diagrams like those of Figure 9.6 more accurately represent sensitivity to several different frequencies.

Microphones with other sensitivity patterns are also available. *Supercardioid, hypercardioid,* and *bidirectional* patterns, for instance, are shown in Figure 9.7. A supercardioid mike has an advantage over a cardioid when elimination of sounds from the 90 degree and 270 degree directions is desired and the 180 degree direction is less important. A hyper cardioid mike is even less sensitive to sound from the sides but might be less useful due to the heightened sensitivity from the rear. A bidirectional mike is desired in some situations (such as when recording the dialogue of two persons facing each other).

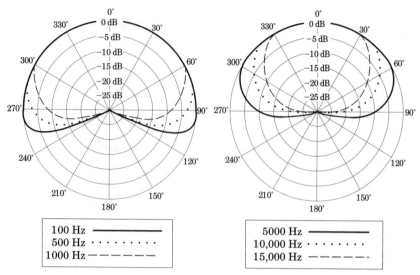

Figure 9.6 Polar response diagrams for multiple frequencies.

Frequency response. Microphones are also rated according to their response across the frequency spectrum. A diagram like that shown in Figure 9.8, a frequency response diagram, is used to express the relationship between frequency of input and amplitude of output. Notice in the figure that relative microphone sensitivity in decibels is graphed on the vertical axis versus frequency on the horizontal axis. Unless otherwise stated, the graph represents measurements made on-axis, from directly in front of the mike. Often, off-axis measurements are made as well, usually including measurements made from directly behind the mike (180 degrees off-axis), but sometimes including other positions. Figure 9.9 shows some off-axis frequency response measurements, with the angle from on-axis noted for each graph.

Notice in Figure 9.8 that below 100 Hz the curve slopes downward. This situation is called *rolloff* and can occur at any frequency; it's usually seen at either the low or high frequencies and represents a slackening of the microphone's response to sounds at those frequencies. An inverse condition might occur when sound at certain frequencies is boosted. *Boost (or peakiness* as it's sometimes called) can be seen in Figure 9.8 for frequencies of more than 7 kHz. Rolloff and boost are usually caused by circumstances of the microphone's design or construction. This doesn't mean, however, that rolloff and boost are merely nuisances to be accommodated—sometimes they're an important and sought-after feature of a microphone. For example, a wide-band microphone, one whose response reaches very low fre-

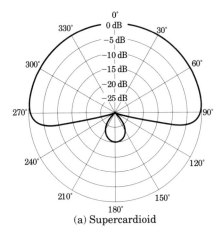

(a) Supercardioid

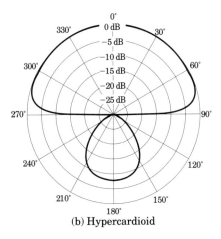

(b) Hypercardioid

Figure 9.7 Polar response diagrams for supercardioid, hypercardioid, and bidirectional sensitivity patterns.

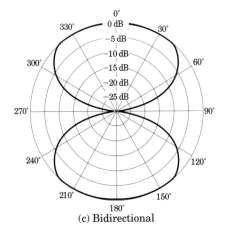

(c) Bidirectional

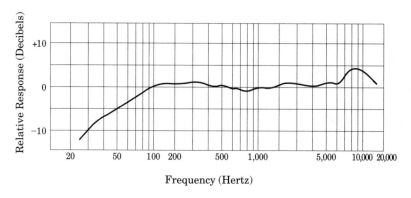

Figure 9.8 On-axis frequency response diagram.

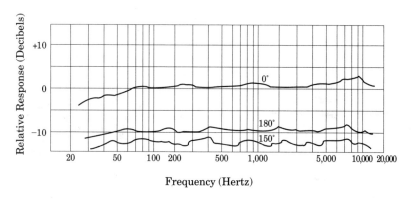

Figure 9.9 Frequency response diagram with on-axis and off-axis measurements.

quencies, might be quite susceptible to low-frequency hum. A bass rolloff in the mike can work to alleviate such problems.

An "ideal" microphone for music features a flat response from about 20 Hz to at least 20 kHz with no more than about 1 dB variation across the spectrum. Such a microphone would be quite expensive—and for voice applications would be unnecessarily expensive. For most voice processing applications, a mike with an essentially flat response curve with no more than about 5 dB deviation from 50 to 8 or 10 kHz would serve quite well.

Proximity effect. When the sound source is very close to a cardioid mike (and some bidirectional mikes), a bass boost occurs. This is known as the proximity effect and doesn't occur with omni mikes. When recording for voice processing systems, the speaker's mouth is within a few inches of the microphone, so the proximity effect is experienced with certain microphones and could cause unacceptable distortion in the resultant recordings. The closer the speaker's mouth is to the microphone, the more pronounced will be the effect—in fact, this relationship is nonlinear, growing rapidly more extreme as the speaker moves closer to the mike.

The proximity effect is a natural result of the design of directional mikes. Sound cancellation in directional mikes is accomplished by allowing sound pressure waves arriving from certain directions to penetrate holes in the mike case to impinge on the rear of the diaphragm. Thus, sounds from the rear are canceled by opposing pressures arriving at both the front and back of the diaphragm. The closer the holes in the case are to the diaphragm, the greater the proximity effect. More expensive cardioid mikes are designed with the holes further toward the back to reduce the effect, and some mikes are equipped with a bass rolloff switch to help flatten out the response curve.

Output impedance. Microphones convert sound energy to electrical voltages available at the microphone's electrical output connector. That output is rated as either a low-impedance or a high-impedance connection. *Impedance* is a measure of the circuit's total opposition to current flow. It's similar to resistance in an electrical circuit but results from a combination of the circuit's resistance, capacitance, and inductance. As with resistance, the unit of measure for impedance is the ohm. Low-impedance mikes are rated at about 200 ohms, while high-impedance devices run about 50,000 ohms. Most other characteristics of a mike are independent of its impedance level—that, by itself, gives no indication of the quality of a mike. There are, however, advantages and disadvantages to each. Low-impedance mikes are less prone to be affected by electrical noise (hum), and longer cables can be used without suffering noticeable loss of high-frequency response. High-impedance mikes, on the other hand, provide greater efficiency—they produce higher voltage outputs for a given sound pressure level but should not be used with cables in excess of 25 feet. Microphone output impedance must be matched to the input impedance of the amplifier or preamplifier at a ratio of about one to three. A low-impedance mike should use an amplifier with an input impedance of about 600 ohms, and a high-impedance mike would require an amplifier input impedance in the neighborhood of 150,000 ohms. Mike inputs are usually noted on the amplifier as either high-level or low-level, and many amplifiers provide both high-impedance and low-impedance microphone jacks.

Microphone types

Various means have been devised for converting sound pressure waves to electrical analogs. The major ones are discussed in the following sections.

Carbon microphone. Operation of the carbon microphone is possible because electrical resistance through a small container (called a *button*) of several hundred packed carbon granules varies in proportion to packing pressure. A metal disk, flexing in response to sound pressure levels, varies the packing pressure and thus the resistance. A power source provides the output voltage, which varies according to the resistance through the button. The carbon microphone is a low-impedance device that usually requires a transformer to step up the output voltage and output impedance and to isolate the mike's power source from the amplifier. The carbon microphone has a restricted frequency response, follows the sound pressure wave sluggishly, and tends to be noisy. It's not well-suited for voice processing applications.

Crystal microphone.   Crystal mikes are physically similar to carbon mikes, but crystal mikes depend upon the piezoelectric characteristic of their crystals. Accordingly, when crystals are deformed by a sound-pressure actuated diaphragm, their electrical characteristics change in proportion to the pressure, allowing the output voltage to be varied accordingly. Crystal mikes are high-impedance devices that also have a relatively strong output voltage. The crystals, however, are easily damaged by high temperature or humidity. Their very limited frequency response makes them unsuitable for many applications.

Ribbon (velocity) microphone.   Ribbon microphones (sometimes called *velocity mikes*) convert sound to voltage by use of a very thin ribbon of corrugated aluminum or other metal stretched longitudinally between the poles of a permanent magnet. These ribbons are typically about 0.001 inch in thickness, ¼ inch in width, and from 4 inches to less than 1 inch in length. The ends of the ribbon are fixed, but the remainder of the ribbon is free to vibrate with the sound pressure wave. A variable current is induced in the ribbon as it moves through the magnetic field. The output voltage corresponds to particle velocity in the sound pressure wave, and frequency follows the sound pressure wave. Ribbon mikes are usually bidirectional (but sometimes hypercardioid) because poor response is obtained when the sound pressure wave is directed across the ribbon rather than along it. The low impedance necessitates a matching transformer to be coupled in the microphone case to step up both the impedance and output voltage. These mikes can have high sensitivity, good transient response, a wide frequency response with low distortion, and minimal self-noise. In older versions ribbons were fragile and magnets large and bulky, but more compact versions with sturdier ribbons are now available.

Moving coil (dynamic) microphone.   Moving coil microphones are part of a class of mikes called *dynamic microphones*. The term dynamic mike has come to be almost universally associated with moving coil mikes, but the word dynamic applies to ribbon mikes as well. A moving coil mike is similar to a ribbon mike because it also moves a conductor through a magnetic field in response to the sound pressure wave. Each of these mikes is named for the moving induction element. Thus, in a moving coil type, a coil of wire is connected to a nonconducting diaphragm that moves in and out with changes in air pressure. These movements cause an equivalent movement of the coil through the magnetic field, inducing a current in the coil whose amplitude and frequency follow the sound wave. The amplitude, however, is greater than that of an equivalent ribbon mike because the coil is much longer than a ribbon. Moving coil mikes are popular for a great many applications because they're sturdy, their transient response can be good, their frequency response curve is wide and reasonably flat, their output signal level is fairly high, and they can be inexpensive compared to other types.

Condenser microphone. Well-designed condenser microphones are used for high-quality recording and are excellent for voice processing applications. These mikes rely on the principle of capacitance to convert sound to an electrical signal. If an electric charge is applied across conducting plates separated by a nonconductor, an electric charge builds up between them. This arrangement of parallel plates and insulating separator is called a *condenser*—it's also called a capacitor. The strength of the charge across the plates depends upon three factors: the distance between the plates, the surface area of the plates, and the insulating characteristics of the separating material. If one of the plates is a low-mass diaphragm, it will move relative to the other in response to a sound pressure wave. The varying charge causes the voltage across a parallel resister to vary accordingly, and is an electrical analog of the sound pressure wave. This voltage is so weak it must be amplified before being output. Thus, an amplifier (preamplifier) is packaged within the mike case. Power for the amplifier and for charging the plates comes either from an on-board battery or is cabled in from an external source (e.g., a dedicated power supply or phantom power from an amplifier or recorder). Because the moving element of the condenser mike has such low mass, the transient response is excellent. Output impedance is very low, and condenser mikes can also feature a wide, flat frequency response with little internal noise.

Electret microphone. An electret mike is basically a condenser mike in that the requirement for capacitor-charging power is removed by using an *electret capacitor*—a precharged capacitor that holds its charge indefinitely. Power for the mike's amplifier is still required and is generally supplied either by a small battery or by an external source.

Microphone for voice processing. Dynamic and condenser microphones are used most often in voice processing applications. Condenser mikes are preferred because they usually have a faster transient response, so output voltage more closely follows the input sound pressure wave. Performance characteristics for some expensive dynamic mikes are close to condenser mikes. Because of the proximity effect, which can be troublesome with cardioid mikes, omni mikes are recommended over cardioid in quiet recording environments, but, if less than ideal surroundings must be used for recording, a directional microphone will help to isolate unwanted sounds. An omni mike should have an even response at least up to 45 degrees off axis. Frequency response for the microphone should be flat within the frequency range of about 50 Hz to 8 kHz (or more if a very high sampling rate is to be used). Whether selecting a condenser or a dynamic mike, a directional or an omnidirectional one, it's especially recommended that inexpensive mikes be avoided. A good mike will come with ratings that include polar response diagrams, frequency response diagrams, and perhaps other information. The better mikes are rated individually rather than as a class—so it's reasonable, for voice processing applications, to insist on a microphone that's rated individually.

Recording equipment

After the microphone, the principal equipment required is a recording device. Factors concerning several types of recording devices are covered in the following.

Tape or digital recorder. Optionally, a digital recorder or an analog tape recorder can be used in the recording session. A good-quality digital recorder, being free of many of the drawbacks of analog recording, can result in the least fidelity loss and produce the highest-quality vocabulary. Reel-to-reel and cassette recorders, using magnetic tape as a storage medium, are subject to many sources of distortion. While certain nonlinearities in a recorded signal might be noticeable to only the most severe audiophile, even the mildest nonlinearity might be enough to confuse speech compression algorithms. Some expensive recorders attempt to compensate for nonlinearities inherent in analog tape recording but introduce additional problems for speech. Dolby, which reduces tape hiss by biasing some frequencies to a different part of the spectrum, is an example. A tape playback machine can readjust Dolby-biased frequencies back to their proper place in the spectrum. Normal compression software would not, however, expect frequency-shifted input. Analog recorders must be aligned to set head position, bias, and equalization. Cassette recorders and consumer reel-to-reel recorders are usually not aligned at the factory and might not even be capable of alignment.

The surface of magnetic recording tape looks perfectly smooth to the eye. It's not. Microscopic defects that occur in manufacture, voids, or protrusions in the oxide surface, can be enough to create immediate but brief reductions in signal level called *dropouts*. The effect of tape surface defects, which can't be totally eliminated even with the most expensive tape, are less crucial the faster the tape moves. Reel-to-reel machines operate at 7½ inches per second (ips), or even faster at 15 ips. Cassette recorders run at a slow 1⅞ ips. A typical aberration in the oxide surface might be about 0.012 inch in length. Using high-speed (15 ips) reel-to-reel tape, this dropout would last about 0.8 millisecond and would probably not seriously affect digital processing. At 7½ ips, the dropout would be 1.6 milliseconds in length and would most likely still not be troublesome. This defect in a cassette tape, on the other hand, would extend over 6.4 milliseconds and would be audible—especially with certain compression algorithms (e.g., differential coding schemes). Another problem, *print-through*, can occur when some of the energy stored on one layer of a wound tape reel leaks through to the adjacent layer. Print-through can be minimized by using thicker tape, recording at medium energy levels, and storing tape at room temperature in the wound (tails-out) condition, away from magnetic fields.

Digital recorders are preferred for speech applications, but if an analog recorder must be used, a professional-level, professionally aligned reel-to-reel recorder running at 15 ips with high-quality recording tape is recommended. Cassette recorders should be avoided for speech processing.

Computer as recorder. Use of a digital device rather than analog tape for recording vocabulary introduces the least distortion. If there's no requirement for long-term storage of analog speech, speech can be recorded by microphone directly to a computer (with appropriate speech hardware and software) for digitization and storage on disk. Speech editor software for the voice board might include an on-screen VU meter to aid in setting record levels. If the voice card doesn't have a microphone input jack, an intermediate amplifier will be required. Manufacturers of speech hardware can explain the best recording procedure and will even recommend auxiliary devices for use with their equipment.

Digitization and editing devices

After an announcer's voice has been recorded, it will be digitized, edited, and organized in files for use by the voice processing system. For this, some additional equipment is needed. Most often, digitization is accomplished with a telephone/voice board identical to that used in the target system. An amplifier and perhaps an audio adapter are used between the analog or digital recorder and the telephone/voice board. Some developers employ an equalizer, compressor, or other audio devices to condition the recorded signal before it's digitized. Finally, monitoring of speech might take place both during and after processing by the telephone/voice board—this requires a set of speakers or headphones. Most of this equipment is discussed in the following.

Amplifier. An amplifier or preamplifier steps up the relatively low amplitude output of a recorder to match it to required input levels of both the telephone/voice board and the speakers. If a modern, high-quality amplifier is used, there will be little concern with specifications. Most good amplifiers manufactured today provide a reasonably flat frequency response from about 10 Hz to almost 50 kHz, a range greatly exceeding normal voices. Other factors such as impedance matching, signal-to-noise ratio, sensitivity, and gain have been anticipated by the manufacturer and will also be adequate for vocabulary production. Manufacturer's instructions should be available with the amplifier, and care should be exercised to properly install all equipment.

Audio/telephone adapter. Some telephone/voice boards don't include an audio-level input circuitry—instead, they introduce audio signals via RJ-11 telephone jacks. When this is done, an audio adapter available from the board's manufacturer is used between the audio equipment and the board to adjust audio to levels compatible with telephone inputs.

Audio conditioning equipment. Use of equalizers, compressors, and other audio conditioning equipment can sometimes improve the quality of digitized voice. However, most conditioning equipment introduces nonlinearities, so the result is very often unsatisfactory. It's important to carefully test and compare the result against nonconditioned versions.

Speech board. In most cases, the same telephone/voice board used in an operational voice processing system is used for vocabulary production. Speech development, however, doesn't require telephone handling—and it certainly doesn't use outbound dialing. The minimum requirement is that vocabulary development hardware and software produce speech in the same data and file formats used by the runtime system. Some board makers offer different versions, making it possible for a speech development system to employ less expensive but compatible hardware from the same manufacturer.

Headphones and speakers. Recorded or digitally processed speech is monitored to evaluate its viability for an application or to edit it as the final production step. Playback of recorded vocabulary is generally accomplished on the same equipment used for recording. Naturally, the microphone is not needed, but either a set of headphones or speakers is required. As you shall see, there's reason to use both. Headphones provide unimpeded sound to the listener, placing the sound source directly on the ears and blocking out external noises. This is an excellent way to listen meticulously for brief imperfections that cause pops, clicks, and similar noises in digitally processed speech. Headphones, however, often mask problems affecting intelligibility and don't enable the best judgments concerning speech quality.

Many developers prefer listening to speech played through loudspeakers because they believe this more accurately mirrors normal use environments. However, this is not always true. First, a listener's head position relative to the loudspeaker greatly affects what is heard. Furthermore, most voice processing systems today speak over the telephone—so the listener does hear speech through an instrument placed next to the ear. Even in this environment, though, the listener's uncovered ear permits ambient noise to interfere. For these applications, neither loudspeakers nor headphones perfectly model the ultimate use environment and listening conditions. The best approach when editing is to first audition speech by loudspeaker to assess its intelligibility and quality. If the speech is judged inadequate, recording problems must be corrected and the speech rerecorded. When intelligible recordings of high quality are available, they can be carefully edited using headphones. For those applications targeted for telephone use, a final telephone audition can be performed.

There are several characteristics of speakers that should be understood by speech developers. Speakers not in an enclosure are inefficient. The enclosure is designed to prevent sound pressure projected forward from wrapping around and canceling sound pressure projected toward the rear. Lower frequencies are more prone to cancellation, so speakers not mounted to a baffle board or those not in an enclosure sound thin and don't accurately reproduce the original sound. A single high-quality speaker doesn't produce a flat spectral response over the entire audio range. For that reason, two or three speakers are mounted together in a single enclosure. Low-range speakers, called *woofers,* cover the frequency spectrum from about 40 Hz to 600 Hz. Woofers are usually 8 inches to 15 inches in diameter. *Midrange* speakers are usually less than 8 inches in diameter and provide flat response from about 600 Hz to 8,000 Hz. High-range speakers are called *tweeters* and handle frequencies from about 8,000 Hz to 20,000 Hz. A fourth type of speaker, called a *horn* because of its shape, is designed to handle frequencies in both mid and high ranges. Speaker enclosures typically house either of two combinations of speakers: a horn with a woofer, or one that includes a tweeter, a midrange, and a woofer. Good-quality headphones can produce a reasonably flat response over a range from about 50 Hz to about 5,000 Hz—adequate for digitally processed voice that's bandlimited between about 50 Hz and 4,000 Hz.

The dispersion of energy around a speaker enclosure is uneven, higher frequencies being more on-axis (focused to the front). Energy at lower frequencies tends to flow around the speaker so that, from behind the enclosure, lower frequencies are more prevalent. Figure 9.10 illustrates this principle. A person located directly in front of the speaker will perceive the flattest spectral response, getting approximately appropriate energy across

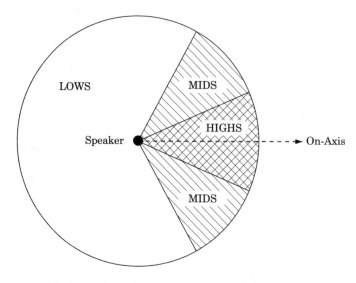

Figure 9.10 Focus of sound energy around a speaker.

the spectrum—the most accurate sound reproduction. Off-axis listeners hear a boosted bass. Because of this energy distribution, placement of the speaker enclosure can be of importance. Positioning an enclosure against the wall results in low-frequency reflections directly forward from the wall, causing discolorations to be perceived at some room locations. Flush-mounting of the enclosure within the wall tends to lessen this effect, as does lining the wall with absorbent materials.

Phase must be considered when two or more speakers are used. Out-of-phase speakers produce sound waves that compete with each other. Sound waves in air are alternating bands of compressed and rarefied air. When a compressed band from one speaker meets a rarefied band from another, they tend to cancel each other, distorting the result. Such sound discolorations are avoided by keeping all speakers in phase (the cones of all speakers moving in the same direction at the same time). Headphone wiring assures that the pair is in phase but care must be exercised to assure that speakers are properly wired.

The Announcer

The person whose voice is recorded is referred to as the announcer. Prototype vocabulary can be recorded by virtually anyone at the time it's needed. A studio and experienced announcer is required only when recording finished vocabulary. It's surprising how little studio time is used for even the most comprehensive scripts. Even if many systems are to be developed, it's unlikely that an announcer would ever be needed full time, but his or her selection should be carefully considered. The following paragraphs discuss qualification and selection of announcers.

Candidates

Announcing for voice processing applications requires skills that are not often possessed by those without vocal training—the best candidates are professionals in the broadcast, theater, record, and movie industries. In some cities, celebrity voices are available. Some performers, incidentally, expect sizable fees and might require royalties for each installed system. Some of these people specialize in recording for the voice processing industry and advertise in industry periodicals. Sound studios in some cities have recognized the broad market for audio production services in the voice processing industry and have begun marketing a spectrum of services to the industry. Their services include professional announcers, and studios can often arrange for celebrity voices to be recorded. Some studios offer a complete audio production service, from script design through production and management of audiotext applications. If your application requires music, sound effects, or other special audio treatment, a sound studio specializing in voice processing should be considered.

For those who wish to handle their own audio production, a very good alternate source of announcer candidates can be found in drama groups and in semantics and theater departments at local colleges. Teachers, students, amateur actors, and others are often anxious for an opportunity to participate in such interesting and out-of-the-ordinary undertakings. Many are seeking part-time employment, and some are willing to forgo royalties and work at a modest hourly rate. Some very talented individuals can be obtained through these channels, but, because many have not yet been exposed to this industry, all should be considered untested. Particularly thorough auditions and evaluations must be conducted before final selection of such candidates.

Because compression algorithms each have their peculiarities, not everyone's voice sounds pleasing and natural after digitization and compression. Furthermore, one speaker's voice and style might be more consistent with a given application than another's. These issues can be pondered in the abstract, but auditions can settle such questions before committing to a specific speaker.

Auditions

Each candidate's voice should be auditioned in the studio using a representative but wide-ranging script and preferably the exact audio equipment to be used in production. A professional studio can be rented for the purpose if an in-house studio is not available. Studios at some radio stations are not used on weekends and might be available for rent. Depending on how many candidates are auditioning, several sessions might have to be scheduled. The product of interest, and the only one that need be evaluated, is the digitized and compressed voice of each candidate. Appearance, public presence and demeanor are technically not of importance. The audition should, as nearly as possible, approximate conditions that will exist during actual production recording sessions. Auditions of any kind can be stressful, so a better performance can be obtained if unnecessary strain is eliminated. In particular, only those people needed should be present. This probably includes only the director, the candidate, and perhaps a technician. Company executives and other interested but extraneous people should be excluded. Waiting candidates can be comfortably situated in an area out of view of the studio.

Candidate evaluation

Each candidate's audition should be recorded so it can be processed and evaluated later rather than at the time it occurs. When judging, listen to each voice over the telephone, if that's how the voice is to be used. Compare the results of all candidates. It's interesting how different a voice can sound when coming from a loudspeaker or a telephone handset rather than from the actual person speaking face to face. Listeners can also be prejudiced if they know the speaker or have an image of the announcer's face while listening to a recording. To avoid favoritism or bias, conduct blind tests with multiple listeners. Don't reveal names of the voices until final selections are made. Male and female voices can be voted on separately and one or more of each selected to provide later choices. It might be useful to have a stable of announcers for varying requirements and as a hedge against the announcer of choice becoming unavailable.

The Recording Session

Production of vocabulary begins with development of a script and selection of an announcer. Once script and speaker are both available, recording sessions can be scheduled. The following sections deal with preparing to record and actual recording sessions.

Preparation

Things will go smoother and expensive announcer time will be saved by preparing the studio and equipment before the recording session begins. Doors and windows should be closed to shut out street noise. If the room does double duty, it will probably have air conditioning and heating systems. These should be turned off and the vents should be closed. Fan motors, the whir of forced air, and other noises transmitted by the ductwork must be eliminated. Computers and other equipment within the room emanate noise, so those not needed for the session should be switched off. Tape recorder heads and rollers should be cleaned, and the microphone, amplifier, and recorder should be tested. The microphone should be set up near the announcer's position. Be sure the mike position is flexible so it can be adjusted to its final position just before recording begins. To save time later, place a glass of water within reach of the announcer.

Script design

Several script design techniques are used to ease recording sessions and improve the resulting vocabulary. Script items sound better when spoken in context. Each script item can be preceded and followed by a sentence or phrase to force the item of interest to be spoken in context. This technique more often results in recordings with proper prosodics (intonation, emphasis, etc.). Any system's voice sounds smoother when entire sentences or phrases are recorded rather than being a concatenation of several words or phrases. For example, the script could contain "Press one," "Press two," and so on instead of "Press," "one," "two," etc. When an item is to be used with more than one intonation, it can be recorded once for each different usage. Pitch contours for numbers, for example, vary according to the position they occupy in a string of digits, so best results are obtained when at least three different versions of each number are available—this means recording each of them three or more times. Finally, the hard copy of the script used during recording should be neat and easy to read, with items listed in the order of recording. Two copies should be made available to the director well ahead of the session.

Microphone techniques

The amplitude and frequency output of most directional microphones are highly dependent on the speaker's position: nonlinearities will be introduced if the speaker's head bobs or turns even slightly. Furthermore, the bass response increases rapidly in a nonlinear manner as the distance between the announcer and the mike decreases. Plosive bursts in close proximity to the mike frequently result in gross and unacceptable distortions. These problems are lessened but not always eliminated with more expensive mikes. Wind screens and pop filters help to reduce pops caused by plosive bursts. Positioning the microphone out of the speaker's airstream so sound energy is not focused directly on axis also helps to minimize effects of plosive bursts. Figures 9.11 and 9.12 show two placements that might be used. Distance from the speaker and orientation depend on the speaker and the exact microphone being used.

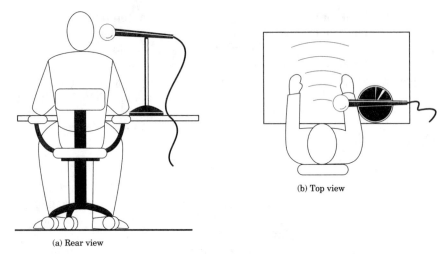

(a) Rear view

(b) Top view

Figure 9.11 Microphone positioned at right angle to announcer.

Figure 9.12 Microphone positioned at oblique angle to announcer.

Direction of a recording session

Recording sessions should be conducted in a professional manner. Multiple sessions can be planned if necessary, but no session should exceed 90 minutes. Twenty minutes at a sitting is about long enough for an announcer and director to concentrate without a break. If possible, the only person in the room during recording should be the announcer. The session director, communicating by intercom, can be positioned outside the room with the equipment—preferably, the announcer and director are able to see each other through a window.

Most announcers use a noticeably different style when repeating an item the first or last time. An acceptable version is more likely to be recorded if the speaker is directed to say each item at least three times in succession.

Directing a speech recording session is similar in a small way to directing a play. A better result will usually be obtained from a speaker if the director explains the context and intended use of an item. Finally, a recording session can be stressful. The desired feeling and tone is more likely to be produced by a speaker who is relaxed. Encouragement, occasional humor, and sincere compliments from the director go a long way toward achieving the desired product.

Prototype Versus Permanent Vocabulary

The initial script, written as the designer tries to "hear" the words in his or her head, almost always undergoes massive changes—system features are added, wording is changed, whole sections are eliminated. When converted to vocabulary and played in a live system, scripts don't sound as originally imagined. It's efficient, therefore, to first install inexpensive prototype vocabulary that can be easily changed as the application develops. Almost any voice will do for prototyping. It is important only that the voice be good enough to give designers the "look and feel" of the finished product. Different versions of prototype vocabulary can be tried, several wordings experienced, and only the best selected. Later, permanent vocabulary can easily replace prototype files.

Some developers, using an application generator, a scripting language, or other development tool, create a system's vocabulary with no more effort than just picking up a telephone instrument and speaking into it. The result can easily be monitored and rerecorded if it's not what's wanted. Vocabulary is sometimes recorded in a room full of computers whose disk drives, printers, circulating fans, and operators add to an already noisy environment. Some systems even support remote recording over the telephone. Indeed, these handy approaches are perfect for preparing vocabulary that's not intended to be permanent, vocabulary that must be changed frequently—and perhaps remotely. These convenient features are quite adequate for creating and revising prototype vocabulary but should never be used to produce permanent vocabulary, which merits more planning and greater care.

Vocabulary Editing

Editing should be conducted in a quiet environment, at times when the session is unlikely to be interrupted. Effective editing requires extreme concentration, focus, and an ability to hear clearly. Use of a loudspeaker will be disruptive and perhaps aggravating to others, so I recommend auditory isolation from people not involved in the process. Use of full-featured speech editor software is required for production and management of permanent vocabulary. It's of inestimable value in converting digitized, compressed data into finished vocabulary and for managing and maintaining vocabulary disk files. Speech editors also support important vocabulary file management functions such as rename, delete, copy, and movement of utterances between files. Editing techniques and special considerations are discussed in the following sections.

The process

Earphones help to eliminate ambient noise during editing and make it easier to focus on distinct sounds. Because the eventual user's listening environment will contain ambient noise, listening through a loudspeaker in a natural environment for editing has some advantages over earphones. As mentioned earlier, both methods should be used: earphones for detail, loudspeaker for intelligibility. Editing should begin with review. All versions of an item can be played in quick succession to compare the sound and "feel" of each—and to identify major irregularities. The recording that sounds best for its intended use and contains the least serious problems should be selected. Further editing concentrates on just that recording as it's played over and over. Listening becomes more focused as each distinct sound is discriminated. Particular attention must be paid to consonants. Every one should be clearly enunciated—some can be difficult to distinguish. If any recording seems unusable, it should be marked for rerecording.

Silence and other unwanted sounds can be trimmed from the beginning and end of an utterance. The speech editor should include one or more display screens that graph an utterance's amplitude versus time in any of several resolutions. Trim, delete, quiet, cut-and-paste, and other editor features are usually executed by moving the cursor on a graph display; these features might be able to remove or otherwise eliminate breath sounds, pops, squeaks, or other troublesome sounds. The editor should not cause permanent changes in speech data until explicitly commanded, so alternative approaches can be tried before committing to any changes. After each utterance is edited and judged satisfactory, it can be installed in an appropriate file. The last step in the development process should be to listen once again to every speech item to assure that amplitude and quality are consistent throughout.

Marginal utterances

Because it's usually inconvenient to schedule additional recording sessions, the editor might be able to rescue an utterance that seems marginal. If the speech editor includes a quieting feature, breathing and other unwanted sounds can be easily removed by locating noisy traces on the graph and quieting them. Many compression techniques, when applied to imperfect recordings, insert various unwanted sounds. Actually, unwelcome sounds can be introduced almost anywhere in the production process. It's often possible to avoid rerecording by deleting short tracts of speech to eliminate such sounds. The result must be carefully monitored, however, because deletion of speech data might introduce discontinuities or other problems. Vocabulary changes can sometimes be accommodated and additional recording avoided by using the editor's cut-and-paste feature to cut a phoneme, syllable, word, or phrase from one utterance for insertion into another.

Indexed files

Vocabulary can reside in indexed files with multiple utterances per file, or each utterance might occupy its own file. Indexed files often result in a smoother, more natural-sounding voice because, for many concatenated utterances, only one file need be opened. For example, by placing all versions of the digits in a single file, any concatenated number can be spoken without opening additional files. A similar situation applies for dates, dollar amounts, time of day, and the like. With an editor geared to indexed files, their handling and maintenance is made simple, and their use is a boon to developers.

Final review

After all speech items are edited and installed in vocabulary files, a few days should be allowed to pass before attempting a final review. This time allows the developer to listen with a fresh ear. After many hours of concentrated focus, it's difficult to evaluate any utterance. A few days away from editing enables the ear to become reaccustomed to normal speech, and edited utterances can be judged from a broader perspective. Later on, each utterance in every vocabulary file should be reviewed to assure consistency. Listening anew also highlights sounds or discrepancies that might have been originally missed due to familiarity and desensitization. Any utterance with persistent problems should be rerecorded, and the entire process should start again. Every utterance in every file should be reviewed and reviewed until nothing can be improved. As each vocabulary file is completed, it can be substituted for the prototype file, and the application can be executed. In this way, the sound and "feel" of the new voice can be experienced by developers and others—whose opinions should be solicited. Every utterance must be reviewed, revised, edited, rerecorded, and reedited until permanent vocabulary is as good as the technology allows.

Conclusion

Because people have learned to expect the very highest quality in audio recording, developers of voice processing systems can help to eliminate callers' negative impressions and create positive ones by producing the best fixed vocabulary possible with today's voice technology.

In this day of impeccable audio, users of voice processing systems will not accept second-best. Developers have set exacting standards for visual display interfaces. You must strive to attain equally high standards in the vocal interface—this means the design and production of high-quality speech. The knowledge is available. The technology exists. You need only recognize its importance and make it happen.

MAX, The Check-In System

Telephone User's Guide

These instructions are for use by security officers and supervisors; the instructions describe features and techniques that can be used to communicate over the telephone with MAX, The Check-In System. MAX knows when check-ins are due. If a scheduled check-in call is not received, MAX will telephone the office to report the fact. Supervisors can telephone MAX to learn about missed check-ins and to send or receive voice messages.

All employees

The telephone keypad. MAX talks to callers much as a human does, but a caller communicates with MAX by pressing the buttons (keys) on a Touch-Tone telephone. The 12 keys on a telephone are called a keypad. There are 10 keys for the numbers 0 through 9, and two special keys, the Asterisk key [*] at the lower-left corner and the Pound key [#] at the lower-right corner. When you communicate with MAX, you'll use these keys to make selections from among the choices he'll offer you, and you'll use the keys to enter the numbers he asks for. Anytime MAX expects you to press a key or keys, he'll explain in detail what you're to do and what keys to use. At the point when MAX wants you to press the key(s), he'll sound a tone.

MAX will tell you what to do. Each step of the way throughout the call, MAX will tell you in his prerecorded voice what to do next. Just follow his prompts, and he'll guide you through the call.

Press keys firmly. When pressing Touch-Tone keys in response to MAX's prompts, press each key firmly and distinctly. Hold the key down for about one second to be sure the telephone network properly transmits your key.

Time limit for pressing Touch-Tone keys. If MAX is expecting you to press a key, he'll tell you what he expects, sound a tone, and wait. If you don't press any key within several seconds—no problem. MAX will simply start again, repeat his instructions, sound the tone again, and wait some more. You generally have about a minute before MAX will assume you're not there and end the call.

Repeat prompts and messages. If you want MAX to repeat something he has just said, press the Asterisk key (the key marked [*] in the lower left corner of your telephone keypad). Pressing this key will, in most cases, cause MAX to back up and repeat his previous prompt.

MAX is resilient. You can't hurt the system even if you make a mistake. MAX will always tell you what to do next, but if you miss it or are unsure, try pressing the [*] key to repeat the previous prompt. Don't be afraid to press a key, even if you're not sure you should. You can't harm the system. If the call doesn't proceed as you expect it to, after trying the repeat key [*], you can always hang up and try the call again.

You can interrupt MAX's speaking. As you become familiar with MAX's prompts, you might not need to listen to them all the way through. You can almost always interrupt MAX's speaking at any time by pressing the next key. When you do this, MAX will stop speaking and go on. (There are only a few places where MAX will not allow you to interrupt.)

Entry of client, post and employee numbers. In order for MAX to identify your client and post, you'll be asked (during calls you place to MAX) to enter your client and post number (see the heading "Entering a string of digits."). On calls that MAX places to your post, he already knows the client and post numbers. Your scheduling office might or might not require entry of employee number during a call. If not, MAX will omit this part of the call and you need not be concerned with it. It's suggested that you know your client, post, and employee numbers. You might want to write them somewhere near the phone at the post.

Entry of the year, month, or day of birth. If your scheduling office requires entry of employee number during calls, the office might or might not also require entry of the year, month, or day of your birth. The purpose of such entry, if it's required, is to prevent unknown callers from having access to the system. If birthdate entry is required, MAX will ask you to press the appropriate digits for the year, month, or day of your birth. He'll ask for only one of these, and he selects which one to ask for on a random basis. If you mis-enter, he'll tell you and ask you to try again. Each time you try again, MAX might ask for a different part of your birthdate.

Entering a string of digits. You might be asked to enter a string of digits to indicate your client, post, or employee number. On each of these occurrences you'll be told how many keys to press (five for client, two for post, six for employee number). As you press each digit, it will be echoed (spoken) on the phone. After you have pressed the correct number of keys, you'll be asked to confirm your entry. You do so by pressing the Pound key (the key marked [#] at the lower-right corner of your telephone keypad). If you make a mistake, you can reenter the digits from the beginning. MAX will allow you to reenter up to four times.

Voice-messages. MAX includes a powerful capability to create, store, and deliver voice-messages. Voice messages can be "recorded" by the Scheduling Office staff or by a supervisor in his or her own voice—much like leaving a message on an answering machine. After recording, the message is "delivered" (read) to people during their phone calls. Some messages will be delivered to everyone who calls or is called. Some messages will be delivered only to those officers manning the posts of a specific client. Others will be delivered only to a specific person. When you call or are called by MAX, after you enter the information he requests, he'll read any voice-messages that you're supposed to hear—those for everyone, those for your client, and those intended for you alone.

Each message will be spoken in turn, starting with the oldest message for everyone. After all messages for everyone have been read, the oldest message for your client will be spoken. Finally, the messages for you individually will be read. After each message, you can either go on to the next one or hear the message again. Messages will not be interrupted by pressing Touch-Tone key (although the key will take effect as soon as the message is finished). The call will not end until you have heard all your messages.

You might actually hear some messages more than once—that is, during more than one phone call. Messages for everyone and messages for a given client are reread during every appropriate call over the period of a day or so. Staff at the Scheduling Office can review and listen to any voice-message that's handled by the system.

Supervisors

Special menu for supervisors. When you telephone or are telephoned by MAX and are asked to enter your employee number, MAX will know that you're a supervisor. If you're making a check-in call, after you check in (immediately if it's not a check-in call) MAX will read a supervisor function menu. This menu includes the functions described in the following. The supervisor menu is not presented by MAX to employees who are not logged as supervisors in his database.

When you hear the special menu, you can select any of the functions it mentions in any order you wish. Simply press the appropriate key on your telephone keypad. As always, you need not listen to the whole menu if you already know which key to press—just press the key and MAX will stop talking and proceed.

For voice-messages—to hear your messages. If there are voice-messages in the system designated either specifically for you or for everyone, they will be spoken over the phone when you request them via the supervisor menu. Each message will be spoken in turn, starting with the oldest message for everyone. After all messages for everyone have been read, the oldest message for you will be spoken. After each message, you can either go on to the next one or hear the message again. Messages will not be interrupted by pressing Touch-Tone key (although the key will take effect as soon as the message is finished). You cannot exit the message function until you have heard every message.

You might actually hear some messages more than once—that is, during more than one phone call. Messages for everyone are reread during every appropriate call over the period of a day or so, specified by the office. Staff at the Scheduling Office can review and listen to any voice-message that's handled by the system.

For voice-messages—to send a message. You can record a voice-message for a specific person, for all posts of any client, for everyone, or for the Scheduling office. When you select this function from the menu, MAX will guide you through the process of recording messages. He'll tell you how long you may speak, and he'll tell you when to press a Touch-Tone key to begin recording. Before you start, he'll remind you to press another key (any key) as soon as you're finished recording.

After you record a message, you can then review the message, send it, rerecord it, or delete it. The message will not be complete until you actually press the key to send it. Once you do send it, it's available to the recipient and will be added to their message list. It will remain in the system until it is automatically deleted after a default period of time, as specified by the office.

When you're done, press nine. When you've finished with everything you want to do, you end the call by pressing the nine key on your Touch-Tone keypad when told to do so by MAX.

Amy Scheduling System

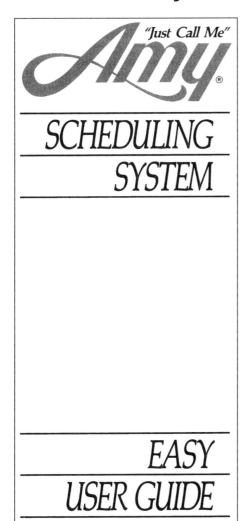

"Just Call Me"

Amy®

SCHEDULING

SYSTEM

EASY

USER GUIDE

GETTING TO KNOW AMY

Welcome to a new world of convenience!

AMY is **your**
personal scheduling secretary —
someone you can call on for
scheduling help any time of the
day or night
from wherever you are.

* AMY's office
  is in a computer.

* Contact is by a
  push-button
  telephone.

* And the key to
  AMY's scheduling
  system is your
  own personal
  identification
  number.

*AMY talks to
you in English.*

You respond by
pressing the keys on
the telephone.

AMY calls this:
"star key" ———
"pound key" ———

TO CALL AMY

*Begin by calling this
special number.*

Amy answers, and
asks for your personal
identification number.

*Use phone push-
buttons to enter your
number.*

AMY repeats your
number and asks you
to confirm it.

Confirm by pressing

*or, if not correct, re-
enter your number.*

AMY reads Option List

- Latest Schedule   **1**
- Absence Report   **2**
- Hang Up   **9**
- To Shorten
  Instructions   **3**
- HELP!   **8**

*When you hear the
option you want, press
the appropriate key.*

TO LEARN YOUR LATEST SCHEDULE

When you select this option, press

1

AMY gives date, time and assignment, beginning with your next shift . . .

Then, she gives choices:

Next day's schedule — **1**

Next week's schedule — **2**

Return to Option List — **7**

To repeat Amy's last message — *****

When you hear the item you want, press the appropriate key:

When finished, return to the Option List by pressing

7

To hang up, press

9

WHEN YOU MUST BE ABSENT

When you select this option, press

2

AMY asks when you'll be absent:
Today — **1**
Tomorrow - **2**

Press appropriate key

AMY acknowledges your message, and asks reason for your absence:
You are ill — **1**
Other reasons —

Press appropriate key

AMY acknowledges date and reason for absence and asks you to confirm.

To confirm, press

#

AMY concludes with the date you are expected back to work.

When finished, return to the Option List by pressing

7

To hang up, press

9

WHEN AMY CALLS YOU

Answer phone:

AMY identifies herself, asks for you and for your personal identification number...

Enter your personal identification number:

AMY gives date, time and job you're expected to work and asks you to accept assignment...
- Accept   **1**
- Decline   **2**
- Repeat the message   *****

Press appropriate key

If you accept the assignment, AMY re-states date, time and job.

If you decline the assignment, AMY acknowledges refusal

AMY says "goodbye."

TO CHANGE SPEED OF INSTRUCTIONS

When you select this option, press

AMY explains:
- To speed up her instructions, press   **1**
- To slow them down, press   **2**

Press appropriate key

AMY confirms she has changed the speed of her instructions

Reminder: The next time you call, AMY will remember and use the speed you selected.

You may go to the option list by pressing

7

To hang up, press

9

Continued on back cover.

HELP

When you have questions about AMY's Scheduling System and how it works — Help is as close as a phone call.

All you have to do is call AMY, and press **8** to get easy step-by-step help.

Try it.

If you still have questions, contact your supervisor.

Standard Codes:

To confirm information

* To repeat AMY's previous message

7 To start over (at AMY's Option List)

8 Help!

9 To hang up (then hang up receiver)

GRANITE SYSTEMS
3732 Mt. Diablo Blvd.
Lafayette, CA 94549

(415) 284-3596

AMY is a registered trademark
of Granite Systems

Printed in the USA · · 1986

C

Sample Scenario for an Auction-Results Telephone System

The following refers to a voice response system that will provide the results of auctions over the telephone. Using the system, a caller can specify any auction that has been held by the sponsor company over the past month and learn, for any item in that auction, whether or not it was sold and the price paid. The caller would also be able to learn whether or not he or she has been successful in an absentee bid, and, if so, the prices paid. The following represents an initial design. The script is meant only to give the reader the gist of the dialogues and provide a "feel" for the system. The actual logic, flow, words, phrases, and sentences to be used can be designed after this scenario has been finalized and approved.

A Possible Scenario

In the following example, it's assumed that callers need not be account holders. It's also assumed that any caller is permitted to hear hammer prices of any item in any auction. A third assumption is that an answering service or device is available when the office is closed. These assumptions might not be valid for many systems. In such situations, appropriate features must be present to account for the differences.

This same scenario can take place on all lines simultaneously. A line rings and is answered. The system says,

"Hello. Welcome to the Auction Results Reporting System. From a Touch-Tone phone, you can receive results of prior sales. Press the keys on your telephone to respond to my prompts. If you want me to repeat anything, just press the Star key at any time."

The system pauses, then continues.

"If you submitted an absentee bid, press the One key. If you did not, press Two. You may speak to someone in our Bid Department by pressing Three. If you don't have a Touch-Tone telephone, please hold the line and I'll switch to our Bid Department." (Tone)

(I've found it helpful to give callers a familiar signal when they're expected to press a key. I recommend sounding a pleasant tone at such times—this will be familiar to callers because they're already used to hearing a tone from answering machines when it's time for them to record their message.)

At this point, if the caller is not using a Touch-Tone phone and waits a few moments, the system will realize the caller has not pressed a key and will automatically transfer the call.

Callers are not required to listen through an entire prompt message. Anytime the caller presses any key, the system will immediately interrupt what it is saying and proceed.

In our sample scenario, the caller had not bid, so he or she presses the Two key on the Touch-Tone telephone and the system continues.

Caller has not submitted an absentee bid

"Please enter the sale number followed by the Pound key." (Tone)

The caller presses the following keys: [4], [0], [9], [5], [P], [#]. The system searches its database for the sale number 4095P. As it turns out, the caller has entered an invalid number (the caller intended to enter 4096P) so the system says,

"I'm sorry. The number you entered, four-oh-nine-five-p, is not a valid sale number. Please try again." (Tone)

The system then returns to the previous prompt "Please enter the sale number followed ···" and proceeds from there.

This time the caller enters the sale number 4096P correctly. On the telephone keypad the P, R, and S are all on the [7] key. Thus, the entry has created a redundancy. The system searches its sale database for all three numbers. It so happens that the system contains two of the sale numbers, 4096P and 4096S. The system has no way of knowing whether the caller meant 4096P or 4096S. So, to resolve the redundancy, the system says,

"If you want 4096P—Paintings, press One. If you want 4096S—Silver, press Two." (Tone)

If all three sale numbers had been found in the system's database, it would have read them all (there can be at most three such numbers).

In our scenario, the caller presses [1] to indicate sale 4096P—Paintings—to which the system responds,

"Paintings. Please enter the Auction Number followed by the Pound key." (Tone)

The caller enters [2], [3], [8], [4], [#], and the system looks up the sale amount for the item in its database and says,

"Sale number four-oh-nine-six-p—Paintings, auction number two-three-eight-four. Nine hundred dollars."

If the item had not been sold, the system would instead say,

"Sale number four-oh-nine-six-p—Paintings, auction number two-three-eight-four. The item was not sold."

In either case, the system would continue with,

"Do you want another item for sale number four-oh-nine-six-p? If so, press One. If not, press Two. Or, you may speak with someone in our Bid Department by pressing Three. To repeat, press the Star key." (Tone)

The caller presses [1] and the system asks for another auction number. The caller enters the number and the system reads the sale amount for that item. It then returns to the previous prompt, which says,

"Do you want another item for sale four-oh-nine-six-p? If so, press One. Otherwise, press Two." (Tone)

This time the caller presses [2].

"Would you like to inquire about a different sale? If so, press One. If not, press Two. Or, you may speak to someone in our Bid Department by pressing Three." (Tone)

If the caller presses [1], the system would return to the previous prompt, which requests that the sale number be entered. Our caller, however, is finished but wishes to ask a question about a future sale. The caller presses [3] and the system says,

"Please hold the line one moment while I transfer the call."

If the office is closed, the call will be transferred to an answering device with the appropriate message. If the office is open, the call will be transferred to a person.

Had the caller not elected to transfer the call but had, instead, ended the call, the caller would hear a closing message such as,

"Thank you for calling. Goodbye."

Caller has submitted an absentee bid

Suppose that the caller had been an absentee bidder in a recent sale. After the greeting message and opening menu, the caller would have elected to enter the absentee bid section. The system would say,

"I'll need your daytime phone number. First, please enter the three-digit area code followed by the Pound key." (Tone)

The caller enters [4], [1], [5], then [#]. If the wrong number of digits had been pressed, the system would ask the caller to try again. The system continues,

"Please enter the rest of your daytime telephone number followed by the Pound key." (Tone)

The caller then enters his or her phone number in much the same way that a caller dials when placing a call. If there are more or less than seven digits entered, the system will prompt the caller to try again. If seven numeric digits are entered, the system will search its customer database for the entire number, including the area code.

If the phone number is not found in the database, the system will say,

"The phone number you entered, 415-283-0232, is not in our database. You may re-enter or press the Pound key to transfer this call to someone in our Bid Department." (Tone)

If some number of incorrect entries (say three of four) are entered in succession, the system will attempt to transfer the call. For example, after the final incorrect entry it will say,

"I'm sorry. If you would like to speak to someone in our Bid Department, press One. To end the call, press Two." (Tone)

If [1] is pressed, the system says,

"Please hold the line one moment while I transfer the call."

If the office is open, the call will be transferred to a person. If it's closed, the call will be transferred to an answering device with the appropriate message.

Had the caller elected to end the call, he or she would hear a closing message and the system would hang up.

If the caller had entered a valid phone number and it is found in the system's database, the system would access a list of all the caller's absentee bids that are contained in the database. The system can either step through all successful bids followed by the unsuccessful ones, or it can simply take the bids in order, regardless of the bid outcome. In either case, it would be best to sub-group them according to sale number and read them in reverse chronological order (within the group or sub-group).

"Sale number four-oh-nine-six-P, Paintings. Auction number two-three-three-four. Your bid was nineteen-hundred dollars."

If the database shows that the caller also authorized bidding to the next highest increment and either the caller's bid was unsuccessful or the caller paid more than his or her bid (e.g., it was necessary to go to the next highest increment) the system will also say,

"You authorized bidding to the next highest increment."

If the caller's bid was successful, the system will say,

"Your bid was successful at a hammer price of two-thousand dollars."

If, on the other hand, the caller's bid was not successful, the system would instead say,

"The item was sold to a higher bidder at a hammer price of twenty-three-hundred dollars."

After a slight pause as a courtesy to the caller, the system presents the following menu,

"To go on to the next item, press One. If you wish to end the call, press Two. To hear the result again, press Three." (Tone)

Of course the caller could also repeat by pressing the Star key, but the caller might want to repeat this message. So, for the sake of clarity, the system gives the caller this extra menu item. The caller presses [1] to go on to the next item. When all bids have been reviewed, the system will say,

"There are no more bids to review. If you'd like to know prices on other items, press One. Or, to speak to someone in our Bid Department, press Two. Otherwise, press Three to end the call."

If the caller wants to hear prices on other items and presses the One key, the system will return to the point in our scenario titled Caller Has Not Submitted an Absentee Bid and proceed from there. If, on the other hand, the caller wants to talk with a person, he or she presses the Two key and hears,

"Please hold the line one moment while I transfer the call."

If the office is closed, the call will be transferred to an answering device with the appropriate message. If the office is open, the call will be transferred to a person.

Had the caller not elected to transfer the call but had, instead, ended the call, the caller would hear a closing message such as,

"Thank you for calling. Goodbye."

D

Top-Level Dialogue
for Guard Check-in System

This dialogue will occur when a guard or supervisor calls the computer system or if it is time to initiate either an outbound check-in call or an outbound alert call. Certain procedures referred to in this dialogue are documented in other files.

```
WAIT_FOR_RING:

Loop through the folowing tests.

    If it's time to place an outgoing check-in call, execute

    Procedure OUTGOINGCHECKIN.

        If (END) is returned, go to ENDTHECALL.

        If (ABORT) is returned, go to ABORTTHECALL.

    If it's time to place an outgoing alert call to a
    supervisor, execute Procedure OUTGOINGALERT.

        If (END) is returned, go to ENDTHECALL.

        If (ABORT) is returned, go to ABORTTHECALL.

        If a ring interrupt occurs, go to ANSWERPHONE

        Go back to WAIT_FOR_RING

    ANSWERPHONE:

    Take the phone offhook.
```

"Hello. This is the Check-in System. If you have an emergency, hangup now and call 555-3535. That's, 555-3535."

Execute Procedure EMPLOYEENUMBER.

If (employee number) returned, go to MESSAGESNOTE.

If (ABORT) returned, go to ABORTTHECALL.

Otherwise, (NOTFOUND) returned.

Set (employee number) = 0.

MESSAGESNOTE:

If there are no voice-messages for this caller,
                                        go to MAINMENU.

"I have x voice messages {or: I have a voice-message} for you."

MAINMENU:

Pause one second.

If this employee is not authorized for supervisor functions, go to NOTASUPERVISOR.

"To get your messages, press one. To access Supervisor Functions, press two. If you are ready to hangup, press nine. You may repeat any of my prompts by pressing the starkey. <Tone>."

If too many timeouts, go to ENDTHECALL.

If a timeout occurs, go back to MAINMENU.

If [*] pressed, go back to MAINMENU.

If [1] is pressed, execute Procedure HEARMESSAGES.

If (END or MENU) is returned, go back to MAINMENU.

If (ABORT) is returned, go to ABORTTHECALL.

If [2] is pressed, go to SUPERVISORMENU.

If [9] is pressed, go to ENDTHECALL.

If any other key is pressed, execute Procedure INVALID.

Go back to MAINMENU.

NOTASUPERVISOR:

"If this is a check-in call, press one. To get your messages, press two. If you are ready to hang up, press nine. You may re-peat any of my prompts by pressing the starkey.<Tone>."

If too many timeouts, go to ENDTHECALL.

If a timeout occurs, go back to MAINMENU.

If [*] pressed, go back to MAINMENU.

If [1] is pressed, execute Procedure INCOMINGCHECKIN.

    If (END or MENU) is returned, go back to MAINMENU.

    If (ABORT) is returned, go to ABORTTHECALL.

If [2] is pressed, execute Procedure HEARMESSAGES.

    If (END or MENU) is returned, go back to MAINMENU.

    If (ABORT) is returned, go to ABORTTHECALL.

If [3] is pressed, execute Procedure PANIC.

    Go back to MAINMENU.

If [9] is pressed, go to ENDTHECALL.

If any other key is pressed, execute Procedure INVALID.

Go back to MAINMENU.

SUPERVISORMENU:

    "To review missed check-in calls, press one. To record a voice message, press two. To setup a temporary post, press three. To go back to the main menu, press seven." <Tone>

If too many timeouts, go to ABORTTHECALL.

If timeout, go back to PASSWORD_CORRECT.

If [*] is pressed, go back to PASSWORD_CORRECT.

If [1] is pressed, execute Procedure MISSEDCALLS.

    If (ABORT) is returned, go to ABORTTHECALL.

    If (MENU) is returned, go back to MAINMENU.

    If (END) is returned, go back to SUPERVISORMENU.

If [2] is pressed, execute Procedure RECORDMESSAGE.

    If (ABORT) is returned, go to ABORTTHECALL.

    If (MENU) is returned, go back to MAINMENU.

    If (END) is returned, go back to SUPERVISORMENU.

If [3] is pressed, execute Procedure SETUPPOST.

    If (ABORT) is returned, go to ABORTTHECALL.

    If (MENU) is returned, go back to MAINMENU.

If (END) is returned, go back to SUPERVISORMENU.

If [7] is pressed, go back to MAINMENU.

If any other key is pressed, execute Procedure INVALIDKEY.

Go back to PASSWORD_CORRECT.

ENDTHECALL:

If there are now no voice-messages for this caller,
go to SAYGOODBYE.

"I have x voice messages {or: I have a voice-message} for
you."

Execute Procedure HEARMESSAGES.

If (END) is returned, go to SAYGOODBYE.

If (ABORT) is returned, go to ABORTTHECALL.

SAYGOODBYE:

"We'll be seeing you. Goodbye."

ABORTTHECALL:

Hang up the phone

Go to WAIT_FOR_RING

C-Language Program Using a Voice Processing Development Toolkit

```
/*------------------------------------------------------------------------*/
/*                                                                        */
/* *                    MAX - TELEPHONE CALL HANDLER                      */
/* *                                                                      */
/* *                         October 24, 1991                            */
/* *                                                                      */
/*------------------------------------------------------------------------*/

#include "stdio.h"          /* io header file              */
#include "dos.h"            /* dos header                  */
#include "vfcns.h"          /* voice file function header  */
#include "applic.h"         /* application header file     */
#include "phones.h"
#include "vocab.h"          /* must be preceded by phones.h */
#include "common.h"
#include "popmenus.h"
#include "video.h"          /* video definitions           */
#include "clock.h"
#include "phone.h"
#include "vmsg.h"
#include "status.h"
#include "allcalls.h"
#include "stack.h"

/*------------------------------------------------------------------------*/
/* EXTERNALS */

extern int    callsdisabled;      /* d41p.c set to 1 to disable calls while database catches up */
extern int    mty_numbers_utt;    /* utterance number of first of numbers */
```

```
extern int     mty_exittodosflag;      /* tells everyone who needs to know that we're exiting */
extern int     mty_demoflag;           /* default=0: 0 means DEMO was not in config.mty, 1 means it was */
extern int     recbadkey[];
extern int     mty_call2makeflag;      /* set flag in eventqtask() when there's an out-call */
extern int     mty_localline;          /* d41/x port to use for local telephone */
extern STATUS  phonestat[NUMPHONELINES]; /* NUMPHONELINES is defined in phones.h */
extern int     mty_localkbflag;        /* tell eventqtask() in d41p.c that local phone is active */
extern int     _TSIZE;
extern int     _MNEED;
extern int     _STACK;
extern int     taskassignment[];       /* task = taskassignment[line]; */
extern int     lineassignment[];       /* line = lineassignment[task]; */
extern char    mty_aborting[];
extern char    mty_dialing[];          /* "Dialing" */
extern char    mty_connect[];          /* "Connect" */
extern char    mty_noconnect[];        /* "No connect" */

DBKEY  callkeys [ NUMPHONELINES +1 ];      /* array to save callkey incase of abort phone call */
int    callendflag [ NUMPHONELINES +1 ];   /* set so call_end() will only be called once per call */
char   *clientnumptr;          /* set in allcalls.c for supcalls.c - if sup, he can get msg */

/*--------------------------------------------------------------------------------------*/

static unsigned checkinmenu1[] =   /* see if this in-call is a checkin call */
{
       9,       /* NUMBER OF UTTERANCES IN THIS ARRAY */
    IF_CKIN,    /* "If this is a checkin call," */
    PAUSE_4,    /* 1/4 second pause */
    PRESS_1,    /* press one. */
    PAUSE_2,    /* 1/2 second pause */
    IF_NOT,     /* If not, */
    PAUSE_4,    /* 1/4 second pause */
    PRESS_2,    /* press two. */
```

```
    PAUSE_2,     /* 1/2 second pause */
    TONE         /* <tone> */
};

static unsigned checkinmenu2[] = /* (SHORT VERSION) see if this in-call is a checkin call */
{
    9,           /* NUMBER OF UTTERANCES IN THIS ARRAY */
    IF_CKIN,     /* Checking in? */
    PAUSE_4,     /* 1/4 second pause */
    PRESS_1,     /* press one. */
    PAUSE_2,     /* 1/2 second pause */
    O_WISE,      /* Otherwise, */
    PAUSE_4,     /* 1/4 second pause */
    PRESS_2,     /* press two. */
    PAUSE_2,     /* 1/2 second pause */
    TONE         /* <tone> */
};

static unsigned panicmenu[] = /* see if this in-call is a panic call */
{
    9,           /* NUMBER OF UTTERANCES IN THIS ARRAY */
    IF_EMERG,    /* If you have an emergency and wish someone to respond right */
    PAUSE_4,     /* 1/4 second pause */
    PRESS_1,     /* press one. */
    PAUSE_2,     /* 1/2 second pause */
    IF_NOT,      /* If not, */
    PAUSE_4,     /* 1/4 second pause */
    PRESS_2,     /* press two. */
    PAUSE_2,     /* 1/2 second pause */
    TONE         /* <tone> */
};
```

```c
/*----------------------------------------------------------------------*/
int mty_outcallflag[ NUMPHONELINES ]; /* flag to tell the task to do an outgoing call */
/*----------------------------------------------------------------------*/

program_1()                            /* telephone function for APS */
{
    int     techdiffabort();
    int     task = 0;
    int     line;

    task = _yield();                          /* get my task number */
    line = getline(task);                     /* assign a telephone line number for this task */
    setabort( techdiffabort, task);          /* setup func to use in backgrnd to abort a call */
    callsetrestart( task );                   /* setup restart func for telephonetask() */
    logcode( START_TASK, line );             /* log event w/ line (logcode.txt) */
    telephonetask();                          /* REENTRANT FUNCTION THAT CONTROLS DIALOGIC HARDWARE */
    _stop();                                  /* if it ever comes here, stop (it shouldnt) */
}

/*----------------------------------------------------------------------*/
callsetrestart( task )       /* set restart for early disconnect */
int     task;
{
    int     telephonetask();

    setrestart( telephonetask, task);
}

/*----------------------------------------------------------------------*/
```

```
telephonetask()                        /* REENTRANT FUNCTION THAT CONTROLS DIALOGIC HARDWARE */
{
    int    task;
    int    line;
    int    numrings;              /* num in-rings before answer a call */

    task = _yield();             /* get my task number */
    line = lineassignment[ task ];

    logcodedata( ENTER_TASK, line, task );

    restphoneline(line);    /* reset phone line to idle */

    onhook(line);           /* go onhook */

    while( 1 )
    {
        numrings = get_numrings();     /* get num rings before ans in-call */

        while ( callsdisabled )        /* wait: db to catch up on startup and missed chkn to clear */
        {
            _yield();
        }

        answer(line, numrings);        /* answer the phone after 1 ring */
        callendflag[ line ] = 0;       /* reset so end_call() can be called */
        cleartones(line);              /* empty the tone buffer */
        toneinton( line );             /* allow dtmf tones to interrupt */

        task = _yield();               /* get task num again in case stack has been clobbered */
        if( mty_outcallflag[ line ] )/* were we awakened to do an outgoing call */
        {
            makeoutcall( line );       /* go to the outcall function */
```

```c
        mty_outcallflag[ line ] = 0; /* reset for next in-call */
        }
    else
        {
        takeincall( line );
        }

    _yield();

    }

/*--------------------------------------------------------------------*/

int get_numrings()                   /* get num rings before ans in-call */
{
    BRANCH branch;

    get_branch( &branch );                    /* get branch info */
    return( (int) branch.answerrings );  /* number of rings before answer in-call */
}

/*--------------------------------------------------------------------*/

takeincall( line )                       /* handle incoming calls */
int line;
{
    DBKEY    callkey;
    DBKEY    got_incall();
    int      ret;
    int      task;
    int      tocount = 0;
    char     menukey[2];
    RULES    rules;                      /* data struct for rules */
```

```
BRANCH      branch;
char        string[5];
int         num;
char        *ptr;
int         i;
EMPLOYEE emplinfo;

task = _yield();              /* get my task number */
logcodedata( INBOUND_CALL, line, task );

callkey = got_incall();       /* report this incoming call to the db mgr */

callkeys [ line ] = callkey;  /* save this incase of abort phone call */

rules.key = find_branch_rules(); /* get branch rule re: allowpanic calls */
get_rules( &rules );

MAINMENU:                     /* MAINMENU = MENU 1 */
    delay( line, 7 );         /* delay 7/10 second */
    if( mty_demoflag )        /* say greeting depending on demo flag set in config */
        speak1(line, 318);    /* "Hello. This is the Security Officer Checkin System" */
    else
        speak1(line, 108);    /* "This is MAX, your checkin system" */

    if( !rules.flag.allowpanic )  /* only say this if branch panic option is disabled */
    {
    get_branch( &branch );

    string[0] = branch.emergency.prefix[0];
    if(( string[0] >= '0') && ( string[0] <= '9' ))  /* make sure phone # numeric */
        {
        speak1(line, 104);    /* "If this is an emergency call, hangup now and call:" */
        ptr = &branch.emergency.prefix[0];
```

```
        for( i=0; i<3; i++)
        {
        num = ptr[ i ] - '0';    /* convert next one byte to integer */
        speakdigitsi( line, num, NO_LEAD_ZERO );
        }

        delay( line, 2 );         /* delay 2/10 second */

        ptr = &branch.emergency.suffix[0];
        for( i=0; i<4; i++)
        {
        num = ptr[ i ] - '0';    /* convert next one byte to integer */
        speakdigitsi( line, num, NO_LEAD_ZERO );
        }

        }

REPEAT:
        delay( line, 4 );         /* delay 4/10 second */

        if( mty_demoflag )        /* say greeting depending on demo flag set in config */
            speak( line, &checkinmenu1[0] ); /* "if this is a checkin call..." */
        else
            speak( line, &checkinmenu2[0] ); /* (SHORT VERSION) "if this is a checkin call..." */

        tocount = 0;
        menukey[0] = 0;
        readtones(line, &menukey[0], 1, TIMEOUTDELAY); /* get one dtmf digit, timeout in 15 secs */

        switch( menukey[0] )      /* parse the key */
        {
        case TIMEOUT:             /* timeout */
            tocount++;
```

```
            if( tocount > MAXTIMEOUTS )
            {
                ret = -1;                                    /* end call */
                break;                                       /* too many timeouts */
            }
            else
                goto MAINMENU;                               /* do it again */

        case REPEAT:                                         /* repeat */
            goto MAINMENU;                                   /* do it again */

        case CHECK_IN:                                       /* this is checkin call */
            ret = checkincall( line, callkey );  /* yes. now do the checkin */
            break;

        case NOT_CHECK_IN:                                   /* this is NOT a checkin call */
            ret = noncheckincall( line, callkey );  /* no. now do the non-checkin */
            break;

        case SPECIAL_USER:                                   /* first digit of privileged access [82633] */
            if( privileged( line ) )                         /* if person will now enters [2633], can get supv priv */
            {                                                /* thus, it takes entry of "82633" */
                emplinfo.flag.issup = 1;                     /* this person may send vm */
                suprvisorfunctions( line, "999999", &emplinfo, callkey );    /* supv phone func menu */
                break;
            }
            else
                goto REPEAT;

        default:
            speak( line, &recbadkey[0] );  /* say "bad key" */
            goto REPEAT;
    }
```

```
cleartones( line );              /* be sure final words are spoken */

if( ret < 0 )                    /* abort */
{
    speak1( line, 157 );         /* "I'm sorry. We can't continue the call" */
    delay( line, 6 );            /* delay 3/10 second */
    speak1( line, 119 );         /* "Please contact the office" */
    speak1( line, 123 );         /* "right away." */
}

delay( line, 7 );                /* delay 7/10 second */

if( mty_demoflag )               /* say greeting depending on demo flag set in config */
    speak1(line, 311);           /* "Thankyou for calling. Goodbye." */
else
    speak1(line, 316);           /* "(SHORTER VERSION) Thanks." */

onhook(line);                    /* go onhook */

if( !callendflag [ line ] )      /* dont call end_call() again if already called */
{
    end_call( callkey);          /* report end of call to db mgr */
    callendflag[ line ] = 1;
}

return;
}
```

/*---*/

```
sendvoicemsgs( line, empnum, emplinfo ) /* send v-mail if supv */
int      line;

char     *empnum;
EMPLOYEE *emplinfo;
{
         int    task;

         task = _yield();                       /* get my task number */
         logcodedata( DELIVER_MSGS, line, task );

         if( empnum[0] )                         /* must be an empl num for all this */
         {
             if( emplinfo->flag.issup )          /* if this empl is supv */
             {
                 recordmsg( line, empnum ); /* speak record-menu -- called in apsback.c */
             }
             else                                /* this empl is NOT supv */
             {
                 delay( line, 4 );               /* delay 4/10 seconds */
                 speak1(line, 10016 );           /* "I'm sorry." */
                 delay( line, 1 );               /* delay 1/10 second */
                 speak1(line, 10018 );           /* "You're not authorized to send voice-messages." */
             }
         }
}

/*----------------------------------------------------------------------*/
```

F

Script Program in
Assembler-Like Language

The following program is implemented as assembler macros.

```
;------------------------------------------------------------------------------
; Telephone Calculator: This program receives incoming calls and performs
;                       arithemetic operations on values the caller enters
;                       on the touchtone keypad. Commands may be entered
;                       on the keypad as follows.
;
; DTMF KEYS      OPERATION
;    0           Clear
;    1           Add
;    3           Subtract
;    5           Say Current Result
;    7           Divide
;    9           Multiply
;   *1           Clear and Start Over
;   *9           Exit Program
;
;------------------------------------------------------------------------------

TITLE   "CALCVOX" PROGRAM IN "VOX" LANGUAGE
        EXTRN EXECVOX:BYTE

DSEG    SEGMENT   PUBLIC  'DATA'
        PUBLIC CALCVOX
```

```
        INCLUDE MACROS.ASM             ;Load MACRO definitions

CALCVOX
        RETURNJUMP  DISPLAY_TITLE      ;Program title to Status Screen
        ANSWER      1                  ;Wait for call -- answer on 1st ring
        DELAY       4                  ;Pause 0.4 seconds
        SPEAK       GREETING           ;Say "Hello. This is Calcvox."

        SETCOMMAND  1,CLEAR_RESTART    ;Go to CLEAR_RESTART whenever [*1] pressed
        SETCOMMAND  9,EXIT             ;Go to EXIT whenever [*9] is pressed

        JUMP        RESTART            ;Go to RESTART

CLEAR_RESTART   EQU $
        DELAY       3                  ;Pause 0.3 seconds
        SPEAK       CLEARUTT           ;Say "Clear."

RESTART         EQU $
        DELAY       4                  ;Pause 0.4 seconds
        SPEAK       PLEASE_START       ;Say "Please Start."
        SPEAK       DOUBLE_TONE        ;Sound the tone twice
        MOVE        DEST,ZEROSTRING    ;'00000000' -> DEST
        JUMP        ADDITION           ;Go to ADDITION
```

```
FUNCLOOP
        SPEAK       TONE                              ;Sound the tone
        READTONES   VAR,FORM11                        ;Wait for one DTMF key -> VAR
        MOVE        FUNCTION,VAR                      ;  put it in FUNCTION

        DELAY       2                                 ;Pause 0.2 seconds
        LOOKUP      FUNCTABLE,FUNCTION,ERRUTT,NOFUNCTION
FUNCTABLE EQU $                                       ;Lookup DTMF key (in FUNCTION) and if:
        TABLE       10,0     ;BINARY TABLE            ;KEY SAY-THIS  JUMP-ADDRESS
        ENTRY       0,NULLUTT,CLEAR_RESTART           ; 0 (Nothing) CLEAR_RESTART
        ENTRY       1,SUBUTT,SUBTRACTION              ; 1 "Minus"   SUBTRACTION
        ENTRY       2,ERRUTT,NOFUNCTION               ; 2 "Invalid" NOFUNCTION
        ENTRY       3,ADDUTT,ADDITION                 ; 3 "Plus"    ADDITION
        ENTRY       4,ERRUTT,NOFUNCTION               ; 4 "Invalid" NOFUNCTION
        ENTRY       5,EQUTT,EQUALS                    ; 5 "is"      EQUALS
        ENTRY       6,ERRUTT,NOFUNCTION               ; 6 "Invalid" NOFUNCTION
        ENTRY       7,DIVUTT,DIVISION                 ; 7 "over"    DIVISION
        ENTRY       8,ERRUTT,NOFUNCTION               ; 8 "Invalid" NOFUNCTION
        ENTRY       9,MULUTT,MULTIPLICATION           ; 9 "times"   MULTIPLICATION

ADDITION  EQU $
        READTONES   VAR,FORM1                         ;Wait for up to 9 touchtone digits
        MOVE        SOURCE,VAR                        ;  put them in SOURCE
        SPEAKNUMBER SOURCE                            ;  read them back

        PLUS        DEST,SOURCE                       ;Add SOURCE to DEST
        JUMP        FUNCLOOP                          ;Go to FUNCLOOP

EQUALS    EQU $
```

```
            SPEAKNUMBER             DEST                 ;Read contents of DEST as a number
            JUMP                    FUNCLOOP             ;Go to FUNCLOOP

SUBTRACTION                         EQU $
            READTONES               VAR,FORM1            ;Wait for up to 9 touchtone digits
            MOVE                    SOURCE,VAR           ; put them in SOURCE
            SPEAKNUMBER             SOURCE               ; read them back

            MINUS                   DEST,SOURCE          ;Subtract SOURCE from DEST
            JUMP                    FUNCLOOP             ;Go to FUNCLOOP

MULTIPLICATION                      EQU $
            READTONES               VAR,FORM1            ;Wait for up to 9 touchtone digits
            MOVE                    SOURCE,VAR           ; put them in SOURCE
            SPEAKNUMBER             SOURCE               ; read them back

MULTIPLY_OVERFLOW_CHECK             EQU $
            COMPARE                 DEST,N2_16           ;Compare DEST to 65536
            JUMPMORE                MULTIPLY_OVERFLOW    ; if DEST > 65536, go to MULTIPLY_OVERFLOW

            COMPARE                 SOURCE,N2_16         ;Compare SOURCE to 65536
            JUMPMORE                MULTIPLY_OVERFLOW    ; if SOURCE > 65536, go to MULTIPLY_OVERFLOW

MULTIPLY_OK                         EQU $
            MULTIPLY                DEST,SOURCE          ;Multiply DEST by SOURCE
            JUMP                    FUNCLOOP             ;Go to FUNCLOOP
```

```
MULTIPLY_OVERFLOW     EQU $
     DELAY            4                        ;Pause 0.4 seconds
     SPEAK            OVERFLOW                 ;Say "Overflow."
     JUMP             FUNCLOOP                 ;Go to FUNCLOOP

DIVISION              EQU $
     READTONES        VAR,FORM1                ;Wait for up to 9 touchtone digits
     MOVE             SOURCE,VAR               ; put them in SOURCE
     SPEAKNUMBER      SOURCE                   ; read them back
DIVIDE_LIMIT_CHECK    EQU $
     JUMPZERO         DIVIDE_OVERFLOW,SOURCE   ;If SOURCE = 0, go to DIVIDE_OVERFLOW

     COMPARE          DEST,N2_16               ;Compare DEST to 65536
     JUMPLESS         DIVIDE_OK                ; if DEST < 65536, go to DIVIDE_OK

     COMPARE          DEST,N2_32M2_16          ;Compare DEST to 4294901760
     JUMPLESS         DIVIDE_LIMIT_CHECK_2     ; if DEST smaller, go to DIVIDE_LIMIT_CHECK_2
     JUMP             DIVIDE_OVERFLOW          ; else, go to DIVIDE_OVERFLOW

DIVIDE_LIMIT_CHECK_2  EQU $
     MOVE             TEMP41,DEST              ;DEST  -> TEMP41
     MOVE             TEMP21,N2_16M1           ;65535 -> TEMP21
     DIVIDE           TEMP41,TEMP21            ;DEST/65535 -> TEMP41

     COMPARE          TEMP41,SOURCE            ;Compare TEMP41 to SOURCE
     JUMPLESS         DIVIDE_OK                ; if TEMP41 smaller, go to DIVIDE_OK
     JUMP             DIVIDE_OVERFLOW          ; else, go to DIVIDE_OVERFLOW
```

```
DIVIDE_OK        EQU $
        DIVIDE   DEST,SOURCE          ;Divide DEST by SOURCE
        JUMP     FUNCLOOP             ;Go to FUNCLOOP

DIVIDE_OVERFLOW  EQU $
        DELAY    4                    ;Pause 0.4 seconds
        SPEAK    OVERFLOW             ;Say "Overlow."
        JUMP     FUNCLOOP             ;Go to FUNCLOOP

NOFUNCTION       EQU $
        JUMP     FUNCLOOP             ;Go to FUNCLOOP

DISPLAY_TITLE    EQU $
        DISPLAY  15,20,'calcVOX........the TELEPHONE CALCULATOR'  ;Display program title on Status Screen
        RETURN                        ;Return to caller

EXIT             EQU $
        CLEARCOMMAND  9               ;Cancel automatic jump on DTMF keys *9
        DELAY    3                    ;Pause 0.3 seconds
        SPEAK    EXIT_UTT             ;Say "Thankyou for Calling. Goodbye."
        HANGUP                        ;Go onhook
        JUMP     CALCVOX              ;Go to CALCVOX

;
```

```
; UTTERANCES

          STRING  8
ADDUTT   EQU     $
         UTTER   237  ;Plus
         UTTER   112  ;(Pause)
         UTTER   112  ;(Pause)
         UTTER   215  ;(Tone)

          STRING  2
CLEARUTT EQU     $
         UTTER   235  ;Clear

          STRING  8
DIVUTT   EQU     $
         UTTER   240  ;Over
         UTTER   112  ;(Pause)
         UTTER   112  ;(Pause)
         UTTER   215  ;(Tone)

             STRING  4
DOUBLE_TONE  EQU     $
             UTTER   215  ;(Tone)
             UTTER   215  ;(Tone)

          STRING  2
EQUTT    EQU     $
```

```
          UTTER    239  ;Is

ERRUTT    STRING   2
          EQU      $
          UTTER    22   ;Invalid

          STRING   2
EXIT_UTT  EQU      $
          UTTER    177  ;Thankyou for calling. Goodbye.

          STRING   12
GREETING  EQU      $
          UTTER    222  ;Hello
          UTTER    112  ;(Pause)
          UTTER    112  ;(Pause)
          UTTER    112  ;(Pause)
          UTTER    223  ;This is
          UTTER    224  ;CALCVOX

          STRING   10
MULUTT    EQU      $
          UTTER    115  ;Time
          UTTER    92   ;-s
          UTTER    112  ;(Pause)
          UTTER    112  ;(Pause)
          UTTER    215  ;(Tone)
```

```
                STRING  2
NULLUTT    EQU     $
                UTTER   0    ;(Say nothing)

                STRING  2
OVERFLOW        UTTER   EQU     241  ;Overflow
                                $

                STRING  2
PLEASE_START    EQU     $
                UTTER   236  ;Please start

                STRING  8
SUBUTT     EQU     $
                UTTER   238  ;Minus
                UTTER   112  ;(Pause)
                UTTER   112  ;(Pause)
                UTTER   215  ;(Tone)

                STRING  2
TONE       EQU     $
                UTTER   215  ;(Tone)

;------------------------------------
; CONSTANTS

FORM1      EQU     $
           FORMAT  1,9,'R',' ',3,'D'
```

```
FORM11   EQU     $
         FORMAT  1,1,'R','  ',3,'D'

         INTEGER 4
N2_16    EQU     $                 ;Constant 65536
         DWORD   65536

         INTEGER 4
N2_16M1  EQU $
         DWORD   65535    ;Constant: 2**16 MINUS 1

         INTEGER 4
N2_32M2_16   EQU $
         DWORD   4294901760 ;Constant: 2**32 MINUS 2**16

         STRING  9
ZEROSTRING   EQU $    ;Constant ASCII String
         ASCII   '000000000'
;------------------------------------------------------------
```

```
; VARIABLES

DEST      INTEGER 4
          EQU     $            ;Arithmetic Destination Operand
          DWORD   0

FUNCTION EQU      INTEGER 2
                  $
                  WORD    0    ;Keypad Selection

SOURCE    INTEGER 4
          EQU     $            ;Arithmetic Source Operand
          DWORD   0

TEMP21    INTEGER 2
          EQU     $            ;Temporary Variable
          WORD    0

TEMP41    INTEGER 4
          EQU     $            ;Temporary Variable
          DWORD   0

VAR       STRING  9
          EQU     $            ;Variable ASCII String
          ASCII   '000000001'

;-----------------------------------------------------------

PROG      EQU     CALCVOX
DSEG      ENDS
          END
```

G

Sample Script
Language Program

```
* SMART ANSWERING MACHINE
*
*    Written in Script Language
*
*    Multitasking, status display, retries, disconnect, call statistics
*    display, error recovery, phone line assignments and other standard
*    features handled automatically.
*
*    This program will run asynchronously on all lines to which it is
*    assigned. Standard displays include Call Statistics Screen,
*    System Status Screen, and Menu Screen (with three items:
*    SYSTEM STATUS, CALL STATISTICS, and QUIT).
*

* - - - - - - - - - - - - - - - - - - - - - - - - - - - - - - - - - - - *
* DEFINE VARIABLES
* - - - - - - - - - - - - - - - - - - - - - - - - - - - - - - - - - - - *

variable    filename, char, public, 'filename'  * Voice message filename field
variable    key, char, private, ' ',             * DTMF input for menu choice
variable    maildb, char, public, 'messages'     * Voice message database name
variable    message, char, private, ' ',         * Voice message filename
variable    pwfixed, char, public, '82633'       * Owners password
variable    pwvar, char, private, ' ',           * DTMF input for owner's password
* - - - - - - - - - - - - - - - - - - - - - - - - - - - - - - - - - - - *
```

```
* DEFINE VOCABULARY

utterance 2end       rec,3    * Press any key to end recording
utterance 2erase     rec,3    * To erase and continue, press 2
utterance 2quit      rec,3    * To return to main menu, press 9
utterance 2recmsg    rec,0    * To record a voice message, press 1
utterance 2repeat    rec,0    * To repeat, press 1
utterance 2save      rec,3    * To save and continue, press 3
utterance 2start     rec,0    * Press any key to start recording
utterance 4apgsumm   rec,3    * For APGEN Summary, press 3
utterance 4vwssumm   rec,3    * For VWS Summary, press 2
utterance apg001     rec,3    * APGEN Summary 1 of 8
utterance apg002     rec,5    * APGEN Summary 2 of 8
utterance apg003     rec,5    * APGEN Summary 3 of 8
utterance apg004     rec,5    * APGEN Summary 4 of 8
utterance apg005     rec,5    * APGEN Summary 5 of 8
utterance apg006     rec,5    * APGEN Summary 6 of 8
utterance apg007     rec,5    * APGEN Summary 7 of 8
utterance apg008     rec,5    * APGEN Summary 8 of 8
utterance both001    rec,0    * Introduce VWS and APGEN Summaries
utterance both081    rec,7    * Play this after both VWS and APGEN Summaries
utterance both091    rec,0    * Play this after both VWS and APGEN Summaries
utterance farewell   rec,0    * Thankyou for calling XYZ Company. Goodbye.
utterance greeting   rec,0    * Hello. This is XYZ Company......
utterance ifdone     rec,3    * If you are finished, press 4
utterance inputpw    rec,0    * Enter your password
```

```
utterance    msgsent     rec,0    * Your message has been sent
utterance    nomore      rec,0    * No more messages
utterance    nomsgs      rec,0    * No messages
utterance    reclimit    rec,3    * Your message may be 90 seconds in length
utterance    tone        rec,0    * <Tone>
utterance    vws001      rec,3    * VWS Summary 1 of 4
utterance    vws002      rec,5    * VWS Summary 2 of 4
utterance    vws003      rec,5    * VWS Summary 3 of 4
utterance    vws004      rec,5    * VWS Summary 4 of 4

*- - - - - - - - - - - - - - - - - - - - - - - - - - - - - - - -*
*
* Setup messages database, set procedure to execute in case of unexpected
* disconnect, the execute the smart answering machine application.
*

Main:
    BEGIN                            * PROCEDURE: Main
    opendb     maildb                * Open messages database
    selectdb   maildb                * Make messages database current
    setdisc    Wait_for_ring         * 'Do' procedure if early disconnect
    setabort   Abort                 * 'Do' procedure on exit from application
    do         Wait_for_ring         * Execute the application
    END                              * PROCEDURE: Main

*- - - - - - - - - - - - - - - - - - - - - - - - - - - - - - - -*
*
* This procedure is entered whenever the application is exited (operator
* invokes QUIT on the standard Menu Screen). This procedure writes any
* messages database records remaining in database buffer then closes database.
*
```

```
Abort:       BEGIN                      * PROCEDURE: Abort
             flushdb                    * Write any remaining records to database
             closedb                    * Close messages database
             END                        * PROCEDURE: Abort

* - - - - - - - - - - - - - - - - - - - - - - - - - - - - - - - *
*
*    Answer phone on first ring. Menu choices: [1] voice message,
*    [2] and [3] software product announcements, [4] quit, [9] hear
*    voice messages (requires password).
*
*    System owner can get messages by phone by pressing [9] at main
*    menu and keying password [82633]. After hearing a message, owner
*    may select repeat, erase, save, or quit. Erase and save both
*    proceed to succeeding message.
*

Wait_for_ring:                          * PROCEDURE: Wait_for_ring
             BEGIN                      * Write previous message if it exists
             flushdb       maildb       * Make sure selected database unlocked
             unlockdb                   * Start with an empty dtmf buffer
             cleardtmf

wait_for_ring:
```

```
        answer      1                             * Wait for ring. Go off hook on 1st ring
        speak1      greeting                      * Speak greeting utterance

main_menu:
        cleardtmf                                 * Start with empty DTMF buffer
        speak                                     * Speak main menu prompts
        BEGIN
        2recmsg, 4vwssumm, 4apgsumm, ifdone
        END                                       * NOTE: owner's key [9] not in menu

        getdtmf     key,end_call,1,9,4            * i/p, abort, 1 key, t/o 9 sec, 4 tries

        switch      key, main_menu                * Interpret key; default to main_menu
        BEGIN                                     * (switch checks variable range)
        1,1         record_msg                    * [1]  record a voice message
        2,2         vws_summary                   * [2]  play SPEECH EDITOR announcement
        3,3         apgen_summary                 * [3]  play APGEN announcement
        4,4         end_call                      * [4]  end the phonecall
        9,9         owner                         * [9]  owner wants to hear messages
        END

record_msg:
        do          Voice_message                 * Record voice message
        goto        main_menu                     * Return to speak main menu

vws_summary:
        speak                                     * Say Speech Editor announcement
        BEGIN
        both001, vws001, vws002, vws003, vws004, both081
```

```
        END

        goto        end_announcement    * Same end as APGEN announcement

apgen_summary:
        speak
        BEGIN
        both001, apg001, apg002, apg003, apg003, apg004,
        apg005, apg006, apg007, apg008, both081
        END

end_announcement:
        speak1      both091             * Say end of both announcements
        goto        main_menu           * Return to speak main menu

end_call:
        speak1      farewell            * Say the farewell
        hangup                          * Put phone on hook
        goto        wait_for_ring       * Go back to wait for next call

owner:
        do          Mail                * Play voice-messages
        goto        main_menu           * Return to speak main menu
        END                             * PROCEDURE: Wait_for_ring
```

--

```
* Request a voice message, record message (using new filename), enter its
* filename into messages database, tell caller the message has been sent.

Voice_message:
    BEGIN                             * PROCEDURE: Voice_message
    cleardtmf                         * Start with an empty dtmf buffer
    speak1                            * Ask for any key to start recording
    getdtmf     2start                * i/p, abort, 1 key, t/o 5 sec, 6 tries
    recmsg      key, quit, 1,5,6      * Create filename, record, 90 sec max
    lockdb      message, 90           * No other task gets db until rec write
    newrec                            * Create a new db rec for this msg
    putfield    message, filename     * Put filename to field in current rec
    writerec                          * Write current record to database
    unlockdb                          * Database access okay for other tasks
    speak1      msgsent               * Tell caller his message has been sent

quit:
    END                               * PROCEDURE: Voice_message

* - - - - - - - - - - - - - - - - - - - - - - - - - - - - - - - - - - - - *
* Ask for entry of password (found in variable pwfixed). If it compares,
* play voice messages in chronological order. After each messages is played,
* it may be repeated, erased, or saved.

Mail:
    BEGIN                             * PROCEDURE: Mail
    cleardtmf                         * Start with an empty dtmf buffer
    speak1      inputpw               * Say "enter password"
    getdtmf     pwvar,quit,5,8,4      * i/p, abort, 5 keys, t/o 8 sec, 4 tries
```

```
        compare       pwvar, pwfixed, no_good, pw_okay, no_good  * Test password

pw_okay:
        toprec        no_msgs           * If db has recs, make 1st one current

get_filename:
        getfield      message, filename * Get current message's filename

repeat:
        cleardtmf                       * Start with an empty dtmf buffer
        play          message           * Play message
        speak                           * Say message disposition menu
        BEGIN
        2repeat, 2erase, 2save, 2quit
        END

        getdtmf       key, quit, 1,8,4  * i/p, abort, 1 key, t/o 8 sec, 4 tries

        switch        key, repeat       * Interpret i/p key; default to repeat
        BEGIN
        1,1           repeat            * [1] Repeat the message
        2,2           delete            * [2] Delete the message and go to next
        3,3           save              * [3] Save the message and go to next
        9,9           quit              * [9] Return to main menu
        END
```

```
delete:
     delmsg       message          * Delete msg file (name is in variable)
     delrec                        * Delete current record from database
save:
     nextrec      no_more          * Go on to the next message
     goto         get_filename     * If next msg exists, make it current
                                   * Go back and play new current message

no_msgs:
     speak1       nomsgs           * There are no messages
     goto quit                     * Tell owner there are no messages
                                   * Exit this procedure

no_more:
     speak1       nomore           * There are no more messages
                                   * Tell owner there are no more messages

no_good:                           * Wrong password entered
quit:                              * Exit from this procedure
     END                           * PROCEDURE: Mail

* ------------------------------------------------------- *
```

Bibliography

Chapter 2

History of Talking Automata

Boorstin, Daniel J. 1983. *The discoverers.* New York: Random House.

Brewster, Sir David. 1832. *Letters on natural magic.* New York: J&J Harper.

Bruce, Robert T. 1990. *Bell, Alexander Graham Bell and the conquest of solitude.* New York: Cornell University Press.

Dickens, Chas. 1870. Talking machines. *All the Year Round* 4 (2): 393.

Dudley, Homer. 1939. Remaking speech. *J. Acoustical Society of America* 11 (2): 169-177.

Dudley, Homer and Otto O. Gruenz, Jr. 1946. Visible speech translators with external phosphors. *J. Acoustical Society of America* 18 (1): 62-73.

Dudley, Homer, R. R. Riesz, and S.S.A. Watkins. 1939. A Synthetic Speaker. *J. Franklin Institute* 227 (6): 739-764.

Dudley, Homer and T. H. Tarnoczy. 1950. The Speaking Machine of Wolfgang von Kempelen. *J. Acoustical Society of America* 22 (2): 151-166.

Flanagan, James L. 1972. *Speech analysis synthesis and perception.* 2d ed. New York: Springer-Verlag.

Flanagan, James L. 1972. The synthesis of speech. *Scientific American* 226 (2): 48-58.

Konig, W., H. K. Dunn and L. Y. Lacy. 1946. The sound spectrograph. *J. Acoustical Society of America* 18 (1): 19.

Kopp, G. A. and H. C. Green. 1946. Basic phonetic principles of visible speech. *J. Acoustical Society of America* 18 (1): 74-89.

Kuecken, John A. 1983. *Talking computers and telecommunications.* New York: Van Nostrand Reinhold.

Pedro the Voder. 1939. *Bell Laboratories Record* 17 (6): 171.

Penzias, Arno. 1989. *Ideas and information.* New York: Simon & Schuster.

Rey, R. F. 1986. Engineering and operations in the Bell system. Murray Hill, N.J.: AT&T Bell Laboratories.

Riesz, R. R. and L. Schott. 1946. Visible speech cathode-ray translator. *J. Acoustical Society of America* 18 (1): 50-61.

Rosenfield, Israel. 1988. *The invention of memory.* New York: Basic Books.

Schott, L. O. 1948. A playback for visible speech. *Bell Labs Record* 26: 333-339.

Tetschner, Walt. 1991. *Voice processing.* Boston: Artech House.

Watson, Thomas A. 1915. How Bell invented the telephone. *Transactions American Inst. of Electrical Engineers* 34: 1011-1021.

Wheatstone, Sir Charles. 1837. Speaking machines, etc. *The London and Westminster Review* 28: 27-41.

_____. 1879. *The scientific papers of Sir Charles Wheatstone.* London: Taylor and Francis.

Witten, I. H. 1982. *Principles of computer speech.* London: Academic Press.

Chapter 3

Speech Technology

Akmajian, Adrian, Richard A. Demers, and Rober M. Harnish. 1979. *Linguistics: An introduction to language and communication.* Cambridge, MA: The MIT Press.

Allen, Jonathan, Sharon M. Hunnicutt, and Dennis Klatt. 1987. *From text to speech: The MITalk system.* Cambridge: Cambridge University Press.

Allen, Jonathan. Fall, 1981. Lingustic-based algorithms offer practical text-to-speech systems. *Speech Technology* 1 (1): 12-16.

Atal, B. S. and M. R. Schroeder. 1970. Adaptive predictive coding of speech signals. *The Bell System Technical Journal.*

Campbell, Joseph P., Jr. 1990. The proposed federal standard 1016 4800 bps voice coder: CELP. *Speech Technology* 5 (2): 58-64.

Chomsky, Noam and Morris Halle. 1968. *The sound pattern of english.* New York: Harper and Row.

Flanagan, James L. 1972. *Speech analysis synthesis and perception.* 2d ed. New York: Springer-Verlag.

Groner, Gabriel F., Jared Bernstein, et al. 1982. A real-time text-to-speech converter. *Speech Technology* 1 (2): 73-76.

Hess, Wolfgang. 1983. *Pitch determination of speech signals.* New York: Springer-Verlag.

Hertz, Susan R. October, 1982. From text to speech With SRS. *J. Acoustic Society of America* 72 (4): 1155-1170.

Honey, Elovitz S., Rodney Johnson, et al. 1976. Letter-to-sound rules for automatic translation of English text to phonetics. *IEEE-ASSP* 24 (6).

Jayant, N. S. and Peter Noll. 1984. *Digital coding of waveforms.* Englewood Cliffs, N.J.: Prentice-Hall.

Keiser, Bernard and Eugene Strange. 1985. *Digital telephony and network design.* New York: Van Nostrand Reinhold.

Klatt, D. H. 1987. Review of text-to-speech conversion for English. *J. Acoustical Society of America* 82 (3): 737-793.

Klatt, Dennis H. 1987. Structure of a phonological rule component for a synthesis-by-rule program. *IEEE-ASSP* 24 (5): 391-398.

Kuecken, John A. 1983. *Talking computers and telecommunications.* New York: Van Nostrand Reinhold.

Gray, Robert M. 1984. Vector quantization. *IEEE ASSP.*

Liberman, A.M., Frances Ingemann, et al. 1959. Minimal rules for synthesizing speech. *J. acoustical society of America* 31 (11): 1490-1499.

Markel, J.D. and A.H. Gray, Jr. 1976. *Linear prediction of speech.* New York: Springer-Verlag.

O'Malley, Michael H. 1990. Text-to-speech conversion technology. *IEEE.*

Rabiner, L.R. and Bernard Gold. 1975. *Theory and application of digital signal processing.* Englewood Cliffs, N.J.: Prentice Hall.

Rabiner, L.R., R.W. Schafer, and J.L. Flanagan. 1971. Computer synthesis of speech by concatenataion of formant-coded words. *Bell System Technical Journal* 50: 1541-1558.

Rabiner, L.R. and R.W. Schafer. 1987.*Digital pricessing of speech signals* Englewood Cliffs, N.J.: Prentice-Hall.

Shannon, C.E. 1948. A mathematical theory of communication. *The Bell System Technical Journal* 27 (3).

Smith, Bernard. 1957. Instantaneous companding of quantized signals. *The Bell System Technical Journal 36* (3).

Winograd, Terry. 1983. *Language as a cognitive process.* Reading, Mass.: Addison-Wesley.

Witten, I. H. and J. Abbess. 1979. A microcomputer-based speech synthesis-by-rule system. *J. Man Machine Studies* 11: 585-620.

Witten, Ian H. 1982. Principles of computer speech. London: Academic Press.

Young, S. J. and F. Fallside. 1980. Synthesis by rule of prosodic features in word concatenation synthesis. *J. Man Machine Studies* 12: 241-258.

Chapter 4

Speech Recognition

Adams, Duane A. and Robert Bistiani. Mar/Apr 1986. The Carnegie-Mellon University Distributed Speech Recognition System. *Speech Technology* 3 (2): 14-23.

Atal, B. S. 1974. Effectiveness of linear prediction characteristics of the speech wave for automatic speaker identification and verification. *J. Acoustic Society of America* 55 (6): 1304-1312.

Baker, James K. 1989. A second-generation large vocabulary system. *Speech Technology* 4 (4): 20-24.

Baker, Janet M. 1981. How to achieve recognition. *Speech Technology*: 30-43.

Baker, Janet M. and James K. Baker. 1983. Aspects of stochastic modeling for speech recognition. *Speech Technology* 1 (4): 94-97.

Doddington, George. 1983. Voice authentication gets the go-ahead for security systems. *Speech Technology* 2 (1): 14-23.

Fallside, Frank. 1989. Progress in large vocabulary speech recognition. *Speech Technology* 4 (4): 14-15.

Hoskins, James. Large vocabulary speech recognition—today at IBM. 1985. *Speech Technology* 3 (1): 16-21.

Johnson, Edith Trager. 1984. Regional dialect recognition is in the offing. *Speech Technology* 2 (2): 29-34.

Kuecken, John A. 1983. *Talking computers and telecommunications*. New York: Van Nostrand Reinhold.

Lamel, Lori F. and Aaron E. Rosenberg. 1981. An improved endpoint detector for isolated word recognition. *IEEE Transactions on ISSP* 29 (4): 777-785.

Lee, Kai-Fu. 1989. *Automatic speech recognition*. Boston: Kluwer Academic Publishers.

Levin, Esther. Connected word recognition using hidden control neural architecture. *Speech Technology* 5 (3): 102-107.

Liang, Marc D. and Krishna Narayanan. 1989. The application of voice recognition to robotic positioning of a hospital bed. *Speech Technology* 5 (1): 30-33.

Levinson. S. E. 1986. Continuously variable duration hidden Markov models for automatic speech recognition. *Computer Speech and Language* 1 (1): 29-45.

_____. 1987. Continuous speech recognition by means of acoustic/phonetic classification obtained from a hidden Markov model. *ICASSP* 1: 93-96.

Levinson, S. E., A Ljolje, et al. 1989. Large vocabulary speech recognition using a hidden Markov model for acoustic/phonetic classification. *Speech Technology* 4 (4): 26-32.

Loken-Kim, K. H., Shinta Kimura, et al. 1990. A large vocabulary Japanese language speech recognition system. *Speech Technology* 5 (2): 14-23.

Makhoul, John. 1989. Toward spoken language systems. *Speech Technology* 4 (4): 34-36.

Mangione, Paul A. 1986. SSI's phonetic engine. *Speech Technology* 3 (2): 4-86.

Meisel, William S. 1986. Developing phoneme recognizers using expert knowledge and statistical analysis. *Speech Technology* 3 (3): 72-74.

Meisel, William S. and Mark T. Anikst. Efficient representation of speech for recognition. *Speech Technology* 5 (3): 96-100.

Pirani, Giancarlo. 1990. Database access using continuous speech understanding. *Speech Technology* 5 (2): 26-29.

Pratt, David. 1990. Automatic voice recognition in the 1990s: With a little help. *Speech Technology* 5 (2): 40.

Rabiner, Lawrence R. 1989. A tutorial on hidden Markov models and selected applications in speech recognition. *Proceeding of the IEEE* 77 (2): 257-286.

Roe, David B., R.P. Mikkilineni, et al. 1991. AT&T's speech recognition in the telephone network. *Speech Technology* 5 (3): 16-22.

Rosenberg, A. E. and A.M. Colla. 1987. A connected speech recognition system based on spotting diphone-like segments—preliminary results. *ICASSP* 1: 85-88.

Roucos, S. and M.O. Dunham. 1987. A stochastic segment model for phoneme-based continuous speech recognition. *ICASSP* 1: 73-76.

Schalk, Thomas B. 1991. Speaker verification over the telephone network. *Speech Technology Magazine* 5 (3): 32-35.

Simpson, Moris M. 1989. The deployment of speech recognition in the telephone network. *Speech Technology* 5 (1): 14-17.

Teja, Edward R., Gary W. Gonnella. 1983. *Voice technology*. Reston, Va.: Reston Publishing Company.

Witten, I. H. 1982. *Principles of computer speech*. London: Academic Press.

White, George M. 1976. Speech recognition: A tutorial overview. *Computer* 9: 40-53.

Zue, Victor W. 1985. The use of speech knowledge in automatic speech recognition. *Proceeding of IEEE* 73 (11): 1602-1615.

Chapter 5

Telecommunications

Bellamy, J. C. 1982. *Digital telephony*. New York: John Wiley & Sons.

Briley, Bruce E. 1983. *Introduction to telephone switching*. Reading, Mass.: Addison-Wesley.

Feher, K. 1981. *Digital communications microwave applications*. Englewood Cliffs, N.J.: Prentice-Hall.

Gurrie, Michael L. and Patrick J. O'Connor. *Voice/data telecommunications systems*. Englewood Cliffs, N.J.: Prentice-Hall.

Harb, M. 1989. *Modern telephony*. Englewood Cliffs, N.J.: Prentice-Hall.

Keiser, Bernard E. and Eugene Strange. 1985. *Digital telephony and network integration*. New York: Van Nostrand Reinhold.

Kuecken, John A. 1983. *Talking computers and telecommunications*. New York: Van Nostrand Reinhold.

Martin, James. *Telecommunications and the computer*. Englewood Cliffs, N.J.: Prentice-Hall.

Rey, R. F. 1986. *Engineering and operations in the Bell system*. Murray Hill, N.J.: AT&T Bell Laboratories.

Rosenberg, Jerry M. 1984. *Dictionary of computers*. Data processing and telecommunications. New York: John Wiley and Sons.

Talley, D. 1979. *Basic telephone switching systems*. Rochelle Park, N.J.: Hayden Book Co.

Welch, Samuel. 1979. *Signalling in telecommunications networks*. London: Institution of Electrical Engineers.

Chapter 6

Requirements and Features

Pelton. Gordon E. 1989. Designing the telephone interface for voice processing applications. *Speech Technology* 5 (1): 18.

_____. 1991. Creating fixed vocabulary for voice processing systems. *Speech Technology* 5 (3): 43.

Chapter 7

Hardware

Adler, Bill. 1990. The new echo DSP offers multiple features on a single board. *Speech Technology* 5 (2): 86-87.

Allen, Jonathan. 1981. Linguistic-based algorithms offer practical text-to-speech systems. *Speech Technology* 1 (1): 12-16.

Bareis, Bern. 1990. The VR-4: Speaker-independent recognition over four channels. *Speech Technology* 5 (2): 88-89.

Binal, Mehmet E. and Stephen J. Leyland. 1991. Next generation voice processing systems. *Speech Technology* 5 (3): 117-119.

Carlson, Gordy. An IEEE floating point DSP for speech applications. *Speech Technology* 5 (3): 110-114.

Gallant, John A. 1989. Speech recognition products. *EDN Magazine* 34 (2).

Groner, Gabriel F., Jared Bernstein, Ed Ingber, et al. 1982. A real-time text-to-speech converter. *Speech Technology* 1 (2): 73-76.

Henderson, Khali. August 1990. Look what's talking. *The 4th Media Journal:* 33-35.

McDonough, K., E. Caudel, and S. Magar. February, 1982. Microcomputer with 32-bit arithmetic does high-precision number crunching. *Electronics:* 105,110.

Morgan, Nelson. 1984. *Talking Chips.* New York: McGraw-Hill Book Company.

O'Malley, Michael H. 1990. Making text to speech portable. *Speech Technology* 5 (2): 70-74.

Peters, Elisabeth W. Sept./Oct., 1990. Listening to E-mail. *Voice Processing Magazine.*

Rabiner, L. R., and B. Gold. 1975. Theory and application of digital signal processing. Englewood Cliffs, N.J.: Prentice-Hall.

Schalk, Thomas B. 1991. Speaker verification over the telephone network. *Speech Technology* 5 (3): 32-35.

Chapter 8

Development Software

Foard, Richard M. March, 1986. Multitasking methods. *PC Tech Journal:* 49-61.

Foard, Richard M. April, 1986. Preemptive scheduling on DOS. *PC Tech Journal:* 99-122.

Chapter 9

Vocabulary Production

Crowhurst, Norman H. 1959. *Basic audio.* New York: John F. Rider.

Everest, F. Alton. 1979. *How to build a small budget recording studio from scratch.* Blue Ridge Summit, Pa: TAB Books.

Jorgensen, Finn. 1980. *The complete handbook of magnetic recording.* Blue Ridge Summit, Pa.: TAB Books.

Nardantonio, Dennis N. 1990. *Sound studio production techniques.* Blue Ridge Summit, Pa.: TAB Books.

Oringel, Robert S. 1983. *Audio control handbook.* New York: Hastings House.

Morgan, Nelson. 1984. *Talking chips.* New York: McGraw-Hill.

Pelton, Gordon E. 1991. Creating fixed vocabulary for voice processing systems. *Speech Technology* 5 (3): 43.

Runstein, Robert E. 1974. *Modern recording techniques.* Indianapolis, In.: Howard W. Sams & Co.

Tremain, Howard M. 1959. *The audio encyclopedia.* Indianapolis, In.: Howard W. Sams & Co.

Van Bergeijk, Willem A. 1960. *Waves and the ear.* Garden City, N.Y.: Doubleday & Company.

Index

ABOUT THE AUTHOR

Gordon Pelton is president of Pelton Systems, a consulting and systems development firm based in Ashland, Oregon and specializing in voice processing. Pelton was President and Founder of Granite Systems, Inc., creator of the first personnel scheduling systems with employee access by telephone. He has more than 30 years experience as a programmer, software analyst, and project manager designing and implementing computer systems. Since the early 1980s, Pelton has specialized in developing voice processing technologies and applications. His projects include a digital speech editor, a voice application generator, and numerous large voice processing applications.